"Fritz West, himself a methodological master of comparative liturgical study, has provided all of us with a great service in the publication of his excellent translation of Anton Baumstark's work. Together with Baumstark's classic *Comparative Liturgy*, which set the methodological agenda for most of contemporary historical-liturgical study, English scholars and students now have another significant Baumstark work on method at their disposal. Not to be overlooked are the fine contextual introduction by West and the preface by the great Eastern liturgiologist in the Baumstark school, Fr. Robert Taft, SJ. This book demonstrates beyond a shadow of a doubt that Baumstark's foundational methods of , also known as 'comparative liturgy,' have a bright future indeed if we are to say anything at all about the history of liturgy. Thank you for doing this, Fritz."

—Maxwell E. Johnson
University of Notre Dame
Notre Dame, Indiana

On the Historical
Development of the Liturgy

Anton Baumstark

*Introduction, Translation,
and Annotation by Fritz West*

Foreword by Robert F. Taft

A PUEBLO BOOK

Liturgical Press   Collegeville, Minnesota

www.litpress.org

A Pueblo Book published by Liturgical Press

Cover design by David Manahan, OSB. Illustration provided by Arca Artium/ Vivarium of Saint John's University. Etching and engraving, 1816, *La messe de St. Martin*, after a painting in the Louvre Museum.

Scripture texts in this work are taken from the *New Revised Standard Version Bible* © 1989, Division of Christian Education of the National Council of the Churches of Christ in the United States of America. Used by permission. All rights reserved.

Library of Congress Cataloging-in-Publication Data

Baumstark, Anton, 1872–1948.
    [Vom geschichtlichen Werden der Liturgie. English]
    On the historical development of the liturgy / Anton Baumstark ; introduction, translation, and annotation by Fritz West ; foreword by Robert F. Taft.
        p. cm.
    "A Pueblo book."
    Includes bibliographical references and index.
    ISBN 978-0-8146-6096-6 (alk. paper) — ISBN 978-0-8146-6259-5 (e-book : alk. paper)
    1. Liturgics. I. West, Fritz. II. Title.

BV176.3.B3813   2011
264.009—dc23   2011038855

To his eminence
the Most Right Reverend
Karl Joseph
CARDINAL SCHULTE
Archbishop of Cologne

Anton Baumstark
(1872–1948)

Contents

Abbreviations

AHMA	*Analecta hymnica medii aevi*. Edited by Clemens Blume and Guido Maria Dreves. 55 vols. Leipzig: Altenburg, 1886–1922; ibid., *Register*, 3 vols. ed. M. Lutolf, Bern and München [Munich]: Francke Verlag, 1978.
ANF	*Ante-Nicene Fathers: The Writings of the Fathers down to A.D. 325*. Edited by Alan Menzies. 10 vols. Peabody, MA: Hendrickson Publishers, 1994. Available online at http://www.ccel.org/ fathers.html and http://www.tertullian.org/ fathers2/.
ARW	*Archiv für Religionswissenschaft*. Vols. 1–37. Leipzig: B. G. Teubner, 1898–1941/42.
Batiffol (Fr. ed.)	Batiffol, Pierre. *Histoire du bréviaire romain*. 3rd ed. Paris: A. Picard, 1911. 1st ed. (1893). Available through Google Books.
Batiffol (Eng. ed.)	Batiffol, Pierre. *History of the Roman Breviary*. Translated by Atwell Marvin Yates Baylay. 3rd ed. London, New York: Longmans, Green, 1912. Available through Google Books.
Bäumer	Bäumer, Suitbert. *Geschichte des Breviers*. Freiburg im Breisgau: Herder, 1895. Available through Google Books.
Baumstark, *Literatur*	Baumstark, Anton. *Geschichte der syrischen Literatur mit Ausschluß der christlich-palästinensischen Texte*. Bonn: Marcus & Weber, 1922. Available through Google Books.
Baumstark, *Messe*	Baumstark, Anton. *Die Messe im Morgenland*. Kempten & München [Munich]: Josef Kösel, 1906. Available through Google Books.

Baumstark, *Perikopenordnungen*	Baumstark, Anton. *Nichtevangelische syrische Perikopenordnungen des ersten Jahrtausends im Sinne vergleichender Liturgiegeschichte.* LF 3. Münster: Aschendorff, 1921.
BKV	*Bibliothek der Kirchenväter. Eine Auswahl patristischer Werke in deutscher Übersetzung.* Edited by Franz Xavier Reithmayr and Valentin Thalhofer. 1st ed. 80 vols. Leipzig: Engelmann-Verlag; Kempten & München [Munich]: Josef Kösel, 1869–88; 2nd ed., 81 vols. in 2 ser. Edited by Otto Bardenhewer, Theodor Schermann, and Karl Weyman. Kempten & München [Munich]: Josef Kösel, 1911–38. Being made available online as of this writing at http://www.unifr.ch/bkv/.
Brightman	Brightman, Frank Edward. *Liturgies Eastern and Western.* Oxford: Clarendon Press, 1896. Reprint, 1967. Available through Google Books.
Brock	Brock, Sebastian P. *A Brief Outline of Syriac Literature.* Mōrān 'Eth'ō 9. Baker Hill, Kottayam, Kerala: St. Ephrem Ecumenical Research Institute, 1997. Reprint of 2nd ed. (2009) forthcoming from Piscataway, NJ: Gorgias Press.
BZ	*Byzantinische Zeitschrift.* Vols. 1–. München [Munich]: C. H. Beck'sche Verlagbuchhandlung, 1892–present.
CE	*The Catholic Encyclopedia.* Edited by G. Herbermann et al. 15 vols. and index. New York: The Encyclopedia Press, 1907–14.
Χρυσοστομικα [Chrysostomika]	Χρυσοστομικα [Chrysostomika]:*Studi e ricerche intorno a s. Giovanni Crisostomo, a cura del comitato per il XV centenario della sua morte, 407–1908.* 2 vols. Roma [Rome]: Libreria Pustet, 1908.
DACL	Cabrol, Fernand and Henri Leclerq. *Dictionnaire d'archéologie chrétienne et de liturgie.* 15 vols. Paris: Létouzey et Ané, 1907–53.
Duchesne, *Origines*	Duchesne, Louis Marie Olivier. *Origines du culte chrétien: étude sur la liturgie latine avant*

	Charlemagne. Paris: Thorin, 1889. 4th Fr. ed. (1908). Available through Google Books.
Duchesne, *Worship*	Duchesne, Louis Marie Olivier. *Christian Worship: Its Origin and Evolution.* Translation of the 5th ed. of Duchesne, *Origines,* by M. L. McClure. London: SPCK, 1956. Available through Google Books.
EB	*Encyclopedia Britannica.* 29 vols. and index (2 vols.). 15th ed. Chicago et al.: Encyclopedia Britannica, 2005.
EEC	*Encyclopedia of the Early Church.* 2 vols. Edited by Angelo di Berardino and translated by Adrian Walford. New York: Oxford University Press, 1992.
ER	*The Encyclopedia of Religion.* Edited by Lindsay Jones. 15 vols. 2nd ed. Detroit et al.: Thomson Gale, 2005.
ERE	*Encyclopedia of Religion and Ethics.* Edited by James Hastings. 12 vols. and an index. New York: Charles Scribner's Sons; Edinburgh: T & T Clark, 1908–27.
Funk, *Didascalia*	*Didascalia et Constitutiones Apostolorum.* Edited by Franciscus Xaverius Funk. 2 vols. Paderbornae [Paderborn]: in libraria Ferdinandi Schoeningh, 1905. Reprinted as a single volume. Torino: Bottega d'Erasmo, 1970.
JLW	*Jahrbuch für Liturgiewissenschaft.* Vols. 1–15. Münster in Westfalen: Verein zur Pflege der Liturgiewissenschaft, 1921–41.
Johnson, *Worship*	Johnson, Lawrence. *Worship in the Early Church: An Anthology of Historical Sources.* 4 vols. Collegeville, MN: Liturgical Press, 2009.
Jungmann	Jungmann, Josef A. *The Mass of the Roman Rite.* Translation of the 2nd German ed. (1949) by Francis A. Brunner. 2 vols. New York: Benziger Bros., 1951–55.
KIT	*Kleine Texte für Vorlesungen und Übungen.* Edited by Hans Lietzmann and Kurt Aland. 192

vols. Bonn: A. Marcus und E. Weber, 1902–26. Published as *Kleine Texte für theologischen und philologischen Vorlesungen und Übungen*. Berlin: W. de Gruyter, 1927–78.

LF *Liturgiegeschichtlichen Forschungen*. Edited by Franz Dölger and Kunibert Mohlberg. 10 vols. Münster in Westfalen: Aschendorff; Freiburg im Breisgau: Herder, 1918–27.

LTK *Lexikon für Theologie und Kirche*. 11 vols. 3rd ed. Freiburg et al.: Herder, 1993–2001.

Mansi *Sacrorum Conciliorum nova et amplissima collectio*. Edited by Joannes Dominicus Mansi et al. 54 vols. Florentiae [Florence]: expensis Antonii Zatta Veneti, 1759–98. Reprint, Paris: H. Welter, 1900–27, and Graz: Akademische Druck-und Verlagsanstalt, 1960–61. Available online at http://www.documentacatholicaomnia .eu/01_50_1692-1769-_Mansi_JD.html.

MEL *Monumenta Ecclesiae Liturgica*. Edited by Ferdinand Cabrol and Henri Leclercq. 6 vols. Paris: Firmin Didot, 1900–12.

NPNF *A Select Library of Nicene and Post-Nicene Fathers*. Edited by Philip Schaff and Henry Wace. Ser. 1 (14 vols.) and ser. 2 (14 vols.). Peabody, MA: Hendrickson Publishers, 2004. Available online at http://www.ccel.org/fathers.html and http://www.tertullian.org/fathers2/.

OC *Oriens Christianus*. Wiesbaden: Otto Harrasowitz Verlag, 1st ser., vols. 1–10, 1901–11; 2nd ser., vols. 1–14, 1911–25; 3rd ser., vols. 1–14, 1927–41; and 4th ser, vol. 1–, 1953–present.

PG *Patrologia Graeca*. Edited by Jacque Paul Migne. Parisiis [Paris]: Migne, 1857–66. Available online at http://www.ellopos.net/elpenor/ greek-texts/fathers/migne-patrologia-graeca .asp.

PL *Patrologia Latina*. Edited by Jacque Paul Migne. Parisiis [Paris]: Migne, 1844–91. Available

	online at http://pld.chadwyck.co.uk/ (subscription required) and at http://www .documentacatholicaomnia.eu/25_10_MPL. html.
RBén	*Revue Bénédictine.* Vols. 1–. Maredsous, Belgique: Abbaye de Maredsous, 1884–present. Past issues available online at http://www .archive.org/details/revuebndictinev00unk ng00g.
Renaudot	Renaudot, Eusèbe. *Liturgiarum Orientalium Collectio.* 2 vols. Pariis [Paris]: Apud Joannem Baptistam Coignard, 1716. 2nd ed. corrected and reprinted. Farnborough: Gregg, 1970. Available online at http://www.archive.org/ details/liturgiarumorie05renag00g.
SGKA	*Studien zur Geschichte und Kultur des Altertums.* Paderborn: F. Schöningh, 1(1907)–23(1942).
TU	*Texte und Untersuchungen zur Geschichte der altchristlichen Literatur.* Leipzig: J. C. Hinrichs, 1(1882)–present.
Zeller	*Die apostolischen Väter. Aus dem Griechischen übersetzt.* Translated by Franz Zeller. BKV 35. München [Munich]: J. Kösel & Pustet, 1918.

Foreword

The inseparable association of Anton Baumstark's name with what
has come to be known as the science of comparative liturgy and its
laws[1] began with this small volume, occasioned by popular conferences, that has at last found a translator into English from the not
always pellucid German at the mercy of Baumstark's pen. Neither the
expression "comparative liturgy," title of Baumstark's later published
conferences on the topic (*Comparative Liturgy*, hereafter referred to as
CL), nor all of its so-called laws originated with him.[2] But they became
immortalized under his name: hence the importance of having this
historic book at long last available in English. For it has time and again
been demonstrated beyond cavil that the solution to some problems
in liturgical history and interpretation is simply impossible except
through the methods of comparative liturgy, some of which were first
adumbrated in this pathbreaking book.

One stellar example is the revolutionary principle, later adopted
by Dom Gregory Dix[3] and now generally accepted, if with nuances,
that "Einheitlichkeit ist nicht der Ausgangspunkt, sondern das Ziel
der liturgischen Entwicklung" (Uniformity is not the point of departure but the result of liturgical evolution), a principle Baumstark first
formulated in this book[4] and later developed in *Comparative Liturgy*

---

[1] On Baumstark's life, œuvre, and scholarly heritage, see the studies in
Orientalia Christiana Analecta 265.

[2] Anglican liturgical scholar John Mason Neale (1818–66) seems to have
coined both the English word "liturgiology" for the scientific study of liturgy
and the expression "comparative liturgy." See J. M. Neale, *Essays on Liturgiology and Church History* (London 1863), 123–24; C. W. Dugmore, *Ecclesiastical
History, No Soft Option* (London 1959), 15, cited in M. D. Stringer, "Style against
Structure: The Legacy of John Mason Neale for Liturgical Scholarship," *Studia
Liturgica* 27 (1997): 235–45, here 235, 242.

[3] G. Dix, "Primitive Consecration Prayers," *Theology* 37 (1938): 261–83, here
279–80.

[4] *Vom geschichtlichen Werden der Liturgie*, Ecclesia orans (Freiburg im Breisgau:
Herder, 1923), 29–36, n. 35.

as his first law of liturgical evolution: that liturgies evolved from variety to uniformity, not vice versa, that the process was toward liturgical unification, not diversification. In short, as time goes on we find fewer, not more, systems of liturgical expression across the horizon of Christendom.

A coherent family of such liturgical usages is what historians of liturgy call a "rite." In the Christian East there are seven such rites still extant: the Armenian, Byzantine, Coptic, and Ethiopian rites, plus the three Syriac rites: Assyro-Chaldean, Syro-Antiochene, and Maronite. But until the liturgical families began to consolidate by the end of Late Antiquity, it would be premature to speak of "rites" in the sense of a coherent, unified corpus of liturgical usages followed by churches within a single ecclesiastical conscription. Before the end of Late Antiquity, this process of the unification of local liturgical usages into a single rite was still under way.

Now formerly there was a popular misconception about how these liturgical rites evolved: I call it "the theory of the diversification of rites," formulated at the end of the nineteenth century by the German Catholic priest-scholar Ferdinand Probst, especially in three books: *Liturgie der ersten drei christlichen Jahrhunderte* (Tübingen, 1870), *Sakramente und Sakramentalien in den drei ersten christlichen Jahrhunderte* (Tübingen, 1872), and *Liturgie des vierten Jahrhunderts und deren Reform* (Münster, 1893). Probst believed there was originally a pristine apostolic liturgy that gradually evolved into distinct rites, much as the multitude of Indo-European languages developed out of the original parent language, Proto-Indo-European.

Now that was all right up to a point. Everything, after all, begins somewhere, and there was an original Christian preaching in apostolic times to which everything Christian can be ultimately traced, including its diverse formulations in the New Testament writings. But as later studies would show, after the initial development of a plethora of local liturgical uses in the first three Christian centuries, what we see from the Peace of Constantine in 312/13 until the end of the first millennium is not greater diversification, but rather an ongoing process of unification within distinct zones of ecclesiastical influence provoked by the development of intermediate administrative church units later called "patriarchates." Just as people speak fewer languages today than they once did, beginning with the fourth century Christians gradually came to worship in fewer diverse liturgical usages or "rites." So Baumstark's principle may have been a bit oversimplified for the pre-Nicene period, but it was verified for the subsequent developments of the liturgical families we call "rites."

The issue, however, is not whether all of Baumstark's methodological principles or every use he made of them was correct. For the heritage he bequeathed to us remains lasting and seminal, and his place in the history of liturgiology assured, regardless of how often he was right or wrong in this or that detail—a paradox Baumstark shares with many pathbreaking thinkers of the past. Of Giorgio Vasari (1511–74), the Cinquecento historian of Italian art, Francis Haskell wrote that "after more than four hundred years of controversy, and the detection in his work of inaccuracies and bias, deceit, ignorance, and intellectual carelessness, it still remains almost impossible . . . not to think of Italian painting, sculpture, and architecture developing along the lines he laid out."[5]

So getting all the facts right is not everything. As Stephen Jay Gould remarks apropos of Darwin: "For those who still cherish the myth that fact alone drives any good theory, I must point out that Darwin, at his key moment of insight . . . was quite wrong in his example. . . . Fact and theory interact in wondrously complex, and often mutually reinforcing, ways. Theories unsupported by fact are empty . . . but we cannot even know where to look without some theory to test. As Darwin wrote in my favorite quotation: 'How can anyone not see that all observation must be for or against some view if it is to be of any service?'"[6]

That is why Yale liturgy professor Brian Spinks could call Dom Gregory Dix (1901–52)—author of *The Shape of the Liturgy* (London 1945), one of the most important books ever written on the topic—"the Charles Darwin of liturgical studies: all his evidence is out of date, and much of it is wrong, but the inspired guesses continue to be useful in explaining the newer evidence."[7] It is also why Eamon Duffy could

---

[5] F. Haskell, "Ah! Sweet History of Life," *New York Review of Books* (April 4, 1996): 32.

[6] S. J. Gould, "Why Darwin?" *New York Review of Books* (April 4, 1956): 11–12.

[7] Review of J. R. K. Fenwick, *The Anaphoras of St Basil and St James. An Investigation into their Common Origin*, OCA 240 (Rome, 1992), in *The Journal of Theological Studies* 44 (1993): 712–15, n. 715. On Dix, see the new biography: Simon Bailey, *A Tactful God: Gregory Dix, Priest, Monk and Scholar* (Leominster, England: Gracewing, 1995); and Kenneth W. Stevenson, *Gregory Dix—Twenty-Five Years On*, Grove Liturgical Study 10 (Bramcote Notts: Grove Books, 1977).

accuse another liturgical giant, Josef Andreas Jungmann, SJ (1899–1975), of disastrous assumptions without in any way detracting from the fact that Jungmann was one of the great liturgical scholars of all time.[8] The issue is not whether Baumstark or Dix or Jungmann were always right, but what we can derive from how they worked and from their liturgical insights.

What we derive from them is a way of working and thinking that remains valid to the present day. Among liturgiologists, Anton Baumstark was one of the first to reflect methodologically and critically on how he worked. In so doing, he provided a model for all practitioners of a science that, like any other scholarly discipline, needs not only objective research but also methodological reflection. Only via the endless process of sifting and resifting hermeneutical presuppositions through the sieve of shared critical reflection can scholars sharpen the tools of their craft and refine its methods via fruitful dialogue within the profession.[9]

Liturgy is a living activity that can never, in Baumstark's words, "be paralyzed into the rigour of an immobile dead formalism" (CL 1). By its very nature, liturgy is subject to a process of continuous evolution. The vocation of the historian of liturgy is "to investigate and describe the origins and variations of the changing forms of this enduring substance of eternal value" that is "the living heart of the Church" (CL 2). This means studying the evidence. And since the evidence presents similarities and differences, its study is perforce comparative. Were there no differences, there would be identity and nothing to compare or explain. Were there no similarities, there would be no basis for a comparative method to begin with. Those who would complain that this is to reduce to text what is per se a living action seem to forget that texts, along with archeological remains, are all of the distant liturgical past that remain to us.

---

[8] E. Duffy, "The Stripping of the Altars and the Liturgy: Some Reflections on a Modern Dilemma," *Antiphon: Publication of the Society for Catholic Liturgy*, vol. 1, no. 1 (Spring 1996): 2–3. Duffy, "The Stripping of the Altars and the Modern Liturgy," *Antiphon*, vol. 2, no. 3 (Winter 1997): 3–12.

[9] For a superb recent example of such disciplinary reflection, see Harald Buchinger, "On the Origin and Development of the Liturgical Year: Tendencies, Results, and Desiderata of Heortological Research," *Studia Liturgica* 40, nos. 1–2 (2010): 14–45.

So what Baumstark called the "laws of comparative liturgy" are not surrogates for the facts of liturgical history, as some of his critics seem to imagine. More importantly, though "an empirical science . . . comparative liturgy is not concerned simply with the determination of facts," but with *explaining* them (CL 15): the "laws of comparative liturgy" are *norms that serve to explain the facts the sources disclose.*

EVALUATING BAUMSTARK'S COMPARATIVE METHOD

So Baumstark's "laws" are heuristic principles: not infallible a prioris to be followed blindly, but aids in formulating hypotheses for the interpretation of data. That, at least, was the teaching imparted to us prospective liturgiologists in "the Mateos School of oriental liturgiology" at the Pontifical Oriental Institute in Rome.[10] I coined the "Mateos School" appellation to describe the way of studying liturgy taught and exemplified by the great Juan Mateos and carried on and further elaborated and formulated by his students and successors. Class notes apart, Mateos himself did no methodological writing, bequeathed us no formulation of his method or any systematic reflections on it. But in his earlier work, Mateos taught us to recognize our debt to Baumstark, while maintaining a certain critical distance from Baumstark's approach.

For as our translator Fritz West has brilliantly shown,[11] Baumstark elaborated his method of explanation within a long since discarded, pseudoscientific philosophical framework very much in vogue in Baumstark's day, when such exploitation of the sciences as the basis for explaining even cultural phenomena was in the air. It is in precisely these terms that Van Austin Harvey describes the philosophical debate among historians concerning the reliability of historical explanation.

---

[10] Cf. Gabriele Winkler, "The Achievements of the Oriental Institute in the Study of Oriental Liturgiology," in R. F. Taft and J. L. Dugan, eds., *Il 75° Anniversario del Pontificio Istituto Orientale. Atti delle celebrazioni giubilari, 15–17 ottobre 1992*, OCA 244 (Rome, 1994), 115–41; R. F. Taft, "Recovering the Message of Jesus: In Memory of Juan José Mateos Álvarez, SJ, 15 January 1917–23 September 2003," OCP 71 (2005): 265–97.

[11] Esp. F. S. West, *Anton Baumstark's Comparative Liturgy in its Intellectual Context* (Ann Arbor, University Microfilms International, 1988). See also West, *The Comparative Liturgy of Anton Baumstark*, Alcuin Club & GROW Liturgical Studies 31 (Bramcote, Nottingham: Grove Books, 1995); and West, "Baumstark's Tree and Thoughts after Harvest," OCA 265: 163–89.

Some would maintain that the credence owed to an explanation is directly proportionate to how much the historical explanation approximates scientific explanations, the hallmark of which is the subsumption of a particular statement under a law.[12] This point of view has been subjected to trenchant criticism from those historiographers who would deny any relevance to the scientific model. For them, the historian does not use laws even implicitly. History is unique, they hold, and explanation-models, while perhaps useful for prediction in science, are irrelevant for history, which has to do with the actions of free human beings, the reasons for which are found within the actors themselves and not in laws extrinsic to them.[13]

Baumstark, a creature of his times like all of us, formulated his methodological principles within the cultural ambience he knew. What has been discredited are not Baumstark's basic insights so much as the intellectual matrix within which he attempted to locate them. In the last analysis, great liturgical scholars like Anton Baumstark (1872–1948), Edmund Bishop (1846–1917),[14] Gregory Dix (1901–52), Josef Andreas Jungmann (1899–1975), and Juan Mateos (1917–2003) advanced our knowledge because they did not just collect facts; they *explained* them.[15] To be content with just editing or describing what is in the sources is to renounce all attempts at writing history.[16] History means perceiving relationships, pointing out connections and causes, hazarding hypotheses, drawing conclusions—in a word, *explaining*. Unless the sources are explained, their editing does not advance our knowledge of history one whit. Knowledge is not the accumulation of data, not even of new data, but the perception of relationships in the

---

[12] V. A. Harvey, *The Historian and the Believer: A Confrontation between the Modern Historian's Principles of Judgment and the Christian's Will to Believe* (New York: MacMillan, 1966), 45ff.

[13] Ibid., 45–46.

[14] See the superb academic biography by Nigel Abercrombie, *The Life and Work of Edmund Bishop* (London: Longmans, 1959). Baumstark himself (*Vom geschichtlichen Werden der Liturgie*, 88) considered Bishop the greatest historian of the liturgy in modern times and fully shared Bishop's insight on the innate conservatism of the Roman liturgy (ibid., 97).

[15] Apropos of Baumstark, see the remarks of Dom Bernard Botte, OSB, in his 1953 foreword to the third edition of CL, vii–viii.

[16] I resume here ideas from my numerous writings on methodology.

data, the creation of hypothetical frameworks to explain new data or to explain in new ways the old.

For the sources alone do not tell us how they got the way they are, nor do later ones tell us why they are not the same as earlier ones. An examination of the sources gives rise not to answers but to questions, and questions cannot be answered by a mere description of what gave rise to them in the first place. The problems of liturgical history are not invented by the historian. They arise from the appearance of changes in the sources themselves, be they additions, omissions, or aberrations that constitute a departure from previously established patterns. The only way these problems can be solved—perhaps only hypothetically—is by sifting and analyzing, classifying and—yes—comparing liturgical texts and units within and across traditions. Only thus can one divine the direction in which things seem to be moving, chart their trajectory, and hypothesize how the gaps in the evidence might be filled in, just as the detective tries to reconstruct a crime from its few remaining clues. For the historian, there is no other way. Since we can have no direct access to the past, our knowledge of it is *inevitably, unavoidably inferential*, based on what Harvey called "the residue of life that remains long after life itself has run its course—the spent oil lamp, the rusted weapon, the faded document, the mutilated coin, the mouldering ruin."[17]

So the "laws," first formulated by Baumstark and Hamm[18] and Engberding[19] and resumed and classified by Baumstark in *Vom geschichtlichen Werden der Liturgie, Liturgie comparée*, and numerous other writings on particular problems in liturgical history and textual or structural analysis, are not blind shots in the dark or a substitute for research. They stand at the end of a long process of research, analysis, synthesis, and subsequent conclusions. Only then do they become presumptions, a way of proceeding from the known to the unknown, which is at the basis of all human reasoning. The evidence shows how liturgies have usually behaved. That permits one to formulate

---

[17] Harvey, *The Historian and the Believer*, 69.

[18] Fritz Hamm, *Die liturgischen Einsetzungsberichte im Sinne der vergleichenden Liturgieforschung untersucht*, Liturgiegeschichtliche Quellen und Forschungen 23 (Münster: Aschendorffschen Verlagsbuchhandlung, 1928), 33.

[19] Hieronymus Engberding, *Das eucharistische Hochgebet der Basileiosliturgie: Textgeschichtliche Untersuchungen und kritische Ausgabe*, Theologie des christlichen Ostens 1 (Münster: Aschendorff, 1931), passim.

hypotheses for reconstructing the evolution of liturgy on the supposition that other liturgies might have behaved in the same way in cases where the evidence to prove it is lacking. All of the humanistic and social sciences like history, sociology, political science, and criminology depend on comparative studies and the generalizations that emerge from them. Generalizations based on observation, analysis, and comparison are so fundamental to all humanistic studies that to challenge them is simply absurd. Just imagine what would happen to art history if comparison were to be banished! I hold the same to be true for *Liturgiewissenschaft*.

ARE BAUMSTARK'S "LAWS" LAWS?

A river of ink has been spilt over Baumstark's use of the term "the laws of liturgical evolution," the product of an era when one still believed in the complete objectivity of the scientific method as applied to the natural sciences. "Laws" says much more than one would say today, long after Gadamer and company laid to rest the myth of absolute scientific objectivity, and Baumstark could have saved us considerable grief had he limited his metaphor to comparative philology or linguistics. But it is a complete distortion of his thought to seize out of context his metaphors of the natural sciences and biology as indicating that he confused the laws of nature with the flow of history. This is clear enough from his assertion that "historical facts ought never to be absent from the mind of the historian of Liturgy. Further, Comparative Liturgy should always be on its guard against preconceived ideas and above all against theories constructed (in the way dear to theologians) in the interests of a system" (CL 7).

Baumstark's abhorrence of preconceived ideas of the sort common to the manual theology of his day, which began with the conclusion and then marshalled the arguments that agreed with it, may be the reason for Baumstark's insistence that Comparative Liturgy is a *science*. For he continues, "This maxim follows from the place we assign to Comparative Liturgy in the totality of the sciences," then goes on to explain what he means by the example of the Anaphora of Addai and Mari and another Mesopotamian anaphoral fragment, which lack the words of institution (CL 8). For Baumstark, such phenomena are facts to be taken at face value and not to be explained (or explained away) in function of some doctrine about the place of the *Verba Domini* in the eucharistic consecration (CL 7–8). So Baumstark's heuristic principles are "laws" only in the metaphorical sense, no more than what Paul Bradshaw calls "observable tendencies"[20] in the growth of liturgies.

The parallel Baumstark stressed most, that of comparative linguistics (CL 15),[21] is a far more apposite and, in my view, valid one. "The first task in the Comparative Study of the liturgical texts is of a purely philological kind," he insisted. "We must begin by finding out their history and as far as possible reconstructing their primitive state on a critical basis" (CL 52).[22] Despite the fact that both liturgies and languages are obviously products not of the laws of nature but of free human beings, one can still extract principles of development from observing how they commonly behave. In languages labials, dentals, and liquids tend to shift according to clearly identifiable patterns. Ts become Ds and Ps become Bs—or vice versa.

The fact that such shifts do not occur in all cases in no way makes the law useless in linguistics any more than exceptions vitiate Baumstark's "laws of comparative liturgy." The rule that in Italian the Latin "bs" between two vowels conflates into "ss" so that *observare* becomes *osservare*, *obsessio* becomes *ossessione*, *absorbere* becomes *assorbire*, *absurdum* becomes *assurdo*, is not at all rendered useless by exceptions like *obsoletum*, which remains *obsoleto*, resisting the expected conflation into *ossoleto*. For there is a "law" to cover that too: just as less frequently celebrated liturgical rites remain resistant to change, evolving more slowly if at all, so too in languages,[23] less frequently used words often resist the common, observable changes, as in the example above.

The same is true of any historico-cultural phenomenon. The fact that English is full of Norman French words and Romanian of Slavic words does not make English any more a Romance language, nor Romanian any less a one. Not to understand that is to miss what is basic to all scientific classification. *Of course* there are exceptions to any rule, *of course* paradigms and patterns are generalizations imposed on reality rather

---

[20] Paul F. Bradshaw, *The Search for the Origins of Christian Worship: Sources and Methods for the Study of the Early Liturgy* (New York: Oxford University Press, 1992), 62.

[21] And earlier, *Vom geschichtlichen Werden der Liturgie*, 5.

[22] See also Hamm, *Einsetzungsberichte*, 93.

[23] On this "law" of comparative liturgy and my extension of it, see esp. R. F. Taft, "Anton Baumstark's Comparative Liturgy Revisited," OCA 265: 191–232, here 206–8; and Taft, "Comparative Liturgy Fifty Years after Anton Baumstark (d. 1948): A Reply to Recent Critics," *Worship* 73 (1999): 521–40, here 527, 535–40.

than the reality itself. *Of course* the Slavic words in Romanian demand an explanation before we can securely label that tongue Romance. But Romance it is, just as surely as English is not. To deny the possibility of generalization, comparison, and extrapolation is to deny the possibility of writing history. And that is what Baumstark and his maladroitly named "laws of comparative liturgy," some of which he first adumbrated in this book, still help liturgical historians to do.

Robert F. Taft, SJ, FBA
Pontificio Istituto Orientale
Piazza S. Maria Maggiore 7
00185 Rome, ITALY

Introduction

ORGANIC THOUGHT AND THE LITURGY

Anton Baumstark (1872–1948) treats comparative liturgy, his liturgical methodology, in two books and few assorted articles.[1] The better-known book, *Liturgie comparée*, was translated into English as *Comparative Liturgy*;[2] the other, *Vom geschichtlichen Werden der Liturgie*, is here translated as *On the Historical Development of the Liturgy*.[3] While one finds overlaps, of course, these two works are essentially complementary. The latter lays out Baumstark's organic model and the former his comparative method, the two components common to all the

---

[1] Two passages and one article by Baumstark dealing with comparative liturgy, in passing or *in extenso*, are Anton Baumstark, "Besprechung: *Die nestorianische Taufliturgie*," ed. Dietrich, OC 3 (1903): 220–21; Anton Baumstark, "Ein liturgiewissenschaftliches Unternehmen deutscher Benediktinerabteien," *Deutsche Literaturzeitung* 40 (1919): cols 903–4; Anton Baumstark, "Das Gesetz der Erhaltung des Alten in liturgisch hochwertiger Zeit," JLW 7 (1927): 1–23.

[2] First delivered as lectures for the Benedictine Monks of Unity at the Priory of Amay–sur-Meuse, these were transcribed and then published by the priory, first in the pages of its journal *Irénikon* in 1934 and 1935 and later as Anton Baumstark, *Liturgie comparée: conférences faites au Prieuré d'Amay* (Chevetogne: Monastère d'Amay, 1939). They were reprinted as *Liturgie comparée: principes et méthode pour l'étude historique des liturgies chrétiennes*, 3rd rev. ed, ed. by Bernard Botte (Chevetogne: Éditions de Chevetogne, 1953); ET: *Comparative Liturgy*, ed. Bernard Botte, OSB, trans. F. L. Cross (Westminster, Maryland: The Newman Press, 1958). Hereafter this work will be cited by its English title.

[3] This book was first published as Anton Baumstark, *Vom geschichtlichen Werden der Liturgie*, Ecclesia Orans 10 (Freiburg im Breisgau: Herder, 1923) and reprinted as *Vom geschichtlichen Werden der Liturgie* (Darmstadt: Wissenschaftliche Buchgesellschaft, 1971). It has been recently translated into Polish as Anton Joseph Maria Dominikus Baumstark, *O historycznym rozwoju liturgii*, trans. Marian Wolicki, Vetera et Nova, Bibliotheke przekładów klasyków liturgiki 6 (Kraków [Cracow]: "Unum," 2001). Already out of print, I thank Father Wolicki for sending me a Xeroxed copy of this work.

comparative sciences of culture, a family of sciences flourishing from the second half of the nineteenth century into the early twentieth. Specifically, these sciences understood their area of study—be it history, law, language, liturgy, or another—to be an "organism" whose internal life is governed by laws producing distinct patterns that require a comparative approach to be fully understood. This methodology Baumstark applied to the liturgy. After commenting upon Baumstark's grasp of the culture of antiquity in the whole Mediterranean basin, the liturgical scholar Theodor Klauser (1894–1984) wrote,

> However, because overall cult constituted the focal point of the culture of antiquity, and moreover because Baumstark was of a religious nature, his predilection was for the problems of liturgical development and in particular the questions about the origins of Christian liturgy. What he accomplished in this area can no longer be separated from the new science of the liturgy. He developed the method of comparative liturgy, whose results he summarized in his book *Liturgie comparée*. He investigated the laws of all liturgical development, whose power he knew how to work out magisterially in his book *Vom geschichtlichen Werden der Liturgie*.[4]

When Anton Baumstark put pen to paper to write this book in 1922, he stepped into a flowing stream. In 1883 Valentin Thalhofer (1825–91), whose liturgical handbook remained in print for half a century, had written that "the liturgy of the church is no loose aggregate, but

---

[4] Theodor Klauser, "Anton Baumstark, 1872–1948," *Ephemerides liturgicae* 63 (1949): 186 (translation mine). For critical treatments of comparative liturgy, see Paul Bradshaw, *The Search for the Origins of Christian Worship* (New York: Oxford University Press, 1992), 57–63; Robert F. Taft, SJ, "Anton Baumstark's Comparative Liturgy Revisited," in *Comparative Liturgy Fifty Years after Anton Baumstark (1872–1948)*, Acts of the International Congress, Rome, 25–29 September 1998, eds. Gabriele Winkler and Robert F. Taft, SJ, Orientalia Christiana Analecta 265 (Roma [Rome]: Edizioni Orientatia Christiana, 2001), 191–232; Taft, "Comparative Liturgy Fifty Years after Anton Baumstark (d. 1948): A Reply to Recent Critics," *Worship* 73 (1999): 521–40; Frederick S. West, *Anton Baumstark's Comparative Liturgy in its Intellectual Context* (Ann Arbor, University Microfilms International 1988); Fritz West, "Baumstark's Tree and Thoughts After Harvest," *Comparative Liturgy Fifty Years after Anton Baumstark*, 163–89; Fritz West, *The Comparative Liturgy of Anton Baumstark*, Joint Liturgical Studies 31 (Bramcote Nottingham: Grove Books, 1995).

rather may be a vital organism governed not merely by the uniform laws of the human spirit, but also by the divine Spirit which lives and works in the Church till the end of time."[5] A year before Baumstark published *On the Historical Development of the Liturgy*, Romano Guardini (1885–1968) wrote, "And indeed the research [into the liturgy] must therefore proceed organically, that is, the method is guided by the assumption—evident both in principle and also from the liturgical data itself—that the liturgy is not an agglomeration of disconnected individual parts, but rather that a powerful life principle created for itself [in the liturgy] a completely homogeneous expression using the greatest variety of material and temporal-spatial particularities."[6] Addressing the general Catholic reading public in 1929, Chrysostomus Panfoeder (1885–1948), an admirer and popularizer of Baumstark, explained in his book *Das Organische*, "The essence of the liturgy is to be found first of all in its historical heart, in its becoming. For the original germs and seeds sown by Christ have grown organically into the magnificent tree of the liturgy, with all its buds, blooms, fruits, shoots, annual rings; they have yielded out of themselves the entire world of liturgical forms, organically incorporating into the essence of the liturgy all that they may have accepted from without."[7] Josef Andreas Jungmann entitled his two-volume work on the Roman Liturgy, *Missarum Solemnia: Eine genetische Erkläring der Römischen Messe*.[8]

---

[5] Valentin Thalhofer, *Handbuch der katholischen Liturgik*, vol. 1 (Freiburg im Breisgau: Herder'sche Verlagshandlung, 1883), 6. This work was reprinted for the last time in a revision by Ludwig Eisenhofer in 1932/33 (translation mine).

[6] Romano Guardini, "Über die systematiche Methode in der Liturgiewissenschaft," JLW 1 (1921): 105 (translation mine).

[7] Chrysostomus Panfoeder, OSB, *Das Organische*, Liturgia 5 (Mainz: Matthias Grünewald Verlag, 1929), 41 (translation mine). See also Fernand Cabrol, *Les origines liturgiques* (Paris: Letouzey et Ané, Editeurs, 1906), 27–35, passim, and Ismar Elbogen, *Der jüdische Gottesdienst in seiner geschichtlichen Entwicklung* (Leipzig: G. Flock, 1913), 1; Kunibert Mohlberg, "The Scientific Study of the Liturgy," *The Placidian* 6 (1929): 53–54; Mohlberg, "Aus der liturgiewissenschaftlichen Forschung," *Zeitschrift für Kirchengeschichte* 41 (1922): 184; Mohlberg, "Vertrauliches aus meinem Umgang mit mittelalterlichen Handscriften," *Miscellanea historica Alberti de Meyer*, vol. 2 (Lewen [Louvain]: Universiteitsbibliotheek, 1946), 1319; and Guardini, "Über der systematiches Methode," 97–98.

[8] Josef Andreas Jungmann, *Missarum Solemnia: Eine genetische Erkläring der Römischen Messe* (Wien [Vienna]: Verlag Herder, 1949), title page. The literal translation of the German title is "Missa Solemnia: A Genetic Explanation of

The use of organic thought in regard to the liturgy is ongoing. Building on Baumstark's methodology, Robert F. Taft (1932–) makes explicit use of an organic framework for explaining comparative structural analysis, the method characteristic of the Mateos School of Comparative Liturgiology.[9] This orientation is apparent, for example, in the title of Taft's article "How Liturgies Grow: The Evolution of the Byzantine 'Divine Liturgy'"[10] and elucidated in others.[11] In contrast to the descriptive use of organic thought found in the Mateos School, some critics of the liturgical reforms of the Second Vatican Council apply it prescriptively to lift up what they count as a necessary ingredient for genuine liturgical development. Alcuin Reid's (1963–) *The Organic Development of the Liturgy* and László Dobszay's (1935–) *The Restoration and Organic Development of the Roman Rite* may serve as examples.[12] This position

---

the Roman Mass," although it was translated into English as *The Mass: Its Origin and Development (Missa Solemnia)*.

[9] Gabriele Winkler, "The Achievements of the Pontifical Oriental Institute in the Study of Oriental Liturgiology," *Il 750 Anniversario del Pontificio Istituto Orientale, atti delle celebrazioni giubilari 15–17 ottobre 1992*, eds. Robert F. Taft and James Lee Dugan, Orientalia Christiana Analecta 244 (Roma [Rome]: Pontificio Istituto Orientale, 1994), 120–36.

[10] Robert F. Taft, SJ, "How Liturgies Grow: The Evolution of the Byzantine 'Divine Liturgy,'" *Orientalia Christiana Periodica* 43 (1977): 355–78, reprinted in Taft, *Beyond East and West: Problems in Liturgical Understanding*, 2nd ed. (Roma [Rome]: Edizioni Orientalia Christiana, 1997), chap. 11.

[11] In chronological order, Taft, "How Liturgies Grow," 355–78, reprinted in *Beyond East and West*, chap. 11; Taft, "The Structural Analysis of Liturgical Units: An Essay in Methodology," *Worship* 52 (1978): 314–29, reprinted in Taft, *Beyond East and West*, chap. 10; Taft, *The Diptychs*, vol. 4 of *A History of the Liturgy of St. John Chrysostom*, OCA 238 (Roma [Rome]: Pontificio Istituto Orientale, 1991), xxix–xxxi; Taft, "Reconstructing the History of the Byzantine Communion Ritual: Principles, Methods, and Results," *Ecclesia Orans* 11 (1994): 355–57; Taft, "Über die Liturgiewissenschaft heute," *Theologische Quartalschrift* 177 (1997): 243–55; Taft, "Comparative Liturgy Fifty Years after Anton Baumstark," 521–40; Taft, "Anton Baumstark's Comparative Liturgy Revisited," 191–232; and Taft, "Cathedral vs. Monastic Liturgy in the Christian East: Vindicating a Distinction," *Bolletino della Badia Greca di Grottaferrata*, series 3, 2 (2005): 173–219. For a critical treatment of the methodology of this school and Robert F. Taft, SJ, in particular, see West, *Anton Baumstark's Comparative Liturgy*, 393–98, and West, *The Comparative Liturgy of Anton Baumstark*, 40–42.

[12] Alcuin Reid, *The Organic Development of the Liturgy* (San Francisco: Ignatius Press, 2005), and László Dobszay, *The Restoration and Organic Development of*

has received the approbation of Pope Benedict XVI (1927–; pope from 2005–), when he observed that these critics insist "that growth is not possible unless the Liturgy's identity is preserved and they further emphasize that proper development is possible only if careful attention is paid to the inner structural logic of this 'organism.' Just as a gardener cares for a living plant as it develops, with due attention to the power of growth and life within the plant and the rules it obeys, so the Church ought to give reverent care to the Liturgy through the ages, distinguishing actions that are helpful and healing from those that are violent and destructive."[13] To maintain the identity of a liturgical tradition, these writers hold and Benedict affirms, liturgical change needs to be organic: gradual and in continuity with previous liturgical life.

As Baumstark was the first to make systematic use of organic thought for the study of the liturgy, an understanding of his methodology can help us think critically about this way of conceiving the worship of the church.

Ernst Cassirer (1874–1945) provides distinctions helpful to a critical assessment of organic thought. Writing about the study of language in the nineteenth century, the first area of cultural studies to use the comparative method, Cassirer distinguished three uses of "organism" as model and metaphor.[14] In a purely metaphorical sense, scholars of language used the term "organic" to depict an integral whole, comprised of interrelated parts. In this sense, a poem can be described as organic. Thalhofer is an example of this, as are those who would reform the reform. Moving from metaphor to model, we encounter two kinds: the methodological (or structural) and the ontological. The use of the

---

the Roman Rite (London and New York: T & T Clark, 2010). See also László Dobszay, *The Bugnini-Liturgy and the Reform of the Reform*, Musicae sacrae meletemata 5, Publications of the Catholic Church Music Associates 5 (Front Royal, VA: Catholic Church Music Associates, 2003).

[13] Joseph Cardinal Ratzinger, preface in Reid, *Organic Development*, 9. See also Ratzinger, "Review: *The Organic Development of the Liturgy* by Alcuin Reid," *Adoremus Bulletin* 10:8 (November, 2004), online edition at http://www.adoremus.org/1104OrganicLiturgy.html; GT: "Liturgie zwischen Tradition und organischem Wachstum," *Una Voce-Korrespondenz* 35:2 (März–April, 2005): 85–90, and Simon Matthew, "Can liturgical 'Reform' Be Reformed?" *AD2000* 7:1 (February, 1994): 12–19. Also available online at http://www.ad2000.com.au/articles/1994/feb1994p12_817.html.

[14] Ernst Cassirer, "Structuralism in Modern Linguistics," *Word* 1 (1945): 99–120.

methodological aspect of the organic model in comparative grammar built upon the similarity between organic and linguistic structure. It asserted that—like an organism—language is an interrelated system, whose parts function to maintain the whole. In a similar fashion, the Mateos School of Comparative Liturgiology attends to the structures of the liturgy, primarily its constituent parts ("liturgical units"),[15] but also whole services.[16] This methodological use of the organic model makes no ontological claim about the liturgy. By contrast, comparative grammar, the "model science" for all other comparative sciences, took this step and asserted that a language was an "organism." It assumed a language lives as an organic being does, discreet from its environment and governed by internal controls. Thinking in such terms, nineteenth-century scholars of language could portray language as a law-governed, hypostasized unity containing a life-principle that, when strong, effected the growth of a language; a weakening of that life-principle might result in the decline or even "death" of a language. These scholars attributed to language the status of an individuated organic being distinct from—and sometimes even independent of— human historical existence. Thus, whereas the methodological use of the organic model stresses structure, its ontological use stresses transformation.

Baumstark makes use of both aspects of the organic model, the methodological (structural) and the ontological. While he certainly attends to structure, thereby making use of the methodological organic model, notably in *Comparative Liturgy*,[17] he also takes the further step of regarding the liturgy as a whole to be a living "organism" in—but not of—history. This he explicates most extensively in the book translated here, *On the Historical Development of the Liturgy*.[18]

---

[15] See Taft, "The Structural Analysis of Liturgical Units," 314–29.

[16] See Taft, "How Liturgies Grow," 355–78.

[17] See Baumstark, *Comparative Liturgy*, chaps. 3–10. For a detailed analysis of these chapters, see West, *Anton Baumstark's Comparative Liturgy*, 295–345.

[18] For a discussion (with bibliography) of the comparative sciences of culture and the use they made of the organic model, see West, *Anton Baumstark's Comparative Liturgy*, 195–251; for brief treatments of the same, see West, *The Comparative Liturgy of Anton Baumstark*, 16–25, and West, "Baumstark's Tree," 168–71.

Karl Anton Joseph Dominikus Baumstark was born in 1872 to an intellectual German family newly converted to Catholicism. After receiving training in classical and oriental philology, he spent five years (1899–1904) in Rome resident at Campo Santo Teutonico, a study house for German Roman Catholics, primarily clerics. While there, he turned his scholarly attention to early Christian history, in particular the literature, liturgy, and art of the Christian East. Anton de Waal (1837–1917), the rector of this study house, was instrumental in obtaining support in 1901 to found the journal *Oriens Christianus*, which Baumstark edited—save for a brief hiatus—until 1941, when World War II caused its publication to be interrupted. During this time he also traveled to the Near East for the better part of a year, studying monuments and collecting documents.

Following his stay in Rome, Baumstark taught for fifteen years in Sassbach, Baden, at a private Roman Catholic secondary school founded by his godfather, Franz Xavier Lender (1830–1913). In 1909 he married Frieda Anna Tröndle (1891–1979),[19] and they raised a family of twelve children. On top of his responsibilities as a schoolmaster, Baumstark kept up scholarly endeavors, working primarily in the fields of the liturgy, literature, and life of the Eastern church. Toward the end World War I, under the influence of Ildefons Herwegen[20] (1874–1946), the abbot of the Abbey of Maria Laach, Baumstark made the liturgy of the Western church a focus of his work as well. His relationship with the abbey offered professional opportunities—including coediting the *Jahrbuch für Liturgiewissenschaft* with Odo Casel (1886–1948)—occasions for publishing articles and books, and an appreciative context for pursuing his organic understanding of the liturgy, which includes the volume translated here.

At this point in his life, the possibility of university teaching presented itself. Baumstark's forthcoming book, *Geschichte der syrischen Literatur*, led in 1921 to a position as *professor honorarius* for the History and Culture of the Christian Orient and Oriental Liturgy at the University of Bonn; in 1925 that institution granted him an honorary doctorate in theology. For a time during the 1920s, Baumstark lectured in Comparative Liturgy and Semitic Languages at the University of Nijmegen in the Netherlands. From 1926 he served as professor for

---

[19] Universitätsarchiv, Münster, Kurator PA Nr. 706, Bd. 3.
[20] On Ildefons Herwegen, see Short Biography, no. 95.

Islamic Studies and Arabic at the University of Utrecht, teaching in an institute that prepared persons for colonial service and employment.

His call to the chair in Oriental Studies at the University of Münster proved fateful for his academic career. An interest in conservative, nationalist politics, intensified by Germany's "ignominious" defeat in World War I and the "shame" of the Versailles Treaty, led Baumstark to join the National Socialist German Workers' Party (NSDAP) in 1932, when he actively campaigned for its electoral success. With Hitler's rise to power in January of 1933, Baumstark threw himself into church and university politics, convinced that the party could forge an alliance with the Roman Catholic Church as well as renew university life. His decision to stand for election to the post of university chancellor sparked vigorous opposition against him in the party of north Westfalen, which led in 1935 to his retirement from Münster and return to Bonn.[21]

Baumstark never recovered from this professional setback. After his retirement from Münster, he continued to hold only the part-time position at the University of Utrecht, which ended when in 1940 the German government withdrew his permission to teach abroad.[22] Over time Baumstark became increasingly isolated, as his politics and actions strained his relationships with some academic colleagues and coreligionists.[23] Feeling alienated from the Abbey of Maria Laach, he

[21] Helmut Heiber, *Universität unterm Hakenkreuz, Teil 1: Der Professor im Dritten Reich* (München [Munich] et al.: K. G. Saur, 1991), 466–72.

[22] Ibid., 471–72.

[23] The family of Paul Kahle (1875–1964), professor of oriental studies at the University of Bonn and editor of *Biblia Hebraica*, was convinced that Baumstark was instrumental in having Kahle's wife denounced by the Gestapo for befriending Jews on the day following *Krystallnacht* (November 9–10, 1938). As a consequence of this incident, Professor Kahle was dismissed from his university position. After months of harassment, the family fled to England as refugees. See Maria Kahle, *Was hätten Sie getan? Die Flucht der Familie Kahle aus Nazi-Deutschland;* Paul Kahle, *Die Universität Bonn vor und während der Nazi-Zeit (1923–1939),* eds. Wilhelm Bleek and John H. Kahle, 2nd rev. ed. (Bonn: Bouvier, 2003), 27 and 142. Friedrich Muckermann, a Roman Catholic priest in active opposition to the NSDAP, who knew Baumstark in Catholic circles, offers a cutting indictment of Baumstark's religiosity. See Friedrich Muckermann, *Die Kampf zwischen zwei Epochen*, ed. Nikolaus Junk, Veröffentlichungen der Kommission für Zeitgeschichte, Reihe A: Quellen, Bd. 15 (Mainz: Matthias-Grünewald-Verlag, 1973), 342–43. On the other hand, August A. den Hollander dismisses as false the suspicion that Baumstark stole the MS of a Dutch

resigned his position as editor of the *Jahrbuch für Liturgiewissenschaft* and turned his scholarly energies toward the Bible, with a particular focus on the textual traditions of Near Eastern biblical texts and harmonizations of the Bible, notably the *Diatesseron*. He did, however, accept an invitation to deliver a series of lectures on comparative liturgy for the monks at the Priory of Amay-sur-Meuse, Belgium, who transcribed and published them, first as articles in their journal *Irénikon* and then in book form as *Liturgie comparée*. Having lost four sons and one son-in-law in World War II, he died of heart failure in 1948.[24]

Baumstark's approach to the study of the liturgy was influenced by Josef Strzygowski (1862–1941),[25] whom he met while in Rome. An art historian born in Austrian Silesia (now Poland), Strzygowski, who taught at the University of Vienna, used the comparative method to solve a problem he discerned in the study of the art of the Near East. While the monumental stone structures built in cities could withstand the ravages of time and remain intact over centuries, structures in the hinterlands constructed of building materials susceptible to decay, such as wood, deteriorated. This physical reality skews the evidence for history of art in the Near East toward the imperial and away from the popular. To write a history of that art, Strzygowski made use of the comparative method, envisioning art as an "organism" manifesting essential features in a variety of cultures and eras. Specifically, he thought he could use the features he found manifest in the surviving monumental structures to infer what had once been extant in the popular forms. By this method, he claimed to be able to reconstruct the development of art in the Near East.[26]

---

harmonization of the gospels, which he had borrowed from the library of the University of Utrecht and upon which he worked in Bonn during the Second World War. See August A. den Hollander, *Virtuelle Vergangenheit*, Bibliotheca Ephemeridum Theologicarum Lovaniensium 25 (Leuven [Louvain]: University Press, 2007), 1–30.

[24] For biographies of Anton Baumstark, see, West, *Anton Baumstark's Comparative Liturgy*, 146–94, and West, *The Comparative Liturgy of Anton Baumstark*, 6–12. See also Hans-Jürgen Feulner, "Bibliography of Anton Baumstark" in *Comparative Liturgy Fifty Years After Anton Baumstark*, 31–60.

[25] On Josef Strzygowski, see Short Biography, no. 169.

[26] Baumstark, *On the Historical Development*, p. 179. For a discussion of Strzygowski's influence on Baumstark, with references, see West, *Anton Baumstark's Comparative Liturgy*, 161–67.

Addressing a similar problem with the same solution and a parallel outcome, Baumstark applied the comparative method to the liturgy of the Christian church. Like the history of art in the Near East, liturgical history has its own peculiar evidentiary problems, gaps of a different kind. Like Strzygowski, Baumstark believed that the comparative method had the methodological power to overcome the problem.

We begin with the two factors at play in the organic development of the liturgy: law and will. For Baumstark, will is that human trait whereby individuals act arbitrarily out of their own conscious intent. Human history, being a function of human will, is therefore arbitrary in itself and exhibits no regular patterns. In marked contrast, historical "organisms," such as language, the liturgy, and (so Strzygowski thought) art, subsist in the natural world and have a life of their own. Being of nature, laws govern liturgical life, that is, its life processes are law-governed, so that its development follows distinct patterns. This development occurs "in profound silence" (*still und geräuschlos*),[27] unbeknownst to those witnessing the liturgical "organism." This is certainly true of biological organisms, in which cells are a vital part of the organism yet unconscious of anything about its life patterns, be they growth, maintenance, or decline. However, mutatis mutandis, it is also true of a cultural "organism." This is reflected in Baumstark's claim that the liturgy is both *ein in bestimmter Form Gegebenes* (a given reality with definite form) and *ein Gewordenes* (a reality that has developed).[28] Though liturgy is perceived phenomenologically as an unchanging, given reality, it is in fact always developing according to its own laws.[29] Of course, Baumstark writes, in the final analysis, this

---

[27] Baumstark, *On the Historical Development*, p. 245 (translation mine).

[28] Ibid., pp. 43–44, 149, 244–45.

[29] This contrast between the synchronic and the diachronic is also found in the study of language, where it was first explicated by Ferdinand de Saussure in lectures delivered at the University of Geneva between 1906 and 1911. Notes from these lectures form the basis for Ferdinand de Saussure, *Course of General Linguistics*, eds. Charles Bally and Albert Sechehaye, with Albert Riedlinger, trans. Wade Baskin (New York/Toronto/London: McGraw-Hill Book Co., 1959), 101–90 and passim. As the assembly regards the liturgy, so the linguistic community regards language, as essentially unchanging, although in fact it is always developing. The field of semiology carried this distinction into cultural analysis, including the study of the liturgy.

is merely appearance and any liturgical change results from the sum of a myriad of actions by individuals.[30] However, being an "organism" within history and yet distinct from it, the laws of the liturgy canalize human will into the life processes that become apparent in the regular patterns liturgical development displays.[31]

Before the sixteenth century, Baumstark argues, liturgical development was universally organic, as it is still in the East. During that fateful century the organic development of the liturgy was disrupted in the West by the exercise of human will. Protestant bodies consciously re-formed the "organism" of the liturgy by acts of will; after the Council of Trent the Sacred Congregation of Rites was established to direct liturgical development with conscious intent, duly recorded in its *acta*.[32] Baumstark writes, "The Christian liturgy was until the time of Luther something unified from its roots. It was locally very diverse, but overall organic, that is, it developed according to laws which originated in its being. A liturgical text can be fully understood only when an historical problem of the liturgy can be properly solved upon the broadest comparative basis."[33]

The quiet stealth of liturgical change impacts the evidence available for studying it. Precisely because liturgical development occurs "naturally" and unbeknownst to liturgical participants, it typically goes unmentioned by those worshipping at the time. The result: a paucity

---

[30] Baumstark, *On the Historical Development*, pp. 149–50.

[31] West, *Anton Baumstark's Comparative Liturgy*, 266–81.

[32] Baumstark's treatment of the Council of Trent is of interest. While one might expect him to criticize it as being a conscious, intentional reform of the liturgy, he in fact praises it, as in this sentence: "Dangers posed by the rampant growth of more recent elements, which threaten the continued existence of venerable ones of an earlier time, were exorcized by the fortunate intervention of authoritative reform." See Baumstark, *On the Historical Development*, pp. 244–45, 247. (As an aside, the reformers of the reform criticize the Second Vatican Council for violating the organic growth of the liturgy but make no similar judgment on the Council of Trent.) On the other hand, Baumstark deems the management of liturgical reform by the Sacred Congregation of Rites following the Council of Trent—for being intentional and conscious—to be counter to the organic growth of the liturgy. See in this introduction the section below on "Liturgical Reform."

[33] Baumstark, "Besprechung: *Die nestorianische Taufliturgie*," 220–21 (translation mine). See also Baumstark, *On the Historical Development*, pp. 244–45.

of secondary sources.[34] Further, liturgical texts, which constitute the bulk of the documentary evidence for the liturgy, are often at variance with praxis. This is because persons—clergy or lay—familiar with a liturgy do not require a change in text to adopt a change in practice. A consequence of celebrating "today's liturgy" using "yesterday's text" is yet another gap in the evidence.[35] Finally, there are times in liturgical history—notably in its earliest period—for which few, if any, texts have survived of any kind, primary or secondary. While this is due in part to texts being lost or destroyed, it may also be due to the character of the liturgy. In certain times and places and for certain aspects of the liturgy, there were no texts, since the liturgy—like epic poems sung by bards—was "stored" in the memory of the community.[36] As a result of all these exigencies, one gets evidentiary gaps or silences in the liturgical record.

While historians have no choice but to accept gaps in the evidence, comparative scholars of culture thought themselves empowered to overcome them. Given the unpredictable and arbitrary character of human will, a history can be written only when there is direct evidence available for it, primary or secondary. Using standard historiographical methods, gaps in evidence necessarily produce gaps in knowledge. Things appeared differently, however, in the comparative sciences of culture, which studied historical "organisms," in—but not of—history. Just as Josef Strzygowski thought himself able to fill in the evidentiary gaps found in the development of the art of the Near East, Baumstark understood himself able to do the same for liturgical development. From the patterns discernible in the available evidence, comparative sciences could deduce the laws at play and then turn around and use those laws to infer what had transpired in times for which evidence is inadequate, sparse, or lacking.[37] Clearly, the comparative method appeared to enhance the methodological power that could be brought to bear upon cultural data.

When we turn to the laws Baumstark actually proposes, however, we find a mixed bag. One does not find here a neat symmetry of method and materials as pertains, for example, between the experi-

[34] Baumstark, "Ein liturgiewissenschaftliches Unternehmen," col. 904.

[35] Ibid. See also Baumstark, *On the Historical Development*, pp. 245–46.

[36] Ibid., pp. 89, 94–95, 150.

[37] Ibid., pp. 45–46, and West, *Anton Baumstark's Comparative Liturgy*, 274–80.

mental method and material reality. In fact, Baumstark uses all manner of reasoning to study the liturgy: philological (agreement/disagreement), biological (genetic), geological (traces of the past in present forms), literary (categorization by genre), et al. Nor is there a clear definition of law as one finds in the natural sciences, that is, a pattern so regular that when repeated experimentally it will recur with a high degree of probability—indeed, so high as to appear without exception (for example, the law of gravity in the Newtonian universe). Indeed, the laws Baumstark presents range widely in their level of generality. The chapter in *Comparative Liturgy* entitled "The Laws of Liturgical Evolution" presents just two: "the *Law of Organic Development* ('Organic' and therefore 'Progressive')"[38] and the law "that primitive conditions are maintained with greater tenacity in the more sacred seasons of the Liturgical Year."[39] Over the course of *Comparative Liturgy*, Baumstark mentions four others. All laws apart from Baumstark's first, the Law of Organic Development, describe particular aspects of the process of liturgical development.[40] Actually, in the framework of the comparative method, the first law is no law at all, but rather an assertion that the nature of the liturgy is such that it is amenable to inferential reasoning. History produced by will can only be described; the historical development of a historical/cultural "organism" can be explored using inferential reasoning. The very use of the term "law" reflects this claim—or rather its reach. It is an expression of Baumstark's confidence in his method, which—in his view—approaches that of the natural sciences, whose laws have predictive power.[41] The other laws mentioned in *Comparative Liturgy* are all observations of patterns

---

[38] Baumstark, *Comparative Liturgy*, 23 (emphasis in the original).

[39] Ibid., 27.

[40] Three of these laws were formulated by students of Baumstark. Fritz Hamm (1872–1948) observed two of them: "that the older a text is the less is it influenced by the Bible and that the more recent a text is the more symmetrical it is." Hieronymus Engberding (1899–1969) observed another yet: "that the later it is, the more liturgical prose becomes charged with doctrinal elements." Apparently Baumstark observed the one remaining law mentioned in *Comparative Liturgy*: "Certain actions which are purely utilitarian by nature may receive a symbolic meaning either from their function in the Liturgy as such or from factors in the liturgical texts which accompany them." Baumstark, *Comparative Liturgy*, 59, 60, and 130.

[41] Ibid., 3.

allowing for inference and may, in that sense, be regarded as corollaries of the first.[42]

The organic model was also helpful to Baumstark for organizing data. Of course, all scholars of the early liturgy must take into account Jewish, Christian, and Hellenistic contributions to the development of the liturgy. For the Roman Catholic scholar of the early twentieth century, however, these three could not be simply analogous historical forms of human invention, comparable to all other such forms in an unbroken series of equal entities. From a doctrinal point of view, Catholic Christian liturgical forms were by (super)nature incomparable, rooted as they are in the historical particularity of the incarnation; the Eucharist was understood to be essentially different from a Jewish Sabbath meal or a Hellenistic symposium. For this reason, the Catholic scholar had to be able to (1) assert the integrity of the liturgy of the Church and (2) weight the factors that shaped it so as to maintain the unique character of the incarnation. The ontological organic model served Baumstark well in this regard. With its bias in favor of the internal life of the liturgical "organism," its genetic understanding of the relationship to Judaism, and its categorization of the Hellenistic cultural milieu as mere "environment," the ontological organic model examined the Church's liturgy in its historical context while maintaining its distinctive character.[43] Within this methodological framework Baumstark found the freedom to exercise his craft, without compromising the historical particularity of Christian revelation.[44]

The ontological organic model organized data within the cultural organism as well. Already as a student of philology, Baumstark recognized that his teachers regarded cultural products of Christianity in the Near East, notably Christian literature, as derivatives of European forms. Baumstark wished to value Christian matters of the Near East in their own right.[45] Once again Baumstark and Strzygowski found themselves in the same camp. When Strzygowski argued that influences in the world of Anatolian art flowed from the East to the West,

---

[42] For a discussion of Baumstark's liturgical laws, see West, *Anton Baumstark's Comparative Liturgy*, 281–95.

[43] In addition to chaps. 2–4 in Baumstark, *On the Historical Development*, see also, for example, Baumstark, *Comparative Liturgy*, 2–14 and 63–70.

[44] West, *Anton Baumstark's Comparative Liturgy*, 268–71.

[45] Baumstark, "Besprechung: Hilgenfeld, ed. *Ausgewählte Gesänge des Giwargis Warda von Arbel*," OC 4 (1904): 209.

Baumstark trumpeted in a review, "The book wishes to prove nothing less than this: that the Romanesque church building of the West is a pure and full-bred son of the Orient. . . . We should learn to recognize Byzantine and Romanesque art as sisters, whose common mother would triumphantly be Hellenistic art. . . . If one keeps in mind the true vital development of medieval church-buildings, be it in the West or in the East, we should accustom ourselves to think of Rome as essentially without influence, the heiress of purely Hellenic tradition."[46] For these two scholars, the organic model proved a powerful methodological framework for organizing their data. A historical/cultural organism functioned as a field of comparison, with all entities within it standing on an equal footing. Art from Anatolia to Aquitaine or liturgies from India to Ireland, Axum to Archangel, and X'ian to Carthage could be evaluated in their own right. This position was not without controversy. At the turn of the twentieth century and earlier, it was common to regard Rome the *primus inter pares* in all things cultural, especially within the church. Not only was Near Eastern literature and art measured against European forms, but law was measured against Roman law, languages against Latin, and liturgies against the Roman Rite. What Strzygowki did for the field of art history, Baumstark accomplished in the field of liturgical history. According to Balthasar Fischer (1912–2001), Baumstark issued a warning to both the academy and the church: "Do not merely believe that the Roman liturgy is *the* liturgy; the Roman liturgy is *a* liturgy."[47]

---

[46] Anton Baumstark, "Besprechung: Josef Strzygowski, *Kleinasien, ein Neuland der Kunstgeschichte*," OC 4 (1904): 415 (translation mine). Baumstark echoes the title of an influential book by Strzygowski, *Orient oder Rom*, in the article title, "Rom oder Jerusalem. Eine Revision der Frage der Herkunft des Lichtmessfestes," *Theologie und Glaube* 1 (1909): 89–105, a topic Baumstark revisits in *On the Historical Development*, pp. 106–8.

[47] Balthasar Fischer, "Schwerpunkte der liturgiewissenschaftliche Forschung im deutschen Sprachgebiet im 19. und 20. Jahrhundert," *Nordisk Kallokvium IV i Latinsk Liturgiforskning 15–17 juni 1978 på Lysebu/Oslo* (Oslo, Institut for Kirkehistorie, Universitet i. Oslo, 1978), 15 (translation mine). For a statement in this vein by Baumstark, see *On the Historical Development*, p. 39. For a critical examination of this, see West, *Anton Baumstark's Comparative Liturgy*, 163–65, 230–32, and 269–72.

In 1921 Baumstark delivered two lectures on the development of the Roman Rite to a gathering at the Abbey of Maria Laach, intended to gain adherents for the German Roman Catholic liturgical movement. Abbot Herwegen offered to publish those lectures, but Baumstark decided to write *On the Historical Development of the Liturgy* instead.[48] Though written for one readership, this book has been valued by another. It was written for a segment of the German Roman Catholic reading public of the early twentieth century, those supportive of the German liturgical movement, but it has been valued for nearly a century by specialists in the field of liturgical studies. This is due to the book being both stimulating and inaccessible. Its inaccessibility stems largely from Baumstark's difficult writing style and penchant for obscure references (see below, pp. 35–36). It is not an easy book to read in the original German. On the other hand, specialists in the field have appreciated its methodological contributions, both the description of comparative liturgy and the portrayal of patterns Baumstark discerns in liturgical development. One might also mention the hypotheses Baumstark proposes and the evidence he brings to bear on problems in liturgical history.

We shall look at Baumstark's understanding of liturgical development before turning to his perspective on reform and the spiritual sustenance he imagined for the liturgical movement.

The Developmental Narrative

It is helpful when reading Baumstark's *On the Historical Development of the Liturgy* to step back far enough to distinguish the forest from the trees. For the trees of this book are densely planted; one can easily get lost amid the myriad examples and references Baumstark brings to bear upon the topics discussed. Stepping back, one can see the narrative of liturgical development, the pattern Baumstark used for planting these trees. This narrative unfolds in the heart of his book, chapters 2 through 16, as depicted in the table on page 17. Much is hidden within the list of chapters 2 through 16. First of all, they reflect the overall pattern of liturgical development: from variety to uniformity. Baumstark writes, "The historical development of the liturgy does not proceed from uniformity at its earliest to an increasing local diversity, but rather from local diversity to an increasing standardization."[49] Second, as

---

[48] Baumstark, *On the Historical Development*, p. 39.

[49] Ibid., p. 89.

On the Historical Development of the Liturgy

Liturgical Narrative

Chapter Number	Chapter Title	OVERALL PATTERN	Early Growth of Liturgy	Formation of Rites: Similarities	Formation of Rites: Contrasts	Malformation of Rites
2	Domestic and Congregational Celebration	FROM VARIETY TO UNIFORMITY	▓			
3	The Legacy of the Synagogue		▓			
4	Impact of Hellenism		▓			
5	Variety and Uniformity		▓			
6	Influential Centers and Regional Definition			▓		
7	Transferal and Blending			▓		
8	Liturgy and Politics			▓		
9	Cathedral and Monastery			▓		
10	The Work of the Individual			▓		
11	Language and Nation				▓	
12	Progress, Persistence, Hardening				▓	
13	Liturgical Language and the Vernacular Priest and Deacon				▓	
14	The Ivy of Poetry					▓
15	The Demands of Personal Piety					▓
16	Reform and Standardization					▓

apparent in the columns indicating phases of liturgical development, the chapters are loosely organized by a chronological sequence, as succeeding factors in the development of the liturgy. Behind all this, however, one also finds a political narrative, the main characters being the imperial liturgies of the East and West. To state the matter more broadly, Baumstark holds that the relationship a liturgy has to imperial power affects how it participates in the narrative of liturgical development. Imperial liturgies have the experience of victory; those "located" on the underside or edges of empire experience life on the margins. At least aware of having less power than others in the wider church, they also often find themselves out of favor, rejected, excluded, or even directly opposed.

In liturgical development, as Baumstark understands it, the earliest forms are the most varied; the later forms are the more uniform (chapter 5).[50] For Baumstark this was merely a fact, a matter of observation. Variety was most prevalent in the earliest period (generally, from the incarnation to the Peace of Constantine in 313),[51] when the seed of the worship of the apostolic community in Jerusalem (chapter 2) grew out of the Jewish motherland (chapter 3) surrounded by a Hellenistic cultural environment (chapter 4). Baumstark noticed this, for example, in the words of institution, which can be traced back to the earliest Christian literature, where they are found to be most varied. This is the mark of a tradition that was originally oral.[52] The variety stemmed also from the local specificity of liturgical forms: the tendency of the liturgy to relate itself to time and place. Found in regard to both text and rite, one telling example of this is the way eucharistic prayers were

---

[50] This observation challenged the traditional view of an apostolic liturgy being the sole origin for all liturgies of the church and the conventional notion that latter forms were more varied. See ibid., p. 89.

[51] While the chapters are loosely organized chronologically, that chronology is fluid. "Domestic and Congregational Worship," (chap. 2) for example, first became apparent in the apostolic church in Jerusalem, but Baumstark perceives it reemerging later in history as a sort of "deep structure," for example, in the evolution of the Breviary (pp. 58–60). Nor was "The Impact of Hellenism" (chap. 4) limited to the first three centuries of liturgical development. While it first made itself felt then, its influence continued, notably in the ritual elaboration of the fourth and fifth centuries. Baumstark dates its influence to the sixth. See ibid., pp. 200–204.

[52] See ibid., pp. 90, 94–95.

"composed" during this period of early growth. They were, according to Baumstark, produced orally and improvised by the presider, who used certain set phrases and pieces, as well as an accepted outline, to organize his thoughts. This approach enabled him to insert local references into the prayer.[53] Yet even in these first three centuries, variety was yielding to uniformity. While the inherited forms rooted in Jewish prayer life provided some uniform patterns in Christian worship, so Baumstark asserted, the propensity toward uniformity was also at work within the liturgical organism as it grew.

As the church filled the social, institutional, and political space afforded by its new legal status following the Peace of Constantine (313), the pace of uniformatization picked up. This proceeded by a number of influences, processes, and dynamics (chapters 6 through 10). It concluded in the ninth century[54] when—according to Baumstark—the two imperial rites took their final forms, the result in each case of predecessor rites being blended to create what came to be known as

---

[53] Ibid., p. 95. In acknowledging early variety, Baumstark recognized the precondition for form criticism (*Formgeschichte*), which already in his day was being applied to biblical texts. Hermann Gunkel (1862–1932), the scholar most closely tied to the emergence of this method in biblical studies, published his commentary on Genesis in 1901, more than twenty years before *On the Historical Development of the Liturgy* appeared in print. Indeed, in chap. four, "The Impact of Hellenism," Baumstark mentions Eduard Norden's "morphology of religious speech used in antiquity" (chap. 4, n. 23) and suggested its application to liturgy. Here we have an instance in Baumstark of cognitive dissonance. To be sure, he acknowledged the varied oral character of the early liturgy. But rather than using form criticism when handling these texts, he continued to use a philological methodological framework. In the case of Jewish prayer, for example, he regards Judaism and Christianity in a mother-daughter relationship, reads later synagogue prayer life back into the first century, and makes textual comparisons using material that was originally oral. For an overview of the methodological issues involved in the relationship of Jewish and Christian worship, see Gerard Rouwhorst, "Christliche und jüdische Liturgie," in *Gottesdienst der Kirche, Handbuch der Liturgiewissenschaft*, pt. 2, vol. 1, *Theologie der Gottesdienst*, eds. Angelus Häußling et al. (Regensburg: Verlag Friedrich Pustet, 2008), 491–513.

[54] Baumstark gives specific dates for when he thought the development of the two imperial rites had concluded: 842 in the East, the conclusion of the iconoclastic controversy, and 843 in the West, the signing of the Treaty of Verdun, which acknowledged the division of Charlemagne's empire.

the Roman Rite in the West and the Byzantine Rite in the East.[55] At the same time that these rites had in themselves become uniform, however, they had also become distinct from one another. Their differences stemmed from how language and culture had shaped them (chapter 11),[56] to what degree they embraced change or valued continuity (chapter 12), how they managed the pastoral question of comprehensibility (chapter 13), and their attitude—prior the ninth century—toward the liturgical embellishment of poetry (chapter 14).[57] Baumstark counts it significant that the imperial rites became firm in form in the very same century that they accepted challenges of evangelism. For in the ninth century both embraced evangelical missions toward the north: the Latin Church among the Scandinavians and the western Slavs, the Greek Church among the eastern Slavs.[58] In this work the imperial rites encountered cultures and languages different from their own. Having already been firmly formed, however, they had the confidence to project their imperial cultures into alien worlds to the north.

At this point another organic process emerged—malformation, with two aspects: (1) the clear lines of the classical liturgy became blurred, and (2) the "natural" processes of the liturgical organism were compromised.[59] The first aspect came to pass with the rampant growth of

---

[55] Baumstark, *On the Historical Development*, pp. 128–29. The Byzantine Rite is a blend of the old Constantinopolitan Rite and the Jerusalem Rite, the Roman Rite a blend of the old Roman and the Frankish rites.

[56] For Baumstark, cultural traits can be distinctive enough to serve as criteria for categorizing liturgical texts. For example, ibid., pp. 69–70.

[57] While the period for the "Formation of Rites: Contrasts" is generally the same as that for "Formation of Rites: Similarities" (313–842/43), there are some differences. Notably, "Language and Nation" (chap. 11) impacted the liturgy from its first days and continues do so on through its history. The characteristics of "Development, Persistence, and Hardening" are set in this period but not limited to it. Finally, chap. 14, "The Ivy of Poetry" pertains both to the "Formation of Rites: Contrasts" and "Malformation." In dealing with poetry prior to 842/43 (an approximate date), Baumstark describes how the East and the West contrasted sharply in their attitude toward liturgical poetry. Following that time, however, liturgical poetry overwhelmed and suffocated venerable liturgical forms in both East and West (see below).

[58] Ibid., pp. 128–29.

[59] The period of "malformation" needs to be qualified as well. The liturgy began to be overgrown by poetry and prayers approximately in the ninth century, but the *terminus ad quem* of this process is different in the West and

liturgical poetry (chapter 14) and the prayers worked into the liturgy to meet the needs of clerical piety (chapter 15). This was not growth but rather overgrowth, in which the crisp profile of ancient liturgical forms was obscured and venerable elements smothered. Textual overgrowth could even break down liturgical frameworks, no longer able to bear the weight of the added material.[60] Secondly, reform can malform (chapter 16). Viewed as human history, reform is conscious, an act of human will, antithetical to the organic character of the liturgy and disruptive to its patterns. In Baumstark's view, this was certainly the case for the Protestant Reformation, as noted above.[61] While Baumstark puts the best light on the actions of the Council of Trent,[62] there is no gainsaying that it can also be understood as contradicting the organic character of the liturgy. True, the decisions of the council itself can be conceived as acts of the Roman Church guided by the Holy Spirit. As we saw above, however, Baumstark observed that the decisions of the instrumentality set up to subsequently handle liturgical affairs, the Sacred Congregation of Rites and is its successor bodies, were and are certainly intentional and conscious.[63]

The pattern of liturgical development just described was written from the perspective of the victors, the imperial rites of the East and the West. There were, and still are, many other rites, those to the south and east of the imperial rites.[64] Since, however, the main characters of Baumstark's

---

the East. In the West it came to a distinct halt with the liturgical reforms of the Council of Trent, which trimmed back much of this material (as well as the sanctoral cycle). There was no such reform in the East, although the use of printed liturgical books beginning at about the same time slowed the "organic" growth of the liturgy there. The time frame for reform needs comment as well. While Baumstark focuses on reforms from the Council of Trent (1570) through the eighteenth century, his examples reach back to the seventh and forward to the twentieth. For him, reform is a factor at play once liturgical forms have developed, from the early Middle Ages to the present.

[60] Ibid., pp. 199–213 passim, esp. 199.

[61] Ibid., p. 245, and Baumstark, "Besprechung: *Die nestorianische Taufliturgie*": 220–21.

[62] Baumstark, *On the Historical Development*, p. 247.

[63] Ibid., pp. 244–5, 231, 244.

[64] To make the point that the imperial rites were oriented north and the nonimperial were found to the south and east, Baumstark must categorize the Ambrosian and Mozarabic rites in the West as "southern," which they were

narrative are imperial, the liturgies of the Oriental, East Syrian, and Indian churches in the East, as well as the non-Roman rites in the West[65] are as marginal to Baumstark's central narrative as they once were to imperial power. Baumstark certainly attends to these other rites, drawing upon them for examples, sometimes extended. He acknowledges their contributions to the liturgical life of the church, sometimes substantial. Their liturgical life was no less vibrant than that of the imperial liturgies; the factors of all aspects of liturgical development play a role in their evolution. Indeed, Baumstark deals with the Oriental and East Syrian rites more extensively than other liturgical scholars of his time. However, these rites fully shared the same narrative of liturgical development only in the first three centuries, prior to the Peace of Constantine, when all of Christendom lived on the edges of or under the empire.[66] Going forward in time, as the two imperial rites of the East and the West started their victorious march toward the ninth century and beyond, the others lived on the raw end of imperial power.[67] They were marginalized, constrained, or suppressed, sometimes by empires—Christian and pagan—sometimes by imperious churches.[68] After the Arab invasions in the sixth and seventh centuries, all of the Oriental churches (with the exception of the Ethiopian) and the East Syrian Church (save the church in India) had to live under Arab hegemony. This experience shaped their participation in the narrative of liturgical development, especially in regard to language and culture (chapter 7). For while the Greek and Latin liturgies projected their imperial cultures against other rites and into new fields of mission, the nonimperial liturgies protected the cultures they had been bequeathed.[69]

---

in the sense that they lay to the south of the area where the Roman Rite was dominant.

[65] Baumstark is referring here primarily to the Ambrosian Rite of Milan and the Mozarabic Rite of Spain, although there were others as well.

[66] The Ethiopian Church is the exception to this generalization, and in this period the church in Persia lived not under the Roman Empire, but rather during a change of empires centered in that region, the fall of the Parthian and the rise of the Sassanian.

[67] The exceptions to this statement are the churches in India and Ethiopia, although ecclesiastically the latter was under the authority of the Coptic patriarch in Egypt, a relationship that continued until 1959.

[68] Baumstark, *On the Historical Development*, pp. 129–34.

[69] Ibid., pp. 130–32. In this regard, Baumstark explicitly mentions the role that the Nestorian Church (ibid., pp. 100, 103–4, 162–63, the Armenian Church

For Baumstark, the Carolingian Empire and Renaissance provide the paradigm for the liturgy's position vis-à-vis politics and culture. To understand this fully we need to acknowledge the place Baumstark gives the individual in history. True, Baumstark regards the liturgical "organism" to be an independent historical entity, whose slow and quiet growth is interrupted by liturgical initiatives driven by human will. However, he also has a chapter on the work of individuals (chapter 10), and over the course of his book he mentions no less than 193 persons. Ironically, we have in Baumstark a representative of both the comparative sciences of culture and the Great Man Theory of History. While Baumstark asserts in all sincerity that liturgical development proceeds by an organic process, the reader of this book also gets the sense that it moves from person to person. Baumstark identified many great men and a few great women in liturgical history: Pachomius (390–46),[70] Ephrem the Syrian (306–73),[71] and Isho'yabh III (580–659);[72] Basil the Great (303–79),[73] Melania the Younger (385–438/39),[74] and Jacob Baradaeus (500–78);[75] Egeria (fl. fourth century),[76] Gregory I (540–604),[77] and Gregory VII (1015–85).[78] None, however, is greater than Charlemagne (742–814),[79] whom Baumstark mentions with more admiration and greater frequency than any other historical figure,

---

(ibid., pp. 102–3), and the Coptic Church of Egypt (ibid., p. 103) played in protecting their cultures while under imperial rule or pressure. It is interesting to note as well that the church in India was using Syriac for its liturgical language when Europeans came upon it in the fifteenth century. The West Syrian Church, located in what Baumstark described as a cultural "transit zone," was not in a position to play this protecting role (ibid., pp. 100, 117–18), although the more isolated Maronite Church in the same area was. So, while the instances of this generalization are mixed, the observation still stands.

[70] On Pachomius, see Short Biography, no. 133.

[71] On Ephrem the Syrian, see Short Biography, no. 66.

[72] On Ishoyabh III, see Short Biography, no. 101.

[73] On Basil the Great, see Short Biography, no. 28.

[74] On Melania the Younger, see Short Biography, no. 122.

[75] On Jacob Baradaeus, see Short Biography, no. 102.

[76] On Egeria, see Short Biography, no. 65.

[77] On Gregory I, see Short Biography, no. 78.

[78] On Gregory VII, see Short Biography, no. 81.

[79] On Charlemagne, see Short Biography, no. 44.

with the emperor's adviser Alcuin (735–804)[80] and son Louis I (778–814)[81] coming in right behind, tying for second.[82]

The place of the liturgy in the Carolingian Empire and Renaissance is paradigmatic for Baumstark because it exemplifies the cultural power of the liturgy being used by a Great Man in the service of an empire. To Baumstark's lights, the Franco-Roman (Carolingian) liturgy (which subsequently became the "Roman") gained its inner strength from combining the classical ideals of Rome with the depth of German feeling. Specifically, the Carolingian liturgy combined Roman restraint, moderation, and sobriety with German valor, virility, and martial spirit. All this is personified in the person of Charlemagne, who brought the liturgy of Rome north to Aachen, instigated the Carolingian Renaissance, and combined in himself Roman and German traits: valor and sobriety, power and restraint, and strength and moderation. Notably, Charlemagne appreciated the value of the liturgy as a cohesive force for unifying the Holy Roman Empire.[83]

There is a decided resonance between the paradigmatic moment Baumstark identified in 1923 for the development of the liturgy and the political vision he espoused later in the same decade. In 1928 Baumstark gave a speech to the fourth annual assembly of the Ring Katholischer Deutscher Burschenschaften, a national association of German Catholic fraternities. While basically a student organization, it welcomed older individuals into its ranks as well. This organization had two central commitments: dedication to the Roman Catholic Church and the creation of a "Greater Germany" (*Grossdeutscher Reich*), by which was meant an empire incorporating all European lands where Germans lived. At the conclusion of the meeting, Baumstark gave a brief talk entitled, "Das wollen wir, das sind wir, das heißt Katholische Deutsche Burschenschaft" (We want this, we are this, this is what Katholische Deutsche Burschenschaft means). He began by praising the German effort during World War I as heroic and complaining that all responsibility for that war had been laid at Germany's doorstep; he went on to declare that Germany was destined

---

[80] On Alcuin, see Short Biography, no. 7.

[81] On Louis I, see Short Biography, no. 119.

[82] Baumstark mentions Charlemagne eight times, Alcuin and Louis I both seven. He only mentions Paul, the Apostle to the Gentiles, so often as Charlemagne.

[83] See Baumstark, *On the Historical Development*, pp. 134–37.

to become a "Greater Germany." For this cause, Baumstark insisted, one must be willing to give up one's life, as Christ had laid down his life for his friends. He notes that Catholics joining in will gain strength for this struggle from God's grace mediated by the church, specifically through the Eucharist. Baumstark concludes, "Said in brief and without any window dressing: Service to *Volk* and Fatherland, by which we mean a Greater Germany, for the sake of God, in the Spirit of Christ, out of the fountains of grace flowing to us from the holy Catholic Church—that is what we want, that is who we are, that is what Catholic German Fraternity means."[84]

In the nationalist, conservative German politics of the 1920s, the paradigm for German empire was the Holy Roman Empire that Charlemagne had brought into being. In this speech Baumstark brings together empire, culture, and church in much the same way as he understands the king of the Franks had done. Just as Charlemagne's Frankish Empire had gained strength and cohesion from the church and its liturgy in the ninth century, so too did Baumstark call upon Roman Catholic German Christians, strengthened by the supernatural grace mediated to them through the church and its Eucharist, to help bring about in the twentieth century a European empire incorporating all Germans. Baumstark's politics and paradigm do not relate as cause and effect, however. Neither were his politics the direct result of his paradigm nor was his paradigm politically motivated. Rather, both politics and paradigm are instances of Baumstark's imperial *Weltanschauung*: that an empire rooted in German culture and the Catholic Church, be it in the ninth century or the twentieth, was positioned to rise.

We need now to step back and look around, shifting our focus from Baumstark's imperial vision to his field of comparison. For in addition to his imperial narrative, he also embraced a comparative approach. In *On the Historical Development of the Liturgy,* he is forever working back and forth between the liturgies of the empires and those on the margins. Indeed, at times he does so puckishly, taking seeming delight in pricking the inflated pretensions of power, particularly those of empire. One might well view in this light his assertion that cultural

---

[84] See Anton Baumstark, "Was wollen wir, was sind wir, was heißt die Deutsche Katholische Burschenschaft," *Der Ring. Mitteilungen des Ringes Katholischer Deutscher Burschencaften* 5 (1928): 51 (translation mine). See also Baumstark, *On the Historical Development,* pp. 134–37.

influence in the Mediterranean basin moves from East to West. Specifically, this challenged the position of Rome, which, though ascendant
in politics and practicality, was (in this view) dependent on the East
for sensibility and cultural refinement.[85] The central point, however, is
this: at the same time that he makes empire central to his developmental narrative, he also directs our attention to the churches and liturgies
of Ireland and India, China and Ethiopia, and others. The very breadth
of this field—the whole "organism" of the liturgy of the church—puts
all liturgies into perspective, including that of the Roman Catholic
Church. When viewing the Roman liturgy by itself, for example, the
standardization effected by the Council of Trent may appear as the
(victorious) end point of the (imperial? imperious?) trend from variety to uniformity. However, in the context of the liturgy of the whole
church, the Roman liturgy appears in an altogether different light. It
is now one among many, sharing a journey of development in common with all other liturgies. In this way, we acquire a sense of propor-
tion about the liturgies produced out of the Council of Trent and even
about Baumstark's imperial passions.

Liturgical Reform

Baumstark expressly presented this picture of liturgical development to further the ends of the liturgical movement.[86] To capture the
whole liturgical "organism" of the Church just discussed, he employed the image of a tree. He wrote that "as a useful tool, comparative liturgical history remains in the service of our ultimate goal: to
awaken and further an appreciation for the growth of that mighty tree
in whose shadow the Catholic community using Latin as its liturgical
language gathers to unite in celebrating liturgical worship according
to the Roman Rite."[87] In Baumstark's view, the most fruitful place for

---

[85] When coupling this assertion with his notion that the Roman Rite gains
its inner strength from German feeling, one can wonder whether Baumstark
sensed an analogy between what Hellenistic culture had to offer Roman rule
and what German culture contributed to the Roman Rite. Or, stated as an assertion, that Rome projects a culture of the head (known for its practicality,
moderation, sobriety, and efficiency), which, to address the breadth of the
human spirit, requires the complement of a culture of the heart (sensibility,
feeling, affect).

[86] Baumstark, On the Historical Development, pp. 49, 193–94 and pp. 240–42.

[87] Ibid., p. 49.

the Roman Catholic liturgical movement to dwell was in the shade of this tree. Here the movement could both gain perspective on liturgical reform and sustenance from the liturgy, the topics of this section and the next.

While in 1921 the German liturgical movement was in its infancy, the question of reform was already in the air. In *On the Historical Development of the Liturgy* Baumstark made clear that the liturgy, while sacred, was not sacrosanct, off-limits to reform. Indeed, the central chapters of this little volume can be read as a historical reflection on liturgical reform: the liturgy's early growth (chapters 2–4), its filling out and shaping (chapters 5–12), its overgrowth (14–15), and its reform (chapter 16). Baumstark held that the Roman Rite, unlike those in the East, had a propensity to reflect upon itself, a necessary prelude to reform.[88] As to the goal of liturgical reform, he wrote, "A return to Christian antiquity, as it was minted in Rome, sober and clear, can be designated as the ultimate and comprehensive goal of such a reforming movement."[89] One must count this as an ideal. Surely Baumstark does not wish to purge the final form of the Roman Rite of the German elements he so greatly admired. In regard to the actions of the Council of Trent, he determined, "Dangers posed by the rampant growth of more recent elements, which threatened the continued existence of venerable ones from an earlier time, were exorcized by the fortunate intervention of authoritative reform."[90] Of the essence was maintaining the venerable forms and clear lines of the liturgy, in this case the final form of the Roman liturgy found in the ninth century. This path certainly leads back toward "Christian antiquity, as it was minted in Rome," but as a norm to be employed, not a golden age to be emulated. Baumstark also wanted to take the growth of the liturgy into account.

Since liturgical reform needs to maintain the organic continuity of the liturgy and honor its venerable forms, a reform driven by human will, conducted without regard for liturgical tradition, violates the liturgy.[91] This was exemplified for Baumstark in the reform of the

---

[88] Ibid., p. 241.

[89] Ibid.

[90] See ibid., p. 247.

[91] Examples of reforms that violated the liturgy are that of the antiphonary by Bishop Agobard of Lyons (see ibid., pp. 123–24), some reforms of the Roman

Breviary conducted by Cardinal Francisco de Quiñones (1475–1540).[92] By contrast, a reform that attends to the continuity of the liturgy, as did those of Gregory VII (1073–85),[93] honors its organic nature. However, the ground shifts in the sixteenth century when the organic growth of the liturgy in the West came to an end. The actions of the Sacred Congregation of Rites reflects this for being (1) wholly conscious and (2) implemented by the authority of the church.[94] Baumstark wrote, "Both features clearly contradict the essence of the liturgy insofar as it manifests itself as a kind of organic growth."[95] At the same time, he holds that the Roman Church can reform the liturgy through conscious acts of authority. With the liturgy no longer growing, the task of reform becomes one of consolidating the strengths the Roman liturgy had previously obtained organically, taking care to walk the fine line between preserving forms unchanged for posterity and introducing innovation that interrupts the continuity of the liturgy's venerable forms. In Baumstark's perspective, the Sacred Congregation of Rites erred to the side of preservation. In particular, they took as their primary task keeping the liturgy as reformed by Trent intact, rather than "consolidating it," that is, "strengthening further certain aspects of liturgical life according to the Roman Rite."[96] The Breviary reform of Pius X (1903–14), on the other hand, erred on the side of innovation, notably in departing from the distribution of psalms over the hours of the week that Trent had preserved untouched.[97]

Any reform, however, ought to be seen in light of comparative liturgy, liturgical language being a case in point. While Baumstark's inclination to conserve is apparent, his knowledge of the various ways the liturgy had been celebrated opened him up to consider the

---

Breviary in the sixteenth and seventeenth centuries, including that of Quiñones (see ibid., p. 235), and the Nikonian reforms in Russian during the seventeenth century (ibid., pp. 230–31). Examples of reforms that honored the liturgy are those of Gregory the Great (ibid., pp. 158–59) and the development of the Carolingian liturgy, ca. 750–840 (ibid., pp. 122–24).

[92] Ibid., pp. 235, 240–41.
[93] Ibid., pp. 232–33.
[94] Ibid., pp. 244–45.
[95] Ibid., p. 245.
[96] Ibid., p. 240.
[97] Ibid., pp. 240–41.

different ways it might be celebrated, even in regard to language. He wrote, "The use of Latin is fundamentally important to the value of the liturgy—and not only as a sign of the unity of church life. It is also crystal clear that, by donning the ancient language of the Roman people for its standard linguistic attire, the Roman liturgy itself gains greatly in dignity and majesty. Nonetheless one cannot deny that celebrating the liturgy in a dead language, which the bulk of the faithful cannot understand, constitutes the main challenge confronting today's vibrant liturgical movement in seeking to attain its ultimate goal."[98] Viewed solely in the context of the Roman Rite, one might well fall toward the side of preserving Latin in the liturgy without exception. We get a different perspective, however, when placing the Roman Rite in the shade of the tree of the whole liturgy of the church. There the Western Rite stands next to those from the East that have consistently been open to using the vernacular in the liturgy.[99] Further, we see the issue of language in the larger framework of comprehensibility, comparable—in this context—to the liturgical ministry of the deacon in the East. Thus Baumstark's criterion of "returning to Christian antiquity, as it was minted in Rome" does not take us down a univocal path to a self-evident answer. True, the use of Latin in the liturgy carries one back to Christian antiquity. But what aspect of that antiquity? In Roman worship of the fourth to sixth centuries, Latin was both expressive of "dignity and majesty" and understood by the assembly. Both values are rooted in Christian antiquity and both strengthened the liturgy of that day. So which aspect should the Roman Church choose to strengthen the liturgy in Baumstark's day? As a Catholic Christian, Baumstark wished to pose this question, but, as a historian, he refrained from answering it.[100]

The Religious Value of Engaging the Liturgy Historically

Baumstark envisioned comparative liturgy as a way to enhance the liturgical piety of the German liturgical movement. Once again Baumstark draws the Roman Liturgy under the branches and into the shade of the gigantic tree, the liturgical "organism" of the whole church. Apart from methodological considerations, the opening and closing

---

[98] Ibid., p. 194.
[99] Ibid., pp. 189–93.
[100] Ibid., pp. 241–42.

chapters of *On the Historical Development of the Liturgy* portray a knowledge of liturgical history, and especially of its comparative study, as a path to greater religious appreciation of the liturgy.[101] To address this question, Baumstark draws upon his German cultural heritage. On the very first page of *Comparative Liturgy*, Baumstark quotes Johann Wolfgang von Goethe (1749–1832), from *Faust*, Part I, "Wirkte [*sic*] der Gottheit lebendiges Kleid,"[102] and applies to the liturgy Goethe's insight into nature. The full text of this passage, which has the Spirit speaking to Faust, reads in English,

> Spirit· In the tides of life, in action's storm,
> > I surge and ebb,
> > Move to and fro!
> > As cradle and grave
> > As unending sea,
> > As constant change,
> > As life's incandescence,
> > I work at the whirring loom of time
> > And fashion the living garment of God.[103]

Baumstark sees "the mysterious power of nature"[104] weaving for the liturgy (being as it is a phenomenon in nature) "a living garment for

---

[101] Ibid., pp. 48–49 and pp. 246–48.

[102] Baumstark, *Comparative Liturgy*, 1.

[103] Johann Wolfgang von Goethe, *Faust I & II*, ed. and trans. Stuart Atkins, *Goethe's Collected Works*, vol. 2 (Princeton, NJ: Princeton University Press, 1984), 480, lines 501–9:
> Geist: In Lebensfluten im Tatensturm
> > Wall' ich auf und ab,
> > Webe hin und her!
> > Geburt und Grab,
> > Ein ewiges Meer,
> > Ein wechselnd Weben,
> > Ein glühend Leben
> > So schaff' ich am sausenden Webstuhl der Zeit,
> > Und wirke der Gottheit lebendiges Kleid.

Johann Wolfgang von Goethe, *Sämtliche Werke nach Epochen seines Schaffens*, vol. 6, pt. 1, Weimarer Klassik 1798–1806, ed. Victor Lange (München [Munich]: Carl Hanser Verlag, 1986), 549, lines 501–9.

[104] Baumstark, *Comparative Liturgy*, 1.

God."[105] The images of this passage from *Faust*—or those in Goethe's poem "Wenn im Unendlichen," whose final couplet reads, "All the straining, all the striving / Is eternal peace in God"[106]—find striking parallels in a sentence from the first chapter of *On the Historical Development of the Liturgy*: "Thundering restlessly, yet resting blessedly in the stillness of God, the waves of that ocean [of communal prayer] swell from earth up to those transcendent heights where the one praying hears the choirs, pure in spirit, join him in singing the *Sanctus* and the souls in purgatory call out 'Lord, have mercy.'"[107] Baumstark has taken Goethe's aesthetic vision and applied it to the Christian liturgy as it plays out in the three-tiered universe. This shift notwithstanding, Baumstark, like Goethe, speaks of the historical and the finite as waves moving and thundering, yet finding quiet rest in the "stillness of God."

For the poet Goethe and the historian Baumstark, the temporal—which is distinct from God—can be revelatory. The distinction is radical: temporal and eternal, finite and infinite, restless and peaceful, rage and repose, straining and striving but still. One finds here *coincidentia oppositorum*—a unity of opposites, a unity transcending opposition. These bold contrasts make the capacity of nature to reveal the Godhead all the more striking. God is revealed through what God is not; the eternal is apparent in the temporal. In commenting upon the phrase *una sancta catholica et apostolica liturgia* (one holy catholic and apostolic liturgy), Baumstark writes, "This phrase is appropriate for describing the intrinsic unity and constancy of the liturgy if used to indicate this and no more: the deep sublimity found at the core of its being. Quite distinct from this core is its form, which changes as

---

[105] In *On the Historical Development of the Liturgy*, Baumstark uses this metaphor repeatedly in regard to the language of the liturgy. See Baumstark, *On the Historical Development*, p. 163 as well as pp. 190 and 194.

[106] Translated by Charles Francis Atkinson in Oswald Spengler, *Decline of the West*, vol. 1, *Form and Actuality* (New York: Alfred A. Knopf, 1959), 140. The German reads:

Und alles Drängen, alles Ringen

Ist ewige Ruh' in Gott dem Herrn.

Johann Wolfgang von Goethe, *Sämtliche Werke nach Epochen seines Schaffens*, vol. 13, pt. 1, *Die Jahre 1820–1826*, eds. Gisel Henckmann and Irmela Schneider (München [Munich]: Carl Hanser Verlag, 1992), 226.

[107] Baumstark, *On the Historical Development*, p. 43.

the liturgy develops, a process going back without interruption to apostolic times."[108] The contrast is understated here. Compared to the "deep sublimity" at its heart, the historical forms of the liturgy are not just changing, but at times are restless or even tumultuous.

With this understanding, presented by Baumstark in the first and last chapters of *On the Historical Development of the Liturgy*, we can appreciate the religious potential of its middle fifteen chapters. A knowledge of the history of the liturgy leads to an appreciation of the eternal apparent in those forms. Baumstark is explicit about this in chapter seventeen. After recounting the various aspects of liturgical development he has surveyed in the book, he writes, "Without the ordering rule of eternal prudence the believing spirit would not have the power to grasp temporal formation, transformation, and passing—even in general terms."[109] Here we return to the contrast between will and law, history and the historical "organism." Since history (being a function of arbitrary will) is unpatterned, patterns in the temporal world are a sign of God's presence, God's "prudence." Baumstark continues, "In regard to the historical development of forms, this soul will doubly sense the possibility of revering that rule, where the finite pays the tribute of his adoration to the eternal and he himself experiences the eternal condescending in grace."[110] Once again we turn to Goethe, notably to his definition of true symbolism in maxim no. 314: "True symbolism arises where the individual represents the universal, not as dream and shadow, but as a vivid, lively revelation of the impenetrable."[111] (A suggestion: instead of "the individual," a better translation of the German word *das Besondere* may be "the particular".) And once again, in Baumstark's religious appreciation of the exchange of

---

[108] Ibid., p. 89.

[109] Ibid., p. 247.

[110] Ibid. The German of this sentence, one of the more difficult to be found in *On the Historical Development*, reads, "Ohne das ordende Walten ewiger Vorsicht vermag gläubiger Geist schon allgemein geschichtliches Werden, Sichwandeln und Vergehen nicht zu begreifen. Doppelt wird er jenes Walten dort meinen verehren zu dürfen, wo es sich um die geschichtlichen Entwicklung der Formen handelt, in denen das Endliche dem Ewigen den Zoll seiner Anbetung entrichtet und die die gnadenvolle Herablassung des Ewigen zu sich erfährt."

[111] ET: Else Marie Bukdahl, *Johannes Wiedewelt: From Winckelmann's Vision of Antiquity to Sculptural Concepts of the 1980s*, Format 10, trans. David Hohnen

prayers and graces in the liturgy, we find a close Christian analogue to Goethe's insight. In the liturgy the Christian acquires an even greater appreciation for the possibility of discerning the eternal in the temporal, for there one has the interaction of the two. The finite and temporal pay tribute to the eternal discerned in history, whereas "the true symbolism" of the liturgy, in which "the [temporal and finite] particular represents the [eternal and infinite] universal," reveals "the impenetrable." For Baumstark, the study of the historical forms of the liturgy is tantamount to a contemplation of the eternal in this world.[112]

A Word of Caution

Zeroing in on Baumstark's specific arguments, one needs to proceed with caution. In the first place, as a historian from another era, Baumstark makes use of dated historiographical concepts and tools, such as German romanticism, German idealism, the Great Man Theory of History, a philological predilection for texts, and—yes—comparative liturgy. He wrote prior to the rise of the social sciences, which play such a significant role in contemporary historiography. Furthermore, Baumstark's strength and weakness lay in his use of hypotheses. With the breadth of his thought, knowledge, and interests, he was able to suggest hypotheses and relationships that might have eluded scholars of narrower focus. Given Baumstark's facility with language, his encyclopedic knowledge, and a prodigious capacity for work, he could bring to bear upon his hypotheses large amounts of data from a variety of cultures, rites, and contexts. While these hypotheses are often stimulating, they are not always carefully crafted. Indeed, at times they are extravagant or, as Olivier Rousseau (1898–1984) termed them, when referring to both his politics and his intellect, "utopian."[113]

(Hellerup, Denmark: Edition Bløndel, 1993), 31. The German reads, "Das ist die wahre Symbolik, wo das Besondere das Allgemeine repräsentiert, nicht als Traum und Schatten, sondern als lebendig-augenblickliche Offenbarung des Unerforschlichen." See Johann Wolfgang Goethe, *Sämtliche Werke nach Epochen seines Schaffens*, vol. 17, *Wilhelm Meisters Wanderjahre, Maximen und Reflexionen*, eds. Gonthier-Louis Fink, Gerhart Baumann, und Johannes John (München [Munich]: Carl Hanser Verlag, 1991), 775, no. 314.

[112] My sincere thanks for Dr. Martin Ulrich of Lakeland College, Sheboygan, Wisconsin, for insight into these similarities between Baumstark's and Goethe's thought.

[113] Olivier Rousseau, "Antoine Baumstark (1872–1948)," *La maison Dieu* 16 (1948): 158.

Bernard Botte (1893–1980) wondered whether Baumstark was able to distinguish between his hypotheses and historical reality, counting this as his "chief limitation."[114] To annotate all those passages in *On the Historical Development of the Liturgy* that might call for comment or correction would require a companion volume, an unwieldy commentary. Suffice it to say that the reader would do well to bring a hermeneutic of suspicion to bear upon Baumstark's historical conclusions.

THIS TRANSLATION

The purpose of this translation is to fulfill Baumstark's intent for *On the Historical Development of the Liturgy*. In the first instance, he intended it for the general reading public, albeit a particular segment: those interested in joining the liturgical movement.

His intention was only partially realized, however, because—from the outset—this work has been relatively inaccessible. This is primarily due to Baumstark's writing style, which is a mannered, turgid *akademisches Deutsch*. In his brief biography of Baumstark, Otto Spies (1901–81), a colleague at the University of Bonn, analyzes this style at some length:

> To be sure his articles are not easy to read because of his elaborate style. One gets the clear impression that one has before one here Latin constructions in German dress. Substantives and substantive abstractions preponderate as well as elaborately pretentious and exaggerated participial constructions in whose place we would simply use a straightforward relative or causal clause. His sentences are too long, too elaborate with one thought packed inside another, so that one no longer knows at the end of a sentence what one read at its beginning. For this reason his popular essays were not able to be effective. A typical example is his letter written for the soldiers on January 1944 about "Die Orthodoxe Kirche": the first printed page consists of two (?) complete sentences. It is also often difficult to find one's way through the scholarly articles. At least in my experience each sentence must be read three times in order to understand and grasp what it was meant to say.[115]

I would only add that his vocabulary can be archaic (for example, *entrücken*), is sprinkled with neologisms (for example, *das Geschlac-*

---

[114] Botte, "Foreword to the Third Edition," in Anton Baumstark, *Comparative Liturgy*, ix.

[115] Otto Spies, "Anton Baumstark (1872–1948)," *Bonner Gelehrte: Beiträge zur Geschichte der Wissenschaften in Bonn: Sprachwissenschaften* (Bonn: Ludwig Röhrschied Verlag, 1970), 349 (translation mine).

tetwerden and *das Sichauswirken*), uses classicisms (for example, *Denkmal*[116] and proper names in their Latin and Greek forms), and draws vocabulary from Austrian and Bavarian dialects (for example, *adelig*, *nurmehr*, *das Muß*, *der Gau*, *ohne weiterer*, and *durchweg*). Because of Baumstark's infelicitous language, I have made no attempt to preserve his style, translating solely for clarity and meaning. In those instances when the sense of a sentence is inextricably bound up in its complexity, I have used various typographical devices to enhance the readability of the text: paragraphs, parentheses, em dashes, numbering, colons, and the outlining of series by the use of numbers and letters.

The text of *On the Historical Development of the Liturgy* is also inaccessible because of Baumstark's penchant for oblique references. In a 1927 review, Hippolytus Delehaye (1859–1941) wrote, "Mr. Baumstark studies the relations of different types of sacramentaries with an exhibition of erudition that is only equal to his disdain for clarity. One would like to be able to analyze these pages where one can clearly see that the author has accumulated treasures of science whose order is more apparent than real. All power to him who would try! We confess to have simply recoiled before the task. Perhaps sometime the author would like to try to write for those less learned than he."[117] To address this problem, I have annotated the text and supplied short biographies for persons mentioned. Only rarely do I comment on conclusions drawn by Baumstark. To avoid multiple citations for the same data, I do not reference information that can be readily found in the standard English encyclopedias of general knowledge, church life, or religion.[118] Information culled from all other works has been duly footnoted.

---

[116] Baumstark, *On the Historical Development*, n. on p. 45.

[117] Hippolytus Delehaye, "Review of K. Mohlberg and A. Baumstark. *Die älteste erreichbare Gestalt des Liber Sacramentorum anni circuli der Römishe Kirche*," *Analecta Bollandiana* 47 (1927): 117 (translation mine).

[118] *Catholic Encyclopedia*, ed. G. Herbermann et al., 15 vols. and index (New York: The Encyclopedia Press, 1913); *The Encyclopedia of Christianity*, ed. Erwin Fahlbusch et al., 5 vols. (Grand Rapids et al.: Wm. B. Eerdmans, 1999–2008); *Encyclopedia of Early Christianity*, ed. Angelo di Berardino, trans. Adrian Walford, 2 vols. (New York: Oxford University Press, 1991); *Encyclopedia of Religion*, ed. Lindsay Jones, 15 vols., 2nd ed. (Detroit et al.: Thomson Gale, 2005); *Encyclopedia of Religion and Ethics*, ed. James Hastings, 12 vols. (New York: Charles Scribner's Sons, 1908–27); *New Catholic Encyclopedia*, 15 vols., 2nd ed. (Detroit et al.: Thomson Gale, 2003); *The New Encyclopedia Britannica*, 32 vols., 15th ed. (Chicago et al.: Encyclopedia Britannica Corp, 2005); and *Oxford Dictionary of*

Annotations are placed below the text as footnotes. Dates for persons and events have been inserted, as well as biblical citations, with the New Revised Standard Version being used for quotations.

Finally, the footnotes that Baumstark provided for the German edition are inaccessible, in that they are highly abbreviated and often reference the series in which a work appeared rather than the work itself. Full bibliographical information has been provided for each of Baumstark's citations and, when available, English translations are cited. In these footnotes the abbreviation ET indicates "English translation" and GT indicates "German translation." I have placed my translator's comments and additions within brackets. These bibliographical notes are indicated in the text by roman numerals and placed at the end of each chapter.

I have no illusion that *On the Historical Development of the Liturgy* will ever have a truly popular appeal, as was Baumstark's intent. I do hope, dear reader, that you will find in this translation a clear path to travel into the thought of an interesting liturgical scholar.

Work on this translation, which has spanned more than a decade, has required the help of many individuals and institutions. In the first instance, I wish to thank Robert F. Taft, SJ, for giving impetus to this project. I deeply appreciate as well the confidence and support offered by the staff of the Liturgical Press, especially Michael Naughton, OSB; Peter Dwyer; Mark Twomey; Hans Christoffersen; Colleen Stiller; and Eric Christensen. I am grateful to Peter Francis, warden of St. Deiniol's Residential Library in Hawarden, North Wales, which has annually provided me with extended periods for quiet study and on two occasions funded my work with grants from the Canon Symonds Memorial Scholarship Fund, designated for biblical and liturgical scholarship; to Luther Seminary Library in St. Paul, Minnesota, with special thanks to librarians Bruce Eldevik and Karen Alexander, who have welcomed me to renew one early twentieth-century German dictionary forty times; to the libraries of the University of Minnesota, especially Wilson Library; the library of Lancaster Theological School; and to St. John's Abbey and University in Collegeville, Minnesota, where I found quiet to translate. With the encouragement of Father Kilian McDonnell, I stayed at the Abbey's Collegeville Institute for Ecumenical and Cultural Research in the fall of 2009.

---

the Christian Church, eds. F. L. Cross and E. A. Livingstone, 3rd rev. ed. (Oxford: Oxford University Press, 2005).

Many have read all or parts of this translation or helped with particular passages: Peter Schwartz, Max Johnson, Hans-Jürgen Feulner, and Martin Ulrich. To that list I wish to add, but also lift up, Gerard Rouwhorst of the University of Tilburg in the Netherlands, who closely read every sentence of this translation and reviewed every footnote, offering ample comments, criticisms, and suggestions. To him, for this most generous act of scholarly collegiality and encouragement, I will remain forever indebted. Others have provided help on particular aspects or questions: Paul Bradshaw; Clemens Leonard; Eileen Stinchfield Lewis; Melanie Lewis; Father Rene McGraw; Father Jonathan Proctor; Tim Robinson; and Gabriele Winkler. Thanks to Patricia Green for preparing the index.

Keeping the best for last, thanks beyond measure goes to my helpmate and bride, Cynthia Evans West, who with unflagging support, patience, and devotion, has been at my side every step of the way.

A FINAL THOUGHT

Baumstark challenges us to think about "the liturgy." Today scholars of liturgical history are wary of generalization. While this stems in part from the sheer volume of data and methods now available for the study of liturgy, it is also due to the postmodern climate of opinion regnant in contemporary academia. In 1970 Helmut Leeb (1906–79) wrote,

> In our time what is required of research in the history of the liturgy is that it produce clear, sure results. In these results, established facts must be clearly distinguished from hypotheses. Because of the refined research methods of today's liturgical scholarship, with its attention to special, detailed questions, a wide-ranging one-author work covering a large area becomes daily more problematic and impossible. Too many uncertain assertions would have to be advanced, too many hypotheses risked, just because one person can no longer keep in view all the diverse sciences. Today the liturgical generalist like Anton Baumstark . . . is becoming more and more a rarity.[119]

These realities notwithstanding, many continue to speak of "the liturgy," or even "the Liturgy"—including Benedict XVI (see above,

---

[119] Helmut Leeb, *Die Gesänge im Gemeindegottesdienst von Jerusalem (vom 5. bis 8. Jahrhundert)*, Wiener Beiträge zur Theologie 28 (Wien [Vienna]: Verlag Herder, 1970), 21. Quoted by Taft, *The Diptychs*, xxxiii–xxxiv.

p. 5)—using the term as a substantive: "a self-subsisting or independent person or thing."[120] For some, the liturgy is a coherent unity. But in what sense? In a social-historical sense, referring to a cluster of similar human activities analogous at any given moment and self-identical through time? In an institutional sense, referring to the ritual activity of the Christian church or an ecclesial community within it? In a structural sense, defined by a series of analogous liturgical and calendrical structures? In a theological sense, understood as an (inter)action of God and the worshiping community? In a dynamic sense, marked by particular processes? Or a combination of some of these or perhaps others? Baumstark's use of the comparative method and organic model challenges us to gain clarity on what we mean by "the liturgy" and wonder what—if any—methodological role it might play today.

On this question and others, Anton Baumstark still offers ample food for thought.

---

[120] *Oxford English Dictionary* (1971), s.v. "Substantive," (B), (2).

Preface

The following pages meet an outstanding obligation. Last September I gave a lecture course at the Abbey of Maria Laach for the purpose of winning adherents for the liturgical movement. As a part of that course I delivered two lectures reviewing the development of the Roman Rite, one covering the period from the reform of Trent back to the Carolingian period and the other from then back to the time of Christian origins.* The initial plan was to expand these two lectures into a small volume for the series *Ecclesia Orans*. The longer I considered the project, however, the more I became convinced that plan was ill-conceived. What one dares to express in the spoken word, whose sounds quickly fade away, will not yet bear the scrutiny given the black and white of the printed page. Before venturing a comprehensive description of the liturgy's development, it must first be examined from an entirely new point of view. Not wanting to flatly decline the honor of being invited to contribute to the series *Ecclesia Orans*, I decided to offer a kind of basic introduction to that development. This approach reflects my own personal scholarly predilections as an orientalist: to set aside the limited perspective whose sole focus is the Roman Rite and instead lay the conceptual groundwork for a comparative study of the liturgy, taking the liturgies of the East as its starting point. I have strived in my scholarly work to put this method to the test.

Having settled upon this approach, the revised plan was carried out during a vacation of just two weeks. This had the benefit of presenting the material in a compact sort of way. I hope, however, that this brevity has not compromised its content.

----

* Baumstark's language in this sentence belies his understanding of the earliest period of Christian history. His use of the phrase *die christliche Urzeit*, translated here as "the time of Christian origins," carries with it the sense of "primal Christian time"; his use of the verb *herauführen*, literally "to lead up to," conveys a sense of approach reflecting the honor in which he held this time, standing above all others.

At the request of the most distinguished editor of this series,* and after some hesitation, I decided to append bibliographical notes. In these notes, for the most part, I do not strive—in keeping with strict scholarly practice—to document the explanations offered in the text so much as to enable the motivated reader to begin to look more closely at problems raised by the historical study of liturgy. Therefore, in the first instance, I have intentionally and consistently cited general histories or overviews of the topic at hand rather than its most recently published primary sources. By using endnotes rather than footnotes, we hope to avoid the impression of a ponderous scholarly tome—unsuitable for a series of this kind.[†]

I have indicated what religious benefits I hope the liturgical movement will gain from a historical engagement with the liturgy in my introduction[‡] and conclusion.[§] To those who do not share my hope for the liturgical movement or to those whose religious sensibilities may even be offended by treating the liturgy from a frankly historical standpoint, I ask them, from my heart, to lay this little volume aside unread. Others will probably do so unbidden, those who may feel compelled to espy an insult to the inherent dignity of historical inquiry when its hard-won results are published for a wider audience and used to further a religious end. In any case I have as little desire to offend anybody's particular religious sensibilities as I do to press my own—or even to give the impression of wanting to do so—on one who is a stranger to religious feeling.[¶]

Bonn, October 14, 1922:
"Callisti in via Aurelia miliario III"**
A. Baumstark

---

* On Ildefons Herwegen, see Short Biography, no. 95.

[†] In this translation, these notes have been placed at the conclusion of each chapter.

[‡] To be found in the opening paragraphs of chap. 1.

[§] To be found in the closing paragraphs of chap. 17.

[¶] Baumstark is here addressing his various constituencies in the Roman Church and the academy. Within the church in the first decades of the twentieth century, there were two perspectives on history. Ascendant before World War I were the neoscholastic theologians, who held theology strictly apart from history and were convicted that the study of history, including liturgical history, could in principle have no theological implications. Emerging after

World War I, in France and Germany in particular, was a new approach to theology that took the historical nature of the church and theology into account. In the circle of the Abbey of Maria Laach, Odo Casel (1886–1948) and Romano Guardini (1865–1968) represented this perspective. At the same time, Baumstark felt compelled to address academic historians, who were still under the influence of positivism, an approach Baumstark embraced. For the most part, these historians disparaged the religious use of historical knowledge as an inappropriate use of scientific discoveries. See West, *Anton Baumstark's Comparative Liturgy*, 54–143, and West, *The Comparative Liturgy of Anton Baumstark*, 9–12.

** "Of Callistus at mile three of the Aurelian Way." In the Roman calendar, both Tridentine and conciliar, October 14 is the feast day of Callistus I (d. ca. 222, pope from ca. 217), a martyr, who was buried in the cemetery of Calepodius on the Aurelian Way.

Chapter 1

The Problem and Its Solution

The liturgy—above all else—is a given reality with definite form. As a given reality, it offers an immediate religious experience. As a given reality with inherent aesthetic values, it triggers aesthetic impressions, intensifying that experience.

However, the liturgy is also a reality that has developed and in this respect may be considered from a historical point of view. By no means is this challenge of interest only to scholars. An understanding the history of the liturgy enhances the religious experience of the liturgy no less than does an awareness of its beauty. The former stems from its being essentially anchored in the notion of community.*

That is to say, the liturgy is anchored just as much in temporal depth as it is in spatial breadth. In the latter sense, the one praying the liturgy understands himself to be set amid an immense multitude, who join him in raising their hands in praise, thanks, and petition, in offering the eucharistic sacrifice, or participating in that offering. A vital inner bond of the deepest sort joins him with them all. As a raindrop falls in the storm-tossed sea, there to dissolve into the cresting waves, so does his prayer, with humble self-effacement, merge into that ocean of communal prayer whose waves surge forth over the whole earth and beyond. Thundering restlessly, yet resting blessedly in the stillness of God, the waves of that ocean swell from earth up to those transcendent heights where the one praying can hear the choirs, pure in spirit, join him in singing the *Sanctus*,† as well as the souls in purgatory calling out, "Lord, have mercy."

---

* In these two opening paragraphs, Baumstark draws a distinction crucial for his understanding of the liturgy. Paralleling the phrase *ein in bestimmter Form Gegebenes*, which we have translated as "a given reality with definite form," with the term *ein Gewordenes*, which we have rendered "a reality that has developed," makes a bold contrast with the use of substantives, which one can only approximate in English translation.

† Baumstark often uses the neologism *das Dreimalheilig* to refer to the *Sanctus*. By employing the same term to refer to the passage from Isaiah 6 found in synagogue prayer, he highlights the continuity between Jewish and Christian forms.

Temporally, he perceives himself to be an ephemeral point between generations going before him and after, between those who have prayed and offered from the time of Christian origins and those who will be praying and offering when the last atoms of his mortal remains have long since loosed their bonds. In this way, for that fleeting moment, he participates in the deepest life of them all: the life of the millenniums. His individual prayer becomes for him an infinitesimally small ringlet in a virtually endless golden chain, stretching from the earthly days of the Son of Man, when Jesus wandered upon the shores of the blue Sea of Galilee, until that final day when he will await the return of the Son of Man in the glory of the Father. Now naturally the elation that the notion of such a trans-historical community produces in the one at prayer increases as his historical understanding deepens, that is, his historical appreciation for the worship he joins in celebrating—both its action and its word.

The liturgy is the product of development, but not like anything human will would ever create arbitrarily, in conscious pursuit of its chosen ends. The liturgy is like the language we speak, the life forms around us, or the earth's surface that is the stage upon which these life forms play out their existence. The first two instances of comparison (language and life) result from an organic process that proceeds according to inner laws and are elucidated by ascertaining those laws. The third instance, the earth's surface, involves a formative process different from human history, at least insofar as its data are concerned. In the nature of the case, pieces of information concerning the development of the earth's crust are not found as they are in the course of human history, passed on from the mind of one human being to another.

In contrast to other areas of historical research, the position of liturgical-historical inquiry is not, like that of geology, completely disadvantaged. Sources providing external evidence for matters of liturgical development are not wholly wanting.* For this reason the collection and critical examination of these sources always remains the first—

---

* No one witnessed the geological formation of the earth to report on it as persons have witnessed the development of the liturgy. Elsewhere, however, Baumstark notes the paucity of external witnesses for the liturgy that results from the tendency of each generation to take the liturgy of its time for granted. Baumstark's emphasis in this passage upon secondary, external witnesses, even ahead of primary documents, also reflects a methodological assumption. Since the lived liturgy cannot be fully deduced from the written document—

and the most pressing—task needing to be done.[1] Indeed, numerous liturgical documents dating from even the earlier stages of development have been preserved for the most diverse rites in both the East and the West.[2] A second essentially philological task is to make these texts available in editions meeting scholarly norms, specifying the relationship between particular texts and, where necessary, providing commentary.* It is tempting to hope that the completion of these two tasks would result in a definitive historical explanation for what the participant in the community of liturgical prayer encounters as the given reality of the liturgy, viz., the continuing existence of liturgical forms. To entertain this hope would be a great mistake, however. Without the use of a method for which we may already have a model—that of the natural sciences, relentless in their exacting observation—this goal will remain beyond reach.

The earth itself furnishes the primary source material for the science of geology, material that functions in that science as archives do in the diplomatic of historical research. The earth's present-day crust provides evidence[†] in its own stratification for the violent upheavals that produced it. In the same way, the liturgy also displays—both in its

---

and indeed might even be contrary to it—external witnesses are crucial for understanding it. Baumstark mentions this anecdotally in the final chapter of this book, pp. 245 and 246, and theoretically in Anton Baumstark, "Ein liturgiewissenschaftliches Unternehmen deutscher Benediktinerabteien," *Deutsche Literaturzeitung* 40 (1919): cols. 903–4.

* From the 1890s, the field of liturgical studies experienced a flurry of activity in the gathering, editing, and publication of primary documents. Edmund Bishop (1846–1917) wrote, "From an increasing recognition of the all importance of the 'document' results that almost crazy activity in search of what has been hitherto unknown; that inquisitiveness as to the inedited [*sic*] which characterizes our time, and not infrequently is the cause of amusement or disdain according to the disposition of the onlooker." See Edmund Bishop, "Historical Critics on the Critical Art," *Downside Review* 18 (1899): 191. On Edmund Bishop, see Short Biography, no. 38.

† Consistently throughout this book Baumstark uses the word *Denkmal* to refer to evidence, in this case of geological events, but more frequently of the liturgy, in which case I have translated it as "document." His use of the word *Denkmal* is a translation into German of the Latin term *monumentum*, which can mean "a written memorial, document, record" (Charlton T. Lewis, *A Latin Dictionary* [Oxford: Clarendon Press, 1980], s.v. "monumentum"). In Baumstark's time, the term was used in the study of history as in *Monumenta*

present form and in those forms evident in this or that older liturgical document—traces of the very process that brought it into being. To meticulously pursue these traces and to compare them with evidence from external sources in order to discern links is also of importance. Above all in this regard, it is crucial to test for an intrinsic conformity to patterns governed by laws: whether or not, and to what extent, from the treasure trove of material available for examination, that conformity can be discerned also in liturgical development. On the strength of such regularity, liturgical development would more or less fall in line with linguistic and biological development.

Research along these lines enjoys a distinct advantage, in that liturgical life has assumed many and varied forms over the course of the centuries. On Western soil, the liturgical use of Rome has attained nearly absolute dominance. Yet even today, standing alongside it, are the Ambrosian liturgy of Milan[3] and the Mozarabic liturgy preserved in Toledo as a venerable antique,[4*] as well as monastic rites and those of the Carmelite and Dominican orders.[†] The liturgical diversity in the East gives a far richer picture still, a reflection of the ecclesiastical divisions that resulted from the doctrinal wars of the fifth to seventh centuries.[5] In terms of liturgical uniformity, the Rite of Constantinople plays a role in the East comparable to Rome's in the West, but only insofar as the Greek-Slavic liturgy is concerned.[6] Next to it, to the north, comes the Armenian national Church, schismatic as well as Uniate.[‡] A

Germaniae Historica, and thus in the study of the history of the liturgy, as in the title of a collection of liturgical documents edited by Fernand Cabrol (1855–1937) and Henri Leclercq (1869–1929) and published from 1900 to 1912, *Monumenta ecclesiae liturgici*. In English, the word "monument" can have this meaning as well: "an indication, evidence, or token (of some fact)" or "anything that by its survival commemorates a person, action, period, or event." Though now rare, this use was still common at the end of the nineteenth century (*Oxford English Dictionary* [Oxford: Oxford University Press, 1971], s.v. "monument"). However, since this has since become an archaic use in English, I have chosen not to translate Baumstark's term *Denkmal* literally, but rather according to context, as "evidence" or "document."

* See n. on p. 102 and n. on p. 132.

† The Council of Trent (1545–63) permitted the continued use in the West of rites with a history of two hundred years or more, be they the rite of a diocese or of an order.

‡ The Armenian Church was the first national church, created when Armenia adopted Christianity as its official religion in 301. In the christological

threesome of Syrian liturgical forms are represented by (1) the Nestorians and (2) the Monophysite Jacobites (whose analogues among the Uniate denominations are [a] the Chaldeans and [b] the Syrians of the so-called pure rite,* respectively) and (3) the Maronites, having originally been Monothelites.[†] In the south the Copts and the Ethiopians carry

---

controversies of the fifth through seventh centuries, it embraced Monophysitism. At the time Baumstark wrote, this theological tradition was being carried forward by the Armenian Apostolic Church, as it is today, while the Armenian Catholic Church, founded in 1742 and now headquartered in Lebanon, is an Eastern Rite church in full communion with Rome. Thus, Baumstark speaks inclusively of the "Armenian national Church," but refers to the schismatic and "uniate" bodies within it. For the christological background of the Armenian Church, see n. on p. 48.

* The Roman Church used the term *Ritus antiochenus Syrorum purus* to refer to both the "Jacobite" Rite and the Syrian or Syriac Catholic Rite. This was in contrast to other rites of West Syrian origin, most immediately the Maronite liturgy, which is related yet different (see n. below). The term belied a precritical understanding of liturgical history, which envisioned the West Syrian Rite as an unadulterated or "pure" version of the original Antiochene liturgy. This terminology reflects the misconception of the liturgy that Baumstark criticizes in chap. 5, "Variety and Uniformity," in which he argues that the liturgy in both the East and the West began with variety and tended toward uniformity rather than vice versa. The understanding of the Antiochene liturgy conveyed in this phrase, on the other hand, begins with uniformity and assumes those liturgies that are related to it but different from it are "impure" and later, differentiated versions of the original. Specifically on this term, see Humphrey William Codrington, "The Syrian Liturgy," *Eastern Churches Quarterly* 1 (1936): 10; = Codrington *Studies in the Syrian Liturgies* (London: Geo. E. J. Coldwell, 1952), 10; and Adrian Fortescue, *The Uniate Eastern Churches* (London: Burns, Oates, and Washburn, 1923), 9. For a discussion of Rome's posture toward Eastern Rites, see Wilhelm de Vries, *Rom und die Patriarchate des Ostens* (Freiburg/München [Munich]: Verlag Karl Alber, 1963), 183–222.

[†] The Maronite Church, an Eastern Catholic church in full communion with Rome, traces its traditions back to the church in Antioch and the ministry there of the apostle Peter (d. 67?). It takes its name from Maro(n) (fl. fourth to fifth century), a monk and mystic, and a group of his followers, which called themselves Maronites, that formed after his death. Holding to the faith articulated by Chalcedon (451), they came under attack by West Syrian Monophysites following that council. This began a troubled history, being only the first of many pressures brought against the Maronite Church, political and religious, Christian and Muslim. These historical pressures drove Maronites to migrate to

on the liturgical traditions of early Egyptian Christianity.[7]* This rich diversity of liturgical life-forms makes possible an approach to research that is comparative, using laws of liturgical development, whose closest parallel is comparative linguistics.

The explanations that follow in the chapters below—taking as their starting point a consideration of the church's worship using the comparative method—attempt to make a wider circle of readers more familiar than they now are with the preconditions for, and the formative influences upon, liturgical development. It is to be expected that, in some instances, revelations about the age and origins of this or that particular feast, custom, or text will create a desire to learn more about

---

present-day Lebanon, where they have intermittently retreated into the mountains, becoming isolated for centuries at a time. The Monophysite attacks on the Maronites also brought support from the church in Rome in the early sixth century, which eventually—centuries later, during the Crusades—resulted in full communion with Rome. The liturgy of the Maronite Church is historically of the Antiochene–West Syrian Rite; their liturgical language is Syriac. Despite antagonism between the Jacobite, Nestorian, and Maronite churches, their liturgies have influenced one another over time. Since the seventh century, the Maronite Church has had a patriarch, whose full title is "Patriarch of Antioch and All the East." While elected locally, the power of this patriarch has—since the Middle Ages—been confirmed by Rome. Although the Maronite Church has consistently maintained its Catholic orthodoxy against the assertion that they were Monothelite (as Baumstark writes), a strong strain of this christological position has been evident among some Maronites. See Matti Moosa, *The Maronites in History* (Syracuse, NY: Syracuse University Press, 1986), 195–216; for a theory relating the West Syrian liturgy to others, see William F. Macomber, "A Theory of the Origins on the Syrian Maronite and Chaldean Rites," *Orientalia Christiana Periodica* 39 (1973): 235–24.

* While the christological declaration of the Council of Chalcedon (451) was widely accepted in the church, the Oriental Orthodox churches did not assent to it. The Council embraced the christological definitions of Nicea and Constantinople, condemning the teachings of Nestorius (427–31) and Eutyches (ca. 380–ca. 456). This led to a theological split with a linguistic dimension. Generally speaking, churches using Latin and Greek accepted the Chalcedonian declaration of the Catholic faith, while those speaking other languages (Syriac, Coptic, and later Armenian) embraced a Monophysite Christology. An exception to this linguistic rule is the Maronite Church, which is Syriac in language but Chalcedonian in faith, although it has had a strong Monothelite element (see preceding footnote). While the Nestorian (Assyrian) Church using the East Syrian Rite

liturgical history.[8] At this point, however, a comprehensive history, be it of the liturgy of the early church in general or of the Roman Rite in particular, cannot be provided with a clear conscience yet, and especially not for the general reading public. Too great and too difficult are the problems that must first be tackled by the selfless labor of monographic research. In the interim, a familiarity with the publications on the course of its general development that are currently available is not without benefit for a deeper understanding of one's liturgical experiences. The reason we take into account the most diverse factual material, from the East and the West, has its roots in the comparative approach to liturgical history. Even so, as a useful tool, comparative liturgical history remains in the service of our ultimate goal: to awaken and further an appreciation for the growth of that mighty tree in whose shadow the Catholic community using Latin as its liturgical language gathers to unite in celebrating liturgical worship according to the Roman Rite.

---

had separated from Antioch and Constantinople before the Council of Ephesus (431), now the Jacobite Church of West Syria separated from Constantinople as a direct consequence of Chalcedon. This opened up the path for an indigenization of the West Syrian Rite, which entailed a shift in liturgical language from Greek to Syriac. Apart from the purely Antiochian elements translated into Syriac from the Greek, the West Syrian rite also borrowed heavily from ritual practices originally composed in Syriac, such as the hymns of Ephrem the Syrian (ca. 306–73) and his disciples. Despite antagonism between the Jacobite, Nestorian, and Maronite Churches, their liturgies influenced one another. See Irenée-Henri Dalmais, *Les liturgies d'orient* (Paris: Les Éditions des Cerf, 1980), 49, and Macomber, "A Theory of the Origins," 235–42.

Notes

On the method for researching liturgical history on a comparative basis, see Anton Baumstark, "Ein liturgiewissenschaftliches Unternehmen deutscher Benediktinerabteien," *Deutsche Literaturzeitung* 40 (1919): 897–905, 921–27. Also, Leo Kunibert Mohlberg provides an excellent overview of all research in the scientific study of the liturgy up to the present: Kunibert Mohlberg, *Ziele und Aufgaben der liturgiegeschichtlichen Forschung*, LF 1 (Münster in Westfalen: Aschendorff, 1919). Francesco Antonio Zaccaria, *Bibliotheca Ritualis*, 2 vols. (Romae [Rome]: Sumptibus

Venantii Monaldini, 1776–81 [repr., New York: B. Franklin, 1964]) is still today indispensable for getting one's bearings in regard to the earlier literature on the history of the liturgy.

[1] At this point, texts for the study of the liturgy have been collected systematically only for the East, and then only to some extent, in the invaluable appendices of Frank Edward Brightman and Charles Edward Hammond, *Liturgies Eastern and Western*, vol. 1 (Oxford: Clarendon Press, 1896 [repr. 1967]), the standard and indispensible work in the field of the oriental Mass liturgy [hereafter cited as Brightman]. The thorough way in which Theodor Schermann handles a treasure store of pertinent material lends lasting value to his works. See Theodor Schermann, *Ägyptische Abendmahlsliturgien des ersten Jahrtausends*, SGKA 6, 1–2 (Paderborn: F. Schöningh, 1912); Schermann, *Die allgemeine Kirchenordnung, frühchristliche Liturgien und kirchliche Überlieferung, Part 2: Frühchristliche Liturgien*, SGKA, suppl. vol. 3, 2 (Paderborn: F. Schöningh, 1915), 137–573. The same can be said above all for the relevant parts of the work by the Anglican Joseph Bingham, *Origines ecclesiasticae or the Antiquities of the Christian Church*, 8 vols. (London: Printed for Robert Knaplock, 1708–22; most recent edition of the original: London: Reeves and Turner, 1878).

[2] An initial attempt at producing a comprehensive catalogue of this material, which yet remains incomplete, was undertaken by the Maronite Joseph Assemani. See *Codex liturgicus ecclesiae universae in XV libros distributus*, ed. Joseph Aloysius Assemani, 13 vols. (Romae [Rome]: Ex typographia Komarek, Apud Angelum Rotilium, 1749–66 [repr., Farnborough: Gregg, 1968]). The multivolume series *Monumenta Ecclesiae Liturgica*, edited by Ferdnand Cabrol and Henri Leclercq, sets out ambitiously to renew this effort. Fundamental for the Eastern Mass liturgy, especially of Syria and Egypt, is Eusèbe Renaudot, *Liturgiarum Orientalium Collectio* (Parisiis [Paris]: Apud Joannem Baptistam Coignard, 1716 [2nd ed., corrected and repr., Farnborough: Gregg, 1970]). Decisive contributions to cataloguing the most important documents for the West are made by Giuseppe Maria Tomasi, *Venerabilis viri Josephi Mariæ Thomasii . . . Opera omnia*, ed. Antonius Franciscus Vezzosi, 7 vols. (Romæ [Rome]: ex Typographia Palladis excudebant Nicolaus et Marcus Palearini, 1747–54 [repr. of 1749 ed.: Farnborough: Gregg, 1969]); Jean Mabillon, *De liturgia gallicana: Libri III in quibus veteris missae* (Luteciae Parisiorum [Paris]: E. Martin et J. Boudot, 1685); Edmond Martène, *De antiquis ecclesiae ritibus*, 1st ed. (Rotomagi [Rouen]: Sumptibus Guellelmi Behourt, 1700–02 [Baumstark erroneously cites the date of publication for first edition of Martène's work as 1748]; [repr., Hildesheim: Olms, 1967–69]); and Ludovico Antonio Muratori, *Liturgia Romana Vetus*, 2 vols. (Venetiis [Venice]: J. B. Pasquali, 1748), published posthumously in an expanded version, along with other liturgies and liturgical writing, in his collected works, *Liturgia Romana Vetus, Opere del proposto Antonio Muratori*, vol. 13 in 3 pts. (Arettii [Arezzo]: Per Michele Bellotti, 1771–73). Add

to that the republication of these texts in *Patrologia Latina*, which is cited by the abbreviation PL throughout these endnotes, in this and the following chapters.

[3] See the comprehensive, but not altogether reliable, article by Paul Lejay, "Ambrosien (rit)," DACL 1, cols. l373–1442. In respect to this same rite, see *Missale Ambrosianum duplex cum critico commentario continuo ex manuscriptis schedis*, ed. Antonio Maria Ceriani (Mediolani [Milan]: R. Ghirlanda, 1913), which came into print through the efforts of the present pope, Pius XI (1922–), Abrogio Ratti, in collaboration with Marcus Magistretti; also see the edition of the oldest preserved Sacramentary (from Bergamo), *Codex Sacramentorum Bergomensis*, ed. Paul Cagin, Auctarium solemnense, Series liturgica 1 (Solemnis [Solesmes]: e typographia Sancti Petri, 1900). For the Pontifical and Breviary, see *Monumenta veteris liturgiae Ambrosianae*, 3 vols., eds. Marco Magistretti and Antonio Maria Ceriani (Mediolani [Milan]: Apud Ulricum Hoepli bibliopolam, 1897 and 1905 [repr., Nendeln, Liechtenstein: Kraus Reprint, 1971]).

[4] For the Missal and Breviary in their final form, see the volumes entitled *Liturgica Mozarabica* in PL 85, containing the *Missale mixtum*, and PL 86, containing the *Brevarium Gothicum*. For the oldest documents of the rite, made available by Marius Férotin, see *Le liber ordinum en usage dans l'église wisigothique et mozarabe d'Espagne du cinquième au onzième siècle*, ed. Marius Férotin, MEL 5 (Paris: Firmin-Didot, 1904), and Férotin, *Le Liber Mozarabicus sacramentorum et les manuscrits mozarabes*, ed. Marius Férotin, MEL 6 (Paris: Firmin-Didot, 1912 [repr., Roma (Rome): CLV, Ed. Liturgiche, 1995]).

[5] See Max Prinz von Sachsen, *Praelectiones de liturgiis orientalibus*, 2 vols. (Friburgi Brisgoviae [Freiburg im Breisgau]: B. Herder, 1908–13). For general information about liturgical life in the East, see as well Konrad Lübeck, *Die christlichen Kirchen des Orients* (Kempten & München [Munich]: Josef Kösel, 1911), and also the much more massive new work by Raymond Janin, *Les Églises orientales et les rites orientaux* (Paris: Maison de la Bonne Presse, 1922).

[6] Along with the textual editions published to celebrate the liturgy, one should still consult Jacobus Goar, *Euchologion Sive Rituale Graecorum* (Lutetia Parisiorum [Paris]: Piget, 1647). The second volume of von Sachsen, *Praelectiones*, is devoted exclusively to the Greek Rite. The liturgical books of "the Orthodox Eastern Church" in their Church Slavonic recensions are offered, with German translations, in a series of handsome publications edited by Aleksei Petrovich Maltsev.

[7] For more recent literature by specialists in the field, one may consult especially Frederick Cornwallis Conybeare, *Rituale Armenorum: being the administration of the sacraments and the breviary rites of the Armenian Church* (Oxford: Clarendon Press, 1905); Anton Baumstark, *Nichtevangelische syrische Perikopenordnungen des ersten Jahrtausends im Sinne vergleichender Liturgiegeschichte*, LF 3 (Münster: Aschendorff, 1921) [hereafter cited as "Baumstark, Perikopenordnungen"]; Baumstark, *Festbrevier und Kirchenjahr der syrischen Jakobiten*, SGKA 3:3–5 (Paderborn: Schöningh, 1910 [repr., New York: Johnson Reprint, 1967]);

Samuel Alfred Browne Mercer, *The Ethiopic Liturgy*, The Hale Lectures, 1914 (Milwaukee: Young Churchman; London: Mowbray, 1915 [repr., New York: AMS Press, 1970]).

[8] In addition to Bingham, *Origines ecclesiasticae*, the works to be consulted above all are Louis Marie Olivier Duchesne, *Origines du culte chrétien: étude sur la liturgie latine avant Charlemagne*, 3rd ed. (Paris: Thorin, 1903) [hereafter cited as "Duchesne, *Origines*"; ET: *Christian Worship: Its Origin and Evolution*, trans. M. L. McClure, 5th ed. (London: SPCK, 1956), hereafter cited as "Duchesne, *Worship*"]; for the Western Mass: Adrian Fortescue, *The Mass. A Study of the Roman Liturgy* (London: Longmans, Green and Co., 1912; 2nd ed. 1914); and also for its earlier history: Ferdinand Probst, *Die abendländische Messe vom fünften bis zum achten Jahrhundert* (Münster in Westfalen: Aschendorff, 1896), the last and probably the best of the many books by this author, a pioneer in the field of liturgical history. For the Eastern Mass, see Anton Baumstark, *Die Messe im Morgenland* (Kempten-Munchen [Munich]: J. Kösel, 1906) [hereafter cited as "Baumstark, *Messe*"]. This work was reprinted in 1921 without the author's knowledge. Naturally, this work is today, in certain respects, thoroughly outdated, as many highly significant sources have come to light since it first appeared. For the Breviary, see Pierre Batiffol, *Histoire du bréviaire romain*, 3rd ed. (Paris: A. Picard [etc.], 1911) [hereafter cited as "Batiffol (Fr. ed.)"; ET: Batiffol, *History of the Roman Breviary*, trans. Atwell Marvin Yates Baylay, 5th ed. (London, New York: Longmans Green, 1912), hereafter cited as "Batiffol (Eng. ed.)"]; Suitbert Bäumer, *Geschichte des Breviers* (Freiburg im Breisgau: Herder, 1895); Fr. ed. in 2 vols., *Histoire du Bréviaire*, trans. Réginald Biron (Roma [Rome]: Herder, 1967). For the liturgical year, see Heinrich Kellner, *Heortologie, oder, das Kirchenjahr und der Heiligenfeste in ihrer geschichtlichen Entwicklung* (Freiburg im Breisgau: Herder, 1901; 3rd ed., 1911).

Chapter 2

Domestic and Congregational Celebrations

"Day by day, as they spent much time together in the temple, they broke bread at home and ate their food with glad and generous hearts, praising God and having the goodwill of all the people" (Acts 2:46-47a). With these words the Acts of the Apostles describe the germ cell of all liturgical development: the ritual life* of the original community in Jerusalem.

This passage tells us two things: (1) that Christians continued to participate in the daily prayer offered in the temple for the whole community of Israel, and (2) that the Eucharist was celebrated in homes at table. As Christian missionaries made inroads into the Jewish Diaspora, they participated in the worship services of synagogues instead of temple prayer. For example, we see Paul (d. 65?) and Barnabas (n.d.) visiting the synagogue, when they were active as missionaries in Antioch of Pisidia (Acts 13:13-52). In the context of these worship services, the oldest kind of Christian sermon, preaching to gain converts for the mission of the church, found its place next to the prayers that were offered. In its infancy the relationship of the church to its Jewish native land was strong. As this original relationship weakened, the first thing to happen—quite naturally—was that the line between these two kinds of worship became blurred, in the sense that congregational celebrations took on the outward appearance of domestic ones. With nothing to replace the synagogue, now become off-limits to

---

* Baumstark regularly uses the word *der Kult*, either alone or in combination, as in this case with the compound word *das Kultleben*. While this is accepted usage in German for writing about Christian worship, a literal translation poses problems in English, given the connotations of the word "cult," which generally refers to non-Christian ritual and may even be pejorative. I have translated this word as "cult" when referring to non-Christian religions, as, for example, with Baumstark's discussion of the Hellenistic mystery religions in chap. 4. However, when Baumstark uses *der Kult* in relationship to Christian worship, I have usually translated it—as in this passage—as the word "ritual."

Christians, the only alternative left congregations was to assemble in houses of individual community members—for prayer and religious instruction as well as the meal. It was during this period, in the home setting, that the word service joined itself to the eucharistic meal. Once again evidence may be cited from the Acts of the Apostles, specifically in its account (Acts 20:7-12)* of the last night in a weeklong stay that Paul, the apostle to the nations, and his companions spent along the coast in the region of Troas.† In this passage Acts graphically illustrates this kind of combination, in which the holy meal was joined to the preaching service. Meal fellowship spread from groups gathered in homes to the congregation itself. Cut off from the Jewish life of the Diaspora, the circle of Christian "brothers" (soon bolstered in ever-increasing numbers by an influx of proselytes from the heathen world) looked to private homes for hospitality. That inevitably remained the case until congregations were allowed to develop a liturgical life outside of private homes, in worship spaces of their own—at which point the process of combination continued in this new setting, that is, the word liturgy combining with the celebration of the Eucharist.

However, the influence exercised by the original custom of celebrating the Lord's Supper in intimate home gatherings did not stop altogether—not just yet. The *Didache*,‡ the oldest Christian writing preserved apart from the New Testament canon, seems to indicate that, alongside the congregation's Sunday worship, with its eucharistic "sacrifice," the Eucharist was also celebrated as of old in homes. The remarkable prayers preserved by this church order, which represent the oldest liturgical texts to have come down to us, may have been in-

---

* The German text mistakenly cites Acts 21:7-12, presumably a typographical error.

† Troas is an ancient region primarily formed by a protrusion of Asia Minor into the Aegean Sea in a northwesterly direction. In addition to Troy, its major urban center, one found there a number of smaller Greek cities as well, including Alexandria Troas, where Paul (d. 65?) stayed before sailing by ship to Macedonia in present-day Greece.

‡ Baumstark refers to the work now called the *Didache* by its full title, *The Teaching of the Twelve Apostles*. While the precise authorship, date, and provenance of this work are unknown, scholarly opinion tends to see it originating from a Syrian Christian community of the later first century or the beginning of the second century. See, for instance, *The Didache in Modern Research*, ed. Jonathan A. Draper, *Arbeiten zur Geschichte des antiken Judentums und des Urchristentums* 37 (Leiden, New York: E. J. Brill, 1996).

tended for home celebration.[1] Evidence for the domestic celebration of the Eucharist can be found in ascetic circles from as late as the fourth century. On the one hand, echoes of that kind of early celebration can be distinctly heard in a table prayer that, with solemn religiosity, bracketed the one meal of the day, which was taken after the ninth hour.[2]* On the other hand, the great Cappadocian Basil (330–79),† at the very least, attests to the practice of hermits administering Communion to themselves, using bread they had set aside from that consecrated for congregational worship.[3] In fact, in Egypt, so he asserts, this practice may have been permitted to any member of the community.

Of course, it was particularly in the bloody times of persecution, under pressure from the "state of emergency" experienced during those periods that older practices were retained or once again revived. Only the final Peace of the Church (313) could—and actually soon had to—effect what appears to have been a ban on any celebration of the Eucharist other than those held in the congregation and joined to a service of teaching and prayer. Thus, not too long after the Constantinian era, the Council of Laodicea in Asia Minor‡ forbade the home celebration of the Eucharist in regions where Greek was spoken.[4] After the end of the great persecution perpetrated by Shapur II (309–79)§ and his immediate successor,¶ the Aramaic-speaking** church in the Sassanian

---

* Two prayers were said before the meal and one following. Before the meal one was said while standing at the table. The other one was said upon being seated, when the bread had to be broken; after making the sign of the cross three times, the ascetic women offered a prayer of thanksgiving. The prayer after the meal also offered thanks. For this reference to Athanasius' discourse *On Virginity*, along with some secondary literature pertaining to it, see Baumstark's n. 2 in this chap.

† On Basil the Great, see Short Biography, no. 28.

‡ Little is known about the Council of Laodicea, save that it did not occur before ca. 345—it probably occurred twenty years later. A set of fifty-nine fourth-century canons entitled *The Canons of Laodicea* are to be found in early collections of church law.

§ On Shapur II, see Short Biography, no. 160.

¶ On Ardashir II, see Short Biography, no. 18.

** Originally the language of the Aramean people, Aramaic is a Semitic language whose many dialects were spoken in Mesopotamia and Syria even before 1000 BCE. Indeed, Aramaic is so diverse that it can be thought of either as a single language or as a family of dialects. Over time it became the lingua franca of the Middle East, eclipsed in some places by the rise of Greek

Empire (227–635)* took a similar action. In that church, the general council of Seleucia-Tesiphon, held at the beginning of February 410, moved against the custom of holding domestic celebrations of the Eucharist.[5] That these measures were taken, however, is a tacit acknowledgment that this practice had been prevalent before.

But even the spirit of the new era was only able to suppress the home celebration of the Eucharist in its old form—as a meal. Clothed in the ritual forms that the sacramental act acquired in the context of congregational worship, it continued to assert itself even during this time, at least here and there. Again this occurred particularly in ascetic circles.

It was during the fifth century that the younger Melania (ca. 385–438/39),[†] a daughter of Roman nobility, created a monastic home on the slopes of the Mount of Olives. At that time the Eucharist was not yet celebrated in the splendid sacred edifices of Jerusalem on a daily basis. This Roman woman held such celebrations, conducted by her house chaplain, Gerontius (395–480/85), within the confines of their own abode for the benefit of herself and her virgins.[‡] Moreover, one

---

following the Hellenization initiated by Alexander (336–23 BCE; on Alexander the Great, see Short Biography, no. 9). Closely related to Hebrew, Aramaic was the language of Palestinian Jews before the Christian era. The particular variety of Eastern Aramaic used by Christian communities in the East is the dialect of Edessa called Syriac, whose name derives from the fact that it was spoken in historic Syria. Syriac became the liturgical language of the Assyrian (Nestorian), Maronite, and Jacobite Churches and developed an extensive literature, notably in the period from the fourth to the seventh centuries. The influence and diffusion of Aramaic began to lessen in the seventh century, following the Arab conquest and the rise of Arabic as the language of prestige.

* The Sassanian (also Sasanian and Sassanid) Empire, founded in 235 by Ardashir I (fl. third century), was named after his grandfather Sasan (fl. second century?). With its capital at Ctesiphon near modern-day Baghdad, it became—along with the Byzantine Empire—one of the two empires to dominate western Asia in the four hundred years prior to the Arab invasion and was regarded as an equal by the Roman Empire. At one time or another, this Persian empire stretched from Armenia and Azerbaijan in the north to the Persian Gulf in the South, from Asia Minor in the west to Afghanistan and parts of Pakistan to the east. Under its rule, Persian civilization flourished, influencing cultures far afield and the Islamic world that followed it. The empire fell before the Arab invasion in 640.

† On Melania the Younger, see Short Biography, no. 122.

‡ On Gerontius, see Short Biography, no. 76.

finds explicit mention that with this practice, she may have been following a custom she had known in Rome.[6] At this time, by dint of necessity, the domestic celebration of the Eucharistic meal had to have been a part of Roman practice.* For in Rome, even at a later date, the daily celebration of the Eucharist by the congregation was still a long way off. Indeed, even during the period of fasting before Easter, the celebration of the Mass was not extended to Thursdays until Pope Gregory II (715–31).[7][†] Before that time, celebrations of the Mass had apparently occurred only four times a week: on Sundays, Mondays, Wednesdays, and Fridays—while Thursday remained "liturgy-less."[8]

One can observe the contrast between home and congregation in the development of the church's daily prayer as well. We learn from first century sources that the Liturgy of the Hours was a thoroughly private affair. Not until the period of peace that followed on the heels of Constantine's consolidation of power (313), when the thrill of victory led to congregational worship being developed with splendor, were liturgical assemblies first allowed to hold daily prayer, morning and evening.[9] From that time on, more and more, daily prayer came to emulate the Easter Vigil, originally closely tied to baptism. While at first vigils were normally celebrated on Sunday, a vigil as such was soon observed every day. At that point the morning prayer of the assembly entered into organic union with the vigil. Finally, even the system of hours moved from the quiet of private devotions observed in the home over into the realm of liturgical events performed in church buildings, where prayer now consecrated specific hours of the day falling between dawn and dusk. A female pilgrim from the West, probably named Egeria (fl. fourth century),[‡] left a report about the worship life of Jerusalem at the end of the fourth century, showing that, by that time, this whole development had already run its course there.[10] If ascetic circles provided the last home for the domestic celebration of the Eucharist, here the opposite was the case: those same ascetic circles were responsible for the liturgical life of daily prayer celebrated

---

* The "necessity" to which Baumstark alludes here is that of participating in the Eucharist on a daily basis. According to this logic, daily Eucharist had to be available to the community in some form. In this passage, Baumstark suggests, if one could not partake of the Eucharist in the churches of Rome, then one must have been able to do so in domestic settings.

† On Gregory II, see Short Biography, no. 79.

‡ On Egeria, see Short Biography, no. 65.

in congregational spaces being elaborated in ways that were increasingly rich. As evidence for this, members of these ascetic communities gathered in those spaces for the various hours of night and day, even at times when the congregation as a whole could not have possibly assembled. With her description of the situation in early Christian Jerusalem, Egeria, this woman from the West, once again provides an instructive picture of its development.

On the other hand, the ascetic world was no less instrumental in paving the way for daily prayer to return from its celebration as public worship back to its practice as private devotion. Naturally, private daily prayer was observed by the hermit, who—at the very most—came into the world out of his seclusion only on Sunday, for the Eucharist. This must have been the case before and after the Peace of Constantine (313), as it had been in the time of Christian origins. Thus in the East, the home of monasticism, we come across texts for the Liturgy of the Hours, for example, in the Syrian language, specifically intended for individuals to use in devotions. In the West, as early as the close of the fourth century, it became evident that circles of female ascetics in Spain were inclined to gather daily for celebrations of the canonical hours, vocally supported by a trained cantor. Since such domestic choir services were conducted without bishop, priest, or deacon, however, the First Council of Toledo,* in the year 400, strictly forbade them.[11]

By another path and in another form, the West turned right back to practicing private daily prayer.[12] In the later monastic world of the West, the idea early gained credence that the individual monk who found himself on the road, away from the intimate circle of communal liturgy he experienced within the monastery, was still obligated to say the prayers required of him in choir.[13] To facilitate reciting the Office apart from the monastic community and under these particular circumstances, a single portable volume was produced. At first the very same texts sung at a full choir service were condensed into a single handy volume, which involved abridging—more or less drastically—texts that, in the monastic setting, were found in series of folio

---

* The First Council of Toledo, held in 400, was directed against Priscillianism, a movement founded by Priscillian, bishop of Avila (d. 386), who urged his followers to regard their baptismal vows as an occasion to dedicate themselves to a life of asceticism. The movement continued to flourish, especially in Galicia where Toledo is located, even after Priscillian's execution as a heretic.

volumes of various kinds. One finds manuscripts of such travel "breviaries," for use by members of the congregations of various orders, starting from the end of the eleventh century.[14]

Meanwhile, in the cathedrals or other nonmonastic churches, the canonical clergy* had assumed the role of the assembly at the church's daily prayer. Applying the same rationale used for monks, canonical clergy were also required to recite the Office in private, at least on occasion. The requirement that absolutely every priest possess a "breviary," from which "they could read their daily Office when they are on journeys," was established for the first time by a synod at Trier, held in the year 1227.[15†] After that beginning, as is well known, the Minorites (Order of Friars Minor)[16‡] gave this new prayer book for Roman priests its final form, edited by Haymo of Faversham (d.1244),§ the General of the Franciscan Order. In 1241 Pope Gregory IX (1227–41)¶ authorized this breviary for use by the order itself. Nicholas III (1277–80),** who himself came out of the spiritual family of the seraphic saint,†† also introduced the use of the Franciscan Breviary at the solemn choir services of essentially every church in the Eternal City. About one hundred years later, Gregory XI (1370–78)‡‡ expressly extended its use even to the Lateran Basilica, the last bulwark of a more ancient form of Roman daily worship.

Throughout this whole development, even when the individual priest prayed in private, the Breviary retained forms rooted in the congregational setting, up to and including the liturgical greeting and

---

* Canonical clergy are those secular clergy belonging to a cathedral or collegiate church and bound to a common life.

† The Latin text that Baumstark quotes and translates here is, "Item praecipimus, etiam districte, ut omnes Sacerdotes habeant breviaria sua, in quibus possint horas suas legere quando sunt in itinere." Canon 9 of the Council of Trier, 1227, in Mansi, v. 23, col. 33. See also Batiffol, (Eng. ed.), 157.

‡ The Minorites is an older name for the Order of Friars Minor founded by Francis of Assisi (1181/82–1226) and now commonly called the Franciscan Order.

§ On Haymo of Faversham, see Short Biography, no. 90.

¶ On Gregory IX, see Short Biography, no. 82.

** On Nicholas III, see Short Biography, no. 129.

†† Francis of Assisi (1181/82–1226) is said to have seen the seraphim in a vision.

‡‡ On Gregory XI, see Short Biography, no. 83.

its reply. Basically we are dealing here with a phenomenon similar to that found in the house-chapel of Melania the Younger, where the private celebration of the Eucharist cloaked itself in forms found in congregational worship. Only one difference pertains, not to be underestimated. In the earlier instance, one finds disguise being used to safeguard the oldest sort of liturgical life of a private nature; in the later instance, one has a kind of unconscious relapse into domestic liturgical life.

Notes

1 *Didache*, 9. GT: Zeller, 11f [ET: *The Didache: A Commentary*, ed. Kurt Niederwimmer and Harold W. Attridge (Minneapolis: Fortress Press, 1998)]. In respect to how these celebrations were conducted, see in particular Paul Drews, "Untersuchungen zur Didache," *Zeitschrift für die neutestmentliche Wissenschaft* 5 (1904): 74–79; and Eduard Alexander von der Goltz, *Tischgebete und Abendmahlsgebete in der altchristlichen und der Griechischen Kirche*, TU 29, 2b (Leipzig: J. C. Hinrichs, 1905), 6ff.

2 Pseudo(?)-Athanasius, Περι παρθεν ίασ, ήτοι περί ασκήσεωσ [*De virginitate, sive de ascesi*], chaps. 12–15, PG 28, cols. 264–69; for a critical edition of this text, see Saint Patriarch of Alexandria Athanasius, Λόγος σωτηρίας παρθένον [*De virginitate*], *Eine echte Schrift des Athanasius*, Eduard Alexander von der Goltz, TU 29, 2a (Leipzig: J. C. Hinrichs, 1905), 45–49 [ET: *Pseudo-Athanasius, On Virginity*, trans. and ed. David Brakke, Corpus Scriptorum Christianorum Orientalium 592–93 (Lovanii [Louvain]: Peeters, 2002); Johnson, *Worship*, II, no. 94-A (selections)]. See also Goltz, *Tischgebete*, 32-36, and more recently Ernesto Buonaiuti, "Evagrio Pontico e il *De virginitate* Ps.-Atanasiano," *Rivista trimestrale di studi filosofici e religioci* 1 (1920): 208–20; = Buonaiuti, *Saggi sul cristianesimo primitivo* (Città di Castello: "Il Solco," 1923), 242–54.

3 Basil, Letter 93, PG 32, col. 485 [ET: Johnson, *Worship*, II, no. 67-E-2]. See Goltz, *Tischgebete*, 36.

4 Council of Laodicea (fourth century), canon 58, Mansi 2, 573 C [ET: Johnson, *Worship*, II, no. 80-C, 2001].

5 General Council of Seleucia-Ctesiphon (410), canon 13: Jean Baptiste Chabot, *Synodicon orientale, ou, Recueil de synodes nestoriens*, Notices et extraits des mss. de la Bibliothèque Nationale et des autres bibliothèques de la France 37 (Paris: Imprimerie Nationale, 1902), 27, see also 267; GT: Oskar Braun, *Das Buch der Synhados* (Stuttgart: J. Roth'sche Verlagshandlung, 1900), 21.

6 No. 46 [Baumstark cites no. 36] in the Syrian biography of the Monophysite Peter the Iberian. See Richard Raabe, *Petrus der Iberer: ein Charakterbild zur Kirchen und Sittengeschichte des fünften Jahrhunderts: syrische Übersetzung einer um das Jahr 500 verfassten griechischen Biographie* (Leipzig: J. C. Hinrichs, 1895),

31 [ET: *John Rufus, the Lives of Peter the Iberian, Theodosius of Jerusalem, and the Monk Romanus,* trans. and ed. Cornelia B. Horne and Robert R. Phenix, Jr., Writings from the Greco-Roman World 24 (Atlanta, GA: Society of Biblical Literature, 2008), 63].

7 *Liber Pontificalis,* ed. Louis Marie Olivier Duchesne vol. 1 (Paris: E. Thorin, 1884–92), 402 [ET: *The Lives of the Eighth-Century Popes (Liber Pontificalis),* trans. and ed. Raymond Davis, Translated Texts for Historians 13, rev. ed. (Liverpool: Liverpool University Press, 2007), 8].

8 It is still to be found in the very interesting remnants of a sacramentary from Salzburg, ed. A. Dold, "Ein merkwürdiges Sakramentarfragment aus Clm 15815," JLW 2 (1922): 102–7.

9 Orders for them alone are found in the eighth book of the *Apostolic Constitutions,* chaps. 35–39. This text is to be found in Funk, *Didascalia* 1, 542–49 [ET: the translation found in ANF 7 is available online at http://www.ccel.org/ccel/schaff/anf07.toc.html; Johnson, *Worship,* II, no. 77, 1822–37].

10 Paul Geyer, *Itinera Hierosolymitana saeculi IV–VIII* (Wien [Vienna]: F. Tempsky, 1898), 35–101; GT: Hermann Richter, *Pilgerreise der Ätheria (oder Silvia) von Aquitanien nach Jerusalem und die heiligen Stätten* (Essen: Baedeker, 1919) [ET: *Egeria's Travels,* trans. John Wilkinson (London: SPCK, 1971), 91–147; Johnson, *Worship,* II, no. 83 (selections)]. Concerning the great antiquity of this document, which has been unjustifiably cast into doubt, see Anton Baumstark, "Das Alter der Peregrinatio Aetheriae," OC, n.s., 1 (1911): 32–76.

11 First Council of Toledo (400?), canon 9, Mansi 3, 1000 A. B. [ET: Johnson, *Worship,* III, no. 128: 3170].

12 Concerning this development, see Batiffol (Fr. ed.), 233–37 [Batiffol (Eng. ed.), 155–60].

13 In this regard, for example, see chap. 89, "De dirigendis in via," of the Cistercian constitution composed by St. Stephen Harding, *Usus Anitquiores Ordinis Cisterciensis,* PL 166, col. 1464.

14 A list of relevant manuscripts can be found in Batiffol (Fr. ed.), 36f, n. 3 [ET: Batiffol (Eng. ed.), 156, n. 5].

15 Synod of Trêves [Trier] (1227), canon 9, Mansi 23, 33 B. C.

16 On this, see Bäumer, 319ff, and Batiffol (Fr. ed.), 242–48 [ET: Batiffol (Eng. ed.), 160–65].

Chapter 3

The Legacy of the Synagogue

In its worship life the early church came into an inheritance from the synagogue, given in equal measure to both of its worship forms, the domestic and the congregational. The result was simply this: the fulfillment of the promise inherent in the forms received from Judaism, which—in the context of the church—were deepened and widened to accommodate the new faith in the Son of God, who appeared in the flesh, was crucified, and rose again victorious from the dead.

The sacramental celebration recalling Christ's death was combined with religious rituals that made every meal shared by a Jewish household sacred, and especially the evening meal that began the Sabbath celebration. The patterns of morning worship used in the synagogue passed over unchanged into the word service of the Christian assembly, which had now moved to the early hours of Sunday morning.

To bless the Jewish meal, a brief prayer was always said over a cup of wine and the broken bread; a more extended discourse served as the thanksgiving following the meal.[1] These formulas, as well as numerous other utterances that Israelites coined in their prayer life, owed their name *berakah*, or "blessing," to the fact that they began—and often ended—with the characteristic formula "Blessed are you, Lord our God." We get a stirring picture of Sabbath morning worship from the account that Luke provides in his gospel of the Lord's appearance in the synagogue at Nazareth (Luke 4:16-30). The public reading of excerpts from the Law and the Prophets* was followed by a discourse,

---

* The phrase "the Law and the Prophets" is used frequently in the New Testament to refer to Jewish Scripture (Matt 5:17; 7:12; 22:40; Luke 16:16; Acts 24:14; 28:23). The Lukan writings refer to Jewish Scripture with a parallel formula as well, "Moses and the Prophets" (Luke 16:29, 31; 24:27; Acts 26:22). Once in the New Testament, the phrase is used to refer to the Scripture read in the synagogue (Acts 13:15), where in time a passage selected from the Prophets followed one from the Law read in course, in Palestine on a biennial cycle, in Babylon on a triennial. Although the Lukan passage describing Jesus' visit to the synagogue in Nazareth neither uses this nomenclature nor makes mention of the Law, Baumstark presumes this pattern for the selection of readings in Nazareth and employs the phrase "the Law and the Prophets" to refer to it.

given for the edification of the congregation, by some member of the synagogue.* Nor did synagogue worship want for a prayer whose type can be heard again and again in the literature of post-exilic Judaism.[2] Its original setting was probably the liturgy used to sacrifice in the Temple. After twice praising God, for (1) creating all things and (2) mercifully guiding the fortunes of Israel, the prayer concludes its series of ideas with intercession.[†] The *Sanctus* sung by heavenly choirs, cited from Isaiah 6:3, must have been woven into this prayer early on. On the other hand, the support that this prayer gives the daily morning recitation of the so-called Shema appears to have developed only later, using an older version in an abbreviated form. Shaped out of the biblical passages Deuteronomy 6:4-9, 11:3-21, and Numbers 15:37-41, the Shema confesses the oneness of God and the covenantal relationship between God and his chosen people. The short form of this prayer, with its embolism quoting the *Sanctus*, survives as support for the Shema in the daily morning prayers of the synagogue.[3] The two readings from the Law and the Prophets have also been preserved in the synagogue to this day, both in the worship service on Sabbath morning and on holy days of celebration and penance.

In the eucharistic text of the *Didache*, the Jewish table blessings appear adapted to the Christian celebration of the Lord's Supper.[4] One finds influence of these Jewish blessings both in the East and in the West. Traces of them can be observed in the table prayers of the East; at times those forms are more closely related to early Christian texts and sometimes wholly unrelated.[5] In the West it is significant to find the pure *berakah* form preserved in the blessings of the liturgical table prayers: "Blessed is God in His gifts and holy in all His works: who lives and reigns forever and ever" (*Benedictus Deus in donis suis et sanctus in omnibus operibus suis: qui vivit et regnat in saecula saeculorum*).[6†]

---

* This is of course an understatement. While it became customary for any literate male member of the synagogue to be asked to read Scripture in the synagogue, Jesus Christ was hardly just any member of the synagogue, being the Messiah himself, that is, the very one whom the Scripture proclaimed.

† The prayer to which Baumstark refers here is likely the blessings preceding the Shema.

‡ As quoted here, this prayer is found in the "Benedictionale," the second section in the appendix of the Tridentine Ritual: "Itinerarium et Benedictio Mensae," among the prayers *post coenam* (after the evening meal). For the Latin and English text of this prayer in the Tridentine Rite, see *Roman Ritual, The Blessings* (Milwaukee: The Bruce Publishing Co., 1946), 474–75. In the

The word service celebrated in the synagogue on the Sabbath served as the basis for the Mass of the Catechumens.[7]* The eighth book of the *Apostolic Constitutions*,[†] reflecting liturgy used in fourth-century Antioch, combines the two readings taken from the Law and the Prophets with a corresponding set of readings, also two in number, taken from the New Testament, one from the gospels and another from the writings.[8] The Nestorian liturgy has in principle preserved the double reading from the Old Testament as a counterpart to two readings from the New Testament, specifically from the letters of Paul and from the gospels. This pattern is only altered through the whole of the Easter Season and on feast days outside of it. The passage from the Pentateuch, normally read in the first position, is suppressed and replaced with a passage from the Prophets, ordinarily taken from Isaiah. The passage from the Prophets in turn, having moved from the second position to the first, makes way for a passage excerpted from the Acts of the Apostles. Here we see the New Testament material cautiously working its way into the liturgy, in this case through the ancient practice of reading the Acts of the Apostles in the Season of Easter.[9] On Egyptian soil we come upon the first indication of a move to exclude the Old Testament reading from the assembly's celebration of the Eucharist outright.[10] Once again we find the quartet of pericopes, but the three nongospel pericopes are all taken from the New Testament, that is, in order, from the Pauline Epistles, the Catholic Epistles, and

---

Conciliar Rite it is found in the *Rituale Romanum* as *De benedictionibus* (Book of Blessings), chap. 30, no. 1036. It also occurs in the *Ordo Benedictionis Mensa* of religious orders such as the Cistercians. See J. Baudot, "Bénédiction de la table et des aliments," DACL 2, cols. 713–16.

* The Mass of the Catechumens is an older phrase used to refer to the Liturgy of the Word. It stemmed from the fact that Catechumens were welcome to the first part of the liturgy, when Scripture was read and proclaimed, but not to the Liturgy of the Meal when prayers were offered and the Eucharist celebrated. Catechumens were invited to depart at the end of the Liturgy of the Word, leaving only the baptized present for the Liturgy of the Meal that followed.

† The *Apostolic Constitutions* is a composite church order in eight books dating from the late fourth century and almost certainly of Syrian provenance. While traditionally ascribed to Clement of Rome (fl. 96) or the apostles, it is in fact a redaction built upon other church orders, notably The *Didascalia Apostolorum* and the *Didache*. The eighth book, itself a composite compilation, includes a complete eucharistic liturgy and the eighty-five "Apostolic Canons."

the Acts of the Apostles. On the other hand, an increase—to varying degrees—in the number of selections read from the Old Testament occurred in the liturgy of the Syrian Jacobites.[11] In most cases, a threesome of Old Testament readings stands vis-à-vis an equal number of New Testament pericopes. In this instance, the latter are taken in order from the Acts of the Apostles or the Catholic epistles, the Pauline Epistles, and the gospels; the Pentateuch, the extra-Pentateuchal Historical Books or Wisdom literature (including Job), and the Prophets provide material for the series of three readings from the Old Testament. In the East, the Armenian liturgy preserves at least one Old Testament lection read before one apostolic* and one gospel reading.[12] In the West, the Ambrosian and Mozarabic Rites, along with older Gallican liturgical documents, do the same thing, except during the Season of Easter when a reading from the Acts of the Apostles replaces the Old Testament lection.[13] In Constantinople, the development of the Mass had reached this point around the turn of the fifth century.[14] At least traces of this practice are preserved in the oldest document attesting to the nongospel reading cycle in Rome: this is a manuscript from Würzburg,[†] whose pericopic references take us back to the time of Pope Boniface IV (608–15)[‡] at the very latest.[15] Only subsequently did the Byzantine and Roman Rites let their stock of Mass readings dwindle down to the modest quantity of two. In this regard, only the former

---

* Baumstark here uses the traditional term "apostolic" to refer to readings from the New Testament writings. In this schema, the Old Testament goes by the name of "the prophet" and the epistle reading is called "the apostle," whereas the gospel is thought to proclaim the voice of Christ.

† This manuscript from Würzburg is the oldest known extant Roman "lectionary," which Baumstark dates to the early seventh century ("at the very latest"), with the system being in use in the sixth century (whereas more recently Martimort dates it to the eighth, with the system going back to the seventh century). It was published in the form of a capitulary, a book listing the scriptural passages to be read during the liturgy, organized according to the liturgical year. See Aimés-Georges Martimort, *Les lectures liturgiques et leurs livres*, Typologie des sources du moyen âge occidental 64 (Turnhout: Brepols, 1992), 31–32. For a facsimile of this manuscript, see *Comes Romanus Wirziburgensis*, ed. Hans Thurn, Codices selecti phototypice impressi 17 (Graz, Austria: Akademische Druck und Verlagsanstalt, 1968); for its list of readings, see Germain Morin, "Le plus ancien 'comes' ou lectionnaire de l'église romaine," RevBén 27 (1910): 41–72.

‡ On Boniface IV, see Short Biography, no. 39.

rite—in agreement with Egyptian use—allowed the reading from the Old Testament to drop out altogether. In Rome, the use of scriptural material for nongospel pericopes—sometimes from the Old Testament, sometimes apostolic—continues to remind us of the older form of a double nongospel reading. What variety we find in this development! Yet again and again, in one way or another, the ultimate relationship to the system of liturgical readings in the synagogue makes itself apparent. Even more! Time and again that relationship is also still evident in the selection of specific Old Testament texts, which one or several rites appoint for particular days in the liturgical year.[16]

The ancient prayer, offering praise for both creation and Israel's salvation,* grew naturally on Christian soil into one praising God for redeeming humankind through Jesus Christ. Eventually this prayer expanded to absorb into itself the old eucharistic *berakah* formulas; this occurred after the time when the word service and the Eucharist had joined together once and for all (the Eucharist having relinquished its old meal character). The basic type for the eucharistic prayer, produced by the fusion of two features inherited from the worship of the synagogue, lives on in the East in all the liturgical documents for the Eucharist—sometimes clearly, sometimes as a faded memory— taking a variety of particular forms. The ideal form found in the eighth book of the *Apostolic Constitutions* (behind which stands the actual use of early Christian Antioch) allows us to see this type at its purest and how it relates to its Jewish native soil.[17]

On Roman soil, one is able to see the prayer of intercession from Sunday's Liturgy of the Word reflected in the open letter sent to the church in Corinth by Clement (fl. ca. 96), a disciple of the apostle Peter.[18]† There is nothing here to indicate that—by the time this letter was written (at the end of the first century)—the Liturgy of the Word had combined with the sacramental celebration. Today we know the oldest texts providing direct evidence for the Roman liturgy are preserved in the prayers of the early (formerly so-called) Egyptian Church Order.[19] For there is no longer any doubt that in this work we have a writing of Hippolytus of Rome (ca. 170–ca. 236).‡ Originally authored by him in Greek, it is now found only in translation, an early one in Latin along

---

* Baumstark uses here the word *Heilsführung*, literally "the leading to salvation."

† On Clement of Rome, see Short Biography, no. 51.

‡ On Hippolytus, see Short Biography, no. 97.

with other versions in various oriental languages. In this document, entitled the *Apostolic Tradition*, the writer provided statutes for a schismatic community, which he himself led—intermittently.[20]* One finds here a rather short eucharistic prayer that, in several respects, reminds us still of the meal prayers in the *Didache* and, for want of the *Sanctus*, unequivocally betrays its independence from the prayer originally found in the Sabbath morning worship of the synagogue.[21] In any case, already before this time, one finds this prayer developing into the main one for the eucharistic celebration. For Justin Martyr (ca. 100–ca. 165),† when writing in his *First Apology* around the year 130,‡ describes this kind of comprehensive prayer of thanksgiving for both creation and redemption, combined with petitions.[22]

The way daily prayer is organized has roots in its Jewish native soil no less than the way the community's eucharistic worship is

---

* Although at the time that Baumstark wrote, the *Apostolic Tradition* was regarded as (1) an integral work, (2) written by Hippolytus, and (3) representative of third-century Roman practice, recent scholarship has called all three of these assertions into question. Indeed, the document known as the *Apostolic Tradition* was first ascribed to Hippolytus only at the beginning of the twentieth century. Currently it is regarded as "living literature," which has integrity as a liturgical corpus containing a variety of documents drawing upon an identifiable tradition in different ways. This common premise notwithstanding, scholars use different approaches for analyzing this liturgical document. Paul Bradshaw et al. see it as a composite of liturgical streams and strata so diverse in time and place that its documentary witnesses can only be presented comparatively in parallel columns *cum* commentary. Recent scholarship has also suggested an Eastern origin; see J. A. Cerrato, *Hippolytus between East and West: The Commentaries and the Provenance of the Corpus* (Oxford: Oxford University Press, 2002). By contrast, Alistair Stewart-Sykes is confident to produce a reconstructed text, which he places in early third-century Rome, but uses redaction criticism to identify three strata within it. See Hippolytus, *On the Apostolic Tradition,* trans. and ed. Alistair Stewart-Sykes (Crestwood, NY: St. Vladimir's Seminary Press, 2002), esp. 11–50, and Paul F. Bradshaw, Maxwell E. Johnson, and L. Edward Phillips, *The Apostolic Tradition: A Commentary* (Minneapolis: Fortress Press, 2002), esp. 1–17. The current state of the question is well summarized in J. A. Cerrato, "The Association of the Name Hippolytus with a Church Order now Known as *The Apostolic Tradition*," *St.Vladimir's Theological Quarterly* 48 (2004): 179–94.

† On Justin Martyr, see Short Biography, no. 113.

‡ *The First Apology* of Justin Martyr is now dated 155.

structured.[23] The liturgy's twosome of morning and evening prayer, *Orthros* and *Hesperinos* in Greek terminology, *Laudes* and *Vespers* in the Roman, harks back to the duty, incumbent upon every Israelite, to recite their confession of faith—the Shema—twice a day, morning and evening. The requirement to pray the Our Father three times a day, already found in the *Didache*, clearly represents a conscious counterpart to the thrice-daily recitation of the so-called prayer of the Eighteen Benedictions.[24]* In the following period, the Liturgy of the Hours continued to develop along these lines. On the one hand, as seen on Syrian soil, the hours of prayer not sung during the night were eventually limited to devotions offered thrice daily: in the morning, at noon, and in the evening. On the other hand, the pattern of praying in the synagogue thrice daily was at least one of the factors in developing the triad found also in the daytime *horae* (hours): Terce, Sext, and None. The African Tertullian (ca. 160–ca. 225)† was already aware of Christian circles observing this practice, although the requirement to keep these *horae* may not have been so strict as praying morning and evening.[25] The Roman Rite shares this practice together with the rest of the Western and most of the Eastern Rites. In whatever way a threefold division of the prayers assigned to actual daylight hours evolved, it in turn produced a propensity (whose influence was nearly universal) to organize the nighttime singing of psalms into three parts. Support for the idea that the way the church consecrated the day is related developmentally to the synagogue is also found on the highest level of generality, however. Namely, the two even agree on when the liturgical day begins: in the evening.

A parallel relationship can be seen in the way the two religions ritually consecrate the week as well and not only in the connections between the Sunday and Sabbath celebrations. The fixed fast days of Wednesday and Friday, which came to have such liturgical significance, also draw upon a Jewish model: two fast days were kept by Jews each week—an occasion for boasting on the part of the Pharisee in the parable of the Pharisee and the tax collector (Luke 18:10-14). In this regard, Jewish practice set Monday and Thursday aside for fasting. Once again we are dealing with an early practice. Already in the

---

* These are "The Eighteen" or "The Eighteen Benedictions" (Hebrew: *Shmone Ezre* or *Shmoneh Esreh)*, which also go by the name of the *Amidah.*

† On Tertullian, see Short Biography, no. 171.

Didache one finds a distinctively Christian way of fasting prescribed, but not without making a polemical comment upon Jewish practice.[26]*

Connections between Jewish and Christian liturgical practices also become apparent in specific liturgical texts, regarding both their formal structure and their content. To assess the overall extent of these connections would require a thorough investigation of the matter, which we still await. For now we may mention two items, which—to our surprise—point in this direction. They are (1) the main section of the *Gloria in excelsis* beginning with the words "We praise you" (which evidently were never related to the angel's song of Luke 2:14),[27]† and (2) the beginning of the *Te Deum*,‡ closely related to the above. Its type in the East finds an echo in a group of Greek evening songs, which originated in early Christian Palestine and date from the fifth century at the latest.[28] Space allows mention of only one significant line in the text of the Gloria. In "We give you thanks for your great glory"§ we hear voiced a remarkable phrase. One of the eucharistic prayers of the *Didache* speaks in a completely similar vein, "For all things, we thank you, Lord, because you are powerful."¶ Just to experience such close contact with the earliest Christian texts, which yet stand so close to Jewish prayer life, would readily give ample food for thought.

---

* "Let your fasts not [take place] with [those of] the wicked. They fast on Monday and Thursday; you, though, should fast on Wednesday and Friday" (*Didache* 8:1). ET: *The Didache: A Commentary on the Didache*, commentary by Kurt Niederwimmer, trans. Linda M. Maloney, ed. Harold W. Attridge (Minneapolis: Fortress Press, 1998), 131.

† *Gloria in excelsis Deo*, known also as the "Greater Doxology," the "Angelic Hymn," or simply the Gloria, became a part of morning prayers in the fourth century, although its origins are earlier. The opening phrases of this hymn have been traditionally regarded as the song of the angels announcing the birth of Christ to the shepherds (Luke 2:13-14), which led to titles such as *Hymnus angelicus*, *Laus angelorum*, and *Laus/Hymnus angeli cum carmine*. On the Gloria, see also p. 200.

‡ The *Te Deum* (known also as *Te Deum Laudamus* or the Ambrosian Hymn) is traditionally attributed to Ambrose (337/40–97) and Augustine (354–430) and thought to have been composed in 387 for the latter's baptism. It is an early Christian hymn combining two genres: a profession of faith and a song of praise. The petitions at the end are widely held to be later additions.

§ Translation by International Committee on English in the Liturgy (ICEL), 2007.

¶ *Didache* 10:4; ET: *The Didache*, Niederwimmer, 155.

However, these two texts, parallel even in how they articulate their thoughts, also point decidedly in the direction of the synagogue, whose prayers—inspired by nationalist and theocratic sentiments— never tired of stressing the kingdom of God. This way of thinking was as inherently foreign to Christian euchological consciousness as it was natural to that of the Jews.* For the deepest impulse of Christian prayer is to give thanks not for power and glory, but rather for the fatherly kindness and favor that the Eternal One has shown humankind.

---

* This sentence reads literally, "This way of thinking was just as inherently foreign to Christian euchological consciousness." I have added the concluding phrase for the sake of clarity.

Notes

Concerning synagogue worship in general, see Emil Schürer, *Geschichte des jüdischen Volkes im Zeitalter Jesu Christi*, vol. 2, 3rd ed. (Leipzig: J. C. Hinrichs, 1886–90; 3rd ed. 1898), 450–63, and above all Ismar Elbogen, *Der jüdische Gottesdienst in seiner geschichtlichen Entwicklung* (Leipzig: G. Fock, 1913); ET: Ismar Elbogen and Raymond Scheindlin, *Jewish Liturgy: A Comprehensive History*, rev. ed. (Philadelphia: Jewish Publication Society, 1993).

[1] This is already known in the *Mishna Berakoth*, VII, 1–3. The Hebrew text is to be found in any Jewish prayer book; GT of the text used for celebrating the Passover meal can be found in Eduard Alexander von der Goltz, *Tischgebete und Abendmahlsgebete in der altchristlichen und der griechischen Kirche*, TU 29, Heft 2b (Leipzig: J. C. Hinrichs, 1905), 8–12.

[2] Anton Baumstark, "Das eucharistische Hochgebet und die Literatur nachexilischen Judentums," *Theologie und Glaube* 2 (1910): 353–70; Baumstark, *Messe*, 24–26.

[3] The Hebrew text of the Shema and its blessings is readily available in *Altjüdische liturgische Gebete ausgewählt und mit Einleitungen*, ed. W. Staerk, KlT 58 (Bonn: A. Marcus und E. Weber, 1910), 4–9; GT: P. Fiebig, *Ausgewählte Mischnatraktate in deutscher Übersetzung*, vol. 3, *Mischnatraktat Berakhôth* (Tübingen: J. C. B. Mohr, 1905), 29–44 [ET: Johnson, *Worship*, I, no. 5; and for text plus commentary, see *The Shema and Its Blessings*, vol. 1 of *My People's Prayer Book: Traditional Prayers, Modern Commentaries*, ed. Lawrence A. Hoffman (Woodstock, Vermont: Jewish Lights Publishing, 1997)].

⁴ It is regarded so throughout the pertinent literature. Perhaps above all see Gottlieb Klein, "Die Gebete in der Didache," *Zeitschrift für die neutestamentliche Wissenschaft* 9 (1908): 132–49.

⁵ See Goltz, *Tischgebete*, 31–65. Old formularies are found in Pseudo(?)-Athanasius, *De virginitate* [*On virginity*], see above chap. 2, n. 2, and in Chrysostomos, "Homilarium in Matthaeum LV al. LVI" in *Ὑπόμνημα εισ τον, ἁγιον ματθαίον τον ευαγγελιστήν* [*Commentarius in Sanctum Mattaeum Evangelistam*], PG 58, col. 545, no. 5 [Baumstark cited col. 561; ET: NPNF (1st ser.), X, 342, no. 6]. Chrysostomos, "Homilarium in Matthaeum LV al. LVI," can also be found in book VII of the *Apostolic Constitutions*, chap. 49, to be found in Funk, *Didascalia* I, 458f [ET: ANF 7, 478, and Johnson, *Worship*, II, no. 77: 1678].

⁶ [The number "6" in superscript is not found in Baumstark's original German text to indicate this footnote.] The fact that there is here at the same time an echo of Ps 145 (144): 13 (and also 17) in no way disproves an ultimate relationship with synagogal prayer, for in just this sort of prayer a kind of interweaving of textual elements from the Bible was very much in vogue.

⁷ Baumstark, *Messe*, 86–91.

⁸ The *Apostolic Constitutions*, VIII, 5, no. 11. See Funk, *Didascalia*, I, 476 [ET: ANF 7, 486, and Johnson, *Worship*, II, no. 77, 1686–87].

⁹ Baumstark, *Perikopenordnungen*, 8–77.

¹⁰ See Brightman, 152–55, 212–19.

¹¹ Baumstark, *Perikopenordnungen*, 78–130.

¹² See Brightman, 425.

¹³ This is the case in the *Lektionar von Luxeuil*, which according to Germain Morin, "Une révision du psautier sur le texte grec par un anonyme du neuvième siècle," RBén 10 (1893): 438–41, offers us the seventh-century Parisian Rite, *Lectionarium Gallicanum*, PL 72, cols. 171–216. See also fragments from Schlettstadt, brought to light by Germain Morin, "Un lectionnaire mérovingien avec fragments du texte occidental des Actes," RBén 25 (1908): 161–66, the pericopes of the Bobbio Missal (the so-called *Sacramentarium Gallicanum*), PL 72, cols. 447–568, and the old Spanish lectionary of Silo, *Liber Comicus sive Lectionarius missae quo Toletana Ecclesia ante annos mille et ducentos utebatur*, Germain Morin, Anecdota Maredsolana 1 (Maredsoli [Maredsous]: Monasterium St. Benedicti, 1893).

¹⁴ This is according to the witness of Chrysostom from his Constantinopolitan period. The passages are to be found in Brightman, 531, n. 5.

¹⁵ Edited by Germain Morin, "Le plus ancient 'Comes' ou lectionnaire de l'église romaine," RBén 27 (1910): 40–74.

¹⁶ Baumstark, *Perikopenordnungen* 17, 60, 92, 99, 116, 120, 124, 174, and 183f. Here consult also a monograph by Venetianer on the origin and meaning of the reading of the prophet in Jewish worship. Though it breaks new ground, it goes too far in supposing relationships: Lagos Venetianer, "Ursprung und Bedeutung der Propheten-Lektionen," *Zeitschrift der Deutchen Morgenländischen*

Gesellschaft 63 (1908): 103–70, available online at http://menadoc.bibliothek
.uni-halle.de/dmg/periodical/structure/2327.

[17] *Apostolic Constitutions*, VIII, chap. 12, nos. 5–60. See Funk, *Didascalia* I,
496–515. See Brightman, 14–23. The relationship of the liturgy found in book
VIII of the *Apostolic Constitutions* to Antioch is corroborated by the liturgical
citations found in the writings of Chrysostom from his Antiochian period [ET:
the collection by Johnson, *Worship*, II, no. 74; for critical evaluation, see Frans
van de Paverd, *John Chrysostom: the homilies on the statues: an introduction*, Orientalia Christiana Analecta 239 (Roma [Rome]: Pontifical Institute, 1991)]. For
the significance and age of the euchological type found here, see Paul Gott-
fried Drews, *Untersuchungen über die sogenannten clementinischen Liturgie im
VIII. Buch der apostolischen Konstitutionen*, 2 vols., Studien zur Geschichte des
Gottesdienstes und des gottesdienstlichen Lebens 2–3 (Tübingen, Leipzig:
J. C. B. Mohr [Paul Siebeck], 1906), where no mention is made of the special
association that in fact pertains to Rome.

[18] Clement of Rome, 1 Cor 20 and 59–61, PG 1, cols. 247 [Baumstark cited
248]–253 [as Migne published the incomplete text of Clement's 1 Cor, PL contains only the first of these four chapters, viz., chap. 20]; GT: Zeller, 39f. 65ff
[ET: *The First Epistle of Clement to the Corinthians*, ANF 9, 235 and 247]. See the
abundant material situating this document in religious history in Theodor
Schermann, *Griechische Zauberpapyri und das Gemeinde- und Dankgebet im I.
Klemensbrief*, TU 34, 3 (Leipzig: J. C. Hinrichs, 1909) [ET: liturgical sections
available in Johnson, *Worship*, I, no. 8].

[19] On ordination prayers and the Great Thanksgiving, see Schermann,
Kirchenordnung, 38–50. [This text, which Schermann attributed to Clement of
Rome and entitled *Ecclesiastica traditio*, follows the Latin text (with lacunae
supplemented by the Sahidic text) of the liturgical strain that has come to
be known as "The Apostolic Tradition" (see p. 67). It is found in a single MS
(*Veronese* LV), which is described in itself and in relation to "The Apostolic Tradition" in *The Apostolic Tradition: A Commentary*, eds. Paul F. Bradshaw, Maxwell
E. Johnson, and L. Edward Phillips (Minneapolis: Fortress Press, 2002), 7–8,
and found in a critical edition in *Didascaliae apostolorum, Canonum ecclesiasticorum. Traditionis apostolicae versions Latinae*, ed. Erik Tidner, TU 75 (Berlin:
Akademie-Verlag, 1963), 117–50; ET: The first column (Latin), supplemented
by the second column (Sahidic), of texts published in Bradshaw et al., *The Apostolic Tradition*, 20, 24, 30, 38, 40, 50, 52, 56, 60, 62, and 68.]

[20] Two scholars, working independently of one another, produced proof for
this: Eduard Schwartz, *Über die pseudo-apostolichen Kirchenordnungen* (Straß-
burg: K.J. Trübner, 1910) and Richard Hugh Connolly, *The So-Called Egyptian
Church Order and Derived Documents*, Texts and Studies, 8, 4 (Cambridge: Cambridge University Press, 1916 [repr., Nendeln, Liechtenstein: Kraus, 1967]). Still
useful in this regard is also Edgar Hennecke, "Hippolyts Schrift 'apostolischen
Überlieferung über Gnadengaben,'" *Harnack-Ehrung-Beiträge zur Kirchenge-*

schichte: ihrem Lehrer Adolf von Harnack zu seinem 70. Geburtstag [7. Mai 1921]
dargebracht von einer Reihe seiner Schüler (Leipzig: J. C. Hinrichs 1921), 159–82.

[21] Though this element of the eucharistic prayer is seen as an apostolic Urform of simply all Mass liturgy, it is nevertheless missing in this instance. In this regard, see Paul Cagin, *L'Eucharistia: Canon primitif de la messe où formulaire essentiel et premier de toutes les liturgies* (Paris: Alphonse Picard et Fils, 1912), and Cagin, *L'Anaphore apostolique et ses témoins* (Paris: Lethielleux, 1919).

[22] On the contrary, R. Devresse, "Revue: Dom. P. Cagin. *L'anaphore apostolique et ses témoins,*" *Revue d'histoire ecclésiastique* 18 (1922): 519–20, has recently demonstrated in a telling way how the language style used in the liturgical formulary is related to that of the genuine writings of Hippolytus.

[23] Bäumer, 31–63. Batiffol (Fr. ed.), 1–23 [ET: Batiffol (Eng. ed.), 1–29].

[24] *Didache*, 8:2, GT: Zeller, *Die Apostolischen Väter* 2, 11 [ET: *The Didache: A Commentary*, ed. Kurt Niederwimmer and Harold W. Attridge (Minneapolis: Fortress Press, 1998)].

[25] Concerning fasting, see Tertullian, *De Ieiuniis* [On fasting], chap. 10 (PL 2, cols. 966–68 [ET: for a liturgically relevant passage, see Johnson, *Worship*, I, no. 26-O].

[26] Didache 8:1 [ET: *The Didache*, ed. Niederwimmer].

[27] On the one hand, a relationship with Luke 2:14 is absent in the case of an evening hymn, which is evidently parallel to the Great Doxology sung in the morning. See *Apostolic Constitutions*, VII, 48; GT: Funk, *Didascalia*, 1, 456–58 [ET: ANF 7, 478, and Johnson, *Worship*, II, no. 77, 1676–77], where in fact Ps 112:1 is placed at the head of the prayer. On the other hand, Luke 2:14 was also moved to the front in prayers that otherwise were on purely formal grounds early Christian, as in the *Martyrdom of Cyprian and Justa*, in Margaret D. Gibson, *Apocrypha Arabica*, Studia Sinaitica 8 (London: C. J. Clay, 1901), 73 [see http://www.archive.org/details/apocryphaarabicaoogibsuoft].

[28] Edited by Paul Maas, "Gleichzeilige Hymnen in der byzantinischen Liturgie: I. Die Abendhymnen," BZ 18 (1909): 310–23, = Maas, *Frühbyzantinische Kirchenpoesie*, vol. 1, *Anonyme Hymnen des V–VI Jahrhunderts*, KlT 52–53 (Bonn: A. Marcus & E. Weber's Verlag, 1910), 3–8.

Chapter 4

The Impact of Hellenism

In its infancy the Christian religion grew out of the soil of its native Palestine and the religion of the Jewish people found there. In search of adherents, Christianity sallied forth into the vast Hellenistic world of late antiquity, known for the intellectual depth of its long-established philosophical traditions, as well as its propensity for new and powerful religious longings. Christianity did this at a time when a varied array of semibarbaric mystery cults was advancing toward the Hellenistic world. Creations like the paintings of Eros and Psyche located near the old entrance to the Roman catacomb of Domatilla reveal how much the art of Christianity continued blithely along paths found tried and true in the art of the Hellenistic world.* It is clearly apparent, already in the prologue to the Fourth Gospel (John 1:1-18), how much Christian thought was soon borrowing from Hellenistic intellectual currents, even for articulating Christian doctrine. From that gospel to the apologists of the second century and the catholic gnosis of a Clement of Alexandria (ca. 150–ca. 215),† and then on to Origen (ca. 185–ca. 254),‡ runs an unbroken intellectual tradition, exhibiting an ever-deepening Hellenistic influence. It is simply inconceivable that the liturgical development of the early church should not also have been influenced by its Hellenistic environment.§

We are frequently still unable to see the influence of Hellenism upon the liturgy as clearly as its relationship to Judaism, with roots in the ritual life of the synagogue. This is because our information about the liturgy of Hellenistic mystery religions themselves is simply in-

---

* Early Christians employed the myth of Eros and Psyche as an image for the resurrection of the body and the eternal blessing of heaven.

† On Clement of Alexandria, see Short Biography, no. 50.

‡ On Origen, see Short Biography, no. 132.

§ The process of Hellenization, which began with the invasion of western Asia by Alexander the Great (336–23 BCE) in the fourth century BCE and reached its apogee in the Hellenism of the seventh century CE, has two aspects. On the one hand, it was identified with the spread of pagan religion, in

adequate.[1] Naturally, our first priority should be to ascertain whether relationships exist between the liturgy of the Christian religion and the mystery cults.[2] Quite often when considering some action or another from early Christian liturgy, some word or another, one may not immediately be able to discern specifically Christian ideas working themselves out (from which the liturgy would have proceeded by inner necessity), any more than one can see a relationship to the synagogue. In such cases, while a presumed connection with the Hellenistic mystery cults may not actually be demonstrable, it at least suggests itself. Despite all of that even now, the contours of quite a few things in this respect are already beginning to take shape.

Of these phenomena, from those that are widespread, only one will be singled out. One form used for the prayers of the faithful entails the leader of the assembly reciting specific petitions, while the congregation answers responsively with an invariable exclamation. This form is common to the Litany of the Saints of the Roman liturgy in the West, as well as to passages, as diverse as one can imagine, in the liturgy of the East. The form in which it reappears in the Gallic-Spanish liturgical area of the West has a closer relationship to the one known in the East. The fact that this type of prayer is prevalent in liturgies everywhere leaves no room for doubting its place among the oldest inventory of liturgical forms. The ritual of the synagogue offers nothing to serve for its pattern. However, now and again in *Metamorphosis*, a novel by

---

evidence even at the end of the fifth century CE. On the other hand, Hellenism was viewed as a carrier of culture, both the social institutions of Greek life and Greek intellectual and literary traditions. Greek served not only as the lingua franca of a large area but also as the language of prestige. While this influence was initially exercised to the east of Greece through a systematic policy of colonization and occupation, over time it established itself as a general cultural influence and norm in both the East and the West. The seventh century CE saw the beginning of the end of this development. A decree issued by Emperor Heraclius (610–41 CE) in 620, which finally replaced Latin with Greek as the official language of the Eastern Roman Empire, proved to be a last-ditch effort at reestablishing Byzantine influence in the face of changing times. This tumultuous century saw an evolution in urban life that weakened the historical centers of Greek influence and also the Arab invasion, which made Arabic the privileged language. From then on, the influence of Hellenism and the use of the Greek language went into decline. For a bibliography, see n. on pp. 230–31. Specifically for Hellenism in Syria, with bibliography, see the same note. On Alexander the Great, see Short Biography, no. 9.

Apuleius of Madaura (ca. 124–after 170),[3]* we learn that this kind of responsive intercessory prayer was practiced in the Mysteries of Isis in just the same way as found in later Christianity. Indeed, as early as the beginning of the second century before Christ, an inscription at Magnesia on the Meander attests to its use in the cult of Zeus Sosipolis.[4]†

Naturally, the ritual forms that non-Christian cults developed in their secret services exercised an influence upon the rites initiating persons into the Christian *mysterium* that was particularly long-lasting. The simple baptism by immersion, which Philip performed for the treasurer of the Ethiopian queen in any old trickle of water found along the way (Acts 8:26-40), saw itself surrounded by an ever-richer ceremonial apparatus, both the prebaptismal rites preparing for baptism and the postbaptismal rites elaborating it. Initiatory exorcisms, the laying on of hands, and anointings by oil undeniably represent a common heritage from the initiation services of the mysteries. A particularly telling motif in this regard has today fallen out of use. At one time, the celebration for the baptism of an adult concluded with the baptized participating in the Eucharist for the first time. After being administered Holy Communion under the forms of bread and wine, the newly baptized was customarily offered a cup containing a mixture of milk and honey.[5] Rome, which shared this practice with Egypt at the very least, probably maintained it into the sixth century,[6] and the introit of the first Sunday after Easter still recalls it, "As newborn babes, crave pure spiritual milk" (*Quasi modo geniti infantes sine dolo lac concupiscite*).‡ One finds explicit confirmation that a cup was similarly administered in the Mysteries of Attis. It is at

---

* On Lucius Apuleius, see Short Biography, no. 17.

† This inscription, dating from the third century BCE and found in Asia Minor at ancient Magnesia on the Maeander River, tells of a ritual held at the beginning of the agricultural year in which a fine bull was dedicated to Zeus Sosipolis, "Zeus, the Savior of the City." Toward the end of the year, the bull, having been well cared for, was led in procession and sacrificed to Zeus, his flesh being shared by those who took part in the procession, apparently as some kind of communion with the god. See ERE, vol. 11, 16a; *Paulys Realencyclopädie der classischen Altertumswissenschaft*, 2nd ser., vol. 5 (Stuttgart: Alfred Druckenmüller Verlag, 1927), s.v. "Sosipolis," esp. col. 1170; and *Zeus. A Study in Ancient Religion*, vol. 1 (New York: Biblo and Tannen, 1964), 58 and 717, n. 2.

‡ In the *Missale Romanum* of the Tridentine Rite, this text reads, "Quasi modo geniti infantes, alleluja: rationabile sine dolo lac concupiscite, Alleuja, alleluja, allejua" (As you are children newborn, alleluia, all your craving must be for

least highly probable that it was done by the cult of Dionysius in southern Italy as early as the fourth to the third century before Christ and perhaps was not unknown in the Egyptian religion of Isis as well.[7]

The outer trappings of the regular celebration of the Eucharist could not avoid Hellenistic influence any more than those of baptism. The Eucharist originally came at the end of a physical meal providing nourishment, religiously consecrated according to Jewish tradition. Only subsequently was the meal united with a word service, whose sensible and sober teaching spoke mainly to the minds and wills of those gathered. Under the influence of ideas prevalent in the mysteries, this composite service was shaped into a kind of coherent holy drama, exercising a powerful hold on the hearts and imaginations of those participating. The essence of this divine play is the appearance of the heavenly "King of all things"[*] in the midst of his own people, to whom he—as both priest and meal—offers himself to be consumed.[8] An undeniable relationship exists between the theater stage wall of antiquity[†] and that closing off the altar room, which thereby becomes mysteriously hidden from the assembly's view; it is through the doors of this enclosing wall that the processions of the liturgical drama of the East move.[9][‡] Just as the drama of the liturgy developed furthest in the East, so too did it appropriate an emphasis on the sacrificial character of the eucharistic celebration. Once again this emphasis, so realistic as to be almost offensive, could only have come about under the influence of Hellenistic sensibilities. Without inhibition one actually spoke of Christ's appearing upon "being slaughtered"[§] anew.[10] In this regard,

_____

the soul's pure milk, alleluia, alleluia, alleluia [cf. 1 Pet 2:2]). *Missal in Latin and English* (Westminster, MD: Newman Press, 1963), 441.

[*] Baumstark is here referring to a phrase from the Cherubic Hymn (*Cherubikon*) sung during the Great Entrance of the Orthodox Divine Liturgy.

[†] The Greek amphitheater had at the rear of its stage the *skene*, a building used for storing stage properties and machinery. The front wall of the *skene* formed the back wall of the stage. Sometimes called the scenic façade, it was pierced by three doors (*thryomata*), used by actors for entry and exit. Baumstark is calling attention to the similarity of this architectural feature of the Greek amphitheater to the iconostasis found in church buildings of the East.

[‡] Baumstark refers here to the iconstasis, the screen of icons, pierced by three doors, which separates the sanctuary from the nave in churches of the East.

[§] Baumstark coined the neologism *Geschlachtetwerden*, which I have translated as "being slaughtered," to convey the meaning of the Greek word

a prominent role was given the image of the Lamb of God, who carries the burden of the sins of the whole world—adopted from the preaching of the Forerunner (John 1:29).[11]* It was no accident that a pope of Greco-Syrian descent, Sergius I (687–701),† introduced the *Agnus Dei* to be sung in the Roman Mass.[12]

Finally, it is of utmost significance that persons participating in non-Christian mystery religions visually contemplated a specific cultic sanctum.‡ It seems that those initiated were saved precisely by this means.[13]§ One cannot separate the ceremonial display of the holy elements in the dramatic structure of the eucharistic mysteries from this kind of thinking. Coming immediately before Communion, this display serves as its effective climax. The Roman Rite has only a rudiment of this display, in the so-called small elevation; in the East the ritual is

---

σφαγιάσηναι, a passive form of the Greek verb meaning "to slay a victim, to sacrifice." It is to be found in the choral introduction to the Cherubic Hymn in the Liturgy of St. James: "Let all mortal flesh keep silence, and stand in fear and trembling, pondering within itself nothing earthly. For the King of kings and Lord of lords cometh to be slaughtered and given as food for the faithful." For the Greek text, see Brightman, 41. Critical edition: *Liturgie de Saint-Jacques*, ed. B. Charles Mercier, Patrologia Orientalis 26, 2 (Paris: Firmin-Didot, 1946; Turnhout: Brepols,1997), 176. For an English translation, see *The Divine Liturgy of the Holy Glorious Apostle James the Brother of God, First Hierarch of Jerusalem* (Basking Ridge, NJ: The Monastery of Saint Mark of Ephesus, 1978), 12, available at http://en.wikisource.org/wiki/The_Divine_Liturgy_of_Saint_James. This choral passage serves as the basis for the first two verses of the English hymn "Let All Mortal Flesh Keep Silence" written by Gerard Moultrie (1829–85).

* The Forerunner is a title for John the Baptist, common in the East, which alludes to John's anticipation of the ministry of Jesus Christ.

† On Sergius I, see Short Biography, no. 158.

‡ I have translated the German word *das Heiligtum* as "sanctum," a word that refers to sacred enclosures of any size, from a sanctuary to a coffer.

§ Though our knowledge of mystery religions is limited by the secrecy of their rites, notably their initiation rites, central to the latter was the "producing and showing" of sacred items, which were taken out of a sacred enclosure and displayed for those participants to see. For example, the initiation rites of the Eleusinian mysteries included drawing from a coffer a sacred object, perhaps a sacred instrument, perhaps an ear of grain, for the initiand and the initiates to view. Baumstark sees a parallel between this aspect of the mysteries' ritual and the "producing and showing" found in the eucharistic rites, the Great Entrance in the East and the elevation in the West.

surrounded by the utmost ceremonial splendor.[14] "Holy things for the holy!"* sounds the call—at once an invitation and a warning—voiced by the priest while performing this action. Already in the *Didache* we find a warning cry in the same context, related in meaning but more detailed: "If anyone is holy, let him come; if anyone is not, let him repent."[15†] However, the congregation answered, at least originally, with a unison confession, "One is holy, one is Lord, Jesus Christ to the glory of God the Father."‡ There is an obvious relationship between this *Urform* of the formula, elaborated later—to some degree—in a trinitarian direction, and the words of the apostle recorded in Philippians 2:11.§ Examining this verse even more closely, perhaps the liturgical formula did not grow out of the words of the apostle Paul (d. 65?), but rather the apostle to the nations was alluding to a liturgical response that congregations had offered from time immemorial.

A feature of the early church was this process of shaping its baptismal and eucharistic celebrations after the spirit of the thought world found in the Hellenistic mysteries. Doubtless this development reached its zenith only deep into the post-Constantinian period, perhaps in the sixth century.[16] But its beginnings surely stretch back into the time of Christian origins.

Naturally, Hellenistic religiosity—through both its sensitivities and its practices—did not only stimulate the development of Christian liturgy through forms specific to the mystery cults. The ancient bridal crown, intended originally to ward off demonic powers, has assumed a commanding place in the marriage rituals of all oriental churches.[17¶] The burial ceremony of the Greek liturgy offers another example. The

---

* *The Liturgy of St. John Chrysostom*, trans. Joseph Rays and ed. José de Vinck (Allendale, NJ: Alleluia Press, 1970), 57.

† *Didache* 10:6; GT: Zeller, 12 [ET: *The Didache: A Commentary*, ed. Kurt Niederwimmer and Harold W. Attridge (Minneapolis: Fortress Press, 1998)].

‡ *Liturgy of St. John Chrysostom*, 57.

§ Phil 2:11 reads, "and every tongue should confess that Jesus is Lord / to the glory of the Father."

¶ Although originally avoided because of its pagan associations, the wearing of bridal crowns by bride and groom came to represent for Eastern Christians both wedding joy and protection from evil spirits. The custom was found already among the Jews (Isa 61:10, Ezek 16:12); the wearing of garlands of foliage or flowers was a variation upon it.

final embrace with which the "brothers" of the deceased bid farewell originates in the ancient customs surrounding the practice of laying the dead out in state, for which the subtle satirist Lucian of Samosata (ca.120–after 180)* gives witness.[18] So also with the melancholy songs that accompany this ceremony. It is not coincidental that the grief they express over the fleeting character of life and beauty resounds with the same elemental power once heard in the elegies of the Ionian Mimnermus (fl. ca. 630 BCE).† A liturgical emphasis upon the character of God and Christ as "Savior" or "Redeemer" cannot be understood without tying it to the cult of Asclepius, which was particularly popular,‡ and other divine "Saviors."§ As in previous examples, this emphasis gained particular importance in the East. Pointing in just this direction are both the loving attentiveness that the intercessions of the liturgy show for the sick as well as a hope for "healing"—for the body just as

---

* Lucian of Samosata (ca. 120–after 180) alludes to funeral practices in *Dialogues of the Dead* and *Charon* in which, by satirizing the failure of humans to appreciate the transience of life, he visits a theme dear to the Cynics. On Lucian of Samosata, see Short Biography, no. 120.

† Mimnermus (fl. ca. 630 BCE) wrote his most important poems as a set of elegies addressed to a flute girl named Nanno. On Mimnermus, see Short Biography, no. 124.

‡ Asclepius, a Greek hero and god of healing, was widely worshiped in the centuries before and after the birth of Christ. The infirm came for healing to an Asklepeion, a healing temple center dedicated to Asclepius, where they underwent purification, performed sacrifice, took baths, and then rested. Asclepius appeared to the patient in a vision or dream, always as a tall, bearded man with a white cloak and serpent staff, the symbol of medicine in our day. The serpent, a dog, or the "healing finger" of Asclepius himself touched the diseased part of the patient's body and the ailment would disappear. The cult spread so widely throughout the Mediterranean world that no large settlement was without its Asklepeion; Christian bishops vigorously opposed it.

§ A pattern found in a number of religions, and in the Hellenistic world in particular, centers upon a savior (σωτήρ; *sotēr*). Examples in the ancient Middle Eastern and Mediterranean world include Asclepius, Isis, Mithra, and Christ. Examples of the same pattern are found in religions of the Far East. In this pattern, human beings are understood to live in a deficient condition that can only be righted by their own efforts or divine intervention, often that of a savior, whose particular concern is ameliorating the condition of the human race through some sort of salvation. Baumstark acknowledges that Christianity fits this pattern found in the Hellenistic world.

much as for the soul—that is tied to consuming the Eucharist.* In contrast to the pagan gods of healing, Christians experienced the Lord in the liturgy as both the exalted one and as the true doctor of all human weakness, just as of old he—whom people supposed to be the son of a carpenter in Nazareth—providing comfort as he walked the roads of Galilee and Judea.

During the last and most difficult bloody persecution,† Christianity had to endure the consequences of refusing to participate in the imperial cult and the cult of the sun, with which—since the early third century—the imperial cult had allied itself as closely as possible.‡ Conversely, as a result of the antagonism between Christianity and these two cults, which were indeed forces in the religion of late antiquity, concepts accrued to the liturgy that exhibited the outstanding vitality inherent to it: (1) the concept of the kingship—one might more accurately say the "emperorship"—of Christ, exalted to rule over all,

---

* This translation assumes a misprint. "In die nämliche Richtung weisen . . ." should read "In die nämliche Richtung weist. . . ."

† In the first years of the fourth century, Roman Emperor Diocletian (284–305) initiated a policy of persecuting Christians that could be fearful, though its severity varied by time and place. It did not finally end until Constantine the Great (306–37) consolidated his power in 313. A key element in this persecution was the requirement that Christians participate in the imperial cult through sacrifice, thus acknowledging the emperor as "Κύριος" (Kyrios). Failing to do so led to punishment.

‡ Sun worship was a popular religion that spread through the Mediterranean world in the last centuries before Christ, and in the first centuries of the Christian era it served as a central rallying point for paganism. Closely tied to the Sun Cult was Mithra, the Sun's ally and agent. Sun worship was especially popular in the army and particularly in the region of the Danube. Emperor Aurelian (270–75), one of the military leaders of stature who came out of that region in the third century, built a magnificent temple to the Invincible Sun (*Sol Invictus*), at Rome in 274. Constantine the Great (306–37), a devotee of the cult before adopting Christianity, declared the Sun to be his comrade and had its image stamped on coins used throughout the empire. See also for this topic M. Wallraff, *Christus verus Solo: Sonnenverehrung und Christentum in der Spätantike*, Jahrbuch für Antike und Christentum Ergänzungsband 32 (Münster in Westfalen: Aschendorffsche Verlagsbuchhandlung, 2001). For the relationship between the Invincible Sun and the feast of Christ´s Birth, see: Susan K. Roll, *Toward the Origins of Christmas*, Liturgica condenda 5 (Kampen, The Netherlands: Kok Pharos Publishing House, 1995), 107–64.

and (2) the idea of him being the true, spiritual sun, the Sun of Righteousness (Mal 4:2). The latter idea was expressed most monumentally in the creation of the feast of Christmas, with its origins in Rome, whereby the celebration of the birth of Jesus was transferred to December 25, the "birthday of the invincible sun."[19]* We find an example even earlier in Alexandria, the city that Alexander the Great (336–23 BCE)† founded to rule the seas. A tie to pagan festal customs was also the deciding factor in the development there of a feast with dual foci, a celebration of both the birth of Jesus and his baptism in the Jordan. Alexandria venerated the god of infinite time, its urban deity, on January 6, the night of Aeon's birth, which the liturgy appropriated as the birth night of him of whom it is written: of his "kingdom, there will be no end" (Luke 1:33).‡[20]

The simple designation "Lord," a translation of the title *Kyrios*, by rights belonged only to Caesar and the sun god. It has been satisfactorily demonstrated that the response *Kyrie eleieson*, along with its pattern of three- or ninefold repetition, found its way into the liturgy from the cult of the sun.[21]§ This assertion is hardly surprising if one

---

* On December 25 the Sun Cult celebrated the birth of the sun with a festival called *dies Natalis Solis Invicti*, the Birthday of the Invincible Sun.

† Alexander the Great died in Babylon. On Alexander, see Short Biography, no. 9.

‡ Alexandria, founded by Alexander the Great (336–23 BCE) in 332 BCE, adopted Aeon as its patron deity. Though used in various, often complex, ways, the concept of Aeon was important to Graeco-Roman religious and philosophical speculative thought. The term, whose primary meaning is a "life" or a "lifetime," came to denote longer periods of time, ages or even eternity. Probably influenced by the Iranian idea of *Zurvan*, both as *Zurvan dareglio chvadata* (Time of the long dominion) and as *Zurvan akarana* (Infinite time), the concept was divinized and Aeon came to be regarded as the supreme deity. The notion evolved further in Alexandria, probably owing to indigenous Egyptian ideas of time and Aeon's association with deities honored there. In that city, the birth of Aeon was celebrated annually on the night of January 5/6. To reconcile the notion of time being born, there arose the odd idea of Eternity being extended, of Aeon being a series of *aeones*. Manichaeism and Gnosticism understood *aeon* differently. Rather than holding Aeon to be a single supreme deity, those religions thought of *aeones* as plural emanations of the godhead, orders of spirits. See *A Dictionary of Comparative Religion*, ed. S. G. F. Brandon (New York: Charles Scribner's Sons, 1970), s.v. "Aeon(s)."

§ This sentence contains a typographical error. The final three "words," *und gefen hat*, should be *und gefunden hat*.

takes into account a fact whose authenticity is utterly beyond dispute. A pagan prayer of considerable extent (preserved in an Egyptian papyrus fragment, intact between genuinely Christian prayer texts) was merely supplied a Christian closing phrase. This prayer stems from a unique genre of religious literature going by the name of "the thrice greatest" Hermes.*[22] How often might prayers, Hellenistic in all other respects, have been simply Christianized at so little cost? However, the meager fragments preserved from the literature of the earliest Christian prayers are so very scanty, and those for the prayers of late antiquity yet more so, that they do not even allow for the possibility of speculation concerning this question.

At any rate, connections between the language employed—at least one with the stylized language of Hellenistic euchology—are found far more frequently than those involving ritual.[†] An outstanding scholar of classical philology has given us the first attempt at a morphology of the religious speech used by antiquity.[23] At some point it would be well worth the effort to peruse at least the *Euchologion* (i.e., a liturgical book approximately analogous to an amalgam of two used in the West, the *Pontificale* and the *Rituale*) of even just one Greek rite, to determine whether the types of that religious discourse, as identified by this scholar, may have survived in it. In particular, it became quite common to multiply the various terms used for addressing the Godhead—and in the process to qualify the divine essence—through apophatic descriptors like "immortal, infinite, inexpressible, incomprehensible," etc. At least this was the case, under Hellenistic influence, in the liturgical language of the East.[24]

It was in particular the eucharistic prayer that was overlaid with a coat of paint in this spirit, and here an influence upon form from

---

* Hermes Trismegistos, the Egyptian god of Thoth, whom Herodotus (ca. 484–ca. 425 BCE) identified with Hermes, was called at times *aa aa ur* (or *paa paa paa*). In Egypt after 200 BCE, this ascription was translated into Greek as *megistos kai megistos theos, megas Hermes* (greatest and greatest god, great Hermes) or Hermes Trismegistos for short. Its origin soon becoming obscured, this shortened title evolved into a proper name, specifically that of the author of a genre of Greek literature (in fact, scripture), presumably translated from the Egyptian and claiming to be the teachings of Thoth, the first Hermes, and of his disciples or descendants, called Hermetics.

† I have added the phrase "than those involving ritual" to this sentence for the sake of clarity.

Hellenistic euchological style intersected with an influence upon content from the thought world of Hellenistic philosophy. As to the doctrines attributable to the various schools of Hellenistic philosophy, those of the *stoa** grew into a philosophical religion of stature, as one can measure by an Epictetus (ca. 55–ca. 130 CE)[†] and a Marcus Aurelius (161–80 BCE), the emperor who donned the philosopher's robes.[‡] Perceiving Stoic thought as akin to their own, Christians had little hesitation being influenced by the spirit breathing through the Stoic ideal, even to the point of opening up their most sacred prayers to its influence. Glowing descriptions of the world, which was thought to be endowed with a soul and identical with the godhead, as well as of the beauty and appropriateness of its parts, had been commonplace in Stoic literature from time immemorial. Cicero (106–43 BCE),[§] Seneca (ca. 4 BCE–65 CE),[¶] and the rhetorician Aelios Aristides (117–after 181 CE)[**] echoed earlier treatments of this theme.[25] In two passages of his work on astronomy, Firmicus Maternus (d. after 360 CE),[††] who later converted to Christianity, shows how—already on pagan soil—this language of inspired description turned into words of prayer.[26] Even in

---

* The philosopher Zeno of Citium (334–262 BCE) founded Stoicism, a Greco-Roman school of philosophy, sometimes taking the form of a philosophical religion, at Athens. By the phrase "those of the *stoa*," Baumstark is referring to the Stoics, whose name derived from Zeno's habit of frequenting the *Stoa Poecile* found in the Athenian *agora*. A *stoa*, essentially a structure with a rear wall and roof supported by a colonnade, was used for all manner of gatherings, from a crowd watching a spectacle to philosophers in discussion. This particular *stoa* took its title *poecile* from panel paintings it housed. The Stoics regarded the world as created and sustained in order and beauty by God, whose energy is immanent throughout it. Indeed, the order and beauty of the world were held to be manifestations of God as the divine reason, world reason, or "Logos." To the Stoics, the good man is the wise man, living in accordance with the laws of nature and conscience, in keeping with the law of the universe rooted in the divine reason. All persons, of whatever rank or class, could live this life conforming to nature.

[†] On Epictetus, see Short Biography, no. 67.

[‡] On Marcus Aurelius, see Short Biography, no. 121.

[§] On Cicero, see Short Biography, no. 48.

[¶] On Seneca, see Short Biography, no. 156.

[**] On Aristides, see Short Biography, no. 19.

[††] On Firmicus, see Short Biography, no. 70.

the liturgy, the Stoic influence may reach the point that its very wording reminds us of these sources. This may occur even in the eucharistic prayer, as is apparent in the eighth book of the *Apostolic Constitutions*, where one finds God being praised as the creator of the world.* There the wisdom of the personal author of all things is glorified in strains that derive from the pantheistic song of songs about the God-world.†

---

* See n. on p. 64.

† Baumstark may be referring here to the "Hymn to Zeus" by Cleanthes (331–232 BCE), a disciple of the Stoic Zeno (334–262 BCE). He held the universe to be a sentient being, whose soul was god and heart the sun. Paul (d. 65?) quotes this hymn in Acts 17:28. I thank Professor Tim Robinson of Saint John's University in Collegeville, MN, for this reference.

Notes

For a general treatment of the topic, see Paul Wendland, *Die hellenistische-römische Kultur in ihren Beziehungen zu Judentum und Christentum* (Tübingen: J. C. B. Mohr, 1907).

[1] Of greatest value is a text, redolent with realizing magical ends, which has been preserved for the mystery cult of Mithras. *Eine Mithrasliturgie*, ed. Albrecht Dietrich (Leipzig: Teubner, 1903; 2nd ed., 1910; 3rd expanded ed., Albrecht Dietrich and Otto Weinreich, eds., *Eine Mithrasliturgie* (Leipzig und Berlin, B. G. Teubner, 1923 [repr., Stuttgart: Teubner, 1966]). ET: This liturgy has been translated and edited by Marvin W. Meyer in *The Greek Magical Papyri In Translation*, ed. Hans Dieter Betz (Chicago & London: University of Chicago Press, 1986), 48–54 (PGM IV, lines 475–834), also available on line at http://hermetic.com/pgm/mithras-liturgy.html].

[2] In this matter, Alfred Loisy, *Les Mystères païens et le mystère chrétien* (Paris: E. Nourry, 1919), goes too far in presupposing a dependence on the part of Christian worship. See the in-depth, critical examination of this book by Marie Joseph Lagrange, "Review: *Les Mystères païens et le mystère chrétien*," *Revue Biblique* 29 (1920): 420–46.

[3] Apuleius, *Metamorphoses* (*Asinus aureus*) [ET: Lucius Apuleius, *The Golden Ass*, trans. P. G. Walsh (New York: Oxford University Press, 1994)], bk. 9, chap. 17. See C. Clemen, "Der Isiskult nach Apuleius, Metamorphosen 11 und das Neue Testament," *Neutestamentliche Studien, Georg Heinrici zu seinem 70. Geburtstage dargebracht*, Untersuchungen zum Neuen Testament 6 (Leipzig: J. C. Hinrichs, 1914), 34f; and Anton Baumstark, "Review: Neutestamentliche Studien (Festschrift Heinrici); Weil (Festscrift Sachau)," OC, n.s., 5 (1915): 323.

[4] *Die Inschriften von Magnesia am Mäander*, ed. Otto Kern (Berlin: W. Spemann, 1900), 83, no. 98, lines 18–21 [ET: Simon R. F. Price, *Religions of the Ancient Greeks* (Cambridge: Cambridge University Press, 1999), 174–75]. See Franz Josef Dölger, *Sol salutis: Gebet und Gesang im christlichen Altertum: mit besonderer Rücksicht auf die Ostung in Gebet und Liturgie*, LF 4, 5 (Münster in Westfalen: Aschendorff, 1920), 71.

[5] More detailed information can be found in Theodor Schermann, *Die allgemeine Kirchenordnung, frühchristliche Liturgien und kirchliche Überlieferung, Part 2: Frühchristliche Liturgien*, SGKA, suppl. vol. 3, 2 (Paderborn: F. Schöningh, 1915), 327–29 (viz. 191–93).

[6] A prayer for the blessing of milk and honey was still used by the so-called *Sacramentarium Leonianum* for the solemn administration of baptism on Pentecost; see *Liber Sacramentorum Romanae Ecclesia omnium vetustissimus S. Leoni Papae in vulgatis tributus*, PL 55, cols. 40–41.

[7] Dietrich, *Eine Mithrasliturgie*, 170–73, 214; Richard August Reitzenstein, ARW 71 (1894): 451–53 [unverifiable citation]; Karl Wyß, *Die Milch im Kultus der Griechen und Römer*, Religionsgeschichtliche Versuche und Vorarbeiten 15, Heft 2 (Gießen: A. Töpelmann, 1914), 52–58; Fr. H. Lehmann, ARW 32 (1917): 1–12 [unverifiable citation].

[8] In this regard, see Gillis Peterson Wetter, *Altchristliche Liturgien: Das eucharistische Mysterium. Studien zur Geschichte des Abendmahles*. Forschungen zur Religion und Literatur des Alten und Neuen Testamentes, n.s., 13 (Göttingen: Vandenhoeck and Ruprecht, 1921). While overstating the case and offering a one-sided point of view, Wetter is highly provocative.

[9] See Karl Holl, "Die Entstehung der Bilderwand in der griechischen Kirche," ARW 9 (1906): 365–84, and Josef Strzygowski, "A Sarcophagus of the Sidamara Type . . . and the Influence of Stage Architecture upon the Art of Antioch," *Journal of Hellenic Studies* 27 (1907): 119.

[10] This is found thus in the Cherubic hymn (*Cherubikon*) of the Liturgy of St. James, which on Good Friday is used throughout the Byzantine Rite: Brightman 41f; GT: Anton Baumstark, "Der Cherubhymnus und seine Parallelen," *Gottesminne, Monatsschriftliche für religiöse Dichtkunst* 6 (1911–12): 12f [see n. on p. 77].

[11] It is thus, for example, in Brightman 62, lines 23ff and 309, lines 8ff and 356, and lines 33–36.

[12] *Liber Pontificalis*, vol. 1, ed. Louis Marie Olivier Duchesne (Paris: E. Thorin, 1884–92), 376 [ET: *The Book of Pontiffs (Liber Pontificalis), The ancient biographies of the first ninety Roman bishops to AD 715*, rev. ed., trans. and ed. Raymond Davis, Translated Texts for Historians 6 (Liverpool: Liverpool University Press, 2000), 89].

[13] Probably the beatitude of Pindar is already to be understood in this sense. See *Pindari carmina cum fragmentis selectis*, ed. Otto Schroeder and Theodor Bergk, Poetae Lyrici Graeci 3, 1 (Lipsiae in Aedibus B. G. Teubneri [Leipzig: B. G. Teubner], 1914), Fragment 137, lines 1–2:

ὄλβιοσ ὅστιζ ἰδὼν ἐκεινα
κοίλαν εἰσί ὑπὸ χθόνα

[14] Baumstark, *Messe*, 157–59.

[15] *Didache* 10:6; GT: Zeller, 12 [ET: *The Didache: A Commentary*, ed. Kurt Niederwimmer and Harold W. Attridge (Minneapolis: Fortress Press, 1998)].

[16] The circumstances concerning baptism are accurately ascertained by Friedrich Wiegand, *Die Stellung des apostolischen Symbols im kirchlichen Leben des Mittelalters. 1, Symbol und Katechumenat* (Leipzig: Dieterich, 1899), 197–260. Concerning the eucharistic liturgy one has to bear in mind a series of texts, which are of the utmost importance and can be shown to have developed only in the sixth century or—at the earliest—in the fifth. Judging from their point of view, Wetter in *Altchristliche Liturgien* claimed these texts for the drama of the mysteries.

[17] See Joseph Köchling, *De coronarum apud antiquos vi atque usu*, Religionsgeschichtliche Versuche und Vorarbeiten 14, 2 (Gießen: A. Töpelmann, 1914), 61–63; and Arnold von Sallis, "Die Brautkrone," *Rheinisches Museum für Philologie* 73 (1920): 199–215.

[18] Lucian of Samosata, Περὶ Πένθους [On mourning], chap. 13.

[19] Indispensable in this regard is Hermann Usener, *Das Weihnachtsfest,* 2nd ed., ed. Hans Lietzmann (Bonn: F. Cohen, 1911). Since Usener's work was published, further light has been shed on the prehistory of Christmas, primarily by two publications: Franz Boll, *Griechische Kalender, herausgegeben und erläutert* (Heidelberg: C. Winter, 1910–20), 40–44, and W. Weber, "Das Kronosfest in Durostorum," ARW 19 (1916/19): 316–41.

[20] This is the case according to K. Holl, "Der Ursprung des Epiphaniefestes," *Sitzungsberichte der Königlich Preussischen Akademie der Wissenschaften* 29 (1917): 402–38. The assessment that the feast of Epiphany is the celebration of ιεποζ γάμος between Christ and his Church is rooted in the religious imagination of Hellenistic antiquity. This above all deserves closer examination as well.

[21] This is discussed by Dölger, *Sol salutis*, 30–80.

[22] Papyrus Berol, 9794, in *Altchristliche Texte*, ed. Carl Schmidt and Wilhelm Schubart, Berliner Klassikertexte hrsg. von der Generalverwaltung der Königlichen Museen zu Berlin, Heft VI (Berlin: Weidmannsche Buchhandlung, 1910), 110–17. Cf. Richard Reitzenstein, "Zwei angeblich christliche liturgische Gebete," *Nachrichten der Königlichen Gesellschaft der Wissenschaften zu Göttingen, Philologisch-historiche Klasse* (Berlin: Weidmannsche Buchhandlung, 1910): 324–29, and Reitzenstein, "Review: *Berliner Klassikertexte* 6: Altchristliche Texte, eds. C. Schmidt and W. Schubart. Berlin: Weidmann, 1910," *Göttingische Gelehrte Anzeigen* [173:1] (Berlin: Weidmannsche Buchhandlung, 1911): 550–68.

[23] Eduard Norden, *Agnostos Theos: Untersuchungen zur Formengeschichte religiöser Rede* (Leipzig: Teubner, 1913), 141–276.

[24] See Schermann, *Liturgien*, 462f.

[25] Cicero, *De natura deorum* [On the Nature of the Gods] [ET: *De natura deorum, Academica*, trans. H. Rackham, Loeb Classical Library, 268 (Cambridge,

MA: Harvard University Press; London: Heinemann, 1967), II, 91f, 98]. Lucius Seneca, *De Consolatione Ad Marciam* [To Marcia, for consolation] [ET: *Moral Essays*, vol. 2, trans. John W. Basore, Loeb Classical Library, 310 (London: W. Heinemann, 1932)], no. 18, and Seneca, De Consolatione ad Helviam [To Mother Helvia, for consolation], [op. cit.] 9, no. 6; and a passage in Aristides, "ΕΙΣ ΔΙΑ" [Regarding Zeus], esp. nos. 7–15, in B. Keil, *Aelii Aristidis Smyrnaei quae supersunt omnia*, vol. 2 (Berolini [Berlin]: apud Weidmannos [Weidmann], 1898) 340–43 [ET: *Aelius Aristides*, trans. Charles Allison Behr, Loeb Classical Library, 458 (Cambridge, MA: Harvard University Press, 1973)].

[26] These citations are to be found in the prefaces to books V and VII. See Wilhelm Kroll, Felix Skutsch, and Konrath Ziegler, *Iulii Firmici Materni Matheseos libri*, VIII, 2 (Leipzig: B. G. Teubner, 1913), 2f and 218f [ET: Julius Firmicus Maternus, *Ancient Astrology: Theory and Practice: Matheseos libri VIII*, trans. Jean Rhys Bram (Park Ridge, NJ: Noyes Press, 1975)]. See also Felix Skutsch, "Ein neuer Zeuge der alterchristlichen Liturgie," ARW 13 (1910): 291–305.

Chapter 5

Variety and Uniformity

Ferdinand Probst (1816–99), one of the most distinguished German scholars of liturgical history in the nineteenth century,* entitled the final chapter of one of his books, "Una sancta catholica et apostolica liturgia" (One holy catholic and apostolic liturgy).[1] This phrase is appropriate for describing the intrinsic unity and constancy of the liturgy if it used to indicate this and no more: the deep sublimity found at the core of its being. Quite distinct from this core is its form, which changes as the liturgy develops, a process going back without interruption to apostolic times. On the other hand, this phrase would be fundamentally mistaken if it implied a *complexus* of forms created by the apostles, which were originally uniform but then underwent a process of increasing differentiation. In actual fact, the historical development of the liturgy does not proceed from uniformity at its earliest to an increasing local diversity, but rather from local diversity to an increasing standardization.

Wherever liturgical development occurred, it necessarily proceeded from the same set of prior conditions: (1) a specifically Christian content and (2) two vital relationships that stimulated its forms to grow, (a) the worship of the synagogue and (b) the influence of the Hellenistic milieu. The universality of these prior conditions inevitably resulted in a certain degree of uniformity, both in the end products and in the developmental processes that produced them. Of the elements inherited from the synagogue and Hellenism, the same ones were everywhere rejected out of hand: those that were incompatible with the contents of the new Christian faith. Inevitably the same elements of this double legacy everywhere acquired the most significance: those particularly well suited to outfit those contents. Beyond that limited extent, liturgical uniformity *ab origine*, at least so far as texts are concerned, was precluded *prime facie* by another factor: in the earliest period the liturgical leader had considerable freedom to coin new wording, enabling him to suit a liturgical text to its particular context.

---

* On Ferdinand Probst, see Short Biography, no. 147.

The *Didache* explicitly grants itinerant prophets, persons endowed with charismatic gifts, the latitude to improvise liturgical texts.[2] Justin Martyr (ca. 100–ca. 165)[*] gives indirect witness to this privilege for the ordained presider as well, when he says that the celebrant offered the eucharistic prayer "to the best of his ability."[3] Apart from wedding Christian content to Jewish and Hellenistic forms, the first step in the process of liturgical development was to pattern the wording of the liturgical speech that had originally flowed freely off the celebrant's lips. This step could be taken only in the midst of individual congregations. It was here that a particular formulation of a text could win lasting acceptance—one that was particularly felicitous or was authored by a particularly respected figure or was offered on a particularly memorable occasion. For example, events experienced under persecution could result in a liturgical text being fixed. We learn that the East Syrian Church gave permanent place to a text—one in its Mass liturgy for Maundy Thursday—that would have been composed just as Shapur II (309–79), king of the Sassanids,[†] first began to persecute the Christians in his realm. Simeon bar Sabbae[‡] (d. 341 or 344), the bishop of the leading see in Persia, Seleucia-Ctesiphon,[§] intoned it while celebrating the holy mysteries for the last time before his martyrdom on April 12, 344, or April 17, 341.[4] This is completely credible, and parallel instances are found quite often in the Roman Empire as well.

One has simply to get used to the idea that the wording of liturgical prayer coalesced into its stereotyped form much earlier than one might at first be ready to accept. Of those traces left from times of persecution, many are found in texts composed during that recent past.[5] Next to a prayer for those who hate and persecute anyone calling themselves "Christian" stands another for the victims of persecution, languishing in prison or at forced labor. Prayers are offered that the faithful suffering persecution might remain steadfast in their confession or ask outright for the opportunity to suffer a martyr's fate. Confessors appear as a distinct class within the community, with a status approaching those of the various hierarchical ministries. Litanies and

---

[*] On Justin Martyr, see Short Biography, no. 113.

[†] On Shapur II, see Short Biography, no. 160. On the Sassanian Empire, see p. 56.

[‡] On Simeon bar Sabbae, see Short Biography, no. 162.

[§] The See of Seleucia-Ctesiphon was "leading" in that it exercised the right of approval over the bishops elected in neighboring sees.

eucharistic intercessions from the Greek East that contain such features have their counterparts in the West and not only in Gallican liturgical documents.* Even the general intercessions of the Roman Good Friday liturgy belong to this category.

Individual worshiping communities also gave birth to the earliest liturgical books. Just as the wording of liturgical speech was first fixed in individual congregations, so too was the whole *complexus* of liturgical life celebrated by a community first put down in writing there. The result of an editorial process of this sort is preserved as a church prayer book from the country town of Thmuis in Egypt. Probably its earliest texts came into being around the middle of the fourth century, for their likely author is the bishop of that city, Serapion[†] (d. after 360), a friend of the great Alexandrian, Athanasius (ca. 296–373).[6][‡] And so, still at this time, even smaller localities in the Nile Valley maintained their own brand of liturgical life, holding their own against the will to power exercised by the mighty Patriarchate of Alexandria. In a parallel example, a letter from Pope Innocent I (402–17)[§] to Decentius, bishop of Gubbio (fl. fourth century),[¶] confirms the fact that, at the beginning of the fifth century, the liturgical practice of this small Umbrian city differed from that of the great Roman Church.[7] At another spot in middle or upper Italy, the unknown author of *On the Sacraments*[8] (which has been ascribed to Ambrose [ca. 339–97])[**] comments upon a form of the text for the eucharistic prayer. Though related to those used in Rome and Milan, this text also differs from them both. Two sacramentaries, preserved from Merovingian Gaul and dating at the latest from the seventh century, appear to have originated in Autun and Auxerre.[9] That liturgical life maintained substantial independence within the old Gallican Rite, even in two cities located not all that far apart,[††] is evident in the considerable disparity of practice apparent from the textual material found in these two liturgical books.

---

* The Gallican liturgies are noted for their Eastern parallels.

[†] On Serapion, see Short Biography, no. 157.

[‡] On Athanasius, see Short Biography, no. 22.

[§] On Innocent I, see Short Biography, no. 100.

[¶] On Decentius, see Short Biography, no. 61.

** On Ambrose, see Short Biography, no. 11.

[††] Autun and Auxerre lie 95 miles, or 153 kilometers, apart from one another in present-day France.

The lesson these particular documents have for us is confirmed by phenomena occurring in general throughout the textual evidence for the liturgy: at its earliest, the process of liturgical formation made for a varied diversity. In this regard we may note *one telling fact*, a prime example. Had an apostolic *Ur*-liturgy, fixed in text, served as the uniform starting point for the liturgy's development, then an element like the words of institution would have had to either (1) recur in a form essentially unchanged in texts of the most diverse sort, or (2) progressively differentiate over time so as to produce variations upon this element's initial uniform shape. However, the opposite is the case. Most varied is the earliest stage to which one can trace the development of the liturgical form of the words of institution. In fact, the variety characteristic of this early stage was at play even back in the considerable diversity found between the four biblical versions themselves (Matt 26:26-29; Mark 14:22-25; Luke 22:15-20; 1 Cor 11:23-26). This state of affairs unleashed a reaction upon the liturgy, with the result that the forms of this text found in the various liturgies entered into a process of convergence that only increased over time.[10]*

By no means did this diversity of the liturgy at its origins involve only the formation of texts. Nor was it limited to specific ritual customs of only minor importance. The second-century Quartodeciman controversy, a dispute between Rome and Asia Minor over the celebration of the Christian Passover, illustrates how a tradition peculiar to a particular locality could prevail when important issues were at stake.[†] The central question was not exclusively, or even predominantly, one of calendar; at issue was the entire ethos of the Christian celebration

---

* The liturgical use of the words of institution was the dissertation topic for Fritz Hamm, one of Baumstark's doctoral students, who set out to apply to the question a strict application of the methods of comparative liturgy. See Fritz Hamm, *Die liturgischen Einsetzungsberichte im Sinner vergleichender Liturgie Forschung untersucht*, Liturgiegeschichte Quellen und Forschungen, 23 (Münster in Westfalen: Verlag der Aschendorffschen Verlagsbuchhandlung, 1928).

† One of several Paschal controversies, this particular one takes its name from the fourteenth day of Nisan, the date of Passover in the Jewish calendar, upon which early Christians in Asia Minor celebrated Easter. Rome, by contrast, celebrated it on the following Sunday. The diversity of liturgical practice was mutually acceptable until Pope Victor I (189–98) took a hard line and tried to suppress Quartodecimanism, excommunicating Polycrates, Bishop of Ephesus (ca. 130–96), in the process. Slowly over time, the Roman calculation for the date of Easter gained wider acceptance.

of Passover. In the final analysis, the debate concerned the festival's proper focus. In Rome, which invariably celebrated the feast on a Sunday, that focus was the historical fact of the resurrection of the Lord, while the facts of Christ's crucifixion and burial were commemorated on the preceding two days of fasting. In contrast to the joy of Easter that followed, one could only regard the events of the two days that preceded it with sorrow. By contrast, the celebration in Asia Minor clung to the fourteenth day of Nisan, the Jewish month of spring. With this date, that celebration was able to do the impossible: tie thoughts of the resurrection to the date of Jesus' death (according to the Fourth Gospel). Today, an early example of Christian writing allows us to infer more details about the shape of that Easter celebration.[11] Apparently written at the time of these controversies, it came to light with translations into Coptic* and Ethiopic (Ge'ez).† According to this work, a daylong fast would have concluded with a Eucharist, celebrated as a festive meal after nightfall. Its festive atmosphere could have only referred to the fact that the economy of salvation had already been accomplished in Christ's death upon the cross. In contrast to the overwhelming import thus ascribed to the cross, the events of Easter morning, even the empty tomb, have only a subordinate meaning. The tomb seems to be left with the significance of an addendum, confirming what had already been revealed on the cross.

---

* Coptic represents the final stage of the ancient Egyptian language, uses an adapted Greek alphabet, and was the standard language for all of Upper Egypt after the fifth century BCE. Sahidic and Bohairic are two of its six dialects. Sahidic (from Arabic *Sa'id*, meaning Upper Egypt) is the oldest, originating in the third century BCE around Thebes. Texts of Scripture and liturgy are found written in it. Bohairic originally evolved in the seventh century BCE in the western part of Lower Egypt, including Alexandria and Memphis. Most Coptic literature is in Bohairic, and since the eleventh century CE it has been the liturgical language for all Coptic Christians. As a living tongue, Coptic was supplanted by Arabic between the eighth and fourteenth centuries CE, eventually dying out.

† Baumstark uses the word "Ethiopic" (an inaccurate term, as other languages are spoken in Ethiopia) for Ge'ez (also Gi'iz), a South Semitic language that originated on the Horn of Africa, in present-day Eritrea and northern Ethiopia. It became the language of the Kingdom of Axum and the imperial court of Ethiopia. Today it exists only as a liturgical language used by both Christians and Jews in Ethiopia and the Ethiopian Diaspora.

This yawning contrast existed not only between Rome and Asia Minor, and the victory of Roman practice over that question in Asia Minor still did not settle the issue once and for all. In the Sassanian Empire, the "Persian Sage" Aphrahat (fl. early fourth century),* who composed twenty-two prose essays in Syriac in the years 337 and 344,[12] expressed an opinion on the celebration of Passover quite close to that held in Asia Minor.[13] In his writings, the date in the month upon which our Redeemer won victory by his suffering death is supplanted by only the day in the week on which it took place.† Various *catenae* of hymns composed in Syriac by St. Ephrem the Syrian (306–73)‡ concern the crucifixion, the festival of the "unleavened bread," the month of spring, and its celebration by the church.[14]§ These hymns appear to assume a one-day celebration for Nisibis and Edessa as well. In this form, the celebration would have recalled on a single day all the discreet events involved in the act of redemption, combined in an integral whole. Even Egypt must originally have shared Asia Minor's idea of Passover. Still, in the year 457, Alexandria administered the festal paschal baptism during the night after Good Friday, rather than celebrating it during the night before Easter Sunday.[15]

Uniformity is not the point of departure but rather the end of liturgical development. Liturgical uniformity gradually impacted various aspects of liturgical life and, more specifically, elements of liturgical texts. Undoubtedly, certain liturgical "assets," texts of a stereotyped nature, were already off-limits to congregational improvisation in the earliest days of the church's worship. The wording of the liturgical greeting and its response, that of the opening dialogue at the start of

---

* On Aphrahat, see Short Biography, no. 16.

† Aphrahat writes, "Our great feast day, however, is Friday," the day upon which Christ died. While he takes pains to place the events of Christ's passion and resurrection in relationship to the date of Passover in the Jewish calendar and encourages the celebration of the Week of the Unleavened Bread following Passover, he does not determine the "feast day" by a date in the month of Nisan. The week begins with a Christian Passover (a commemoration of the Last Supper), is marked throughout by fasting, and celebrates "the great feast day" whenever Friday falls within it, without regard for the date of the month. On Sunday, as the day of resurrection, fasting is not permitted. See the work of Aphrahat cited in Baumstark's n. 13 at the conclusion of this chapter.

‡ On Ephrem the Syrian, see Short Biography, no. 66.

§ For the sets of hymns in Ephrem's corpus, see Ephrem the Syrian, *Hymns*, trans. Kathleen E. McVey (Mahwah, NJ: Paulist Press, 1989), 49.

the eucharistic prayer, how that prayer opened, the way the *Sanctus* was introduced and the words that follow on from it, the wording of the *Sanctus* itself, and the form of the concluding doxology: undoubtedly, all these elements were already established by each locality as inviolable at a time when the celebrant was still allowed to compose, more or less freely, the wording needed to fill out a fixed framework of this kind. Custom also dictated early on, and just as indisputably, the sequence of thought to be followed in that "filling." The organic significance of a framework of introductions, transitions, and conclusions, each fixed in stereotyped speech, lay precisely in the fact that they set out, as it were, signposts to direct the celebrant's train of thought along a particular path. At this point, this whole approach was soon uniformly established for wider areas as well. In its present position before the preface, where it introduces the eucharistic prayer, the opening dialogue has its first witness for Rome in the *Apostolic Tradition* of Hippolytus (ca. 170–ca. 236),* and, a few decades later, with the same wording, Cyprian (d. 258) † provides evidence for North Africa.[16] As early as in Tertullian's (ca. 160–ca. 225) ‡ treatise *On Baptism*,[17] which describes practices dating from even before 201, we catch a glimpse of the euchological train of thought used in North Africa for blessing the baptismal waters. This shows a close affinity with that found in certain sections of the text now used in Rome.

---

* On Hippolytus, see Short Biography, no. 97. On *The Apostolic Tradition* see n. on p. 67n.

† On Cyprian, see Short Biography, no. 57.

‡ On Tertullian, see Short Biography, no. 171.

Notes

[1] Ferdinand Probst, *Liturgie des vierten Jahrhunderts und deren Reform* (Münster in Westfalen: Aschendorff, 1893), 319–54.

[2] *Didache*, chap. 10:7 [Baumstark incorrectly cited chap. 10:6]; GT: Zeller, 12 [ET: *The Didache: A Commentary*, ed. Kurt Niederwimmer and Harold W. Attridge (Minneapolis: Fortress Press, 1998)].

[3] Justin Martyr, Ἀπολογία Πρώτη Ὑπέρ Χριστιανῶν [*First Apology*], chap. 67, PG 6, col. 429; GT: *Frühchristliche Apologeten und Märtyrerakten aus dem Griechischen und Lateinischen übersetzt*, vol. 1, ed. Anselm Eberhard, Gerhard Rauschen, and Richard Cornelius Kukula, BKV 12 (Kempten & München [Munich]: Josef Kösel, 1913), 136 [ET: ANF 1, 185–86; Johnson, *Worship*, I, no. 14-A (selections)].

⁴ This text by Simeon bar Sabbae, edited by M. Kmosko, with Latin translation, is found in *Patrologia Syriaca* 1, 2, ed. René L. Graffin (Parisiis [Paris] Firmin-Didot et socii, 1907), 1050. See Baumstark, *Literatur*, 30.

⁵ Texts of this kind are collected and discussed in Anton Baumstark, "Liturgischer Nachhall der Verfolgungszeit," *Beiträge zur Geschichte des christlichen Altertums und der byzantinischen Literatur, Albert Ehrhard zum 60. Geburtstage dargebracht* (Bonn: Röhrscheid, 1922), 53–72.

⁶ Serapion of Thmuis, *Altchristliche liturgische Stücke aus der Kirche Aegyptens nebst einem dogmatischen Brief des Bischofs Serapion von Thmuis*, ed. George Wobbermin, TU 17, 3b (Leipzig: J. C. Hinrichs, 1899). A Latin translation may be found in Funk, *Didascalia* 2, 158–95; GT: *Griechische Liturgien*, trans. Remigius Storf and Theodor Schermann, BKV 5 (Kempten & München [Munich]: Josef Kösel, 1912), 135–57 [ET: *The Sacramentary of Serapion of Thmuis: a text for students*, trans. R. J. S. Barrett-Lennard (Bramcote, Nottingham: Grove Books, 1993); Johnson, *Worship*, II, no. 88-A]. See Anton Baumstark, "Die Anaphora von Thumis und ihre Ueberarbeitung durch den heiligen Serapion," *Römische Quartalschrift für christlichen Altertumskunde und für Kirchengeschichte* 18 (1904): 123–42.

⁷ Innocent I to Decentius, Bishop of Gubbio, *Epistola XXV*, PL 20, cols. 551–61 [ET: Johnson, *Worship*, III, no. 108-A-4 (selection)].

⁸ Ambrose, *De sacramentis*, chap. 5, no. 21 through chap. 6, no. 27, in PL 16, cols. 443–45 [ET: *On the Sacraments* (Chicago, Loyola University Press, 1960); Johnson, *Worship*, II, no. 53-M].

⁹ The so-called *Missale Gothicum* in PL 72, cols. 225–318, and accordingly the *Vetus Missale Gallicanum* in PL 72, cols. 339–82.

¹⁰ One finds a good compilation of these texts in an otherwise highly unsatisfactory work by K. J. Merk, *Der Konsekrationsmoment der Römischen Messe: Eine liturgiegeschichtliche Darstellung* (Rottenburg am Neckar: Bader, 1915).

¹¹ ["Epistula Apostolorum" is available in] *Gespräche Jesu mit seinen Jüngern nach der Auferstehung. Ein katholich-apostoliches Sendschreiben des 2. Jahrhunderts*, ed. Carl Schmidt, TU 43 (Leipzig: J. C. Hinrichs, 1919 [repr., Hildesheim: Olms, 1967]). See here the "Excursus III" on the celebration of Pascha in the church of Asia Minor, 587–795 [ET: "The Epistle of the Apostles" (Epistula Apostolorum) in *The Apocryphal New Testament*, ed. James Keith Elliot (Oxford: Oxford University Press, 1993; repr. 2005), 555–88; Johnson, *Worship*, I, no. 17 (selections)].

¹² Baumstark, *Literatur*, 30f [see Brock, 19–22 and 124–25].

¹³ This text, with GT by Georg Bert, is no. 12 in the collection *Aphrahat's des Persischen Weisen Homilien*, ed. Georg Bert, TU 3, Heft 3 (Leipzig: J. C. Hinrich, 1888), 179–95 [ET: "Demonstration XII: On the Paschal Sacrifice," chap. 3 in Jacob Neusner, *Aphrahat and Judaism; the Christian-Jewish argument in fourth-century Iran, Studia post-Biblica* 19 (Leiden, Brill, 1971), 31–40; Johnson, *Worship*, II, no. 75-A (selections)]. Cf. *Gespräche Jesu*, 179–95 [*sic*].

¹⁴ These texts [*De crucifixione* (On the crucifixion) VIII and *Hymnni azymorum* (Hymns on unleavened bread) XV] can be found in Syriac, with Latin translation, in *Sancti Ephraem Syri hymni etsermones*, vol. 1, ed. Thomas Joseph Lamy (Mechlin: H. Dessain, 1882–1902), cols. 637–714 and cols. 567–636, respectively; [*Hymni de resurrectione Christi* (Hymns on the resurrection)] can be found in ibid., vol. 2, cols. 741–74 [available through Google Books].

¹⁵ *Der Papyruskodex saec. VI/VII der Philippsbibliothek in Cheltenham*, ed. W. E. Crum, with a contribution by Albert Ehrhard (Straßburg: K. J. Trübner, 1915), 47 (Translation 68). See Ernst Wilhelm Hengstenberg, "Pachomiana (mit einem Anhang über die Liturgie von Alexandrien)," *Beiträge zur Geschichte des christlichen Altertums*, eds. Albert Ehrhard and Albert M. Koeniger (Bonn; Leipzig: K. Schroeder, 1922 [repr., Amsterdam: Rodopi, 1969]), 243–47. Admittedly, in this article Hengstenberg thoroughly misunderstands the situation when he hypothesizes that the celebration of baptism may have been shifted from Easter night to a second location on Holy Saturday and from there finally onto the evening of Good Friday.

¹⁶ See the passage of Cyprian in "Letter 63" (PL 4, col. 384) [ET: Johnson, *Worship*, I, 27-E-13 (selection)].

¹⁷ Tertullian, *De baptismo* [On baptism], PL 1, cols. 1197–1224; GT: *Tertullians ausgewählten Schriften 1: Private und katechetische Schriften*, trans. and ed. Karl Adam Heinrich Kellner, BKV 7 (Kempten and München [Munich]: Josef Kösel, 1912), 274–99 [ET: ANF 3, 669–79; Johnson, *Worship*, I, no. 26-E].

Chapter 6

Regional Definition and Influential Centers

A series of various factors led to a gradual decrease in the variety characteristic of the liturgy at its origins. One of decisive importance was the tightly organized system of church administration that evolved in the Roman provinces following the state's embrace of Christianity. As the church came to enjoy a relationship to Rome as close as could be imagined, it modeled its organization upon the system of political administration used throughout the empire. During its earliest days, the Christian world had conceived church organization to be simply the community with its bishop. The church of the empire, emulating the Roman organization of governance, created layers of hierarchy to arch over these communities. A metropolitan was placed over a number of dioceses, a primate above metropolitans, and finally a patriarch above primates. With a zeal characteristic of new initiatives, these hierarchical entities extended their influence over every aspect of ecclesial and religious life. The liturgy could not possibly escape this influence. From this time on, it was only to be expected that these higher entities would take the lead in developing the liturgy, which had previously been primarily the prerogative of individual congregations. Those ecclesiastical centers whose bishops were raised to positions of privilege shaped the liturgy of the whole area falling under their oversight, as their worship—in practice and text—became models for the rest. At first they didn't pressure the areas under their jurisdiction to accept their particular liturgical forms hardly at all. They didn't have to. One does nevertheless find examples to the contrary. In 517 a Council at Gerona, Spain, declared that the liturgical practice of the Spanish church province of Tarraconsensis should conform to that of Tarragona.[1]* For the most part, however, things evolved gradually and quietly, as a matter of course. This was facilitated from the very beginning by the natural kinship between liturgical forms celebrated in proximity to one another.

---

* Tarragona, a city located on the Mediterranean Sea in eastern Spain and southern Catalonia, was the metropolitan see for the province of Tarraconensis.

Alongside these inclinations to conform, however, there grew up complementary differences, or even contrasting practices. The more distant an area lay from the main cities of a new megadiocese, the more likely it was for these differences to occur. The liturgies of regions that were remote from the episcopal see of their own diocese, yet close to the boundary of a neighboring one, developed after the manner of those areas in the adjacent diocese that lay just over that border. For this reason, an ecclesiastical area with natural boundaries inevitably enjoyed an advantage in the effort to standardize its liturgy. When the boundaries of a church district coincided closely with geographical ones, those efforts were sure to meet with success and firmly take hold. From time immemorial Egypt has constituted a unity strictly defined by geographical features: its unique lifeline, the Nile River, and the surrounding deserts. Its historical significance from the days of the first pharaohs (ca. 1500 BCE) is due to this. No metropolis in the Christian world was able to exercise authority more readily than Alexandria. For this reason, it is easy to understand why time and again one is struck—in comparison to the liturgical styles of other traditions, at least those of the East—by how firmly established and entirely unique the Egyptian liturgy is. The following are only a few of the most significant features unique to the Egyptian variety of worship: a liturgical greeting offering the fellowship of the "Lord" rather than "peace"; eucharistic intercessions originally located before the *Sanctus* rather than after the eucharistic prayer's consecratory section; the *Sanctus* sung without continuing on to the "Hosanna," the shout of Palm Sunday;* the development of a type of eucharistic liturgy that systematically directs all prayers to Christ rather than to God the Father;[2] and a form of the litany of general intercessions in which the deacons originally played a minor role. In the early days of Egyptian Christianity, influence clearly moved along the merchant sea routes connecting Alexandria with the ports of Carthage, Ostia,† and Masilia (Marseilles).‡ It comes as no surprise, then, that—unlike all other Eastern liturgies—parallels repeatedly appear between this same Egyptian

---

* By this Baumstark means singing the *Sanctus* without the *Benedictus*.

† Ostia served as the port for Rome.

‡ Masilia (Marseilles) was founded by Greeks and eventually populated by persons from Phocis, a central Grecian province. Although annexed by Rome in 49 BCE, for generations the population remained largely Phocian and culturally Greek.

liturgy and the kind of worship found in the West, sometimes that of Rome and proconsular North Africa, at other times that of Gaul. This marked pattern in the flow of influence was clearly apparent in other aspects of the life and mission of the church as well.

Syrian history was shaped by the lack of geographical definition just as much as its prominence influenced the history of Egypt. As in the case of Egypt, the historical circumstances affecting Syrian liturgy reflect the influence geography exercised on the overall historical situation.[3] Of course, Antioch had great influence on particular aspects of the liturgy. One can trace ties to this patriarchal see as far away as the Tigris River, Constantinople, Rome, and Gaul—especially in regard to lectionaries.[4] However, there was never a strictly defined Antiochene liturgical area. We learn about the indigenous liturgical style of Antioch from Chrysostom (ca. 347–407)* and from the eighth book of *The Apostolic Constitutions*.[†] But this liturgical style was supplanted early on in Antioch itself by foreign ones, first that of Jerusalem and later that of Constantinople.[5]

Political boundaries were just as effective in creating liturgical uniformity as natural ones. Many of the features of the Nestorian East Syrian Rite present a picture just as idiosyncratic as the liturgical variant peculiar to Egypt. This is because there lives on in that rite the liturgical form once found in the "Christendom" of the Persian Sassanian Empire (227–635).[‡] This kingdom was isolated from Christianity in the Roman Empire and on the Mediterranean littoral by political boundaries that were being contested constantly by warring parties.

Inevitably, political borders acquired particular significance where—unlike Persia—they were those of a Christian nation-state. That was originally the case with Armenia. The same pattern occurs in the West.

---

* In this passage, Baumstark has in mind references to the liturgy of Antioch made by Chrysostom in homilies he delivered during his years there as priest (386–98). See Frans van de Paverd, *Zur Geschichte der Messliturgie in Antiocheia und Konstantinopel gegen Ende des vierten Jahrhunderts: Analyse der Quellen bei Johannes Chrysostomos*, Orientalia Christiana Analecta 187 (Roma [Rome]: Pontificium Institutum Orientalium Studiorum, 1970). On John Chrysostom, see Short Biography, no. 47.

† See n. on p. 64.

‡ See n. on p. 56.

As early as 563, the First Council of Braga* decided to introduce liturgical uniformity into the Suevian kingdom of Gallicia[6]—the immediate consequence of the Suevian royal family's return to Catholicism.[†] The Visigothic kingdom of Spain (and then still also of southwestern Gaul) provides a similar instance. After its ruling house turned from Arianism[‡] to the Catholic faith, this kingdom saw its liturgy standardized nationwide.[§] For that principality, the Fourth Council of Toledo in 633 laid down the principle of "one kingdom, one liturgy" in respect to psalmody and the celebration of the Mass.[7] Of course, in its actual implementation, one finds exceptions to the rule. This is apparent when comparing the Mozarabic Mass book to documents for the early liturgy of Toledo. The former was published through the efforts of the

---

* Braga, in the northern part of modern Portugal, was the archbishopric for the province of Gallicia in which the Suevi tribe held power. The council was held in the year 561, not 563.

† Although once Catholic, under King Remismund (464–69) the Suevian (Suebian) Kingdom in Gallicia turned to Arianism in 465. Martin of Braga (ca. 520–80), whom Venantius Fortunatus (ca. 530–610) called "the apostle to Gallicia," arrived there in 550. With a mission to convert the Suevi (Suebi), Martin founded a monastery near Dumio, becoming abbot. He was later elected bishop. King Chararich (550–58/59) and his household embraced the Catholic faith after the healing of his son. The Suevian (Suebian) people followed. At the Second Council of Braga (572), over which Martin presided as the Archbishop of Braga and metropolitan of all Gallicia, the bishops declared, "There is no doubt now that through the grace of Christ, there is but one faith in the province."

‡ Named after Arius (d. 336), this heresy denies the divinity of Christ, holding that he was not eternal but created by God and therefore capable of change. Though condemned by the Council of Alexandria (ca. 320), Arianism continued to spread and was famously condemned by the Council of Nicea (ca. 325), which asserted the coeternity and coequality of the first two Persons of the Trinity, the Father and the Son. It was not finally quashed in the East until the Council of Constantinople (381), which in turn resulted in a division between the Orthodox (Chalcedonian) and Oriental (Monophysite) Churches. In the West it gained a foothold among the German tribes, including those that had settled into Gaul and Spain, and declined only after the conversion of the Franks to the Catholic faith in 496.

§ Leovigild (525–86, king from 569), king of the Visigoths of Spain and an Arian, had his son instructed in the Catholic faith. Once on the throne, Recared (586–601) renounced his family's heresy and by example led his people to adopt the faith of Rome.

notable Cardinal Jiménez (1436–1517);[8]* the latter is preserved in a series of manuscripts appended to a lectionary from the monastery of Silo, one of which even dates to the seventh century.[9] The comparison reveals differences for which a linear process of development cannot give adequate account.

While in the West the idea of liturgical uniformity was found in these German kingdoms on the Iberian Peninsula, in the East it was known in the phenomenon of churches distinguished by national roots and heretical beliefs. In the case of Armenian Christianity, a national church inherited from the monarchy the responsibility for safeguarding the treasure of Armenian national culture. It assumed this responsibility as early as the year 428 and shouldered it until the monarchy was revived, not until the three ruling dynasties† of the Bagratid (885–1054),‡ the Ru-

---

* Cardinal Francisco Jiménez de Cisneros (1436–1517) worked to ensure a future for the Mozarabic Rite. Finding the Mozarabic liturgical books to be old and imperfectly understood, he arranged for editions of both the Missal and Breviary to be printed. The work was directed by a canon named Alfonso Ortiz (fl. ca. 1500), with the Missal coming out in January of 1500. Jiménez also endowed a chapel in the Toledo cathedral for the celebration of the Mozarabic Rite, the *Capilla Muzárabe*. Regarding the suppression of the Mozarabic Rite, see n. on p. 132. On Cardinal Franciso Jiménez de Cisneros, see Short Biography, no. 107.

† In the early Middle Ages, Armenia was divided, with Western Armenia being a part of the Byzantine Empire from 386 and Eastern Armenia a part of the Sassanian Empire from 428. While Western Armenia shared Christianity with the Byzantines, the Sassanians did not grant their Christian subjects the freedom to worship until 484. (See pp. 116–17 and p. 179.) In 639 the Arabs invaded Greater Armenia (Western and Eastern Armenia combined), controlling it for two centuries following the mid-sixth century.

‡ Although the Bagratids were Armenian noblemen in the first century and even claimed to descend from King David, they emerged as a royal dynasty only in the ninth century, with branches of the dynasty in Armenia (Armenian: Bagratuni) and Georgia (Georgian: Bagrationi). Ashot I (Prince of Princes 862–84, King of Armenia 884–90) founded the Armenian dynasty when he was crowned King of Armenia following a successful revolt against Arab hegemony. Externally, the Bagratids played the Byzantine and Persian Empires off against each other; internally—through intermarriage and conquest—they tried to create a united Armenia. With the Bagratids reduced in power through the loss of lands, Greater Armenia was annexed by the Byzantines in 1045 and invaded by the Seljuk Turks in 1064.

benides (1080–1342),* and the Western Lusignans (1342–75)† came into power. Being Monophysite and Coptic-speaking‡ both belief and language served to isolate the indigenous church of Egypt in the orthodox, Greek-speaking empire of Byzantium. The Egyptian Coptic Church felt compelled to keep its unique liturgy intact at a time when the Orthodox Grecophone Church in Egypt—which maintained vital ties with other parts of the Greek-speaking Christian world—was open to influences from abroad. A similar development occurred in the eastern part of the area where the Christian liturgy was found, where Aramaic was

---

* While Armenians started migrating toward the southwest from Greater Armenia in the sixth century, the events that ended Bagratid rule increased this flow, so that by the eleventh century there were numerous Armenians settled in Cilicia. Ruben (or Ripen or Rouen) I (ca. 1081–95), founder of the Rubenid dynasty, established the Armenian Kingdom of Cilicia ca. 1080, which in time gained independence from the Byzantine Empire. Also called Little Armenia, with its capital located at Sis, this kingdom proved a buffer on the eastern edge of Christendom, holding out against warring Islamic neighbors, first the Seljuk Turks and then the Marmeluks of Egypt. Although Baumstark dates the Rubenid dynasty to 1342, in fact their power declined and the Hethumids ruled the kingdom from 1126 to 1341 or from 1226 to 1373, depending on how one dates this transition.

† The Lusignan dynasty originated in France, where, in the early tenth century, the family rose to prominence near Lusignan. Becoming active in the Crusades, a branch of the family—through intermarriage and inheritance—gained ascendancy in the two kingdoms of Jerusalem and Cyprus during the twelfth century. They maintained good relations with the Armenian Kingdom of Cilicia, which had given hospitality and succor to Crusaders en route to the Holy Land. In the fourteenth century the Lusignans came to power in that kingdom through marriage, whereupon they sought to impose upon the populace the Roman Catholic faith and European customs. While making inroads into Armenian leadership circles, resistance by the peasantry led to violence. The Armenian liturgy does show signs of Roman influence, however, exercised both by the Crusaders and the Dominican branch of the Order of the Brothers of St. Gregory the Illuminator (*Fratres Unitores*), whose influence reached its apogee under the Lusignans (see p. 179 and pp. 221–22). Following a Mameluk invasion in the fourteenth century, Lusignan rule and the Kingdom of Cilicia came to an end. The capital city of Sis fell in 1375 and the Lusignan rulers returned to their home in France.

‡ On the Coptic language, see n. on p. 93. For christological controversies and language, see n. on p. 48.

spoken.* Since being overrun during the Arab conquest and having its Roman-Persian border—once this area's western edge—erased from the map, the Nestorian confession, with its uniform liturgy, offered the one form able to lend this area some coherence.

Whether rooted in national or ecclesial identity, the cohesion that a liturgy provided an area had both internal and external effects, cutting it off from the outside just as much as uniting what lay within. Thus, while providing liturgical uniformity in its own setting, it precluded the possibility of achieving a yet broader uniformity. The exception to this rule is the impact exercised by a handful of ecclesiastical centers, whose significance for liturgical history is simply inordinate. These are only three in number: Jerusalem, the holy "city of our God," as even a liturgical prayer calls it;[†] Constantinople, the capital of the Roman Empire, renewed by Justinian's western conquests;[‡] and Rome, the city of popes.

In terms of immediate influence, the role Jerusalem played was the most important of the three.[10] A worship life unfolded in its magnificent holy edifices, unique in character and overwhelming in splendor. Since the days of Constantine (306–37),[§] these church buildings have proclaimed the triumph of the cross. Built in ever-increasing numbers, they can be found both in the city and its environs. The deeply moving celebrations held in these structures sought to let the facts[¶] of the New Testament *Heilsgeschichte* be experienced anew, on the very spot where

---

* On the Aramaic language, see n. on p. 55.

[†] The Liturgy of St. James prays, "Remember, Lord, the holy city of you our God, the queen of cities, every city, town and village, and those who with Orthodox faith and devotion dwell in them, and their peace and security." For the Greek text, see Frederick E. Brightman, 45; ET: *The Divine Liturgy of the Holy Glorious Apostle James the Brother of God, First Hierarch of Jerusalem* (Basking Ridge, NJ: The Monastery of Saint Mark of Ephesus, 1978), 29, or visit http://en.wikisource.org/wiki/The_Divine_Liturgy_of_Saint_James.

[‡] Justinian I (483–565) sought to reestablish the political and religious unity of the Roman Empire. Toward that end, he reconquered North Africa from the Vandals and Italy from the Goths, the "western conquests" to which Baumstark refers. On Justinian I, see Short Biography, no. 114.

[§] After granting Christianity legal status in the Roman Empire, Constantine, with the active participation of his mother, Helena (246/50–330), had churches constructed, notably at the purported holy places in the Holy Land, particularly in and around Jerusalem. On Constantine the Great, see Short Biography, no. 53.

[¶] Baumstark uses the word *Tatsachen* here, meaning "facts." Although it could be translated as "realities," the word "facts" befits his positivist orientation.

they took place, in a form as dramatic as possible. Often stirred to the point of tears and loud sobs, pilgrims participated in these services from every part of the world that had been evangelized, every region that Christian missionaries had visited to that point. These pilgrims took back to their homelands the profound impressions Jerusalem made upon them. Without intending to promote the use of these services in their home settings, they did so inadvertently by the animated way they recounted what they had seen and heard. Though only yesterday the Roman colony of Aelia,* overseen by a suffragan bishop subordinate to the metropolitan of Caesarea, the "new Jerusalem" now attained such importance as a center of piety that its influence spread to the shores of the Atlantic Ocean and the gates of India, to the British Isles and the edge of the Sahara Desert.

The eucharistic liturgy used in Jerusalem was held to be the work of the apostle James, "the Lord's brother" and the first bishop of that city.[†] In its Greek *Urtext*, this liturgy was occasionally used as far north as Thessalonica.[11] Textual fragments from this liturgy, embedded in the Greek and Coptic versions of the Egyptian liturgy,[12] attest to the favor it once enjoyed to the south as well. Two Syriac versions became the primary forms for celebrating the Eucharist in the Monophysite communities of the Julianists[‡] and the Jacobites,[§] respectively.[13] The form

---

* After suppressing a Jewish rebellion, the Romans razed Jerusalem, including much of the Second Temple, in 70 CE. In 130 Emperor Hadrian (117–38) had a pagan city built on the ruins of Jerusalem, but did not incorporate into it a large portion of the ancient city. He named it Aelia Capitolina, Aelia being a family name of Hadrian and Capitolina reflecting its pagan character, as the city was dedicated to Jupiter Capitolinus and a temple to him was placed on the Temple Mount. To wipe Judaism from the map, Hadrian gave the new name Syria Palaestina to the old province of Judaea. Following Constantine's (306–37) consolidation of power in 313 CE, the empire honored Jerusalem as the Holy City.

[†] On James, see Short Biography, no. 105.

[‡] The Julianists were a Monophysite group named after Julian (d. after 518), Bishop of Halicarnassus in Caria (modern-day Bodrüm, Turkey), who upheld the incorruptibility of the body of Christ. Upon being deposed from his see ca. 518, he took refuge in Alexandria, where his activity in the church once again won him theological opponents. The Julianists were attacked both by adherents of the Catholic faith and by other Monophysites.

[§] "Jacobites," a term no longer current in scholarly circles, refers to the West Syrian Orthodox Church. It stems from Jacob Baradaeus (d. 578), who in the

of the text used by the former was retranslated into Armenian; that used by the latter into Ethiopic (Ge'ez).[14]* Translations into Georgian and Church Slavonic came out of the Greek original.[15] In the West, individual prayers from this eucharistic liturgy, in various Latin translations, even found their way into Mass books used in the early and high Middle Ages.[16]

In addition to the Liturgy of St. James, Jerusalem's lectionary and festal calendar also spread widely throughout the East, initially as a whole complex encompassing all the ritual used in the liturgical year celebrated there.[17] A lectionary in the dialect of Syriac spoken by Christians in Palestine was used by an Aramaic-speaking community in Egypt, an indication that this community celebrated worship in the former language according to the Rite of Jerusalem.[18] That same rite, in the form used around the middle of the fifth century, provided the basis for the festal and pericopic cycles of the old Armenian Church calendar.[19] The stage of development reached by those orders in the period immediately following the Arab conquest of Palestine† is reflected in Georgian liturgical documents.[20] The liturgies that the early church in Jerusalem used for the feasts of the liturgical year served as a model for the West, at least in some particulars. Egeria's (fl. fourth century)‡ description of this usage, which she reported already in the fourth century, agrees with the later Eastern documents discussed above as evidence for the Jerusalem calendar and lectionary. Concerning the procession on Palm Sunday and the veneration of the cross on Good Friday, their influence upon the West is crystal clear to anyone who—at one time or another—has read this pilgrim woman's vivid descriptions of the Holy Week services as celebrated in Jerusalem.

Another example is provided by the procession of lights held on Candlemas, which gained acceptance in the West a few decades after Egeria's visit to Jerusalem.[21] It is clear that this ritual, along with the feast itself, also made its way there from its home in Palestine. This is so even though apparently in reality the rites used for the feast in the

---

sixth century was instrumental in establishing a Monophysite hierarchy in Syria alongside that of the official church, which embraced the Chalcedonian teaching on the person of Christ. On Jacob Baradaeus, see Short Biography, no. 102.

* On Ethiopic (Ge'ez), see n. on p. 93.

† Palestine fell to the Arabs in 636, Jerusalem a year later.

‡ On Egeria see short biography, no. 65.

East blended in Rome with an older Roman propitiatory procession, rooted in indigenous heathen ritual practice.[22] Be that as it may, the Roman practice of celebrating Mass three times on Christmas was also inspired by the way the feast of Christmas—according to Egeria and the old Armenian lectionary—continued to be conducted in Jerusalem on January 6. The Mass celebrated at night in the "manger" church of Santa Maria Maggiore‡ is modeled after a Eucharist celebrated in the Church of the Holy Nativity in Bethlehem at the conclusion of a nocturnal liturgical vigil; that celebrated during the day in the Vatican at the tomb of the apostle§ emulates one that occurs the following morning in the Constantinian Basilica of the Holy Sepulcher.[23] The third time the Holy Sacrifice is offered, in between the other two at the first light of day, stems from local Roman custom. This takes place where the procession, which goes from the place where the Eucharist was celebrated at night (Santa Maria Maggiore) to that during the day (St. Peter's Basilica), makes a stop en route at "a Church of the Resurrection" located at the foot of the Palatine Hill. (The name of this church is something of a misnomer, since it had been consecrated to the martyr Anastasia [d. ca. 300]¶ rather than named after the resurrection event.) This addition to the procession's Mass schedule took place, presumably under Pope John III (561–74),** at a time when the shrine to Anastasia had become the court church for the representatives of the Byzantine emperor, who

---

‡ When Pope Sixtus III (432–40) reconstructed the Roman basilica Santa Maria Maggiore, he added a small oratory resembling the cave in Bethlehem where tradition holds that the birth of Christ took place. It serves as the station for the first papal Mass at Christmas.

§ The reference is to the tomb of Peter (d. 67?), who is buried under the altar of St. Peter's Basilica.

¶ Santa Anastasia, a basilica church near the Circus Maximus in Rome, was originally named the *Titulus Anastasiae*, perhaps the name of its founder. However, the name association with Anastasia (d. ca. 303/13) resulted in its later dedication to this Eastern martyr, who died during the Diocletian persecution (303–13). Although allegedly she died in Sirmium (in the Balkans) and her relics were translated to Constantinople, Anastasia has been venerated as a Roman martyr since the fifth century. The name certainly does not refer to Christ's resurrection.

** Baumstark appears to link John III (561–74) with the church that came to be dedicated to Anastasia (d. 303/13), because that pope was the son of the *vir illustris* named Anastasius (n.d.). On Pope John III, see Short Biography, no. 108.

had taken up residence in the palaces on the Palatine.[24] The psalm text used as the gradual for this new Mass, a free composition drawn from Psalm 117:23, 26ff, was the very one Egeria heard sung while processing from Bethlehem to Jerusalem at the first light of day.*

The liturgical influence Constantinople exercised prior to the outbreak of the first iconoclastic controversy[†] does not compare with that of Jerusalem. Nevertheless, one has to assume that the liturgy of this capital city spread quite early, at least throughout the region around the Aegean Sea. It is hardly coincidental that the liturgies peculiar to numerous churches that apostles founded in this area have disappeared without a trace. In point of fact, almost no evidence has come down to us of the liturgical life that originally pulsed through the Pauline communities of Asia Minor,[‡] Macedonia,[§] and Héllas,[¶] or in the cradle of Johannine Christianity.[**] Only in the last prayer of Polycarp

---

* Although Baumstark offers no specific citation for the text of this gradual psalm, the *graduale* sung in the Tridentine Rite for the Second Mass at Dawn for Christmas is a composite text (in order) of Ps 117: 26, 27, and 23, which reads,

"R̊. Benedictus qui venit in nomine Domini: Deus Dominus, et illuxit nobis.
Ꝟ. A Domino factum est istud: et est mirabile in oculus nostris"

(R̊. Blessed is he who comes in the name of the Lord! The Lord is God; he has given us light.
Ꝟ. This is the Lord's doing, and it is marvelous in our eyes).

In her description of the liturgical celebrations for Epiphany in Bethlehem and Jerusalem (no. 25), Egeria in her travel diary specifies no psalm. *Egeria's Travels*, trans. John Wilkinson (London: SPCK, 1971); Johnson, *Worship*, II, no. 83 (selections).

[†] The first phase of the iconoclastic controversy dates from ca. 725 to 813; the second phase lasted from 814 to 842.

[‡] The congregations in Asia Minor that were founded by Paul (d. 65?) and are known to us are Antioch at Pisidia, Derbe, Ephesus, Iconium, Lystra, Troas, and those in Galatia. To those one could perhaps also add Colossae, Philadelphia, Hierapolis, and Laodicea.

[§] The congregations known to us that were founded by Paul (d. 65?) in Macedonia were Beroea (?), Philippi, and Thessalonica.

[¶] The congregations known to us that were founded by Paul (d. 65?) in Héllas were Corinth and Athens (?).

[**] The reference here is to western Anatolia. By tradition, John the Evangelist is the author of the Revelation to John, composed on the Island of Patmos for the "Seven Churches of Asia": Ephesus, Smyrna, Pergamum, Thyatira, Sardis, Philadelphia, and Laodicea.

(ca. 69–155),* preserved in the report of his martyrdom, do we hear from one of these churches, that in Smyrna, a weak echo of the early Christian liturgy.[25] With this prayer, Polycarp prepared himself for death. In the course of the seventh century, the three great Marian feasts—her birth (September 8), the annunciation (March 25), and her assumption into heaven (August 15)—came to the West from Constantinople. In the same century and by the same route, there followed the Exaltation of the Cross (September 14). Pope Sergius I (687–701)† organized the Roman celebrations for all of these feasts.[26] In yet another example, the fathers of the Third Council of Toledo, held in Spain in 589, clearly had the capital city of the Byzantine Empire in mind when they appealed to the custom of "oriental churches" as justification for introducing the recitation of the Niceno-Constantinopolitan creed into the Mass.[27]

The Roman liturgy had influenced the development of worship on the Iberian Peninsula even earlier. The incident in question constitutes the earliest instance of the Roman liturgy extending its reach beyond the borders of Italy. One Profuturus, bishop of Braga (n.d.),‡ brought a series of questions concerning liturgical matters§ before Pope Vigilius (537–55).¶ The answer from the pope, dated 538, is probably preserved only in an interpolated form; unfortunately, two invaluable appendices that were at one time attached to it are no longer extant, even in part.[28] These contained the texts that the Roman Rite then used for baptism as well as the Canon of the Mass (including the embolisms for Easter). However, these two appendices do not appear to have exercised a direct influence upon the formation of the liturgy in the Suevian Kingdom in Gallicia. At a national council assembled in 561 in the city Profuturus served as bishop, only the papal decretal was read out.[29]** On the other hand, the Roman liturgy as a whole was

---

* On Polycarp, see Short Biography, no. 146.

† On Sergius I, see Short Biography, no. 158. This pope, of Greco-Syrian descent, also introduced the *Agnus Dei* into the Roman liturgy (see p. 78).

‡ On Profuturus, see Short Biography, no. 148.

§ For the Letter of Pope Vigilius to Profuturus, see, Johnson, *Worship*, IV, no. 159-A (selections).

¶ On Pope Vigilius, see Short Biography, no. 187.

** Properly speaking, this *Nationalkonzil* was a regional assembly of a church province dealing with issues of the Suevian (Suebian) "nation" (read: German tribe, ethnic group). The only reference to Profuturus is found in 538 with regard

introduced into Britain from when the mission sent there from Rome began evangelical work among the Angles and the Saxons. Subsequently, people in England cherished the belief that the liturgical books they possessed came from the pope himself, Gregory the Great,* who had entrusted them to Augustine (d. 604/5) when dispatching him on his evangelical mission to Britain.[30†] Be that as it may, it would have been the Roman Rite, among other things, that the monk Theodore,[‡] a Greek born in Tarsus, was ordered to implement when Pope Vitalian (657–72)[§] dispatched him as archbishop of Canterbury to finish the job of organizing life in the Anglo-Saxon Church.[31] When Abbot Hadrian of Naples (d. 709)[¶] was named to accompany Theodore to Britain, the task of keeping the Easterner on the straight and narrow as far as the liturgy was concerned was hardly the least of the assignments entrusted to that Westerner.

On top of all this, there had in the meantime already begun a movement that—in terms of significance—finds no parallel in the whole history of liturgical development: the "Romanization" of the liturgy in Merovingian Gaul. To grasp the import of this development for the West requires an analogy from the East. The impact of the Roman liturgy upon Gaul was equivalent to its Eastern counterpart: the influence of Jerusalem upon Constantinople.

---

to this decretal of Pope Vigilius (537–55). Canon 4 of the Council (or Synod) of Braga explicitly states that Profuturus was at that time "formerly the metropolitan of Braga." ET: Johnson, *Worship*, IV, no. 181: 4742.

* On Pope Gregory I (or the Great), see Short Biography, no. 78.

† On Augustine of Canterbury, see Short Biography, no. 24.

‡ On Theodore of Tarsus, see Short Biography, no. 176.

§ On Vitalian, see Short Biography, no. 188.

¶ On Hadrian of Canterbury, see Short Biography, no. 88.

Notes

For an overview of this topic, see Anton Baumstark, "Vorbyzantinische Kulturzentren des christlichen Morgenlands," *Hochland* 3 (1905/6): 440–55.

[1] Council of Gerunda [Gerona], canon 1, Mansi 8, 549A [ET: Johnson, *Worship*, IV, no. 180-B: 4717].

² This euchological type is represented above all by the Divine Liturgy of Gregory (Nazianzus) the Theologian, extant in Greek, Arabic, and Bohairic Coptic texts. See Renaudot I, 95–115, and accordingly 25–37. In addition, see fragments of related formularies in Sahidic Coptic in Jacob Krall, "Aus einer koptischen Klosterbibliothek Mittelägyptens," *Mitteilungen aus der Sammlung des Papyrus des Erzherzogs Rainer,* vol. 1, ed. Josef Karabacek (Wien [Vienna]: Hof und Staatsdruckerei, 1887), 69–72, and Henri Hyvernat, "Fragmente der altkoptischen Liturgie," *Römische Quartalschrift für christlichen Altertumskunde* 2 (1888): 20–22 [ET: *The Divine Liturgy of Saint Gregory the Theologian* (Sydney: Coptic Orthodox Theological College, 1999 AD, 1715 AM), or see http://www .copticchurch.net/topics/liturgy/stgregory.pdf].

³ See Anton Baumstark, *Festbrevier und Kirchenjahr der syrischen Jakobiten,* SGKA 3, 3–5 (Paderborn: Schöningh, 1910 [repr., New York: Johnson, 1967]), 10–24.

⁴ Ibid., *Perikopenordnungen,* 17, 20, 43, 69, 95, 153, 174, and 177.

⁵ In Brightman, compare "Appendix D: The Syrian Liturgy from the Fifth to the Eighth Century," 481–87, with "Appendix C: The Liturgy of Antioch from the Writings of S. Chrysostom," 470–81. See Cyrille Korolevskij [Charon], "Le Rite byzantine et la liturgie chrysostomienne dans les patriarcate melchites (Alexandrie-Antioch-Jerusalem)," χρυσοστομικα [*Chrysostomika*], 485–94.

⁶ Council of Braga (561), canons 1–19, Mansi 9, 777 C [ET: Johnson, *Worship,* IV, no. 180-F: 4739–52 (under Synod of Braga I, ser. 2)].

⁷ Fourth Council of Toledo (633), canon 2, Mansi 10, 617 C, D.

⁸ *Missale Mixtum,* pars prima, PL 85, cols. 109–656.

⁹ See above, chap. 3, n. 13.

¹⁰ For a summary of the significance of Palestine in the time of the early Christian and the Byzantine Empire, see Anton Baumstark, "Die geschichtliche Beden tung des christlichen Palästina vor dem Zeitalter Kreuzzüge," *Wissenschaftliche Beilage zur "Germania"* (1910): 293–97, 363–67.

¹¹ The MS Codex Paris, Biblioth. Nationale Graec. [Bibliothéque Nationale Greek] 2509, found today in Paris, developed in the first half of the twelfth century, in this case under the archbishop Theodolus. For a description of the MS, see Brightman, L–LI, no. F. The Divine Liturgy of St. James has remained in use on the island Zante [Zakynthos] up to the present time. For a description of this MS, see Brightman, Ll, no. J.

¹² Renaudot I, 58 and 73; see also 12 and 19f.

¹³ See Baumstark, *Literatur,* 40f. For a critical edition, see *Die syrische Jakobosanaphora nach der Rezension des Ja'Qôb(h) von Edessa. Mit dem griechischen Paralleltext,* ed. Adolf Rücker, LQ 4 (Münster in Westfalen: Aschendorff, 1923).

¹⁴ A translation of the Armenian text, compared with the other recensions, can be found in Anton Baumstark, "Denkmäler altarmeinischer Messliturgie 3. Denkmäler Rezension der Jakobusliturgie," OC, n.s., 7–8 (1918): 1–32. For an edition of the Ethiopic text, with translation, see Sebastian Euringer, "Die Anaphora des hl. Jacobus, des Bruders des Herrn," OC, n.s., 4 (1914): 1–23.

[15] A translation of the former is available by Frederick Cornwallis Conybeare and O. Wardrop, "The Georgian Version of the Liturgy of St. James," *Revue de l'Orient Chrétien* 18 (1913): 396–410 and 19 (1914): 155–73; a translation of the latter is available by Heinrich Goussen, "Die georgische 'Petrusliturgie,'" OC, n.s., 3 (1913): 2f.

[16] Evidence for this is to be found in Brightman, LIV. Up until the *Decretum Gratiani* (III. Distinct. I c. 47) knowledge of the foundational significance of the Divine Liturgy of St. James was conveyed by canon 32 of the Sixth Ecumenical Council [Constantinople, 680–81].

[17] See Baumstark, *Perikopenordnungen*, 131–72.

[18] *A Palestinian Syriac Lectionary, containing lessons from the Pentateuch, Job, Proverbs, Prophets, Acts and Epistles*, eds. M. D. Gibson, Agnes Smith Lewis, and Eberhard Nestle. Studia Sinaitica 6 (London: Cambridge University Press, 1897 [available through Google Books]). Additional material of the greatest interest, which is drawn from the information available for the stational churches of Jerusalem, is to be found in Agnes Smith Lewis, *Codex Climaci rescriptus*, Semiticae 8 (Cambridge: Cambridge University Press, 1909). Over the Egyptian origin of this lectionary, see J. T. Marshall, "Remarkable Readings in the Epistles Found in the Palestinian Syriac Lectionary," *Journal of Theological Studies* 5 (1904): 437–45.

[19] This lectionary was brought to light by Frederick Cornwallis Conybeare, *Rituale Armenorum* (Oxford: Clarendon Press, 1905), 507–27.

[20] This is evident in the document made available in *Иерусалимский канонарь VII века: (Грузин. версия)* [Transliteration of title: Ijerusalimskij Kanonar' VII veka (Gruzinskaja Versija); ET of title: The Jerusalem Canonary of the Seventh Century: Georgian Version], Прот. Корн. С. Кекелидзе [transliteration of editor: ed. Kornelij S. Kekelidze (Baumstark cites V. Kekelidze)], Тифлис: изд. архим. Назария, 1912 [ET of publication information: Tiflis: Losaberidze, 1912]. For an article by Theodor Kluge, containing translations of the sections concerning Lent, Good Friday, and the Season of Easter, with an introduction and footnotes by Anton Baumstark, see "Quadragesima und Karwoche Jerusalems im 7. Jahrhundert (in Verbindung mit Th. Kluge)," OC, n.s., 5 (1915): 201–33, 359–63; 6 (1916): 223–39. [For a more recent critical edition, see: Michel Tarchnischvili, *Le Grand Lectionnaire de L'Église de Jérusalem*, 2 vols., CSCO 188 and 204 (Louvain: Secrétariat du Corpus scriptorum christianorum orientalium, 1959–60)]. Heinrich Goussen will soon publish additional material of the greatest value.

[21] Standing in need of correction in this regard is Hermann Usener, *Das Weihnachtsfest*, 2nd ed., ed. Hans Lietzmann (Bonn: F. Cohen, 1911), 34ff. He conceives this development erroneously, in fact as the reverse of what is the case: that the introduction of the procession of lights, which occurred in Jerusalem in the fourth century, was prompted by Rome. See Anton Baumstark, "Rom oder Jerusalem? Eine Revision der Frage nach der Herkunft des Lichtmessfestes," *Theologie und Glaube* 1 (1909): 89–105.

[22] The publication by Donatien de Bruyne, "L'Origine des processions de la chandeleur et des rogations a propos d'un sermon inédit," RBén 34 (1922): 14–26, will henceforth be regarded as decisive in this respect.

[23] In this regard, see also the evidence in the Armenian lectionary, viz. Conybeare, *Rituale Armenorum*, 507–27. Unfortunately, only the final part of the account relating the celebration in Jerusalem on this day is preserved in Egeria, chap. 25, nos. 6–10. See Paul Geyer, *Itinera Hierosolymitana saeculi IV–VIII* (Wien [Vienna]: F. Tempsky, 1898), 75f; GT: Hermann Richter, *Pilgerreise der Ätheria (oder Silvia) von Aquitanien nach Jerusalem und die heiligen Stätten* (Essen: Baedeker, 1919), 58f [ET: *Egeria's Travels*, trans. John Wilkinson (London: SPCK, 1971), 126–27; Johnson, *Worship*, II, no. 83: 2172–74]. See Anton Baumstark, "Die Formulare der römischen Weihnachtsmessen and die Liturgie des frühchristlichen Orients," *Cäcilienvereinsorgan. Fliegende Blätter für katholischen Kirchenmusik* 45 (1910 [Baumstark cited 1919]): 159–64.

[24] This is discussed in Hartmann Grisar, *Analecta Romana: dissertazioni, testi, monumenti dell'arte riguardanti principalmente la storia di Roma e dei Papi nel medio evo: volume primo con una tavola cromolitografica, dodici tavole fototipiche e molte incisioni* (Roma [Rome]: Desclée Lefebvre Cie., 1899), 608–10.

[25] "The Martyrdom of Polycarp," chap. 14; GT: *Frühchristliche Apologeten und Märtyrerakten aus dem Griechischen und Lateinischen übersetzt*, vol. 2, trans. Gerhard Rauschen, BKV 14 (Kempten & München [Munich]: Josef Kösel, 1913), 305 [ET: ANF I, 42]. See Hans Lietzmann, "Ein liturgisches Bruckstück des zweiten Jahrhunderts," *Zeitschrift für wissenschaftliche Theologie*, 54 = n.s., 19 (1912): 56–61.

[26] *Liber Pontificalis*, vol. 1, ed. Louis Marie Olivier Duchesne (Paris: E. Thorin, 1884–92), 376 [ET: *The Book of Pontiffs (Liber Pontificalis), The ancient biographies of the first ninety Roman bishops to AD 715*, rev. ed., trans. and ed. Raymond Davis, Translated Texts for Historians 6 (Liverpool: Liverpool University Press, 2000), 89].

[27] Third Council of Toledo (589), canon 2, Mansi 9, 993 A [ET: Johnson, *Worship*, IV, no. 180-H: 4765 (listed as Capitulum 2, Series 2, of the Synod of Toledo III)].

[28] "Incipit Epistola Decretalis Vigilii Papae ad Profuturum Episcopum," *Decretales Pseudo-Isidorianae et Capitula Angilramni*, ed. Paul Hinschius (Lipsiae [Leipzig]: B. Tauchnitz, 1863), 710–12 [available through Google Books]. This part of the document was handed down by the so-called Collectio Hispana, which came into being soon after 633.

[29] Canons 4 and 5, Council of Braga (561), Mansi 9, 777 A [ET: Johnson, *Worship*, IV, no. 180: 4742–43 (under the Synod of Braga I, ser. 2)].

[30] This was the case with the so-called Gregorian Evangeliary, now at Cambridge. See Stephan Beissel, *Geschichte der Evangelienbücher in der ersten Hälfte des Mittelalters* (Freiburg im Breisgau: Herder, 1906), 86–91.

[31] Venerable Bede, *Historia ecclesiastica gentis Anglorum*, bk. IV, chap. 1 (PL [95], cols. 171–73) [ET: bk. 4, chap. 1, in Bede, *A History of the English Church and People*, trans. Leo Sherley-Price, rev. R. E. Latham (Harmondsworth, Penguin, 1968), 203–5]. The pericopic notations of the renowned *Book of Lindisfarne* (so-called) and, in the final analysis, also those found in the Evangeliary of St. Burchard of Würzburg are based upon the gospel books that came to England at that time, some of which were of Roman origin and some of Neapolitan. See Stephan Beissel, *Entstehung der Perikopen des Römischen Meßbuches. Zur Geschichte der Evangelienbücher in der ersten Hälfte des Mittelalters* (Freiburg im Breisgau: Herder, 1907), 109–27.

Chapter 7

Transferal and Blending

In both the East and the West, from the time of the iconoclastic controversy in the former and the Carolingian epoch in the latter, there occurred a decisive expansion of rites that should not be confused with the influence that prominent liturgical centers—Rome and Constantinople as well as Jerusalem—had already exercised for some time in their own right. In contrast to earlier instances of liturgical expansion, whether of a particular influential center or of a defined region, the expansion that now occurred, of the Byzantine rite on the one hand and the rite portraying itself as Roman on the other, was not that of two pristine liturgies. Rather, both of these rites were the results of blending two other liturgies from two different areas, each with their own distinctive character.

Initial indications of this trend were apparent early on. As a matter of fact, individual liturgical texts were transferred from one area to another even though a major center, which could have exercised influence from afar, does not present itself as a possible source. In the age of the great christological controversies,* the association (whether justified or not) of particular texts with the name of a leader of a theological party was always sufficient to bring about such a transfer. Thus did the Persian Mar(j) Ab(b)a (540–52),† who later headed up the Nestorian Church, collaborate with a citizen of Edessa named Thomas (d. before 544)‡ to translate two eucharistic prayers into Syriac from the Greek. Bearing the names of Nestorius (after 351–d. after 451)§ and Theodore of Mopsuestia (350–428),¶ respectively, these two prayers have remained family heirlooms of the Nestorian Mass liturgy ever since. In the one case, the Mopsuestian may actually have edited the text; the other text is a form of the eucharistic prayer from the city of Constantinople that is older than the Byzantine Divine Liturgy of St.

---

* On the christological controversies, see n. on p. 48.
† On Ab(b)a I, see Short Biography, no. 1.
‡ On Thomas of Edessa, see Short Biography, no. 182.
§ On Nestorius, see Short Biography, no. 127.
¶ On Theodore of Mopsuestia, see Short Biography, no. 175.

John Chrysostom (347–407). The reputation, not of the capital city of the Eastern Roman Empire, but rather of the heresiarch on his bishop's throne, opened the way for this latter prayer to travel into the Persian kingdom and thence to India and China.[1]*

Another phenomenon that deserves mention here is the rivalry that could be sparked when two different liturgical areas extended their missionary efforts into one and the same region. Inevitably, both liturgical traditions left a mark upon the liturgy eventually celebrated in the new territory, won for Christianity by their separate missionary efforts. The liturgy resulting from this process is from the outset the product of some sort of blending. In the context of the Ethiopian Rite, which essentially goes back to the Coptic Rite of Egypt,† the translation of the Syrian-Jacobite liturgy illustrates this point. It is evidence, confirmed by legendary traditions, for the role that Aramaic Christianity played in the evangelization of the Abyssinian kingdom of Axum.‡ The fact that even stronger doses of Syrian and Greek extraction mix in the Armenian liturgy reminds us how much Armenian Christianity in

---

* "[T]he heresiarch on his bishop's throne" refers back to Nestorius (b. after 351, d. after 451). Following the Council of Ephesus (431), the Eastern bishops who refused to accept its position gradually formed themselves into the Nestorian Church, with its center in Persia and its see at Seleucia-Ctesiphon on the Tigris River. Over time this church carried its message in missions as far afield as India and Arabia, Mongolia and China, where the Xian-Fu Stone gives direct evidence for their activity. See n. on p. 192.

† The original evangelization of Ethiopia received support from the Egyptian Church, when Athanasius (293–373) in 328 (according to tradition) conferred episcopal consecration upon Frumentius (d. ca. 383), the "Apostle of the Abyssinians," who returned to Ethiopia to convert it. This relationship between the two churches continued, with the Ethiopian Church becoming dependent upon the Monophysite patriarch when the ancient patriarchate of Alexandria was transferred to Cairo ca. 640. On the Coptic language, see n. on p. 93.

‡ Toward the end of the fifth century, "Nine Roman [i.e., Eastern Roman or Byzantine] Saints" (Aragawi, Pantaleon, Garima, Alef, Saham, Afe, Libanos, Adimata, and Oz or Guba), perhaps from Syria, came to strengthen the faith of that country. Axum, where a cathedral was built, served as the religious capital of Ethiopia. See Archdale King, *The Rites of Eastern Christendom* (Rome: Catholic Book Agency, 1948; repr., Piscataway, NJ: Gorgias Press, 2007), 501–2.

Armenia, when it was first emerging, vacillated between Aramaic*
and Greek Christianity.[2][†]

To complete this picture, an example of liturgical blending of the
utmost significance took place in the homeland of the Syrian-Jacobite
Church. This church, like Syria itself from time immemorial, functioned as an immense transit zone, with cultures streaming across
it, as different as can be imagined. That earns it—and the national
characteristics it forged—a place of importance in the cultural history of humankind. It gives it the right to claim its sure (although not
to be exaggerated) place in that history through such figures as the
learned Jacob of Edessa (ca. 633–708)[‡] and the great Mafrian Gregory
the Hebrew (1126–1286)[§]—the Jerome (ca. 342–420)[¶] and Albertus
Magnus (1200–80),[**] respectively, of the Christian Aramaic world.[3] The
characteristics that generally mark this birthplace of culture also gave
the liturgy of the Jacobite Church its peculiar character. Antioch, Jerusalem, and Edessa have contributed, in about equal measure, the elements that comprise its liturgy. That this rite is anchored in these three
liturgical centers reflects the historical circumstances from which the
Jacobite Church emerged. The church is named after Jacob Baradaeus
(ca. 500–78) in honor of his efforts to found it anew.[††] He was raised to
the episcopal see of Edessa in name only when, in 542 or 543, he was
consecrated bishop in Constantinople at the urging of the Arab prince
Harith (529–69)[‡‡] and under the protection of the Empress Theodora I
(ca. 500–47).[§§] He endeavored in the area where Aramaic was spoken,

---

* On the Aramaic language, see n. on p. 55.

[†] See pp. 102–3.

[‡] On Jacob of Edessa, see Short Biography, no. 103.

[§] On Gregory Bar Hebraeus, see Short Biography, no. 27.

[¶] On Jerome, see Short Biography, no. 106.

[**] On Albertus Magnus, see Short Biography, no. 5.

[††] On Jacob Baradaeus, see Short Biography, no. 102.

[‡‡] On Harith, see Short Biography, no. 89.

[§§] Empress Theodora I (ca. 500–47) played a major role in the theological
controversies of her time, notably in support of the Monophysite party. Al-
Harith ibn Jabalah (529–69) begged her to fill empty sees in the Monophysite
Syrian Orthodox Church. Theodosius of Alexandria (d. 567), also in exile in
Constantinople, secretly consecrated Jacob Baradaeus or Bûrde'ânâ (ca. 500–
78) and a companion as bishops of Edessa and Bostra, respectively. Neither
was able to take up residence in their sees. On Theodora I, see Short Biography, no. 172.

with indefatigable zeal, to reestablish the Monophysite hierarchy of the Antiochene patriarchate, which had been in ruins since 518.* For a very long time, the real stronghold of Monophysite thought had been Jerusalem and the Palestinian monastic community.[†]

Similar to the liturgical blending found here between the legacies of the holy city,[‡] the metropolis of Hellenized northwest Syria,[§] and the capital of the Mesopotamian province of Osroene,[¶] there came later on also the blending of Jerusalem and Constantinople in the east and that of Rome and Gaul in the west.

During the first phase of the iconoclastic controversy,[**] Jerusalem was the real bastion of the iconophile monastic world. Under the protection of the caliphate, it was able to hold out against the power of the iconoclastic Byzantine state.[††] With the Studios Monastery[‡‡] as its bridgehead, that monastic world smoothed the way for the Palestin-

---

* Although the Byzantine Emperor Anastasius I (491–518) had supported the Miaphysite hierarchy, his successor Justinian I (527–65), who held to the Chalcedonian creed, ousted it, leading to the split in 518 between the Syriac and Eastern Orthodox Churches. This led to the decline of the hierarchy of the Syrian Church. After Justinian banished Severus (512–38) to Egypt, there was no patriarch resident in Antioch again until Jacob Baradaeus or Bûrde'ânâ (542–78), as the bishop of Edessa, consecrated Sergius of Tella (544–46). On Jacob Baradaeus, see Short Biography, no. 102.

† The Armenian liturgy reflects the political tug-of-war in which Armenia found itself, stretched as it was between the Eastern Roman Empire to the west and the Persian Empire to the east. See pp. 102–3 and p. 179.

‡ Jerusalem.

§ Antioch.

¶ Edessa.

** The first phase of the iconoclastic controversy dates from ca. 725 to 813; the second phase lasted from 814 to 842.

†† The caliphate of Jerusalem was established in 637. When Umar I (581?–644), an associate of Muhammad (ca. 570/71–632), first took the city, he set a pattern of leniency in the treatment of Christians. Only when the Egyptian Fatimid Caliphs became rulers of Jerusalem in 969 did the situation for Christians in Jerusalem under the Muslims worsen seriously.

‡‡ According to tradition, this famous monastery in Constantinople, also called Hagios Ioannes Prodromos en tois Stoudiou (Saint John the Forerunner at Stoudios), was founded in 463 by Studios, a former Roman consul (fl. fifth century). Dedicated to John the Baptist, the monastery was located in the western part of the city, not far from the Golden Horn. See also Theodore the Studite, Short Biography, no. 177.

ian liturgy to wield influence in Constantinople. Not until the veneration of icons had proved victorious could that influence successfully break into the worship of the imperial city.* It was strong enough to make Jerusalem quite simply the authoritative model, for example, of the celebration of Holy Week in the parochial Byzantine Rite, already being shaped under its influence. At the same time, however, Constantinople's liturgical character could not simply be shunted aside; it was too well established, due to its political significance. Between the state's center of power and the religious center of piety we can observe reciprocal interaction at work. A manuscript dated to 1122 preserves a comprehensive order of worship from Jerusalem for Holy Week and the week after Easter, whose basic stratum dates back to the late eighth century.[4] It shows that, already at this time, the indigenous early Christian Palestinian Rite no longer retained its pristine form, but instead was interspersed with elements of Constantinopolitan origin. From this time on, these two streams of liturgical life, one out of the worldly capital of Greek Christianity and the other from its spiritual center, flowed into a single channel, their waters commingling.

Despite some obvious differences, the developmental parallels between the West and the East are simply astounding. With two apostles entombed there,[†] Rome was for religious sensibility in the West what Jerusalem—with its holy sites—represented for the East. It is certainly true that the Frankish state may have fallen into ruinous disorder under the later Merovingians.[‡] However, as early as the conversion of Clovis I (481–511) to Catholic Christianity,[§] it embraced the calling to revive the notion of the Roman Empire for the West. It is particularly instructive to observe how, in the liturgical texts of Rome, the "king-

---

* The end of the iconoclastic controversy in 842 was celebrated in 843 and every year subsequently on the feast of Orthodoxy.

† It appears that Peter (d. 67) was originally buried in the Vatican and Paul (d. 65?) on the Ostian Way, under his basilica. Greek and Latin graffiti from the early third century, found in the catacombs, attest that both were venerated from very early times. Reputedly their relics were translated to the catacombs in 258. Presently, the remains of Peter lie below the high altar in St. Peter's Basilica; Paul is entombed below the altar of St. Paul's Outside the Walls.

‡ The Merovingian dynasty ruled the Franks from 481 to 751. As the last strong Merovingian ruler was Dagobert I (ca. 629–39), Baumstark is here speaking of the period between the death of Dagobert in 639 and the fall of the dynasty in 751.

§ On Clovis I, see Short Biography, no. 52.

dom of the Franks" shoved aside the "Roman Empire," and the king
of the Franks usurped the emperor just as soon as those texts pushed
over the Alps.[5] It is hard to say how far back into Merovingian history
the diffusion of Roman liturgical material may go. Be that as it may,
one finds among its liturgical imports textual material that may have
originally sprung up in Rome itself during the first half of the sixth
century. In keeping with this, it was possible for the name of Pope
Gelasius I (492–96)[*] to be tied, albeit by a more or less legendary association, to the liturgical form that the Franks knew from the other
side of the Alps.[†] Otherwise of little note, this Roman bishop did in
fact author, even according to Roman tradition,[6] at least prayers for
the Mass as well as, purportedly, a codification of the liturgy in three
books. In addition to a very comprehensive inventory of variable texts
for celebrating the Eucharist and a text for the Canon of the Mass
(already essentially identical to the one used today), the codification
contains the most important texts of a Ritual.[7] This allegedly Gelasian
Sacramentary exists in a single complete manuscript, while another
preserves a fragment of its table of contents.[8] However, in its present
form, this work, when taken as a whole, is a far cry from a Mass book
for the city of Rome that would have come over the Alps to be used
throughout the Merovingian kingdom. Next to Roman prayers, which
are undoubtedly genuine, stand prayers that are no less undeniably
Gallican.[9] Thus, at this early date, we have in this book the fruit of a
blending of the two rites.

Such a blending of Roman and Gallican forms also came about
in upper Italy, probably even earlier. From the monastery at Bobbio
originates a Mass book whose text goes back to the Gallican liturgy
of Ireland.[10‡] Its texts for the Mass only reach up to the beginning of
the Canon. From that point on, it assumes that the holy celebration
proceeds according to the Roman Rite. Likewise, a form of the Roman
Canon, somewhat more ancient, gained entry into the essentially Gallican structure of the Ambrosian Mass of Milan.[11] Only two insertions,
on Maundy Thursday and Holy Saturday, respectively, recall an older
construction, as it gained a footing in the Mozarabic Mass of Spain

---

[*] On Gelasius, see Short Biography, no. 75.

[†] As a Roman presbyteral sacramentary from the seventh century, the *Gelasianum* could not have been his work.

[‡] On the liturgy of Ireland, see n. on p. 207.

and the manuscripts of the Mass liturgy indigenous to the Frankish kingdom.[12]

The transfer of royal power to the new Carolingian ruling house took place in the kingdom of the Franks in 752, with the approval of Pope Zacharias (741–ca. 752).[*] Following his coronation, apparently posthaste, Pepin (751–68)[†] began to work single-mindedly toward adopting Roman usage for the worship life in his empire.[13] His first efforts concentrated in the area of choral music. As early as 766 or 767, he could decree the introduction of Roman choral music throughout his kingdom, replacing the early Gallican. Previously, the episcopal brothers[‡] Chrodegang of Metz (d. 766)[§] and Remigius of Rouen (d. ca. 771)[¶] had created in their cathedrals influential training centers for Roman choral music. Naturally, melodies could be adopted only in conjunction with the Roman hymn texts composed for them. Between 758 and 763, Pepin had received one copy each of two liturgical books sent to him by Pope Paul I (757–67), a responsory and an antiphonary,[**] containing the hymn texts for the Office and the Mass.[14] On top of this, the form of the Roman Rite then in use also began to exercise an influence on the Mass prayer texts. Just as the form of the Roman liturgy first known to the Franks had been associated with the name of Gelasius I (492–96), so too was this one associated with the name of Gregory the Great (590–604).[††] Once again blending occurred, this time between the new Gregorian usage and the older one represented by the Roman-Frankish Sacramentary. The result was Mass books with a mixture of "Gregorian" and "Gelasian" texts. Books of this kind, one coming from Chur and another from Angoulême, recently published in exemplary critical editions, belong to the beginning of the ninth century.[15]

---

[*] On Zacharias, see Short Biography, no. 193.

[†] On Pepin III or the Short, see Short Biography, no. 137.

[‡] Although these two bishops may have been related, Baumstark is referring here to an ecclesial rather than biological fraternity. Remigius (d. ca. 771) was a son of Charles Martel (716–41), and an anonymous life makes Chrodegang of Metz (d. 766) his grandson, born to one of Charles' daughters. The latter claim is widely regarded as legendary, however.

[§] On Chrodegang, see Short Biography, no. 46.

[¶] On Remigius of Rouen, see Short Biography, no. 153.

[**] On Paul I, see Short Biography, no. 134.

[††] See n. on pp. 134–35.

Between 784 and 791, Charlemagne (king from 768; emperor 800–14),* had Pope Hadrian I (772–95)[†] send him an authentic exemplar of the "Gregorian" Sacramentary then being used in Rome.[16] It was deposited in the *Pfalz* (palace) at Aachen with a mandate to become normative for the celebration of the holy mysteries throughout his kingdom—from the Spanish border up into the land of the Saxons, from the North Sea to as far south as the valleys of the Alps.[17] This implementation of a pure Roman Mass rite universally throughout the Frankish Empire did not come to pass in actuality, however. Between the spring of 801 and his eventual death in 804, the most learned man in Charlemagne's entourage, an Anglo-Saxon by the name of Alcuin (735–804),[‡] worked on a kind of critical new edition of the "Gregorian" Sacramentary. To it was attached a comprehensive supplement containing texts taken from the older usage, which were soon incorporated into the book itself. It was precisely this new mixed form, produced by Alcuin through this editorial process, that became the sole standard for the whole period that followed.[18] The adoption of the hymn and prayer texts of the Roman Mass was completed when the Frankish Church adapted its lectionary to that of Rome. Although there is direct evidence for Alcuin's involvement only in regard to the epistle readings, there is no doubt that it was once again he who gave the system of epistle and gospel readings a new form, the so-called *comes*,[§] with its two cycles of readings. The very temperament of the author seemed to ensure that this work also would not adopt the Roman urban order without thought or change, in a way oblivious to the needs of the territory to the north where it was to be authorized for use. Helisachar (d. after 837),[¶] chancellor to Louis the Pious (814–40),[**] apparently facilitated a new edition of this book. Once again, like Alcuin's revision of the Sacramentary, it includes a text supplemented by an appendix.[19] To complete this picture, Charlemagne had Paul the Deacon (ca. 720–ca. 800)[††] produce another innovation for the liturgy

---

* On Charlemagne, see Short Biography, no. 44.

[†] On Hadrian I, see Short Biography, no. 86.

[‡] On Alcuin, see Short Biography, no. 7.

[§] A *comes* is a book listing the scriptural passages to be read during the liturgy, organized according to the liturgical year.

[¶] On Helisachar, see Short Biography, no. 91.

[**] On Louis I or the Pious, see Short Biography, no. 119.

[††] On Paul the Deacon, see Short Biography, no. 136.

of the time. Between 786 and 797 this native of Lombardy assembled a collection of patristic sermons to be read aloud at the night office.[20]

The reign of Charlemagne's son Louis* also saw blending take place between the older and the new, this time in regard to the choral texts of the Office. Exemplars of the Roman antiphonary brought to Corbie by Abbot Wala (ca. 755–836)[†] during the papacy of Gregory IV (827–44),[‡] at least some of which date back to the time of Hadrian I, contain a version of that book that already deviates in significant ways from the one that came into the Frankish Empire during the papacy of Paul I.[21] One of the most distinguished men in Louis' court, Helisachar by name, initially undertook the revision of this Roman hymn-book.[22] This was deemed necessary because the style of performance then being used was at variance with the Roman urban practice. In the responsorial singing of psalms according to the Roman style, the entire response was repeated after the verse or else, accordingly, after the trinitarian doxology. Probably modeled on patterns in the Greek East, the Gallican-Frankish practice (still found in today's Breviary) is content to repeat only the second part of the response or to alternate this with the whole. It was Amalarius of Metz (ca. 780–ca. 850)[§] who worked hard to effect a blending between the antiphonary's two versions, the older Gallican one and the more recent Roman version. In his invaluable book *De ordine antiphonarii* (Concerning the Order of the Antiphonary), Amalarius accounts for the procedure used in this revision.[23][¶] Bishop Agobard of Lyons (ca. 769–840),[**] a bitter adversary of Amalarius, tried to put in place a frankly radical reform. Almost like a schoolmaster, he took offense at the poetic freedom exercised in not a few of the Roman texts. For this reason he placed a corrected edition of the antiphonary in the hands of his clergy. The criterion used for this

---

* Louis I or the Pious or le Débonnaire (814–40).

[†] On Wala, see Short Biography, no. 190.

[‡] On Gregory IV, see Short Biography, no. 80.

[§] On Amalarius of Metz, see Short Biography, no. 10.

[¶] While Baumstark calls this "a book," it is actually the prologue to the antiphonary that Amalarius (ca. 780–ca. 850) composed. The text can be found in *Amalarii Episcopi Opera Liturgica Omnia* I, ed, J. M. Hannssens (Vatican City: Biblioteca Apostolica Vaticana, 1958), 361–63; an English translation by W. L. N. North is available by searching "Amalarius" on the Carleton College website: www.carleton.edu.

[**] On Agobard, see Short Biography, no. 4.

revision was clear: admit only those chants based strictly upon the biblical text. Demonstrably, subsequent development continued to rely on this exaggerated puritanism no less. In *De Correctione Antiphonarii* (On Revising the Antiphonary), the open letter that introduces his work, Agobard cited a string of questionable texts from the uncorrected antiphonary, examples he deemed to be particularly egregious.[24]* In the Roman Rite of the following period, and thus in today's Breviary, actually only one of these texts is yet to be found.[25]

Precisely this Frankish-Roman Rite, which took final form in the Carolingian period, then became standard for the Frankish Empire and, subsequently, the medieval political world of central Europe that ultimately emerged after its collapse. But it was not found only there. It also gained acceptance in Rome itself—just as in the East the indigenous liturgy of Jerusalem fell prey to the Byzantine Rite, which was itself a mixture of the Hierosolymitan Rite and the one originally found in Constantinople. Use of the Frankish-Roman Rite became widespread in Rome, especially during the era of the Ottonian† and Salian‡ dynasties, when German and French popes occupied the throne of the Prince of the Apostles§ with their imperial protectors appointing themselves to lord over the Roman Church and rule it according to their own willful desires. Even the doors of the Eternal City's venerable basilicas had to be opened more and more to the "Roman" liturgical use, dominant on the other side of the Alps' glacial wall. One instance in particular exemplifies this trend toward the exercise of German influence upon the Roman urban liturgy. It was reported by

---

* The authenticity of the ascription of this attack on the liturgical work of Amalarius of Metz (ca. 780–850) is in doubt.

† The Ottonians were a line of Saxon kings who reigned from 936–1024. Notably Otto I (912–73, reigned from 936) came to the aid of the pope against ambitious nobles from the north, the Byzantine Greeks in the east, and the Saracens to the south. Following Otto's victory in Italy, Pope John XII (955–64) crowned him emperor in 962. The relationship was sealed in a treaty called the Ottonian Privilege, in which popes were required to swear fealty to the emperor in exchange for his protection of papal lands.

‡ The Salians were one of the most influential families in Rhenish Franconia, which, with the assumption of Conrad II (990–1039), came to the German throne in 1024. Marked by struggles between the empire and the church, the dynasty's rule ended when the last Salian, Henry V (1086–1125, reigned from 1098), died childless in 1125.

§ This phrase refers to the pope sitting on the throne of St. Peter.

a contemporary witness to the event, Berno, the abbot of Reichenau (ca. 978–ca. 1048),* who came from Prüm;[26] it took place on February 14, 1014, after the last in the Saxon line,† Henry II (1002–24),‡ received the imperial crown from the hands of Pope Benedict VIII (1012–24).§ The king himself made the request of the pope, in a certain sense as a gift honoring the occasion, that from henceforth the Niceno-Constantinopolitan Creed¶ be sung in the Mass also at Rome, just as Henry was accustomed to hearing it in his homeland to the north. In this way a custom from the East, first introduced on its native soil at Antioch by the Monophysite Patriarch Peter the Fuller (471–88),** found entry into the city of the popes by a circuitous route through Germany.††[27]

---

* On Berno, see Short Biography, no. 36.

† The Ottonian dynasty was also known as the Saxon dynasty after its founder, Henry I (876–936; duke of Saxony from 912; king of the Germans from 919).

‡ On Henry II, see Short Biography, no. 92.

§ On Benedict VIII, see Short Biography, no. 31.

¶ As Henry II (1002–24) requested that they recite in Rome the version of the Niceno-Constantinopolitan Creed used in Gaul, which had incorporated the *filioque* clause, this became the first instance of its use in Rome.

** On Peter Fullo, see Short Biography, no. 138.

†† According to Theodore the Lector (early sixth century), Peter Fullo (d. 488), introduced the Niceno-Constantinopolitan Creed into the liturgy of Antioch sometime between 476 and 488, to be recited after the reading of the gospel. From Antioch it spread gradually throughout the East and West, although it was not adopted in Rome until 1014.

Notes

[1] See Baumstark, *Messe*, 54 and 57f. Baumstark, *Literatur*, 119f. On the Nestorian liturgy, see Baumstark, "Die Chrysostomos-Liturgie und die syrische Liturgie des Nestorios," *Chrysostomika*, 771–857. Baumstark, "Zur Urgeschichte der Chrysostomosliturgie," *Theologie und Glaube* 5(1913): 299–313. For an attempt at reconstructing the Greek text, see, Baumstark, *Liturgische Texte: I Die konstantinopolitanische Meßliturgie vor dem 9. Jahrhundert*, KlT 35 (Bonn: A. Marcus und E. Weber, 1909).

[2] Baumstark, *Messe*, 63–65.

[3] Baumstark, *Literatur*, 248–56, 312–20.

[4] For the *typikon* of the Church of the Resurrection at Jerusalem dated 1122, see Ἀνάλεκτα Ἱεροσολυμιτικῆζ Σταχυλογίασ [*Analekta Heirosolumitikēs stachyologias*],

vol. 2, ed., Athanasios Papadopoulos-Kerameus (En Petrupolei [St. Petersburg]: Kirschbaum, 1894 [repr., Bruxelles (Brussels): Culture et Civilisation, 1963]), 1–254. See Anton Baumstark, "Die Heiligtümer des byzantinischen Jerusalem nach einer übersehenen Urkunde," OC 5 (1905): 227–89.

[5] This is especially evident in the prayers in time of war and in the general petitions for Good Friday. Concerning the former, see Anton Baumstark, "Friede und Krieg in altkirchlicher Liturgie," Hochland 13 (1915–16): 265.

[6] Liber Pontificalis, vol. 1, ed. Louis Marie Olivier Duchesne (Paris: E. Thorin, 1884–92), 265 [ET: The Book of Pontiffs (Liber Pontificalis), The ancient biographies of the first ninety Roman bishops to AD 715, rev. ed., trans. and ed. Raymond Davis, Translated Texts for Historians 6 (Liverpool: Liverpool University Press, 2000), 45; Johnson, Worship IV, no. 163: 4223 (selections)].

[7] Sacramentarium Gelasianum, PL 74, cols. 1050–1244. For a critical edition, see Henry A. Wilson, The Gelasian Sacramentary (Oxford: Clarendon Press, 1894).

[8] The complete MS is Vatican Codex Reg. 316. For the fragment, which has been preserved on two folios and is found in Reims, see Dom André Wilmart, "L'Index liturgique de Saint-Thierry," RBén 30 (1913): 437–50.

[9] Essential in this regard is Suitbert Bäumer, "Über das sogenannte Sacramentarium Gelasianum," Historisches Jahrbuch 14 (1893): 241–301.

[10] Sacramentarium Gallicanum, PL 72, cols. 447–568. Over the origin of the Bobbio Missal, see Dom André Wilmart, "Bobbio (Missel de)," DACL 2, 939–62, and Wilmart, "Le palimpseste du missel de Bobbio," RBén 33 (1921): 1–18.

[11] The example of the series of saints mentioned in the "Communicantes" section of the Roman Canon is instructive for the light it sheds upon the relationship of the Milanese text of the Canon to the Roman one. See Hans Lietzmann, Petrus und Paulus in Rom: Liturgische und Archäologische Studien (Bonn: Marcus und Weber, 1915), 66–70. Anton Baumstark, "Das Communicantes und seine Heiligenliste," JLW 1 (1921): 24–30.

[12] Duchesne, Origines, 215 and 218 [ET: Duchesne, Worship, 215–18].

[13] For an account summarizing this development in broad strokes, see Duchesne, Origines, 96–105 [ET: Duchesne, Worship, 102–5]. For the Mass, see H. Netzer, L'introduction de la messe romaine en France sous les Carolingiens (Paris: Alphonse Picard, 1910), and Adrian Fortescue, The Mass: A Study of Roman Liturgy (London: Longmans, Green, 1912), 177–79; in reference to the Office, see Bäumer, 228–40, and Batiffol (Fr. ed.), 100–103 [ET: Batiffol (Eng. ed.), 64–65].

[14] For the letter from Paul I, see Epistolae Merowingici et Karolini aevi, ed. Societas aperiendis fontibus rerum Germanicarum medii aevi, Monumenta Germaniae historica: Epistolae, vol. 1, pt. 3 (Berolini [Berlin]: Weidmann, 1892), 529.

[15] Das fränkische Sacramentarium Gelasianum in alemannischer Überlieferung, ed. Leo Kunibert Mohlberg, LQ 1/2 (Münster in Westfalen: Aschendorff, 1918), and Le Sacramentaire gélasien d'Angoulême, ed. Paul Cagin (Angoulême: Société Historique et Archéologique de la Charenté, 1919 [Baumstark cites 1918]).

[16] *Epistolae Merowingici et Karolini aevi*, 626.

[17] *Das Sacramentarium Gregorianum nach dem Aachener Urexemplar*, ed. Hans Lietzmann, LQ 3 (Münster in Westfalen: Aschendorff, 1921), is based on the oldest copy of the Sacramentary, now found in Cambrai, France.

[18] Alcuin's version of this sacramentary, whose oldest manuscript exemplar is Vat. MS Ottobon lat. 313, more or less forms the basis for the older editions of the *Sacramentarium Gregorianum*, as can be seen in *Sancti Gregorii Magni Romani Pontificis Liber Sacramentorium*, PL 78, cols. 1–240, as well as in Henry A. Wilson, *The Gregorian Sacramentary under Charles the Great* (London: Harrison and Sons, 1915). These versions have a purely practical advantage over Lietzmann's methodically planned and strictly scholarly work: they also offer the appendix added by Alcuin. [In *Patrologia Latina*, the sacramentary actually begins in col. 25; the appendix, found in cols. 239–64, in fact follows the section Baumstark cites.]

[19] Concerning the Helisachar edition of the epistolary, *Comes Albini*, see Germain Morin, "Une Rédaction inédite de la préface au supplément du comes d'Alcuin," RBén 29 (1912): 341–48. In reference to the Alcuin *comes* of gospel readings, see Stephan Beissel, *Entstehung der Perikopen des römischen Meßbuches* (Freiburg im Breisgau: Herder, 1907), 127–41.

[20] In regard to this, see Bäumer 287f. The text of the homilary, which is found as Paul the Deacon, *Homilarius* in PL 95, cols. 1159 [Baumstark cites 1154] to 1566, was reconfigured in the eleventh and twelfth centuries through additions.

[21] Bäumer, 279. Batiffol (Fr. ed.), 103–5 [ET: Batiffol (Eng. ed.), 68–70].

[22] Bäumer, 281f.

[23] Amalarius, *Liber de ordine antiphonarii*, PL 105, cols. 1243–1316 [Baumstark cites 1314; ET: available by searching Amalarius on the Carleton College website: www.carleton.edu]. See Bäumer, 279–85, Batiffol (Fr. ed.), 105f [ET: Batiffol (Eng. ed.), 65f], and Max Manitius, *Geschichte der lateinischen Literatur des Mittelalters* (München [Munich]: Beck, 1911), 380–90.

[24] Agobard, *Liber De Correctione Antiphonarii*, PL 104, cols. 329–40. See Bäumer, 283.

[25] The antiphon for the *Magnificat* sung in the first vesper for Christmas, "Cum ortus fuerit. . . ." Here Agobard objected especially to the *procedentem a Patre*, which allegedly took the place of an earlier *a matre*.

[26] Berno of Reichenau, *De officio Missae*, PL 142 [Baumstark cites vol. 113], cols. 1060–61.

[27] On this topic is a valuable short note in Theodoros Anagnostes [Theodor the Lector], Εκλογαι εκ της Ἐκκλησιαστικῆς ἱστορίας [Excerpts from church history], bk. 2, 48, PG 86, pt. 1, col. 209.

Chapter 8

Liturgy and Politics

With the creation of two influential liturgical types, the Byzantine on the one hand and the Frankish-Roman on the other, a linear development with origins in the Christian *Urzeit* comes to an end in the Greek East and the Latin West—almost simultaneously. For the historical significance that both of these worship forms were destined to achieve, it is of utmost importance that their development ended before both of them, Byzantine Orthodoxy in the East and the Catholic Church of the West, were presented with new opportunities to evangelize and the huge tasks that challenged them as a result.

The era of liturgical blending came to a close in two consecutive years. That between Constantinople and Jerusalem ended in 842, when—through the efforts of Empress Theodora*—the iconoclastic era came to a close on the first celebration of the feast of Orthodoxy;[†] the blending between Gaul and Rome came to an end in 843, when the Treaty of Verdun buried all hope of uniting the greater Frankish kingdom.[‡] Even before these events, Ansgar (801–65) had begun his northern mission among the Danes and the Swedes.[§] A few years later, the brothers Cyril (826–69) and Methodius (815–85) began to work among the Khazars of Crimea, a prelude to their greater achievement:

---

* On Theodora the Armenian, see Short Biography, no. 173.

† Acting as regent for her son, Theodora called the Synod of Constantinople in 842, which condemned the iconoclasts and reinstated the decisions of the Seventh Ecumenical Council (787), including the veneration of icons. The first session of the Synod ended with a procession from the Church of Blachernae to Hagia Sophia to place icons in that church once again. This occurred on February 19, 842, the first day of Great Lent, upon which the feast of Orthodoxy has been celebrated ever since.

‡ This treaty was signed in the city of Verdun (now in France) by the three surviving sons of the Carolingian emperor Louis I (814–40): Lothair I (817–55), Louis the German (817–43), and Charles the Bald (840–77). It ended their contest for the Frankish Empire by dividing its possessions among them.

§ On Ansgar, see Short Biography, no. 14.

the establishment of Slavic Christianity.* The curious connection that these two Byzantine missionaries had with Rome notwithstanding,† the events they set in motion resulted in the whole eastern Slavic world, including the linguistically Slavic Bulgarians,‡ becoming a gigantic mission field for Constantinople. For Rome, the western Slavic peoples,§ along with those of the Scandinavian North, acquired a similar significance. Hungary and the Wend peoples south of the Baltic Sea¶ came to complete this picture. Taking this Christianizing movement as a whole, oriented as it was toward the north, the accepted liturgical form from the outset for all the territory newly won in the east was the Byzantine, and in the west, the Frankish-Roman. The former simply became the Greco-Slavic Rite, the latter the Western Rite.

From its beginning, this historical development endangered the older liturgical forms that kept the liturgy's relationship with Christian antiquity intact. These lay to the south. The Ambrosian and Mozarabic Rites were celebrated to the south in the West; the liturgies of St. James and St. Mark, along with the early Antiochene Rite, had their homes to the south of Eastern Orthodoxy.** In a word, the two major liturgical areas, now growing to colossal proportions, threatened to crush the older forms. Under any circumstances, the Byzantine and

---

*On Cyril and Methodius, see Short Biography, no. 59.

†The two brothers were invited to Rome, where they were honored. Although Cyril (826–69) died there, Methodius (815–85) was consecrated archbishop of Sirmium (Pannonia) by the pope and returned to Moravia, where he continued his missionary work under the aegis of Rome, though celebrating the Divine Liturgy of St. John Chrysostom.

‡ Baumstark is contrasting the "Slavic Bulgarians" to the original Asiatic Bulgar peoples, who migrated to southeastern Europe from Central Asia beginning in the second century. This latter group spoke the now-dead Bulgar language, which was a member of the Oghuric branch of the Turkic language family.

§ Baumstark is here referring to the Poles, Czechs, and Slovaks.

¶ During the Middle Ages, Germans used the name "Wends" for all the Slavic tribes that lived in the territory bounded roughly by the Elbe and Saale Rivers on the west and the Oder River on the east. After fighting with them for centuries, the Germans succeeded in conquering them in the twelfth century, converting them to Christianity. They continue to exist as a discreet ethnic group, centered around Bautzen, to this day.

** All of these rites date from the period before the Council of Chalcedon (451).

Frankish-Roman Rites would have unceasingly challenged the liturgical independence of Antioch, Alexandria, Milan, and Spain. This threat was only intensified by the imperial political power in the East and the world stature of the papacy in the West.

For the Byzantine Empire, the Arab conquest created a unique situation vis-à-vis Orthodoxy in Syria and Egypt.* The trunk of the imperial tree remained in Europe and Asia Minor, but shorn of its branches: the provinces to the east and south.† From that time on, the sole remaining tie to these areas was the religious connection maintained through the church. The first priority required for an effective imperial foreign policy in these regions was to make this bond as strong as possible. Now nothing strengthened that ecclesial relationship more than the establishment of liturgical uniformity. The interests of the "ecumenical patriarch" of Constantinople, the bishop to the court, went hand in hand with those of the court. After thoroughly sidelining Ephesus,‡ and doing the same to his colleagues in Antioch, Jerusalem, and Alexandria,§ the "ecumenical patriarch" could lay claim to an unrivaled position. He occupied the see of the new Rome, Constantinople, allegedly established by Andrew, the "first called" of the apostles.¶ Nothing demonstrated this ascendancy more emphatically than

---

* Syria fell to the Arabs in the 630s; Egypt was occupied in 640.

† As a consequence of the Arab invasions, the Byzantine Empire lost its provinces in Syria, Egypt, North Africa, and on the islands of the western Mediterranean. Various reconquests notwithstanding, this left as its "trunk"—now shorn of its "branches"—only Asia Minor and parts of southeastern Europe. However, it did have sovereignty over parts of the Italian peninsula and the island of Sicily for extended periods.

‡ Prominent in the early Christian world, Ephesus was the place where, by tradition, John "the beloved disciple" and Mary, the mother of Jesus, settled; it was visited by Paul (d. ca. 65?). An ecumenical council was held there in 431. However, it never acquired the status of a patriarchal see.

§ While equal in ecclesiastical status, the five patriarchal sees (Antioch, Jerusalem, Alexandria, Constantinople, and Rome) were unequal in political power, with Rome dominating the West and Constantinople the East. Baumstark is here referring to the fact that Constantinople exercised inordinate influence over the three patriarchal sees located to its south and east.

¶ Andrew is portrayed in John 1:40-42 as the first disciple to be called by Jesus. An early medieval forgery attributes to him the founding of the church in Constantinople. After Constantine (306–37) had Andrew's relics translated there in 337, the eastern Roman capital could compare its apostolic standing to

imposing the liturgy he celebrated upon the other patriarchates in the East. On top of that came the relationship of the Byzantine Church to "old" Rome and the West. Initially Photius (858–95) ripped open the wound of schism in 867;* Michael Cerularius (1043–59) rendered it irreparable in 1054.[†] So, vis-à-vis the papacy as well, everything necessarily turned on enabling the Eastern Orthodox Church to stand as united as possible. Ever present was the danger that, in a fight, the patriarchates of the South would side with Rome, as they had during the first iconoclastic controversy.[‡] The only way to address this danger was to curtail their independence as much as possible. But this meant, above all, robbing their liturgies of their individuality.

The manuscript copies of the Liturgy of St. James preserved from the patriarchates of Jerusalem and Antioch offer scant evidence for sustained resistance, the kind that one might have expected Constantinople's attempts at liturgical politics to have encountered there. This is because the venerable liturgy of "the brother of our Lord" was permitted for use alongside the Byzantine Rite, even in the domain of the Constantinopolitan patriarchate.[1] Documents attesting to the liturgical reading of Scripture in the dialect used by the Christian population in Palestine are valuable for what they can tell us about Jerusalem: they suggest the opposite of resistance. Naturally these documents originally exemplified the traditional Palestinian Lectionary. However, the pericopic notations in a gospel book,[§] copied in the year 1030 at Gerasa east of the Jordan,[2] are already in complete agreement with the Byzantine order. Numerous manuscripts and fragments of manuscripts, from the ninth down into the seventeenth centuries, shed light upon the liturgical history of the orthodox patriarchate of Antioch.[3] Yet, in this whole documentary stratum, one finds only isolated traces of a remaining pre-Byzantine rite.[4] Apparently Egypt put up the strongest resistance to the wholesale displacement of its indigenous rite by the Byzantine. The eucharistic liturgy of Alexandria, attributed to Mark

---

that of Rome, where Peter (d. 67?) and Paul (d. 65?) had ministered, died, and were buried.

* On Photius, see Short Biography, no. 141.

[†] On Michael I Cerularius, see Short Biography, no. 123.

[‡] The first phase of the iconoclastic controversy dates from ca. 725 to 813; the second phase lasted from 814 to 842.

[§] In this instance, pericopes for reading were indicated by notes written in the gospel book itself, typically in the margins.

the evangelist, was still being used in 1203. Only in that year did the Antiochene Patriarch Theodore Balsamon (ca. 1140–after 1195),* resident in Constantinople, render a canonical verdict declaring its inadmissibility—in the most trenchant possible terms.[5] He had in effect sounded the death knell for the Alexandrian Liturgy of St. Mark.

As for the West at this time, during the second half of the eleventh century, popes were as ruthless as Balsamon. In Spain, Popes Nicholas II (1059–61),† Alexander II (1061–73),‡ Gregory VII (1073–85),§ and Urban II (1088–99)¶ strove to replace the Western Gothic Mozarabic Rite with the Roman.[6] In this case, Rome's dogged efforts were not without success.** Pope Nicholas II at least made an advance against the Ambrosian Rite of Milan as well, this attack being renewed by Pope Eugene IV (1431–47)†† around 1443.[7] In the time between these two skirmishes, Milan apparently felt that Pope Gregory VII had also challenged its right to possess an inherited local liturgy. At that time,

---

* On Theodore Balsamon, see Short Biography, no. 174.
† On Nicholas II, see Short Biography, no. 128.
‡ On Alexander II, see Short Biography, no. 8.
§ On Gregory VII, see Short Biography, no. 81.
¶ On Urban II, see Short Biography, no. 183.
** The four popes Baumstark mentions oversaw a replacement of the Mozarabic Rite by the Roman that was virtually total. In 1060, during the pontificate of Nicholas II (1059–61), a council held in the cathedral city of Jaca, Aragon, decreed the exclusive celebration of the Roman Rite and the banning of all others, including the Mozarabic. Alexander II (1061–73) effected the establishment of the Roman liturgical rite and the abolition of the Mozarabic in the province of Aragon through the office of the papal legate, Hugh Candidus (fl. twelfth century), whose work also resulted in its spread to Navarre. Despite considerable discontent and opposition, Gregory VII (1073–85) insisted upon Roman use in Castile. After Toledo had been taken back from the Arabs (1085) and the Roman Church asserted itself in that city, devotion to the Mozarabic Rite necessitated compromise. While the Roman Rite was used in general, the Mozarabic Rite was permitted for use in just seven parish churches of venerable age. Though no longer celebrated in any of those churches, it has lived on since 1504 in a chapel dedicated exclusively to its celebration, the *Capilla Muzárabe*, built under a tower of the cathedral in Toledo, Spain. For a discussion of the suppression and survival of the Mozarabic Rite, see Archdale A. King, *Liturgies of the Primatial Sees* (Milwaukee, WI: Bruce Publishing Company, 1957), 503–22.
†† On Eugene IV, see Short Biography, no. 68.

around 1080, a miracle story was circulated,* apparently by design,[†] that would have caused even Charlemagne (king from 768; emperor 800–814)[‡] and Pope Hadrian I (772–95)[§] to give up trying to suppress the form of worship bearing the name of Ambrose.[81¶]

---

* The following summarizes a report of this event written by Landulf the Elder during the eleventh century in his *Historia Mediolanensis*, bk. 2, chaps. 10–13, PL 147, cols. 852–56: "Some bishops at a synod in Rome in the time of Charlemagne, runs the narrative, had protested against the Milanese liturgy, since it differed from the Roman rite. Whereupon the Emperor decided to abolish all Ambrosian usages, sending an order to Milan for the destruction or 'exile beyond the mountains' of the books of the rite. In the meanwhile, a certain Eugenius, a 'bishop from the other side of the Alps' [*transmontanus episcopus*], pleaded with the Pope and Emperor for the preservation of the Ambrosian liturgy. It was finally arranged that the decision was to rest on a 'miracle': closed copies of the two liturgies were laid on the altar in the Vatican basilica, and it was agreed that the book, which at the end of three days should open of its own accord, should be preserved, while that which remained closed should be destroyed. The two manuscripts opened simultaneously, and Eugenius returned triumphantly to Milan, only to find that the Ambrosian books had been already destroyed, with the exception of a missal that a priest had hidden for six weeks in mountain cave. A *manuale* was drawn up from memory by certain priests and clerks, and with the aid of these two books the Ambrosian rite was saved from extinction." Quoted from King, *Liturgies*, 304–5.

[†] Baumstark is suggesting here that the Milanese circulated this story to generate support for their use of the Ambrosian Liturgy.

[‡] On Charlemagne, see Short Biography, no. 44.

[§] On Hadrian I, see Short Biography, no. 86.

[¶] The first record of incursion against the Ambrosian Rite by a pope dates to the papacy of Nicholas II (1059–61), when Peter Damian (ca. 1007–72) attempted to suppress it as a part of a broader assertion of Roman authority. This attempt was reversed under Pope Alexander II (1061–73), himself of Milanese origin. An attempt by Pope Gregory VII (1073–85) followed, when the legend recounted in a footnote above may have been circulated in support of the Milanese rite. The final move came in 1443 during the papacy of Eugene IV (1431–47), who sent Cardinal Branda da Castiglione (d. 1448) as legate to Milan. In trying to reconcile the Duke of Milan with the Holy See, he set out to replace the Ambrosian Rite with the Roman. Rioting, which may have been a protest against the legate in general, brought this attempt to an end. The Ambrosian Rite was not threatened again until the Council of Trent in the sixteenth century, when Milan was able to save the Ambrosian Rite on the basis

Significantly, the most vigorous opposition to local liturgical rites continuing to be used came from the leading standard-bearer for papal supremacy. This was Pope Gregory VII, who promoted the idea of the papacy being a worldwide spiritual monarchy placed above kings and princes. However, the Curia was not the first in the West to use its position of power to pursue a deliberate liturgical politics. Even in the Carolingian era, the liturgy was cultivated essentially to help achieve ambitions of power. This was already the case with Pepin (751–68),* who had the Pope's blessing to thank for his crown. Concerning the liturgy, he was clearly guided by the desire to secure lasting support for his throne. By associating himself with Rome liturgically, Pepin sought to ally himself as closely as possible to the spiritual superpower.[†] Though Charlemagne surpassed Pepin in greatness, in matters of liturgical politics the son—with absolute clarity of purpose—continued down the paths mapped out by his father. Implementing both Rome's liturgy and its canon law in the kingdom of the Franks was in complete accord with the idea guiding all of Charlemagne's political thought: the renewal of Roman imperial glory through German strength. Moreover, the Roman Use was the only conceivable candidate for attempting a liturgical settlement in the imperial superpower. It was the only rite that the empire as a whole—comprised of parts so diverse and far-flung—could assent to accept. For an empire forcibly united by the power of the sword, the possibility of strengthening its internal cohesion by means of a liturgical agreement of this sort must have been a *desideratum* of the highest order.[9] From this perspective one can easily understand the keen interest that the royal entourage—

---

of the ruling by that council that local liturgies may continue in use if they had been so for two hundred years or more. Holding on to the Milanese Rite took effort, however. With papal permission to have the Roman Mass said in any church he might attend, the Governor of Milan made a move against the rite that Cardinal Charles Borromeo (1538–84) was able to defeat. While the cardinal accommodated Rome with some changes in the rite, he was careful to preserve its essence. On Charles Borromeo, see Short Biography, no. 41. For a discussion of the history of the Ambrosian Rite, see King, *Liturgies*, 296–312, and "Ambrosian Liturgy and Rite," CE, 374–97, esp. 395.

* On Pepin III (the Short), see Short Biography, no. 137.

[†] In this passage, Baumstark takes the position that Pepin sought to consolidate the support that the pope had given him by associating the liturgy of his kingdom with that of Rome.

after having acquired territory along the Spanish border*—took in the text of the Mozarabic liturgy, specifically on the question of its dogmatic correctness.[10] No less understandable would have been a concerted and earnest effort on Charlemagne's part to in fact suppress the Ambrosian liturgy, if he had ever been called upon to do so. On the other hand, it is also not by chance that Alcuin's (735–804)[†] new edition of the Gregorian Sacramentary followed, so to speak, hard on the heels of the event that took place on the feast of Christmas in the year 800,[‡] when the diadem of the Roman Augustus came to adorn Charlemagne's head and grace his temples.[§] With this new edition making considerable concessions to the Gallican "golden" past, one gets the clear impression that the goal of keeping the imperial liturgy absolutely faithful to Rome may have lost all significance for the mighty Frank, once he had no more to gain from it.

From a historical perspective, however, the most curious thing about Carolingian liturgical politics may be something else altogether: it preserved the Roman liturgy and its Western character at a time when there was real danger of it being essentially "orientalized." Political circumstances created this threat as well. For two centuries Rome had been the capital city for a *Ducatus* of the Exarchate of Ravenna.[¶]

———————————

* This acquisition was made in 778.

† On Alcuin, see Short Biography, no. 7.

‡ Baumstark understood Alcuin to have produced his new edition of the Gregorian Sacramentary between 801 and 804 (see p. 122). As this work begins with prayers for Christmas, specifically *In vigiliis domini* (December 24) and *Natale Domini ad S. Mariam maiorem* (December 25), one could surmise that it would have first been used for that feast, which would also have been the first anniversary of Charlemagne's coronation. It may be in this sense that Baumstark speaks of the Sacramentary following closely on the heels of the coronation, indeed perhaps on the first anniversary of it.

§ On Christmas day in 800 at St. Peter's Basilica in Rome, Pope Leo III (795–816) placed a diadem upon the head of a kneeling Charlemagne (768–814, emperor from 800), whereupon the congregation said in acclamation, "Long life and victory to Charles Augustus, crowned by God, great and peaceful Emperor of the Romans." For a discussion of the coronation event, see Robert Folz, *The Coronation of Charlemagne, 25 December 800* (London: Routledge & K. Paul, 1974), esp. 143–50, and *The Coronation of Charlemagne: What Did It Signify?* ed. Richard Eugene Sullivan, Problems in European Civilization (Boston: Heath, 1959).

¶ Under the Byzantine Emperors, provinces distant from Constantinople were designated as exarchates. From ca. 580 to 751, Italy was governed as the

During this period, to prop up its control over Italy, the Byzantine imperial administration systematically exploited the Roman Church.[11] Again and again under its influence, scions of high imperial officials, Syrians as well as Greeks, from the East as well as Sicily, ascended to the See of Peter. Elements of the same extraction occupied the uppermost ranks of the clerical circles surrounding these oriental popes.[12] Already around the middle of the seventh century, oriental monasticism had become a power in Rome, supremely confident of its position.[13] Inevitably all this had a formative influence on the city's liturgy. During this time numerous translations of Greek texts, recognizable as such yet today, found their way into the inventory of antiphons and responses used by the Roman liturgy. Probably more numerous still are those whose true origins can no longer be identified with confidence.[14] As the number of Roman church buildings honoring oriental saints increased, so did the importance of these saints for the whole liturgical system. One need only recall, perhaps, the miracle-working doctors, who "healed without remuneration," Cosmas and Damian (d. ca. 287), whose names even found their way into the Canon of the Mass.* What is now Trinity Sunday was for a time celebrated according to Byzantine custom as the Sunday "of all Saints."[15]† And when Pope Paul I (757–68)‡ had two stone tablets (extant yet today) inscribed with the feast days of saints whose relics he had deposited in his new Sylvester Church,§ they were now listed according to the Byzantine festal calendar rather than the Roman.[16] Once Gregory the Great (540 to 604)¶ almost angrily rejected the allegation that he had accommo-

---

exarchate of Ravenna, with that city serving as its administrative center. The exarchate was divided into dukedoms (Middle Latin: *ducatus*). In this administrative system, the importance of Rome, as the capital city of a dukedom or duchy, was only secondary.

* On Cosmas and Damian, see Short Biography, no. 56.

† All Saints' Sunday (Άγίων Πάντων), the Sunday following Pentecost, is the occasion in the Byzantine tradition for collectively honoring all saints. It brings the paschal season to a close.

‡ On Paul I, see Short Biography, no. 134.

§ Although Pope Stephen III (752–57) built the Church of San Silvestro in Capite inside the walls, his successor, Paul I (757–68), oversaw the translation of relics to it. These included the remains of Sylvester I (314–35), from whom the name San Silvestro comes, and the reputed head of John the Baptist, from which the phrase "in Capite" in its name is derived.

¶ On Gregory I or the Great, see Short Biography, no. 78.

dated local liturgical practice.[17]* In fact, fully a century and a half later, Rome came close to replacing its traditional sanctoral cycle with that of the Greek East.

When reestablishing imperial power in the West, Charlemagne cultivated a liturgical relationship between the Frankish Empire and Rome that was as close as possible. Could it be that in so doing he also wanted to create a counterweight against such an alliance with the East, one between the Byzantine Empire and Rome? Could it be that, on the eve of this development, it was in his best interest to blast Rome loose from the East—liturgically speaking? Whatever the answers to these questions may be, the fact is that Charlemagne did remove the danger that political realities posed for the Roman liturgy during the era of Byzantine hegemony over Italy. While the Byzantine Rite could not have been simply substituted for the liturgy of even one city in the West, it would have been possible for the liturgy of a city, even that of the popes, to have been thoroughly orientalized to the core of its being. It is simply unimaginable that a liturgy of that sort could have served as the imperial liturgy for a political entity uniting the whole of the Christian West.

---

* This sentence is enigmatic. Although Baumstark failed to provide the reference for this sentence (see n. 17), one is tempted to relate it to Gregory's letter to Bishop John of Syracuse, in which he does just the opposite of what this sentence states—that is, he protests that the innovations he made in the Roman liturgy were not inspired by Constantinople. See n. 21, p. 158.

Notes

[1] See above, chap. 6, n. 6.

[2] *Evangeliarium Hierosolymitanum*, 2 vols., ed. Francesco Miniscalchi-Erizzo (Verona: n.p., 1861). Republished by Paul Anton de Lagarde in *Bibliothecae Syriacae* (Göttingen: L. Horstmann, 1892), 237–402, the first edition with Latin translation. The manuscript, which is now in Rome (Vat. Syr. 19), was published with variants found in MSS discovered on Mt. Sinai. This may be found, with one MS published in parallel and the variations found in another MS noted, in Agnes Smith Lewis and Margaret Dunlap Gibson, *The Palestinian Syriac Lectionary of the Gospels* (London: Kegan Paul & Co., 1899) [available through Google Books].

[3] A list of the material that has come to light up to this point may be found in Cyrille Korolevskij [Charon], "Le rite byzantine et la liturgie chrysostomienne

dans les patriarcate melchites (Alexandrie-Antioch-Jerusalem)," Χρυσοστομικα [*Chrysostomika*], 506–16. For material of the utmost value, which has come recently to light, see, *Antiquariatskatalog K. W. Hiersemann 500. Orientalische Manuskripte* (Leipzig: Eigenverlag, 1922), and Anton Baumstark, "Neue handschriftliche Denkmäler melkitischer Liturgie," OC, n.s., 10/11 (1923): 157–68. See also Baumstark, *Literatur*, 337–39.

[4] Material from this period is found especially in two Psalters and two fragments of choral books. See *Antiquariatskatalog*, nos. 41, 42, 48, and 29.

[5] For the pertinent letters exchanged between the Antiochene patriarch Theodor Balsamon and patriarch Mark III of Alexandria, see PG 138 [Baumstark cited 135], cols. 953–56.

[6] A good overview of this development is found in Pierre C. Lebrun, *Explication littérale historique et dogmatique des prières et des cérémonies de la messe* (Paris: Florentin Delaulne, 1716), a work that has been reprinted numerous times and that, even today, is consistently useful. In the Italian edition that I use, see dissertation V, article 2, in Pietro Lebrun, *Spiegazione letterale, storica e dogmatica delle preci e delle cerimonie della messa*, vol. 2, trans. Anton Maria Donado (Verona: Dionigio Ramanzini, 1752), 120f [its most recent French edition is *Explication de la messe*, Lex orandi 9 (Paris: Editions du Cerf, 1949), available through Google Books].

[7] Dissertation III, article 1, in Lebrun, *Spiegazione della messa*, vol. 2, 79–84.

[8] Reported by Durandus, "Rationale divinorum officiorum," bk. 5, chap. 2, no. 5 [the 1574 edition is available through Google Books. For a critical edition, see Guillelmi Duranti, *Rationale divinorum officiorum, V–VI*, = Guillelmi Duranti Rationale divinorum officiorum, 2nd vol., ed. Anselme Avril and Timothy M. Thibodeau, Corpus Christianorum, Continuatio mediaevalis, 140A (Turnholti [Turnhout]: Brepols, 1998), 15–16].

[9] In a book review, Ildefons Herwegen makes some very stimulating connections in this vein with Lietzmann's edition of the *Sacramentarium Gregorianum*. See Ildefons Herwegen, "Besprechung: *Das Sakramentarium Gregorianum*, ed. Hans Lietzmann," *Zeitschrift der Savigny Stiftung für Rechtsgeschichte, Kanonistische Abteilung* 43 (1922): 493–95.

[10] See the *acta* of the Council of Frankfurt (794), Mansi 13, 863–926, and Alcuin, *Contra Felicem*, bks. 8, 13 in PL 101, cols. 226–27.

[11] See Charles Diehl, *Études sur l'administration byzantine dans l'exarchat de Ravenne (568–761)*, Bibliothèque des Écoles françaises d'Athènes et de Rome, fasc. 53 (Paris: E. Thorin, 1888), 369–86.

[12] For details, see ibid., 251–66.

[13] The Greek monastery in Rome appeared en masse at the Lateran Synod of 649. See Mansi, 10, 903–10.

[14] For examples, see, "Antiphonarium Ambrosianum du Musée Britannique (XII siècle); Codex Additional 34209," *Palèographie musicale* 5 (1896): 6–9; Henri Leclercq, "Carthage," DACL, 2, col. 2294f; Anton Baumstark, "Rom oder

Jerusalem? Eine Revision der Frage nach der Herkunft des Lichtmessfestes," *Theologie und Glaube* 1 (1909): 102f; Baumstark, "Die Hodie-Antiphonen des römischen Breviers und der Kreis ihrer griechischen Parallelen," *Die Kirchenmusik* 10 (1909): 153–60; Baumstark, "Uebersetzungen aus dem Griechischen in den Responsorien der Metten des Triduum Sacrum," *Der Katholik* 1 (1913): 209–20; and Baumstark, "Der Orient und die Gesänge der Adoratio crucis," JLW 2 (1922): 1–17.

[15] Germain Morin, "Le plus ancient 'Comes' ou le lectionnaire de l'église romain," RBén 27 (1910): 73.

[16] Mentioned by Mariano Armellini, *Le chiese di Roma dal secolo IV al XIX*, 2nd ed. (Roma [Rome]: Edizione del Pasquino, 1891), 299.

[17] [Although this footnote is numbered in the text, Baumstark provided no accompanying citation.]

Chapter 9

Cathedral and Monastery

Liturgies indigenous to different localities were not the only forms
in the liturgical life of the church to experience blending. Yet another
instance stands out as significant in the development of the liturgy. In
this case, blending occurred not between liturgies from different localities, but rather between those from two kinds of ecclesial communities: monastic and episcopal (that is, those that had been under the
oversight of a bishop from the outset).

The influence of both of these liturgical types was already being felt
by the time the early liturgical forms of Constantinople and Jerusalem
were undergoing amalgamation. But the influence of monasticism—as
the spiritual "superpower" in both the medieval West and the Christian churches of the East—was simply far too great to be significant for
only one instance in liturgical history, even one of such great moment
as the Byzantine Rite. Viewed in this broader context, we find further
demonstration of how significant this influence is as we pursue other
problems in liturgical development. This is especially the case when
dealing with one question in particular: How did the Mass develop in
the East?

Of the Mass formularies coming out of monastic communities, only
one attained a stature equal to that of Jerusalem's Liturgy of St. James,
that is, only one was able to reach across confessional divisions and
national boundaries. This was the eucharistic liturgy attributed to
Basil (330–79),* the great monk from Cappodocia, who in all probability did in fact originally compose it. Recensions of the Basilian liturgy
in old Armenian and Syriac[1] are quite independent of the Greek recension that surfaced in the liturgical area using the Byzantine Rite.[2] For
its part this Greek recension, like its sister rite ascribed to Chrysostom,
was translated into several other languages to actually be used in the
liturgy: Georgian, Church Slavonic, Armenian, Syriac, and Arabic.[3]
In turn, individual prayers from this liturgy, in Latin translation, also

---

* On Basil, see Short Biography, no. 28.

became familiar in the West.[4] Egyptian Monophysite Christianity* possessed a recension of the Basilian liturgy (found in Greek, Coptic,[†] and Arabic translations),[5] which from there was taken over onto Ethiopian soil and translated into Ethiopic (Ge'ez).[6‡] In its expanded order, this recension, sharply abbreviated, takes into account the Egyptian patterns for celebrating the Eucharist. Oriental monasticism embraced as their own—albeit not universally—this liturgy by the author of the two monastic rules,[§] a fact that guaranteed the Basilian formulary would enjoy such a wide distribution throughout the Christian world.

The Liturgy of St. Basil spread into Constantinople and, once there, blended into the liturgy celebrated in its cathedral. True, the final form of that city's eucharistic formulary, bearing the name of John Chrysostom (ca. 347–407), "the one with the golden tongue,"[¶] held its own for ordinary use. However, the Cappadocian monastic formulary did so as well. It turned up not only on the author's feast day (January 1) but also on occasions of special significance: the Sundays in the Season of Lent, Maundy Thursday, and the great vigils of Epiphany and Easter. In Egypt the Basilian liturgy experienced a similar blending, which showed even more favor to this monastic liturgy in the end. In fact, that version of the Liturgy of St. Basil became standard in the Coptic Rite for celebrating the Eucharist, whereas the Coptic recension of the Liturgy of St. Mark—traditional for the city of Alexandria and attributed by the Monophysites to Cyril (376–444)**—was relegated to a position analogous to that of the Byzantine text of Basil in Constantinople.

In regard to the daily prayer of the church, the characteristic contrast between cathedral and monastery is not only a phenomenon common to the East. Rather, its absolutely classic expression is found nowhere else than in the West, where—even up to the present day—two kinds of breviaries exist side by side. From the outset the circumstances prevailing in monastic communities—traditionally being more intimate—were essentially different from those found in the congregation itself

---

* On the christological controversies, see n. on p. 48.

† On Coptic, see n. on p. 93.

‡ On Ethiopic (Ge'ez), see ibid.

§ Basil wrote two successive versions of the *Asketikon,* his rule for monastic communities, one shorter and the other longer.

¶ On John Chrysostom, see Short Biography, no. 47.

** On Cyril of Alexandria, see Short Biography, no. 58.

(or those who later came to represent the congregation: the cathedral or collegiate clergy). For this reason, the monk's obligation to pray could be—indeed had to be—much more rigorous. In fact, the monk's proper daily work was the "Opus Dei," essentially to pray without ceasing (1 Thess 5:17).* The only activities allowed to interrupt it—and then only as briefly as possible—were the physical necessities of rest and food and the work required to survive.

For the monk, praying the Night Office or Vigil had the potential of becoming his most demanding and strenuous obligation. Pachomius (ca. 290–346), founder of coenobitic monasticism in Egypt,[†] was reportedly instructed by an angel to use the grouping of twelve psalms for nightly prayer,[‡] the pattern adopted by the Rule of St. Benedict as canonical.[7] Elsewhere that number was even greater—indeed, much greater! According to a witness from the turn of the seventh century, the monks of Sinai[§] were not the only ones to recite the whole Psalter every night, along with all of the biblical canticles.[8] We hear that in Syria the Nestorian monks were equally rigorous in fulfilling their obligation of night prayer.[9] Likewise, Benedict (ca. 480–ca. 550), the patriarch of Western monasticism,[¶] knew how zealous the prayer practices of previous generations had been. The whole Psalter—at the very least—was recited over a twenty-four-hour period. The rigor of the pattern he organized, the recitation of the Psalter over the course of a week, paled by comparison.[10] Again it was monasticism that, in various ways and increasingly, elaborated the structure of the whole round of

---

* *Opus Dei* is the term used by the Benedictine Order for the Divine Office, connoting that the monk's primary "work" is daily prayer.

† On Pachomius, see Short Biography, no. 133.

‡ Pachomius used to withdraw into the uninhabited desert, to Tabennisi on the upper Nile, in the diocese of Tentyra. On one visit there, an angel provided him with instructions relating to monastic life. In Egyptian monastic tradition, this vision lives on in "the rule of the angel," an interpretation of the Pauline command to "pray without ceasing" (1Thess 5:17), specifically to pray at every hour of the twenty-four in the day, twelve during the day and twelve at night.

§ The region around the mountain that tradition regards as Mount Sinai early became a center for Christian monasticism, with Emperor Justinian I (483–565) building the Monastery of St. Catherine on the traditional site of the burning bush around 557. In the eighth century, the isolation of this monastery saved its icons from being destroyed by the iconoclasts.

¶ On Benedict of Nursia, see Short Biography, no. 30.

daily prayer. Frequently this resulted in the number of Morning Offices being doubled. This development may have originated in a practice of urban cathedrals, whereby the Morning Office was performed by two different groups, one after the other: the congregation as a whole and the ascetics living in the area.[11] On the other hand, the situation within monasteries—starting with Bethlehem around 382*—led to the addition of the hour of Prime, placed before the three older hours sung during the day.[12] A similar doubling occurred in the evening offices, when a final hour of prayer was inserted between supper and bedtime. Basil is the earliest witness to this practice, which became simply universal.[13] In the Armenian Rite, one even finds a tripling of the evening hours.[14] In the Greek-speaking areas, monastic rigor doubled the series of daylight hours by inserting the intermediate hours (*Mesoria*) after Prime, Terce, Sext, and None. Similarly, after the early Christian vigil service in the middle of the night had merged with the morning celebration of *Orthros*, there developed a new worship service to take its place.[15] With an exuberance characteristic of the zeal found in Spanish monasteries, the Mozarabic Office was elaborated in a similar fashion.

Material differences appeared in how parochial clergy and monks sang the Divine Office. In the West, the practice of singing hymns was initiated in the monastic choir service. In the Greek world, at a time when sung poetic compositions had long since gained a firm foothold in the worship life of urban cathedrals, the monks on Mount Sinai forbade this decorative embellishment from entering their vast store of nocturnal psalmody. Today, just the opposite is the case in the monasteries on Mount Athos.† There psalmody lives on in all its ancient grandeur, where forms as opulent as can be imagined are used to combine poetic insertions with the singing of psalms.[16]

---

* The monastic presence in Bethlehem to which Baumstark alludes in this passage is not the better-known Latin communities, the monastery and convent founded in 386 by Jerome (ca. 342–420) and Paula (347–404), respectively. Rather, he has in mind a report by John Cassian (ca. 360–after 430), who even earlier lived in a hermitage there.

† Mount Athos, called the "Holy Mountain," is located at the end of a peninsula, which extends out into the Aegean Sea from the coast of Macedonia. This peninsula has long been the property of monasteries of the Eastern Orthodox Church. While one finds historical records of monastic life on Mt. Athos only from the ninth century, tradition places it there further back in time. There are currently twenty functioning monasteries on the mountain.

When monastic liturgical usage first took shape, it naturally relied upon forms found in cathedrals, whether those accepted generally throughout the church or those bearing the distinctive stamp of a particular individual. Of course, the grouping of twelve psalms sung by the night choir, which had been introduced by Pachomius and was adopted by the Benedictines, cannot be considered apart from the grouping of twelve biblical readings that congregations used in the oldest celebration known for the hours of the night.* The significance of this grouping of twelve for this celebration's structure becomes apparent when we note its presence elsewhere; it is common to both the Epiphany and Easter Vigils of the early church in Jerusalem, as well as to the Good Friday liturgies of Rome and Gaul.[17] In regard to the pattern used for distributing the biblical canticles sung in the service of Lauds over the particular days of the week, the Rule of St. Benedict expressly directs that the Roman system be used.[18] That schema, encountered here in Benedict as early as the first half of the sixth century, and preserved in the weekday office for Lauds in the Tridentine Breviary, slipped out of there to find its way into the alternate schema of today's Breviary.† The one-of-a-kind Dominican Breviary is based upon the diocesan rite used in Paris during the high Middle Ages.[19]‡ As early as 1223 the rule governing the newly formed Franciscan order

---

* Baumstark is here referring to the Easter Vigil.

† In 1911 the Breviary of Pius X (1903–14) was promulgated, a thorough revision of the Tridentine Breviary. Baumstark was critical of this revision for departing from early Roman tradition preserved by the Tridentine Breviary. In this paragraph, Baumstark is taking the biblical canticles of Lauds as a case in point. While in the Tridentine Breviary biblical canticles were always said at Lauds on weekdays according to the ancient pattern, the Breviary of Pius X appointed them as an alternate schema. Baumstark shows his hand by the verb *sich retten*, which literally means "escape" and is translated here as "slipped out." He is alluding to the "survival skills" that he attributes to ancient elements of the liturgy. In this case, he is suggesting that the ancient pattern for distributing the canticles at Lauds slyly slipped past the redactors' disregard for the venerable past. See Anton Baumstark, "La Riforma del Salterio Romano alla luce della Storia Liturgia comparata," *Roma e l'Oriente* 3 (1911/12): 217–28 and 289–302, = Anton Baumstark, *La riforma del Salterio Romano alla luce della storia della Liturgia comparata*, Studi liturgici, fasc. 2 (Grottaferrata: Tip. "Nilo," 1912).

‡ Baumstark is here referring to a short uniform rite created by four appointed friars working in Rome ca. 1250. It was passed on by general chapters

required the recitation of the Office. The obligatory form was that used by the papal court, as distinct from the older rite sung in Rome's major churches. Thus, already for Franciscans—the poor of Assisi—the use "of the Roman Church"* meant simply this papal form.[20]

As the Divine Office developed, further blendings took place that consistently favored the monastic rite. Without exception more recent creations of the monastic world, elements added to the order of the Liturgy of the Hours, have enjoyed wide acceptance. Since the time of the Mongolian invasions (thirteenth century), the way the Nestorian Rite sings the Divine Office has been standardized, through adopting the practice of one monastic community in particular, the one used in the "upper" Monastery of St. Gabriel and Abraham,[†] a stronghold of monasticism near Mosul in northern Mesopotamia.[21] Manuscript sources reveal a form of Byzantine daily prayer diverging markedly from that accepted today, that is, diverging from that found in the modern editions of the liturgical books printed for use in the Greco-Slavic Rite.[22] A comparison demonstrates irrefutably that this rite has come under monastic influence, while the old system of worship used

---

of the Dominicans, revised by Humbert of Romans (ca. 1200–1277), and formally approved by Clement IV (1265–68) in a bull dated July 7, 1267.

* Chap. 3 of *The Rule of the Franciscan Order* (1223) reads, "Clerics are to perform the divine office of the Roman Church, except for the Psalter, and they can have breviaries for that purpose." Available online at http://www.fordham. edu/halsall/source/stfran-rule.html. See p. 59.

† The Dayra 'Alita or Upper Monastery derived its moniker from being located on the highest point above the Tigris River in the city of Mosul. It was established by Gabriel of Kashkar (fl. seventh century), who founded several monasteries in the region, and its proper name honors him: the Monastery of Mar Gabriel. After Abraham bar Dashandad (fl. eighth century) became renowned as a teacher at the monastery, its name was changed to the Monastery of Mar Gabriel and Mar Abraham. The most prominent monastery in the East Syrian Church, it was significant for its liturgy, providing both stability and reform. The monastery reached the height of its strength and influence in the ninth and tenth centuries. The conversion of the Mongol dynasty to Islam in 1295 resulted in Nestorian Christianity being greatly reduced by the fourteenth century and the monastery disbanded in the sixteenth. On the Upper Monastery and its liturgical role, see Adolf Rücker, "Das 'Obere Kloster' bei Mossul und seine Bedeutung für die Ostsyrische Liturgie," *Oriens Christianus*, 3rd ser., 7 (1932): 180–87. See also http://adultera.awardspace.com/CHRON/ SYR/index.html.

at Hagia Sophia in Constantinople represents the earlier style.[23] For a very long time the rite used in the city of Rome firmly rejected the practice of singing hymns found in Western monasteries. It was not yet permitted in the Basilica of St. John Lateran when its prior, Bernard (d. 1176), who was elevated to become Cardinal Bishop of Porto in 1145,* wrote an *ordo officiorum*—as detailed as one can imagine—a comprehensive description of the worship celebrated there.[24†] In fact, for the singing of hymns to gain final acceptance into the Roman Breviary, the offices of an intermediary were required: the private chapel of the pope. But even that papal rite could not vanquish the rites celebrated in the ancient basilicas of Rome without the powerful support of the Franciscans, the popular order of mendicant friars. Radulf of Rivo (1350–1403) recognized this reality.‡ Time and again this valiant Dutch dean leveled bitter accusations against the Order of Friars Minor (the Franciscan Order). [25] Though hopes for reviving the ancient use of Rome were in vain, he fought a last-ditch effort right up to the turn of the fifteenth century.

---

* Baumstark's date is incorrect. Bernard (d. 1176) was elected bishop of the See of Porto and Santa Rufino in the suburbs of Rome in 1158; in 1145 he became cardinal priest of San Clemente. On Bernard, Bishop of Porto, see Short Biography, no. 34.

† Pope Alexander II (1060–72) brought canons regular from the canonry of San Frediano at Lucca in present-day Italy to the Basilica of St. John Lateran to care for its liturgy. Eventually they assumed pastoral duties as well. Being both the cathedral of the diocese of Rome and the residence of the popes when Bernard served as prior (see previous footnote and Short Biography, no. 34), the Lateran liturgies exercised great influence. His customary, *Ordo officiorum ecclesiae Lateranensis*, provides a most detailed description of the worship celebrated in this church. See "Canons Regular of St. John Lateran" on http://www.augustiniancanons.org/About/houses_and_congregations_through_copy(1).htm#First%20John%20Lateran.

‡ On Radulf of Rivo, see Short Biography, no. 152.

Notes

[1] A translation [into Latin] of the latter can be found in Renaudot, 2, 243–56. For the former text, see *Die Liturgien bei den Armeniern*, ed. Joseph Caterghian and P. J. Dashian (Wien [Vienna]: n.p., 1897), 120–58, although this work is not yet widely available.

2 For the oldest form in which this text has been preserved, see Brightman, 309–44.

3 Baumstark, *Messe,* 60f and 64f.

4 See, for example, the evidence assembled by Anton Baumstark in "Review: G. Richter, A Schönfelder, *Sacramentarium Fuldenses saeculi X,"* Roma e l'Oriente 5 (1912/13): 180.

5 Renaudot, 1, 57–85, and similarly 1–25.

6 See Brightman, LXXIV.

7 This is according to the *Life of Pachomius,* for example, in its Latin recension, *Vita Sancti Pachomii,* PL 73, col. 243.

8 This is according to the highly interesting report over the visit of John Moschus and Sophronius to Mt. Sinai. See Jean-Baptiste Pitra, *Juris ecclesiastici Graecorum historia et monumenta,* vol. 1 (Roma [Rome]: Bardi, 1868), 270.

9 Bk. 3, chap. 5, of the extensive liturgical commentary of Pseudo(?)-George of Arbela deals with a recitation of "the whole David" in the Night Office for feasts: Gïwargïs (Metropolitan of Arbela and Mosul), *Anonymi auctoris expositio officiorum ecclesiae Georgio Arbelensi vulgo adscripta,* vol. 1, ed. Richard Hugh Connolly, Corpus scriptorum Christianorum orientalium 64, = Scriptores Syri 25 (Parisiis [Paris]: E Typographeo Reipublicae, 1911 [repr., Louvain: L. Durbecq, 1954]), 225–31.

10 *Regula Sancti Benedicti,* chap. 18; GT: *Des heiligen Benediktus Mönchsregel,* trans. Pius Bihlmeyer, BKW 20 (Kempten & München [Munich]: Josef Kösel, 1914), 275 [ET: *The Rule of Saint Benedict,* trans. Leonard J. Doyle, ed. David W. Cotter (Collegeville, MN: Liturgical Press, 2001); Johnson, *Worship,* IV, no. 155: 4111–17].

11 Perhaps details in Egeria's description of Jerusalem worship in the fourth century point in this direction. Egeria, chap. 25, nos. 8–11. See Paul Geyer, *Itinera Hierosolymitana saeculi IV–VIII* (Wien [Vienna]: F. Tempsky, 1898) 75f; GT: Hermann Richter, *Pilgerreise der Ätheria (oder Silvia) von Aquitanien nach Jerusalem und die heiligen Stätten* (Essen: Baedeker, 1919), 55f [ET: *Egeria's Travels,* trans. John Wilkinson (London: SPCK, 1971), 127; Johnson, *Worship,* II, no. 83: 2174–75].

12 According to the witness of Cassian, *De coenobiorum institutis,* bk. 4 in PL 49, cols. 126–32 [Baumstark cites cols. 26–32. ET: John Cassian, *The Institutes,* trans. Boniface Ramsey, Ancient Christian Writers 58 (New York (u.a.): Newman Press, 2000). The text (as published in NPNF) is available online at http://www.newadvent.org/fathers/3507.htm; see also Johnson, *Worship,* III, no. 118-B (selections)].

13 Basil, Ὅροι κατά πλάτος [Greater *Asketikon*], chap. 37, nos. 2–5, PG 31, cols. 1011–16 [ET: Anna M. Silvas, *The Asketikon of St. Basil the Great* (Oxford: Oxford University Press, 2005); see also Johnson, *Worship,* II, no. 67-B and 67-C (selections)].

14 *Breviarium Armenium . . . nunc primum in latinam linguam translatum* (Venezia [Venice]: In Insula S. Lazzari, 1908), 239–90 [available through Google Books].

[15] The Μεσονυκτικόν, in which on Sundays the κανόνεσ Τριαδικοί songs in praise of the triune God were sung.

[16] In reference to the so-called ἀσματικὸς ῎Ορθροσ, see, for example the article by L. Petit, "Catacombes (les arts)," DACL 2, col. 2483.

[17] This is according to evidence from the old Armenian Lectionary. See Frederick Cornwallis Conybeare, *Rituale Armenorum* (Oxford, Clarendon Press, 1905), 507–27. For the Easter Vigil of the early Gallican Rite, apart from the pericopes of the Lectionary of Luxeuil (see in *Lectionarum Gallicanum* in PL 72, col. 194f.), the relevant series of prayers in the sacramentaries from Autun (see in *Missale Gothicum* in PL 72, cols. 270–73) and Auxerre (see in *Missale Francorum*, PL 72, cols. 365–67) needs to be considered.

[18] Baumer, 253.

[19] Ibid.

[20] Ibid., 319. Batiffol (Fr. ed.), 242f [ET: Batiffol (Eng. ed.), 160–65].

[21] Baumstark, *Perikopenordnungen*, 14–70. Baumstark, *Literatur*, 198.

[22] For a profound article offering some instructive revelations on this topic see, L. Petit, "Antiphone dans la liturgie Grecque," DACL 2, 2461–88.

[23] This was published by А. А. Дмитриевсий [transliteration of ed.: A. A. Dmitrievskij], Описание литургических рукописей, храняшихся в библиотеках Православного Востока. Т. 1: *Τυπικά* [transliteration of title: *Opisanie liturgičeskix rykopisej, xranyaščixsja v bibliotekax Pravoslavnogo Vostoka. T. 1: Τυπικά*; ET of title: *A Description of Liturgical Manuscripts Preserved in the Libraries of the Orthodox East*, vol. 1: *Typica*] (Киев [transliteration: Kiev]: n.p., 1895). [For a more recent critical edition of the same, see *Le Typicon de la Grande Église: Ms. Sainte-Croix no. 40, Xe siècle*, 2 vols., ed. Juan Mateos, Orientalia Christiana Analecta 165–66 (Roma [Rome]: Pontificium Institutum Orientalium Studiorum, 1962–63).]

[24] Bernhardi Cardinalis et Lateranensis ecclesiae Prioris, *Ordo officiorum ecclesiae Lateranensis*, ed. Ludwig Fischer, Historische Quellen und Forschungen 2, 3 (München [Munich]-Freising: Dr. F. P. Datterer & Cie. [A. Sellier], 1916).

[25] On this remarkable man and his literary legacy, see Leo Kunibert Mohlberg, *Radulph de Rivo der letzte Vertreter der altrömischen Liturgie*, vol. 1: Studien, vol. 2: Texte (Louvain: Bureaux de recueil, 1911).

Chapter 10

The Work of the Individual

The liturgy has—as an essential feature—the character and quality of an object. In importance this feature of the liturgy ranks only after the fact that the liturgy is anchored in the *sensus communis* of the church and an immediate consequence of that fact.* When the communion of the faithful encounters God, there is no room for subjectivism. For every individual soul participating in that communion, the experience of the encounter subordinates and integrates each and every stirring, from the most sublime to the most profound. The way the liturgy develops is also impersonal in the main. Rather than being a conscious creation, something an individual wills into being, the liturgy and its forms—what is said and what is done—grow. It doesn't seem like the work of individuals, but rather like a product of universal preconditions, forces stimulating its growth, and contrasts. In the final analysis, of course, the impersonal character of liturgical development is only apparent. For in the end, all apparently impersonal development is actually only the sum of numerous efforts by individuals whose names are now lost to history. Every single turn of phrase must

---

* *Sensus communis* is a philosophical concept originating with Aristotle (384–22 BCE), who held it to be the sixth sense, integrating the input of sight, hearing, taste, smell, and touch into coherent notions. Christian thinkers of the nineteenth century employed it to refute the challenge Enlightenment thought posed for revealed truth. Hugues Félicité Robert de Lamennais (1782–1854) drew upon it to assert the certitude of the faith and tradition, arguing that certitude is to be found in the *raison générale* or *sens commun*, the conviction held by men in general, which itself participates in the omniscience of God and is therefore infallible. De Lamennais further claimed that the church expresses truth at its most sublime. In this passage, Baumstark desires to assert the objective nature of the liturgy within the communal context of the church and its faith. For a discussion of *sensus communis* as a philosophical concept, see CE, s.v. "Common Sense, Philosophy of," and LTK, s.v. "Sensus communis." For Lamennais, see *New Catholic Encyclopedia* (Detroit: Thomson/Gale; Washington, DC: Catholic University of America Press, 2003), s.v. "Lamennais, Hugues Félicité Robert de."

at one time or another have been uttered by a particular individual; every single ritual movement must have first been introduced by a specific person. When the innovation of these individuals hardens into form, their words and gestures live on for centuries. But as individuals they disappear. Just as itinerant poets recede behind epic poems that are genuinely of the people, so too do these individuals recede behind their liturgical creations.

To be sure, there are exceptions. By no means are all liturgical texts, even those in prose form, anonymous—either as they have been handed down, or even as they were originally conceived. It goes without saying that whenever compositions of liturgical prose are attributed to a particular author, that claim must be judged—on prin-ciple—with a healthy dose of skepticism. The attribution of eucharistic liturgies to particular personages often indicates no more than its place of origin, that is, the liturgical center where it came into being. This is the case, for example, with eucharistic liturgies whose origins lie in apostolic times or epochs of intense dogmatic controversy. The formulary of a particular ecclesiastical center was associated with the actual or legendary apostolic founder of the church there or with its leading figure (in the opinion of the dogmatic party concerned). One should understand the attributions of liturgies to particular persons in this light: the Liturgy of St. James, the Liturgy of St. Mark, the Liturgy of St. Cyril, the Liturgy of Nestorius, and the Divine Liturgy of St. John Chrysostom.* In other cases, the reasons for choosing the banner of

---

* For most items on this list, the liturgy and the person are associated with the same place. Thus St. James and the liturgy named after him are associated with Jerusalem, and St. Mark and St. Cyril and the liturgies named after them with Alexandria. The Liturgy of St. Cyril is the old Alexandrian Anaphora of St. Mark, one of the three Coptic liturgies of Egypt. Finally, both John Chrysostom and the Divine Liturgy named after him are associated with Constantinople. In each case, the person to whom the liturgy is ascribed lived (in fact or by tradition) in the city from which the liturgy derived. The exception to this rule is Nestorius (on Nestorius, see Short Biography, no. 127) for whom a liturgy is named in the East Syrian Church. He neither lived in Persia nor spoke Syriac; he was not a leading personage in the East Syrian Church, in the sense that James (on James, see Short Biography, no. 105), Mark, Cyril (on Cyril, see Short Biography, no. 58), and Chrysostom (on Chrysostom, see Short Biography, no. 47) were for their respective cities. While the East Syrian Church has been referred to in the West as "the Nestorian Church," this church itself does not claim the name. On the other hand, adherents to Nestorianism did flee to

one person or another to fly as a false flag over a liturgy or prayer remain unknown. While undoubtedly no less pseudo-epigraphical, what led to the choice remains lost to history. Thus we are left to wonder why the Egyptian type of eucharistic liturgy, which directs all prayers to Christ, was linked directly to Gregory of Nazianzus (330–89/90);* why the Roman Pope Gregory the Great (590–604)[†] is regarded as the editor of the Byzantine Mass of the Presanctified;[1] why the Alexandrian Athanasius (296–337)[‡] is held to be the author of the liturgy ordinarily celebrated by the Armenians;[2][§] why particular eucharistic texts, used later by the Jacobites, specified as their authors this or that particular apostle, follower of an apostle, Roman pope, or Greek theologian. The names of these authors made their appearance above these texts at the beginning of the seventh or at the turn of the eighth centuries, when they were translated—some of them even twice—out of the Greek into Syriac.[3] A similar question has to remain unanswered also about documents of the eucharistic liturgy in Armenian and Ethiopic (Ge'ez).[¶]

In some instances, however, the accuracy of authorial attribution is beyond doubt, as in the case of certain Eastern texts containing liturgical formularies for the Mass. Falling into this category is certainly the eucharistic prayer of Serapion of Thmuis (d. after 360)** (dating from the early days of the liturgy), as well as very probably the Liturgy

---

the east and one of the three liturgies used by the East Syrian Church (along with the Liturgy of the Apostles and the Liturgy of Theodore of Mopsuestia) is known as the Liturgy of Nestorius. What city Baumstark may have had in mind as a home for the Liturgy of Nestorius is less clear. He might have meant Edessa, the historical center of this church and a center for learning, although the ecclesiastical center for the East Syrian Church became Seleucia-Ctesiphon. On the other hand, this liturgy may simply be an example of one named after a person held to be important, as Baumstark writes, "in the opinion of the dogmatic party concerned" (p. 150).

* On Gregory Nazianzus, see Short Biography, no. 84.

[†] The Liturgy of the Presanctified, used on those days in Lent when the Divine Liturgy is not celebrated, bears the title "The Liturgy of St. Gregory the Great." On Gregory the Great, see Short Biography, no. 78.

[‡] On Athanasius, see Short Biography, no. 22.

[§] This is the Liturgy of St. Athanasius, known in Armenia and West Syria.

[¶] On Ethiopic (Ge'ez), see n. on p. 93.

** On this prayer, see p. 91. On Serapion, see Short Biography, no. 157.

of Basil (330–79)* and perhaps the Liturgy of Theodore of Mopsuestia (350–428).[4†] Neither should we in any way ignore this question: Why could certain Syrian princes of the Jacobite Church not have actually authored eucharistic texts for its use? These were handed down as their creations, sporadically from the seventh to ninth centuries, but mainly just between the eleventh and the fifteenth. In Spain—just as reliably—one learns the identities of particular individuals who authored a series of Mass formularies, inaugurated by one Bishop Peter of Lerida (fl. fifth to sixth centuries),[‡] around the middle of the sixth century at the very latest.[5] We also ought not to question the credibility of the claim that Pope Gelasius I (492–96)[§] authored some formularies of the Roman Mass.[¶]

As with liturgical prose, texts of liturgical poetry are frequently passed on anonymously, or with a great deal of uncertainty about the reliability of the tradition that ascribes them to a particular poet. In this regard, the branch of liturgical tradition that brings us poetry in old Syriac offers very few guarantees. Of the Latin hymns that the Middle Ages held to be Ambrosian, only the smallest fraction can claim to actually stem from the great Milanese (ca. 339–97).[**] However, the authenticity of those few hymns actually written by Ambrose can still be definitively ascertained.[6] No less incontestably, Ephrem the Syrian (306–73)[††] is the genuine author of elements in the Jacobite[‡‡] and Maronite[§§] liturgies. One determines their authenticity by comparing them with poetry whose literary transmission, guaranteed by manuscripts dated as early as the fifth to sixth centuries,[7] has an excellent claim to being actually composed by the Syrian poet. From the thirteenth to the sixteenth centuries a late spring of song flourished in the Syriac lan-

---

* For a discussion of this liturgy, see pp. 140–41. On Basil, see Short Biography, no. 28.

† This is the Liturgy of Theodore of Mopsuestia, a liturgy in the sphere of the Antiochene Rite of West Syria, but also translated into Syriac for use in the East Syrian Church. On Theodore of Mopsuestia, see Short Biography, no. 175.

‡ On Peter of Lerida, see Short Biography, no. 139.

§ On Gelasius, see Short Biography, no. 75.

¶ On liturgy attributed to Gelasius, see p. 120.

** On Ambrose, see Short Biography, no. 11.

†† On Ephrem the Syrian, see Short Biography, no. 66.

‡‡ See n. on p. 105.

§§ See n. on p. 47.

guage, some of which made its way into the inventory of hymns used by the Nestorian Office. Despite some instability in this tradition, the attribution of those latter hymns to individual poets remains firmly documented.[8] As to the authorship of the texts of liturgical poetry that flooded into the Byzantine Rite: this tradition does not warrant our fundamental distrust—at least as a general stance.[9] To eliminate any possibility that the tradition of their authorship might be lost to obscurity, these poets frequently stated their names acrostically.[10] Equally well attested are the authors of poetic texts for some Latin hymns, in many cases valued as the jewels in the crown of this tradition and used in the liturgy to this day.[11] It will suffice to recall the following hymns from an earlier time: the Lenten hymns of Venantius Fortunatus (ca. 530–610);* the Palm Sunday hymn of Bishop Theodulf of Orléans (ca. 750–821) (notwithstanding an ahistorical legend associated with it);† "Veni Creator" by Rabanus Maurus, Archbishop of Mainz (ca. 780–856);‡ the Easter sequence§ authored by Wipo (ca. 990–after 1048),¶ the court chaplain of the first two Salian emperors, Conrad II (1024–39), and Henry III (1026–56);** or "Salve Regina." This heartfelt salutation is the creation of Herman the Lame (1013–54),†† endowed with a lively spirit. Every hour

---

* Baumstark is here likely referring to *Vexilla regis* and *Pange lingua gloriosi*, which were sung in the Office of the Roman Rite in Holy Week and in the liturgy on Good Friday. Outside of Holy Week, they were sung at various feasts of the cross. Baumstark incorrectly dates Fortunatus' death as 606. On Fortunatus, see Short Biography, no. 71.

† The hymn referred to here is *Gloria, Laus, et Honor*, known in English as "All Glory, Laud, and Honor," which became the processional on Palm Sunday for the Western church. The legend to which Baumstark refers recounts that Theodulf composed this hymn while imprisoned in Angers for conspiring against Louis I or the Pious (781–840; emperor from 814). One day, as Louis was riding past the prison, he heard Theodulf singing the hymn from his cell window. Struck by its beauty, Louis freed him and restored his bishopric. On Theodulf of Orléans, see Short Biography, no. 178. On Louis I, see Short Biography, no. 119.

‡ On Rabanus Maurus, see Short Biography, no. 151.

§ The sequence referred to here is *Victimae paschali laudes*, which was sung in the Western church on Easter Day and used by Luther (1483–1546) in his hymn *Christ lag in Todesbanden*.

¶ In the German text, Baumstark gave his death date as 1046. On Wipo, see Short Biography, no. 191.

** On the Salian dynasty, see n. on p. 124.

†† On Herman the Lame, see Short Biography, no. 94.

of his earthly life this noble monk of Reichenau battled with a most miserable affliction. As a stepchild of nature, lame from birth, Herman had to overcome the weakness and malformation of a crippled body. It is from his exile "in this vale of tears"* that "Salve Regina" seeks, with yearning, the sweet queen of heavenly mercy.

During later centuries, in regions where Greek was spoken, individuals, whose names are often still known, also composed complete *acolouthias* (so-called),† services incorporating all of the material sung on a particular saint's day. During the second millennium a corresponding development is found in the West as well, on "Roman soil," where more and more often the whole Office was reworked by individuals known by name. That the Office for the feast of Corpus Christi was authored by Thomas Aquinas (1225–75)‡ is only the best-known example of this development. The prince of scholasticism created this thoughtful office, including its sonorous hymns, in 1264.§ The oldest example of this development is the creation of the Office of the Holy Trinity¶ by Bishop Stephen of Liège (ca. 850–920),** completed well before the turn of the millennium, between 903 and 920.[12]††

These liturgical creations appeared in both the East and the West at a time when the cathedral of Christian liturgy, its foundations having been laid in early Christian times, had only just been completed. The

---

* This is a translation of a line from the hymn *Salve Regina*, which reads, "in hac lacrimarum valle."

† The Byzantine Rite employs the term *acolouthia* (also transliterated *akalouthia* and *akolouthia*) to refer to an order of service for the Divine Office. However, the term may also connote the fixed sequence of any liturgical service. In other writings, Baumstark uses the term in this broader sense. See Anton Baumstark, *Comparative Liturgy*, trans. F. L. Cross (London: A. R. Mowbray & Co., 1958), 31.

‡ On Thomas Aquinas, see Short Biography, no. 180.

§ According to a disciple of Thomas, Pope Urban IV (1261–64) asked Thomas Aquinas (1124–75) to compose this office for Corpus Christi, newly created by the pope in 1264.

¶ The *Micrologus*, written during the pontificate of Gregory VII (1073–85), calls the Sunday after Pentecost a *Dominica vacans*, one with no special office. It goes on to say, however, that on this day some places recite the Office of the Holy Trinity composed by Stephen, bishop of Liège (ca. 850–920). On Gregory VII, see Short Biography, no. 81.

** On Stephen of Liège, see Short Biography, no. 167.

†† Stephen became bishop of Liège in 901, not 903 as Baumstark states.

question of paramount importance for liturgical history is whether individual efforts at organizing the liturgy also decisively affected how the liturgy developed in its formative periods. Did individual efforts at organizing the liturgy redirect its course? And did that even occur back in those very periods when the liturgy was taking shape? Although it was certainly always something of an anomaly for individuals to intervene in the development of the liturgy, this question should—without a doubt—be answered in the affirmative.

The liturgical activity of Musaeus (d. 457/61),* a presbyter in Marseilles, extends back beyond the middle of the fifth century.[13] Masilia (Marseilles) was the harbor for the early Phocian colony, a merchant power in its day,† which must once have functioned as the natural gateway for Christian missionaries working their way into Gaul. Upon the urging of his bishop, Venerius (431–52),‡ Musaeus chose biblical passages for the liturgical year to be read at daily prayer, along with corresponding antiphons for the psalmody to be sung. Indeed, a "Sacramentary," which Musaeus dedicated to Eustasius (fl. fifth century), Venerius' successor as bishop in Marseilles,§ was in fact nothing less than a sort of plenary missal,¶ the earliest known of its kind. In addition to offering propers for prayer texts, this volume also provided ones from Scripture (the biblical pericopes to be read) and the psalm verses to be sung at each Mass celebrated on a particular day or occasion. Thus, at a remarkably early date, the liturgies for the Office and Mass celebrated in that Phocian colony underwent a conscious reconfiguration executed by a single individual for the purpose of introducing an element of uniformity.

Apparently the reign of Severus (ca. 465–538), the Monophysite patriarch of Antioch from 512 to 518,** carried a similar significance for the

---

* On Musaeus, see Short Biography, no. 126.

† See n. on p. 99.

‡ On Bishop Venerius, see Short Biography, no. 185.

§ On Bishop Eustasius, see Short Biography, no. 69.

¶ A plenary missal was a missal containing all the parts required to celebrate the Mass: those for the celebrant, liturgical ministers, and choir. Previous to its development, these parts had been divided among various liturgical books: Sacramentary, Epistolary, Evangeliary, and Antiphonary. Plenary missals came into wide use by the second half of the ninth century. Cyrille Vogel expressly rejects Baumstark's categorization of this document as a *missale plenum*. See Cyrille Vogel, *Medieval Liturgy: An Introduction to the Sources*, trans. and rev. William Storey and Niels Rasmussen (Washington, DC: Pastoral Press, 1986), 51.

** On Severus, see Short Biography, no. 159.

church in West and East Syria. In the sphere of the Jacobite Rite, a series of liturgical texts bearing his name has been preserved in Syriac translation. Of two eucharistic items: (1) A formulary for the Liturgy of the Mass of the Presanctified belongs to texts that had already undergone translation, some of them even for a second time, around the turn of the eighth century at the latest.[14] (2) From a Mass liturgy there are preserved—in addition to fragments in Syriac—one in the original Greek and others in translation (one each into Sahidic and Bohairic Coptic*). In both cases, there is every reason to regard their attribution to Severus as authentic.[15] Concerning a redacted version of the Jacobite baptismal liturgy, the relationship of its prayer for consecrating the water to that found in the Byzantine Rite is actually only one indication of its very great antiquity. Even the write, Pseudo-Dionysius the Areopagite (fl. ca. 500)[†] appears to refer to these words, which are said as the holy oil is mixed with the baptismal waters.[16][‡] The hymnbook of Severus,[§] translated into Syriac around 619, experienced some further additions, but only later, in the Thomas Monastery at Qenneshre[¶] on the Euphrates.[17]

---

* For Sahidic and Bohairic Coptic, see n. on p. 93.

† On Dionysius the Pseudo-Areopagite, see Short Biography, no. 63.

‡ The liturgy to which Baumstark alludes (see n. 16 of this chap. and Denzinger, *Ritus orientalium*, 276, 307, and 314) directs the priest to pour oil into the water of the baptismal font in the form of a cross with the words (translated into Latin) "Ecce effundimus sanctum chrisma super aquas istas baptismi, ut per eas vetus homo in novum evadat" and provides the prayer to follow. As Pseudo-Dionysus describes the ritual without quoting any prayer, Baumstark can only surmise that this writer is alluding to the prayer found in the order ascribed to Severus (on Severus, see Short Biography, no. 159).

§ It is reported that Severus of Antioch (ca. 465–538) composed a book in the sixth century containing eight Sunday offices, one for each tone. Of the 365 hymns found in the *Octoeches* of Syria, 295 are attributed to Severus (on Severus, see Short Biography, no. 159). Paul of Edessa (fl. seventh century) translated it into Syriac between 619 and 629. Jacob of Edessa (ca. 633–708) revised it in 675 (on Jacob of Edessa, see Short Biography, no. 103).

¶ This monastery on the Euphrates is distinct from the St. Thomas Monastery located outside of Antioch in Seleucia on the Orontes. Forced to flee from western Syria on account of his Monophysite beliefs, John bar Aphtonia (475/80–537) withdrew to Qenneshre (ET: "eagle's nest") on the left bank of the Euphrates, opposite Europus (or Oropus). As superior, he developed this monastic community into a center of study for Greek and Syriac letters, and it remained so for generations. Although the exact site of this monastic founda-

The historicity of one last example is confirmed plain for all to see: a reconfiguration of the whole Nestorian Rite, the result of an individual effort around the middle of the seventh century. This undertaking, which primarily involved providing an organizing principle for the liturgical year and the festal breviary,* was implemented by the Catholicos Ishoyabh III (647/50–59),† who stood at the helm of the Nestorian Church from 647 to 648, or 650 to 651, or 657 to 658.[18] Soon after completion,‡ it became the subject of a commentary by one Gabriel from Bet Qatraye§ (fl. sixth to seventh centuries).[19]¶ The effect of Gabriel's commentary was enduring, still evident even in an extensive

––––––––––

tion is no longer known, its place-name suggests a high location in the mountains. See A. S. Atiya, *A History of Eastern Christianity* (London; Methuen Co., 1968), 195–96, n. 3; EEC, s.v. "John bar Aphtonia"; and Jules Leroy, *Monks and Monasteries of the Near East* (London: George G. Harrap & Co., 1963), 147–48. For Quenneshre or Kennesrin (Chalcis ad Belum), see Arthur Vööbus, *History of Asceticism in the Syrian Orient*, vol. 2, Corpus Scriptorum Christianorum Orientalium 197 (Louvain: Secrétariat du Corpus SCO, 1960), 248–50.

* This festal breviary (*Hudra* or *Kudra*, literally meaning "circle" in English) contains the variable chants and prayers (propers) for the Office and Mass of all the days of the year, of the Feasts of the Lord, and during the Ninevite Feast. See Mateos, *Lelya-Sapra; essai d'interprétation des matines chaldéennes*, Orientalia Christiana Analecta 156 (Roma [Rome]: Pontificium Institutum Orientalium Studiorum, 1959), 489.

† On Ishoyabh III, see Short Biography, no. 101.

‡ Contrary to Baumstark's claim, Gabriel of Qatar (fl. sixth/seventh century) wrote his commentary before the liturgical reforms of Ishoyabh III (647/50–59). See Sebastian P. Brock, "Gabriel of Qatar's Commentary on the Liturgy," *Hugoye: Journal of Syriac Studies* 6:2 (2003): 1–25, also available online at http://syrcom.cua.edu/Hugoye/Vol6No2/HV6N2Brock.html#S4; and Adam H. Hecker, *Fear of God and the Beginning of Wisdom* (Philadelphia: University of Pennsylvania Press, 2006), 1–6.

§ Bet Qatraye (ET: The Islands) is a province of the Nestorian Church located on the Arabian Peninsula to the northeast. It lies along the Persian Gulf and includes present-day Bahrain—along with the coast opposite it, the al-Hasa' oasis—and present-day Qatar, which takes its name from it. This province, with its mixed Aramaic and Persian culture, contained a number of bishoprics. It flourished during the Sassanian period (see n. on p. 56) and for some time after the Arab invasion. Geoffroy R. King, "The Coming of Islam and the pre-Islamic Period in UAE," *The United Arab Emirates: A New Perspective*, ed. Ibrahim Abed and Peter Hellyer (London: Trident Press, 2001), 79.

¶ On Gabriel of Qatar, see Short Biography, no. 73.

liturgical commentary written in the tenth or eleventh century, where its influence is striking for being so direct.[20]

The three examples just discussed—the work of Musaeus, Severus, and Ishoyabh III—all run counter to the impersonality that normally characterizes the development of the liturgy. They lead us to reflect upon one of the most important questions in the history of the Roman Rite. In a letter to one Bishop John of Syracuse (fl. sixth to seventh centuries),* Gregory the Great personally attests to innovations he introduced to the Roman liturgy and defends them against the contention that they were inspired by the example of Constantinople.[21] At present, we do not know how far this visionary pope carried the liturgical innovations he embraced as his life's work. The fact is that the copies of the Roman liturgical books—the Sacramentary and books containing chants—that made their way across the Alps during the Carolingian era, traced their texts back to Gregory. He is also named as editor of a scheme of versification in dactylic hexameter, which in various forms was placed at the front of these chant books. This scheme was held in such high esteem that a series of verses taken from it were sung to introduce the introit of the Mass, even in worship services on the First Sunday in Advent.[22] This practice was initiated during the papacy of Hadrian II (867–72)† at the very latest.

How plausible is this traditional view, taken on its own merits? Did the first Benedictine to occupy the throne of Peter have the latitude to do for the Roman liturgy what Musaeus had done—fully a century and a half earlier—for the liturgy of Marseilles? This much is clear: one finds no reason in the tradition to mistrust it. Only a misguided hypercritic could wish to dispute that the Roman liturgy bears the stamp of an individual. Like the Nestorian liturgy under Ishoyabh III, the Roman liturgy was systematically organized upon the initiative of Gregory the Great. It is true that the copies of Gregorian books that later came into the Frankish kingdom—one and a half to two centuries after this pope's death—show signs of development. However, this observation alters our conclusion not one iota. The interpolations incorporated into these books were due to the liturgical progress that had taken place as a matter of course in the interim. Thus, by way of example, (1) the Sacramentary included the Mass for Thursdays in

---

* On John of Syracuse, see Short Biography, no. 110.
† On Hadrian II, see Short Biography, no. 87.

Lent introduced by Gregory II (715–31),* and (2) all liturgical books accommodated the various feasts that had enriched the calendar since the time of Gregory the Great.[23]

---

* For a discussion of this liturgical development, see p. 57. On Gregory II, see Short Biography, no. 79.

Notes

[1] Brightman, 345–52.

[2] For an English translation of the Armenian, see Brightman, 434–55.

[3] Baumstark, *Literatur*, 266f.

[4] For a Latin translation of the Greek Text, see Renaudot 2, 610–19.

[5] According to Isidore of Seville, *De viris illustribus*, chap. 13 (PL 83, 1090).

[6] In *Hymnographi latini: lateinische Hymnendichter des Mittelalters*, 2nd ser., eds. Clemens Blume and Guido Maria Dreves, AH 50 (Leipzig: O. R. Reisland, 1907; repr. Frankfurt am Main: Minerva, 1961), 10–21 [ET: (with Latin text and commentary) Matthew Britt, *The Hymns of the Breviary and Missal* (New York, Cincinnati, Chicago: Benziger Brothers, 1924), nos. 1–18].

[7] See Baumstark, *Literatur*, 40f.

[8] Ibid., 302–6, 321–25, and 329–35.

[9] Yet—from a critical perspective—compare this with the uncertainty that weighs upon the material that is found in the liturgical books attributed to John of Damascus. See Wilhelm Weyh, "Die Akrostichis in der byzantinischen Kanonesdichtung," BZ 17 (1908): 30ff.

[10] See the foundational works by Karl Krumbacher, "Die Akrostichis in der griechischen Kirchenpoesie," *Sitzungsbericht der Bayrischen Akademie der Wissenschaften 1903* (München [Munich]: Franz in Komm, 1903), 551–691, and Weyh, "Die Akrostichis," 1–69.

[11] The best collection of these is to be found in Blume and Dreves, *Hymnographi latini und Thesauri hymnologici hymnarium: Die Hymnen des Thesaurus hymnologicus H. A. Daniels und anderer Hymnen-Ausgaben*, vol. 1, *Die Hymnen des 5.–11. Jahrhunderts und die irisch-keltische Hymnodie aus den ältesten Quellen*, eds. Hermann Adalbert Daniel and Clemens Blume, AH 51 (Leipzig: Reisland, 1908 [repr. Frankfurt am Main: Minerva, 1961]).

[12] Batiffol (Fr. ed.), 201; ET: Batiffol (Eng. ed.), 134.

[13] According to Gennadius of Massilia, *De Scriptoribus Ecclesiasticis* [Baumstark cites this work as *De vir. Ill.*, an abbreviation for *De viris illustribus*], chap. 79 in PL 58, cols. 1103–4 [ET: Jerome and Gennadius, *Lives of Illustrious Men*, NPNF, 2nd ser., vol. 3, 398, cited as chap. 80; Johnson, *Worship*, III, no.124-B: 3068 (selection)].

[14] With a translation published by Humphrey William Codrington, "The Syrian Liturgies of the Presanctified," *Journal of Theological Studies* 4 (1903): 73–81. See also Baumstark, *Literatur*, 267.

[15] See Anton Baumstark, "Die syrische Anaphora des Severus von Antiocheia," JLW 2 (1922): 92–98.

[16] Pseudo-Dionysius the Areopagite, *Τῆς ἐκκλησιαστικῆς ἱεραρχίας* [The Ecclesiastical Hierarchy], chap. 2, no. 2, VII, PG 3, col. 396; GT: *Des Heiligen Dionysius Areopagita, Angebliche Schriften über die beiden hierarchien*, ed. Josef Stiglmayr, Hermann Bourier, and Leonhard Fendt, BKV, 2nd ser. (Kempten & München [Munich]: Josef Kösel, 1911), 106 [ET: *The Ecclesiastical Hierarchy*, trans. Thomas L. Campbell (Washington, DC: University Press of America, 1981); Johnson, *Worship*, IV, no. 185-A: 4862]. A Latin translation of the Severus formulary itself is found in Heinrich Denzinger, *Ritus orientalium, Coptorum, Syrorum et Armenorum in administrandis sacramentis*, vol. 1 (Wirceburgi [Würzburg]: Stahel, 1863 [repr., publishing the 2 vols. in 1, Graz: Akademische Druck- und Verlagsanstalt, 1961), available through Google Books], 302–16.

[17] For a translation, see *The Hymns of Severus and Others in the Syriac Version of Paul of Edessa as revised by James of Edessa*, ed. and trans. Ernest W. Brooks, Patrologia Orientalis 6, fasc. 1 (Paris: Firmin-Didot, 1909 [repr., Turnhout: Brepols, 2003]), 593–802. See also Anton Baumstark, *Festbrevier und Kirchenjahr der syrischen Jakobiten*, SGKA, vol. 3:3–5 (Paderborn: Schöningh, 1910 [repr., New York: Johnson Reprint, 1967]), 45–47, and Baumstark, "Ein Kirchengesangbuch des frühen sechsten Jahrhunderts," *Wissenschaftliche Beilage zur "Germania" Blätter für Literatur, Wissenschaft und Kunst* (1912): 129–34 [this citation could not be confirmed], and Baumstark, *Literatur*, 253.

[18] Baumstark, *Literatur*, 197–200.

[19] Ibid., 200f.

[20] See chap. 9, n. 9. See also in *Anonymi auctoris expositio officiorum ecclesiae Georgio Arbelensi vulgo adscripta*, vol. 1, ed. Richard Hugh Connolly, Corpus Scriptorum Christianorum Orientalium 64 = Scriptores Syri 25 (Parisiis [Paris]: E Typographeo Reipublicae, 1911 [repr., Louvain: L. Durbecq, 1954]), 239 [ET: for an article including the Syriac text, the text in English, and a bibliography, see Sebastian P. Brock, "Gabriel of Qatar's Commentary on the Liturgy," *Hugoye: Journal of Syriac Studies* 6:2 (2003): 1–25, also available online at http://syrcom.cua.edu/Hugoye/Vol6No2/HV6N2Brock.html#S4].

[21] For the passage referenced in this letter of Gregory the Great to Bishop John of Syracuse, see *Registri Epistolarum*, Liber IX, Epistola XII, PL 77, cols. 935–38 [ET: Gregory the Great, "Epistle XII," in Schaff and Wace, NPNF, ser. 2, vol. 13, 8–9; see also Johnson, *Worship*, IV, no. 165-A-17 (selection)].

[22] Various recensions of this piece can be found in *Tropi Graduales*, vol. 2, *Tropen zum Proprium Missarum*, ed. Clemens Blume, AHMA 49 (Leipzig: Reisland, 1906), 19–42 [the section dealing specifically with the First Sunday in Advent is to be found on pp. 9–25].

²³ However, one must reject altogether the view that Louis Marie Olivier Duchesne represents concerning the Sacramentary sent by Hadrian I to Charlemagne and the actual Gregorian Sacramentary. Rather than tracing the former back to the latter, he hypothesizes that a difference exists between the two that goes to their very core, whereby the Gregorian Sacramentary—interspersed with Gallican material—is in fact to be found in the so-called *Gelesianum*.

Chapter 11

Language and Nation

In both the East and the West, liturgical development proceeded from the same set of preconditions, was governed by the same dynamics, and frequently manifested forms that corresponded closely to one another, even in particulars. Yet, when taken as a whole, the final product of that developmental process presents a bold contrast, that between the Byzantine Rite and the Frankish-Roman Rite. How does one explain this? A comparison of the liturgy of the West with that of the East reveals features that are—without any question—quite pronounced. What brought this about? What conditioned the kind of liturgy characteristic of Rome and the Western church that it led?

Without any doubt the key for answering these questions is language and race.* These two cultural forces create—in every case—the strongest bond able to hold a nation together, but also—and for that very reason—the sharpest division able to hold two nations apart. From the moment that the Good News was proclaimed beyond the borders of Palestine, a region of miniscule size, the mother tongue of Christian worship and preaching was Greek, the language of the New Testament. Then the gospel was proclaimed further afield, beyond the areas where Greek was spoken, primarily eastward into Aramaic-speaking Mesopotamia and neighboring Adiabene,† and westward where Latin was the dominant tongue. Given this pattern one cannot deny that the position held by the Nestorian Rite is absolutely unique,

---

* Here and elsewhere in this chapter, Baumstark uses the word *Blut*, which I have translated each time as *race*.

† Once a northern province of Mesopotamia, in the Christian era Adiabene was a small kingdom to the east of the Tigris River, roughly in the area of the Little Zab and Great Zab Rivers in present-day Iraq. Ca. 45 CE its ruler, Izates (d. 55 CE), along with his mother and brother, converted to Judaism. It subsequently became Christian. See *The Oxford Dictionary of the Jewish Religion*, eds. R. J. Zwi Werblowsky and Geoffroy Wigoder (New York and London: Oxford University Press, 1997), s.v. "Adiabene"; see also *The Times Atlas of World History*, 4th ed., ed. Geoffroy Barraclough (London: Hammond, 1994), 102–3.

even among liturgies in the East. Its position stems from the rite being heir to the early Christian liturgy of the Sassanian Empire (227–635) and is based upon the contrast, present from the outset, between Greek and Aramaic,* the former language being used in West Syria, the latter spoken to the north and east.†

In the West, the true homeland of Latin Christianity was not Rome but North Africa. Cornelius (251–53)‡ was the first pope to have a Latin inscription on his grave—not immediately after his death in 253, but only when this martyr's remains were returned to Rome. Well into the second half of the third century, the official language of the Christian community in Rome was Greek. The oldest echo of its liturgy we come across is written in Greek, a passage from Clement's Letter to the Corinthians.§ Also, at least one of the prayer texts found in the *Apostolic Tradition* of Hippolytus, the prayer for the consecration of a bishop, is preserved in its Greek original.¶ Neither in this Greek text, nor in pieces Hippolytus wrote for the liturgy found only in translation, do we encounter anything that stands out noticeably for its Roman character in a liturgy that was, in all other respects, Greek. The quality that came to mark Roman liturgical speech evolved only after the Roman liturgy had changed clothes—linguistically speaking. The difference one hears between the liturgies of Rome and those in the East stems fundamentally from linguistic genius. The *ordo* and Canon of the

---

* On the Aramaic language, see n. on p. 5. On the Sassanian Empire see n. on p. 48.

† For the christological controversies that have relevance here, see n. on p. 48.

‡ On Cornelius, see Short Biography, no. 54.

§ The echo of which Baumstark writes is a possible reference to the *Sanctus* (1 Cor 34:6f). Baumstark discusses this letter on p. 66. On Clement of Rome, see Short Biography, no. 51.

¶ On the literary tradition referred to as "The Apostolic Tradition," see n. on p. 67; on Hippolytus, see Short Biography, no. 97. The passage of *The Apostolic Tradition* that could possibly be extant in the original Greek is the prayer for consecrating a bishop found in the epitome of book 8 of the *Apostolic Constitutions*. However, this prayer has also been seen as a translation into Greek from another language. See Christoph Markshies, "Wer Schrieb die sogenannte *Traditio Apostolica*? Neue Beobachtungen und Hypothesen zu einer kaum lösbaren Frage aus der altkirchen Literaturgeschichte," in Wolfram Kinzig, Christoph Markshies, and Markus Vinzent, *Tauffragen und Bekenntnis*, Arbeiten zur Kirchengeschichte 74 (New York: de Gruyter, 1999), 15–19.

Roman Mass have often been translated into Greek. Perhaps it is these translations that bring out most clearly the difference in style between liturgical speech stemming from Latin and Greek. The artistry at work in the older prayers of the city of Rome is unrivaled. Expressing thought with economy and precision, these prayers could only have evolved in that part of the world where Latin was spoken.

Such a contrast is not seen in the East, that is, between liturgies in Greek—the root language form of all liturgical speech—and those in other languages. Indeed, one does not find in the East a contrast in style arising out of differences in language that even begins to be so strong as that found between the liturgy of Rome and those in Greek. This is because Eastern liturgy was touched to its very soul by Hellenization, a pervasive influence experienced throughout the Orient.* Stranger still, even the non-Roman (that is, the pre-Roman) liturgies of Gaul and Spain, stylistically speaking, are far closer to the East than to Rome—despite their use of Latin. This last example helps us gauge the importance of the Roman race for liturgical formation.

One process can be seen to be everywhere at work: national customs, which reflected the orientation and values of their own root cultures, but had been suppressed with the rise of Christianity and seemingly buried under a Hellenistic veneer, acquired renewed importance. Two different aspects of culture show this process in equal measure at work: the way the art of Christianity evolved and how Christian literature flourished in languages other than Greek.[2] It will come as no surprise that the historical law governing this process worked to the benefit of not only the Semitic and Coptic "barbarians"[†] but also the Roman people, with their distinctive national character and religious sensibilities. That national character sustained the

---

* On Hellenization, see n. on p. 74.

† In applying the word "barbarian" to the Semitic and Coptic language groups, Baumstark is eliciting its original connotation. On the impression that non-Greeks spoke gibberish, sounding to them like "bar-bar-bar-bar," Greeks came to refer to them as such. Thence the root *barbar* and a variety of words: *barbaros, barbarismos, barbarophonos,* and so on. Later this root departed from its initial linguistic connotation, as Romans used it to describe "uncivilized" tribes, those who had no Greek or Roman accomplishments. See Henry George Liddell and Robert Scott, *A Greek-English Lexicon*, rev. ed. Henry Stuart Jones and Roderick McKenzie (Oxford: Clarendon Press, 1940), s.v. "βάρβαρος, ον," or online at http://www.perseus.tufts.edu/.

grandchildren of Romulus* as they grew to maturity, at a time when oriental civilization streamed like a flood from Greece into the Roman heartland and unnerved them. Nature had endowed Romans with the native gifts of sobriety and clear thinking as well as practicality. Their speech sounded plain and concise to the ear. They had been an agrarian people, worshiping their gods to confer a simple blessing on the annual cycle governing the farmer's life. Along with military power, the Roman people were significant for world history because of the strict civil code and national law they had crafted. From the Greeks they acquired the skill of oratory—to speak in the forum before judges and popular assemblies.[†]

The character of the Roman liturgy brings all this to mind. Its most characteristic feature was the negative impulse to reject—for the most part—the Hellenistic influence that, from the outset, had streamed into the legacy bequeathed to the church by the synagogue.[‡] The use of name upon name for addressing God, or of phrase upon phrase in an attempt to define God's essence: these rhetorical devices were alien to it. It avoided, apparently assiduously, apophatic language for expressing something about God.[§] It spoke with simple directness to the "all-powerful," "eternal," and—still, in any event—"merciful" "God" or "Lord." When addressing God in prayer, it at most mentioned his holiness and fatherhood. However, the liturgy spoke readily of his "majesty," as one had once spoken of the majesty of the Roman people and subsequently of the majesty of Caesar (as well as of the crime of insulting it). Bridal crowns for marrying couples and the final embrace of the dead were unknown in Rome. In the celebration of the Eucharist, it consciously kept all theatricality at arm's length; no stately processions symbolizing the entry of the ascended Christ developed in the struc-

---

* This image proposes three "generations," with Romulus as the grandparent, agrarian peasantry on the Italian peninsula as the parents, and Roman civilization as the child.

† Physically, a forum was a centrally located open space defined by public buildings and colonnades. In ancient Roman cities, it served socially as a place for public gathering. The most significant forum in the city of Rome was the *Forum Romanum*, located on swampy ground between the Palatine and Capitoline Hills. During the Republic (ca. 509–44/27 BCE), it was the site for public assemblies, law courts, and gladiatorial contests. Under the Roman Empire (44/27 BCE–476 CE), the forum was used largely for ceremonial purposes.

‡ See pp. 77–79 and 204–5.

§ See pp. 83–85.

ture of its liturgy. Once again Rome discarded any screen concealing the altar room.* It is noteworthy that the mention of Christ's role as Savior recedes into the background of genuinely Roman prayer, while in Gallican prayer it even became a regular feature of the concluding eucharistic doxology.[3] Gregory the Great (590–604) may have been the first to plant the cry *Kyrie eleison* in Roman soil.[4†]

Just as genuine Roman sobriety exhibited such obstinacy in resisting the Hellenistic liturgy of Eastern Christianity, so did the Roman practical temperament take a distinctive approach to the dogmatic content of liturgical prayer. Eastern formularies, like the liturgies of Basil (330–79)[‡] and Nestorius (after 351–after 451),[§] indeed even that of Serapion of Thmuis (d. after 360),[¶] constructed the eucharistic prayer as a kind of instructional discourse, which at the same time sounds like a hymn and focuses upon dogma, notably those of the uncreated God and his only-begotten Son. In the Nestorian formulary one even encounters expressions taken from the polemics of an actual christological controversy,[5] while others articulating the opposing position are found in texts of the Syrian Jacobite Mass.[6] Rome's interest does not lie in this direction. In its prayers one hears far more often distinct echoes of the disputes conducted in the fifth and sixth centuries over the doctrine of grace.** Even on Easter Sunday, the feast celebrating the resurrection of our Lord, the Gregorian collect offers no petition more specific to the feast than that the power of grace might help complete the work initiated by the firstborn from the dead.[7]

Annual rituals in the ancient agrarian religion of Rome were simply Christianized. The celebrations of Ember Days have their roots here.[††] In the texts of its "liturgies," one still finds today some reference to

---

* For a discussion of these aspects of Eastern liturgy, see pp. 77–79.

† On Gregory I or the Great, see Short Biography, no. 78.

‡ On Basil's liturgy, see pp. 140–41. On Basil the Great, see Short Biography, no. 28.

§ On Nestorius, see Short Biography, no. 127.

¶ On Serapion of Thmuis, see Short Biography, no. 157.

** Baumstark is here referring to the controversy occasioned by Pelagianism, in which Augustine of Hippo (354–430) was engaged. It continued into the fifth century in Gaul, coming to a conclusion at the Second Council of Orange (529).

†† Ember Days were a time for fasting and abstinence three days in length, observed four times a year. They fell on the Wednesday, Friday, and Saturday after the feast day for St. Lucy (December 13), Ash Wednesday, Pentecost, and

the seasonal worries and labors of the peasant farmer, the focus of the pagan models for these days of penance and prayer. They were originally observed only three times a year: before the grain harvest, before the grape gathering, and after the winter cultivation of the fields.[8] It is common knowledge that the procession through the countryside, held on the feast of St. Mark, is rooted in that of the ancient festival of Robigalia, celebrated by the city of Rome.* Similarly, the ancient festival of Ambarvalia, an observance that enjoyed wide acceptance, lives on as a celebration that originated in Gaul: the three Rogation Days observed before Ascension Day.[9†] This link between the agrarian customs of

---

Holy Cross Day (September 14), respectively. Spreading throughout the Western church from Rome, their origins and initial purpose are unclear.

* Baumstark traces the procession on the feast of St. Mark to Robigalia, a festival of ancient urban Rome celebrated on April 25 to protect the crops from blight. This pagan festival involved a procession from the center of Rome to the fifth milestone of the Via Claudia outside the city, where a red dog and a sheep were offered in propitiatory sacrifice to Robigus, the Roman spirit of wheat rust. The feast of St. Mark also falls on April 25, and the celebration on that day (called variously the Major Rogation, *Litania Maior*, and *Romana*) also offered prayers of petition for good crops. According to documentary evidence from Gregory I (590–604), this rogation procession had become a yearly celebration by 598. Like Robigalia, whose route it followed when starting out, this ceremony was geographical and processional. Specifically, it commenced at S. Laurentii in Lucina in Rome, traveled north into the countryside along the Via Flamina on the east bank of the Tiber, crossed over the west bank at the Milvian Bridge, whence it moved south, ending at St. Peter's Basilica. Liturgies were celebrated at stations along the way.

In addition to articles in English-language encyclopedias, see D. E. Moeller, "Litanies majeurs et Rogations," *Questions liturgiques et paroissiales* 23 (1938): 75–91; LTK, s.v. "Bittprozession"; and *Reallexikon für Antike und Christentum* (Stuttgart: Hiersemann Verlag, 1954), s.v. "Bittprozession, A. Nichtchristlich, I. Griech.-römisch."

† Baumstark roots the rogation processions made on the Monday, Tuesday, and Wednesday preceding Ascension Day in Ambarvalia, a rural pagan ritual that came to be observed in the city of Rome. This festival, celebrated in May, entailed a circumambulation of the most ancient *Romanus ager*, the territory of the primitive city only, offering petitions to avert blight and disease and to ensure the fertility of the fields. Such ceremonies were decidedly intended for purification and expiation. On the days prior to Ascension Day, also celebrated in May, rogations were offered containing similar petitions. To distinguish these rogations from those offered on the feast of St. Mark, they were called

ancient Rome and Rome's current Christian liturgy allows us to understand in historical terms a Western liturgical form with no Eastern counterpart. Though the East witnessed a marked increase in the ritual veneration of the saints, in its liturgical prose prayers it never called upon them directly. The Roman West did so in its Litany of the Saints, a prayer rooted in the procession through the countryside. The formal genre used by the Litany of Saints finds its model in a prayer style with direct, external evidence in the agrarian cult of ancient Rome; this genre is immediately recognizable in the inscriptions of the *acta* of the Arval Brethren.*[10]

The verbal formulas found in popular agrarian prayer, which Marcus Porcius Cato the Elder (234–149 BCE)[†] has preserved in his book *On Agriculture*,[‡] illustrate the strategy employed for securing a petition's success: heaping up parallel wordings by repeatedly rephrasing a petition. By this strategy, these agrarian prayers sought, so to speak, to block any possible escape route by which the godhead could deny their requests.[11] Undeniably, that method suits the Roman legal mind

---

Litaniae Minores. Introduced into Gaul ca. 470, they were adopted for all of Gaul at the Council of Orléans (511) and for use at Rome by Leo III (795–816). See ERE, s.v. "Landmarks and Boundaries, 5: Beating the Bounds," s.v. "Litany, 5: Processions in the West," and s.v. "Purification, 2: Common Acts of Purification"; LTK, s.v. "Bittprozession"; Moeller, "Litanies majeurs et Rogations," 75–91; *The Oxford Classical Dictionary*, 3rd rev. ed., ed. Simon Hornblower and Anthony Spawforth (Oxford and New York City: Oxford University Press, 2003), s.v. "Ambarvalia"; and *Reallexikon für Antike und Christentum* (Stuttgart: Hiersemann Verlag, 1954), s.v. "Bittprozession, A. Nichtchristlich, I. Griech.-römisch."

* The *Fratres Arvales* (ET: Arval Brethren or Brothers) was a priesthood of ancient Rome that each year offered prayers for the fertility of the fields and the preservation of the imperial house. It consisted of twelve members from senatorial families elected for life and always included the emperor. While the literary evidence for the brotherhood is sparse, inscriptions in stone of ninety-six *acta*, or minutes of their proceedings, have been found near Rome on the site of their sacred grove. See *The Oxford Classical Dictionary*, s.v. "Fratres Arvales."

† On Cato the Elder, see Short Biography, no. 43.

‡ Rather than dealing with agriculture in general, *De agricultura* offers advice to the proprietor of a midsized estate, including the use of slave labor and the production of wine and olive oil. An eclectic work, it incorporates recipes, religious formulae, prescriptions, and sample contracts. See *The Oxford Classical Dictionary*, s.v. "Porcius (RE9) Cato (1) Marcus."

even better than the naïve cunning of peasants. This mind-set had an effect upon the Roman Canon and the verbose wording it uses to petition for the miracle of transubstantiation.* Using the exact same linguistic style found in the agrarian prayers of old, this section, which precedes the account of the Lord's Supper, asks that the bread and the wine become the Body and Blood of God's Son.[12] Equally characteristic is the stylistic form Rome used to construct prayers. The regularity of syntactical members increases to the point that each one contains the same number of words and syllables. The most elaborate word order imaginable and the adherence to ancient rules of meter, required to produce euphony through rhythm, sought[†] to create a powerful rhetorical affect. Such a technique was obviously learned in the schools of rhetoric where Roman jurists were trained. Throughout the Roman Canon one finds a fondness for certain rhetorical devices that bears the telltale mark of an individual, in that those devices are used to the point of becoming downright pretentious. It is no coincidence that Gregory the Great (590–604), who evidently still knew the identity of the Canon's "author," referred to him as a "certain *scholasticus*," that is, as a guild member of the legal fraternity.[13]

Along with the Roman racial type, the Germanic one also played a role in determining the liturgical style of the West. Germans not only produced liturgical elements after Visigothic rituals, like celebrations modeled on the rituals for sending a king marching off to war and welcoming him back home in victory.[14] Most important: Germans influenced the essence of the Frankish-Roman liturgy in the final stage of its development. With a morale characteristic of valiant Germanic warriors, happy to have an opportunity to fight, the liturgy sings with Venantius (ca. 530–610),[‡]

---

* The phrase Baumstark employs here is *die Wesenverwandlung von Brot und Wein in Leib und Blut des Gottessohnes*, which translates literally as "the transformation of the essence [being or nature] of the bread and the wine into the Body and Blood of the Son of God." This phrase I have translated with the single word "transubstantiation." See nn. on p. 218, and p. 246 for other instances in which Baumstark uses *die Wandlung* in a eucharistic context.

† The word *abzieenden*, a typographical error in the German edition, has been translated here as *abzielenden*.

‡ See n. on p. 153.

Abroad the regal banners fly,
now shines the Cross's mystery.*

The idea held here of Christ's kingdom is entirely different from
that found in the Byzantine liturgy—heir in the East to the Hellenistic
imperial cult. What matters here is the personal moral qualities con-
nected with the ideal of the Germanic *Volkskönig*, the sacred devotion
of a sovereign to his people, heard in German song. With this devotion, Dietrich, the hero of the epic poem, pledges his life on behalf of
his men and in atonement for their deaths.† It is also found at work
in the line of a sequence by Wipo (ca. 990–after 1048),‡ in which the
"Prince of Life"—who was "dead, but lives and reigns"—does battle
with Satan.§ When Germany's new culture was just emerging, its
world was harsh, filled with *Meintat* and *Fehde*.¶ This world waited

---

* These are the first two lines of the hymn by Venantius Honorius Clementianus Fortunatus (530–610), "Vexilla regis prodeunt/fulget crucis mysterium." See Matthew Britt, *The Hymns of the Breviary and Missal* (New York,
Boston, Cincinnati, Chicago, San Francisco: Benziger Bros., 1948), 115–19. On
Fortunatus, see Short Biography, no. 71.

† Dietrich of Berne (Verona) is a hero figuring in German legend, apparently
inspired by Theodoric the Great, a king of the Ostrogoths (471–526), ruler of
Italy (493–526), and regent of the Visigoths (511–26). His exploits are extolled
in a number of southern German songs that can be found in *Das Heldenbuch*
[*Book of Heroes*], whose themes are loyalty and sacrifice, notably in *Dietrichs
Flucht* [*Dietrich's Flight*], the *Rabenschlacht* [*The Battle of Ravenna*], and *Alpharts
Tod* [*Alphart's Death*]. See *Dietrichs Flucht*, ed. Elisabeth Lienert, Texte und
Studien zur mittelhochdeutschen Heldenepik 1 (Tübingen: Niemeyer, 2003);
Rabenschlacht, ed. Elisabeth Lienert and Dorit Wolter, Texte und Studien zur
mittelhochdeutschen Heldenepik 2 (Tübingen: Niemeyer, 2005); and *Alpharts
Tod*, ed. Elisabeth Lienert and Viola Meyer, Studien zur mittelhochdeutschen
Heldenepik 3 (Tübingen: Niemeyer, 2007).

‡ On Wipo, see Short Biography, no. 191.

§ Baumstark refers here to the phrase *dux vitae mortuus regnat vivus* found in
the eleventh-century paschal sequence *Victimae paschali* ascribed to Wipo. See
Britt, *Hymns*, 129–31.

¶ These are technical terms of medieval German jurisprudence, which defined an offense as any action damaging to the social order, understood in
terms of *peace*. Indeed, German tribes then held *law* and *peace* to be virtually
synonymous: to break the law was to break the peace; to be an outlaw was to
be "out of peace" with the community. In the time before courts and penal institutions, both judgment and punishment proceeded according to communal

with longing for the royal judge and peacekeeper to march through every district of the land, settling strife. The image of the divine-human "King of Peace," which emerges as the dominant theme of the

---

norms of jurisprudence but could be carried out by an individual on behalf of the tribe or clan. In broad strokes, offenses were categorized according to what group was offended: the community as a whole or a clan within it.

Meintat is a collective term for any serious crime against the law and custom of the group as a whole (synonyms: *Firntat, Freveltat, Meingewerk, Meinwerk, Missetat, Übeltat*). It carried the connotation of being a "base," "vile," and "mean" outrage against the community. Since a *Meintat* was understood ultimately to put the community at risk from the wrath of a god or gods, it had a sacral dimension. For the more serious infractions, priests sought to determine the will of the god(s) and were involved in judging and punishing the criminal. While any action disrupting social order (breaking the peace) fell into the category of *Meintat*, specific instances were sorcery, treason, and slaying in secret. Being an outlaw ("out of peace" with the community) was punishable by either loss of all community status and banishment into the woods (*in sylvam*) or death by any number of means: hanging, burying alive, burning alive, or decapitation for men; drowning and stoning for women. Nor was the property of outlaws spared; their goods were distributed throughout the tribe and their dwellings were burned. As German jurisprudence came to differentiate specific crimes in this general category, the term fell into disuse.

Fehde (feud) referred to offenses on the level of the clan. In the Middle Ages, *feud* did not have the connotation of frontier justice that it carries in American English today: retribution taken outside of the law. Then it referred to a legal institution by which a clan gained redress for damages or a grievance without involving a higher authority to mete out justice. *Fehde* allowed for the damaged party to gain satisfaction directly and immediately by appropriating property or by killing in cases of blood and honor. Stated plainly, *Fehde* was a legalized form of vendetta, whereby the tribe sanctioned a war between two clans, until one or the other was no longer able to fight. As slaying a person in secret was *Meintat, Fehde* had to be public. This legal institution slowly passed out of use as forms of compensation (*compositio*) evolved, with damages going to the aggrieved party and "peace money" going to the community.

In this passage Baumstark juxtaposes the "peace" maintained through the harsh mechanisms of the early legal German system to the peace Christ brings.

Deutsches Rechtswörterbuch: Wörterbuch der älteren deutschen Rechtssprache, vol. 3, ed. Eberhard von Künßberg (Weimar: Verlag Hermann Böhlaus Nachfolger, 1999), s.v. "Fehde"; ibid., vol. 9, s.v. "Meintat." See also Claudius Freiherr von Schwerin, *Germanische Rechtsgeschichte: Ein Grundriss* (Berlin: Junker und Dünnhaupt Verlag, 1944), 40–45, and Munroe Smith, *The Development of European Law* (New York: Columbia University Press, 1928), 24–33, 66–68.

Advent and Christmas liturgies, is born out of these miseries. An astute expert cogently pointed out how closely this image relates to the *City of God*, the treatise on the philosophy of history written by St. Augustine (354–430),* the great bishop of Hippo, which—incidentally—was also one of Charlemagne's favorite books.[15] For the liturgy of the city of Rome, the Sunday opening Holy Week was originally a quieter day, an anticipation of the celebration of the Passion marked more by gravity, and it has remained just that to the present in the Office and in the formulary of the Mass. When this Sunday's celebration using palms, with its strong emphasis upon the concept of "king," made its way from the East through even to Rome, that did not happen by chance but came—as can be demonstrated—on a detour through Frankish Gaul.[16]

The readings in the Roman Breviary from the First and Second Books of Maccabees make for a singular impression, with their responses containing prayers for times of war and expressing a soldier's delight upon seeing sunlight reflecting off of golden shields.† Had the German people not become the preeminent guarantor of the Roman liturgy's preservation and dissemination, these readings would have been hard put to maintain their impressive position in the lectionary of the Office. Now they stand there as a towering monolith, recalling the proud days of the Vikings and bearing public witness against all who

---

* On Augustine of Hippo, see Short Biography, no. 25.

† The Roman Breviary (1911) appoints passages from 1 and 2 Macc throughout the month of October. Baumstark here refers to a passage from 1 Macc 6 that is used as a responsory three times in each week of that month (the seventh responsory on Sundays, the first on Wednesdays and Saturdays). It is a composite of vv. 39, 40, 41, and 42 that reads in part:

> ℟. Refulsit sol in clipeos aureos, et resplenduerunt montes ab eis: Et fortitudo gentium dissipata est.
> ℣. Erat enim exercitus magnus valde et fortis: et appropiavit Iudas et exercitus eius in proelio. Et fortitudo gentium dissipata est.

> ℟. The sun shone on the shields of gold, and the mountains glittered with them; and the strength of the nations was destroyed.
> ℣. For their army was very numerous and strong; and Judas and his army moved in for the battle. And the strength of the nations was destroyed.

See *The Hours of the Divine Office in English and Latin*, vol. 3 (Collegeville: Liturgical Press, 1964), 1202–3.

would confuse the virile spirit of the church with programs for world peace, born of a weak and weary spirit. Could a nation in fact collapse utterly when suffering the heaviest blow fate could mete out in a national war of desperation, if—in that decisive hour of its history—that nation were able to experience firsthand the Breviary prayer for the month of October in a liturgical setting?*

And next to this ominous image of war—a pleasing, tender picture. One can be moved by the verses of Greek poetry dedicated to the Mother of God, which the Eastern church has amassed. The Byzantine Rite never tires of stringing together images and metaphors, one after another—continually new verbal displays—in praise of the ever-virgin *Theotokos* (God-bearer). Then compare that approach to Western Marian hymns, unpretentious in their sincere affection! In these hymns, written by spiritual troubadours, one senses immediately, waving on the wind, the spirit of chivalry in service to a lady, without which the German Middle Ages would be simply unimaginable.

Without exception it was emotional values that the German people contributed to their adopted Roman liturgy. Making an attempt to account for everything that pertains here requires noticing fine lines and listening for colorations of sound fast fading away. The kind of liturgy found in Rome has remained what it purports to be, something genuine and laid out in plain sight for all to see. Not only in the Latin West but also in the Aramaic East the relationship between language and nation was decisive for the liturgy's development. However, in the Latin West this relationship was the inverse of that found in the Aramaic East. This resulted in the liturgy of the Aramaic East being less different from the Greek liturgy than the Roman liturgy was from the same. Although both the Aramaic East and the Latin West used foreign languages for their liturgies, in the former case this language was not rooted in a national character, and, for that reason, it did not always fend off the profound influence of Hellenism.[†] In the West,

---

* Like many Germans of a conservative bent after World War I, Baumstark regarded the aggression expressed in this passage to be a fitting response to the "humiliation" of the Versailles Treaty, which they felt had dealt harshly with Germany for its aggression in World War I and required reparation payments that were unduly onerous. The sentiments expressed in this passage reflect Baumstark's belief that Roman Catholicism had a role to play for German culture, strengthening and edifying it.

[†] For footnote on Aramaic and Syriac, see p 55.

however, the full actualization of the German national character in liturgy was fettered by the use of Latin, a foreign language. Yet another comparison may shed light on the significance of this conjunction of language, culture, and liturgy. The Byzantine liturgy has remained strictly untouched among the eastern Slavs, Bulgarians, and Romanians, who celebrate it as one does in Constantinople or in Athens or on Mt. Athos.[*] This is so, despite the fact that it has been translated into Church Slavonic for use in the mission field, and indeed even into Romanian, a living tongue.[†] On the other hand, one can only imagine how the Roman liturgy would have developed on German soil had the dialect of the Saxon troubadours, who chanted *Heliand*,[‡] had the opportunity of becoming the language it used for worship![§]

---

[*] See p. 143.

[†] The Romanian Orthodox Church uses for its liturgy both Church Slavonic and Romanian. For more on liturgical language in the Romanian Orthodox Church, see n. on p. 190.

[‡] *Heliand* (meaning *Savior* in Old Saxon) is an epic life of Christ in alliterative verse dating from ca. 830. An evangelistic tool for converting the warlike Saxons, it used familiar Saxon surroundings and mores for telling the life of Christ; for example, it pictured Christ as a Germanic king bestowing armbands upon his retainers (disciples). For an edition of this work in Old Saxon, see *Der Heliand*, ed. Burkhard Taeger, Altdeutsche Textbibliothek, 95 (Tübingen: Niemeyer, 1984); ET: *The Heliand*, trans. G. Ronald Murphy (New York u.a.: Oxford University Press, 1992).

[§] Behind this whole discussion stands volkish thought, a strain of German nationalist thought that provided Germans with a sense of national identity for more than a century, beginning with the rise of romanticism and ending (discredited) by the Nazi defeat at the end of World War II. This thought provided Germans with a corporate sense when Germany existed only as "a nation of the imagination" and after the rise of the German Empire (1871). An aspect of volkish thought rooted German national traits in a mythic past. It imagined the tribes occupying "Germania" after the birth of Christ to be a cohesive ethnic group, exhibiting admirable traits of valor, loyalty, and honor, with the strength to defeat the Roman Empire. These martial and communal qualities were held to serve "Germany" well as it came to participate in European (i.e., Roman) civilization. The book *Germania* by Publius Cornelius Tacitus (56–117 CE), an example of classical ethnology, was interpreted in support of this mythic history. Baumstark was introduced to volkish thought by his grandfather and namesake (1800–76), who wrote extensively on Tacitus' *Germania*. Following World War I, Baumstark became a member of the

Deutschnationale Volkspartie, a political expression of volkish thought that re-acted nationalistically to Germany's "ignominious" defeat. Baumstark's judg-ment that the Frankish-Roman liturgy merges Roman refinement and German feeling can be read as a volkish interpretation of the Roman liturgy. The classic study of the volkish movement, originally published in 1964, is George L. Mosse, *The Crisis of German Ideology: Intellectual Origins of the Third Reich* (New York: Howard Fertig, 1998). A most stimulating study of the role of Tacitus' *Germania* in German nationalist thought is Christopher Krebs, *A Most Danger-ous Book: Tacitus's* Germania *from the Roman Empire to the Third Reich* (New York: W. W. Norton & Co, 2011). In addition to preparing a student's edition and an extensive commentary on *Germania*, Baumstark's grandfather used it to reflect upon the primal German state. See Anton Baumstark, *Urdeutsche Staatsalterthümer zur schützenden Erläuterung der Germania des Tacitus* (Berlin: W. Weber, 1873).

Notes

As early as 1899, no less a liturgical scholar than Edmund Bishop em-phatically pointed out one of the most important challenges possible for the historical study of the liturgy: in order to recognize the significance of differences "freely and fully," races and peoples must be fundamen-tally taken into account. For a recent citation, see his essay on "The Roman Canon" in Edmund Bishop, *Liturgica Historica* (Oxford: Claren-don Press, 1918), 115.

[1] In the so-called parallel text to the eighth book of the Apostolic Constitu-tion, "Traditio Apostolica," chap. 3. GT: Schermann, *Kirchenordnung*, 38–41 [ET: *The Apostolic Tradition. A Commentary*, ed. Paul F. Bradshaw, Maxwell E. John-son, and L. Edward Phillips (Minneapolis: Fortress Press, 2002), 31].

[2] For a comprehensive treatment of this response by the Orient, see Anton Baumstark, *Die christlichen Literaturen des Orients*, vol. 1 (Leipzig: G. J. Göschen, 1911), 14–18.

[3] "Salvator mundi, qui vivis et regnas (vivit et regnat) in saecula saeculo-rum" [ET: Savior of the world, you who live and reign (who lives and reigns), forever and ever]. Today in the Roman sphere this usage is encountered only at the conclusion of the second oration for Prime, which makes its Gallican origin readily apparent. [See *The Hours of the Divine Office in English and Latin*, vol. 1 (Collegeville: Liturgical Press, 1963), 94 and passim; ibid., vol. 2, 94 and passim; ibid., vol. 3, 94 and passim.]

[4] See Bishop, "Kyrie Eleison: A Liturgical Consultation," in *Liturgica His-torica*, 116–36.

[5] See Anton Baumstark, "Die Chrisostomosliturgie und die syrische Liturgie des Nestorios," Χρυσοστομικα [*Chrysostomika*], 848–54.

⁶ An example of this can be seen in the anaphora of Severus of Antioch (see above, chap. 10, n. 15). A further example may be seen in an anaphora attributed to Gregory of Nazianzus. See Assemani, *Codex liturgicus ecclesiae universae in XV libros distributus*, 7, ed. Joseph Aloysius Assemani (Romae [Rome]: Ex typographia Komarek, Apud Angelum Rotilium, 1749–66 [repr., Farnborough: Gregg, 1968]), 193–95.

⁷ See Germain Morin, "L'origine des Quatre-Temps," RBén 14 (1897): 337–46, and Hartmann Grisar, *Geschichte Roms und der Päpste im Mittelalter*, vol. 1 (Freiburg im Breisgau: Herder, 1901), 768–71.

⁸ See Hermann Usener, *Das Weihnachtsfest*, 2nd ed., ed. Hans Lietzmann (Bonn: F. Cohen, 1911), 304–10; Grisar, *Geschichte Roms*, 854f.; and finally Donatien de Bruyne, "L'origine des processions de la Chandeleur et des Rogations apropos d'un sermon inédit," RBén 34 (1922): 14–26.

⁹ According to Fabius Pictor, as cited by Servius in his commentary on Book I, 21, of Virgil's *Georgics* [see *Servii Grammatici qvi fervntvr in Vergilii Bvcolica et Georgica. Commentarii*, ed. Georg Thilo, = Servius Maurus Honoratus Grammaticus, *Servii Grammatici qui fervntur in Vergilii carmina commentarii*, ed. Georg Thilo and Hermann Hagen, vol. 3, pt. 1 (Lipsiae [Leipzig]: in aedibvs B.G. Tevbneri, 1902; repr., Hildesheim: Olms, 1986), 137, lines 21–25].

[Nn. 10–17 have been rearranged in the English text. In the German text, n. 10 was placed too early, and each note from n. 11 to 14 was placed where the previous note should have been. N. 16 was placed where n. 15 should have been, without any citation provided. I have removed n. 16 found in the German text and moved nn. 10–15 forward, renumbering n. 17 in the German text as n. 16 in the English.]

¹⁰ Wilhelm Henzen, *Acta fratrum Arvalium* (Berolini [Berlin]: Reimer, 1874), 42–47, 93f, 107, 140–43, 186, 202, and 224. This material is also available in Georg Appel, *De Romanorum precationibus*, Religionsgeschichtliche Versuche und Vorarbeiten 3, 2 (Gießen: Impensis Alfredi Toepelmanni, 1909).

¹¹ Marcus Porcius Cato the Elder, *De agricultura*, chaps. 139 and 141; see Appel, *De Romanorum precationibus*, 29f [ET: Marcus Porcius Cato, *On farming*, = *De agricultura*, trans. Andrew Dalby (Blackawton: Prospect Books, 1998), also available online at http://penelope.uchicago.edu/Thayer/E/Roman/Texts/Cato/De_Agricultura/I*.html].

¹² "Quam oblationem." In this regard, see Odo Casel, "Quam oblationem," JLW 2 (1922): 98–101, which is still in no way the last word on the subject.

¹³ For the passage referenced in this letter of Gregory the Great to Bishop John of Syracuse, see *Registri Epistolarum*, Liber IX, Epistola XII, in PL 77, col. 957 [ET: Gregory the Great, "Epistle XII," in NPNF, 2nd ser., 3, 9; Johnson, *Worship*, IV, no. 165-A-17 (selection)]. While in no way specifically choosing one name over another, one is easily reminded of Prosper of Aquitaine's (ca. 390–ca. 455) manner of thought, whom the Venerable Bede characterized as *sermone scholasticus et assertionibus nervosus*. [N.b., this phrase is used by Gen-

nadius of Massiliensis to describe Prosper in "On Illustrious Men," chap. 84 of *Liber De Scriptoribus Ecclesiasticis*.] Though one could just as well go back earlier to the *causidicus* Minucius Felix (second or third century) and Tertullian (ca. 160–ca. 220 CE), who throughout his life essentially remained a jurist and rhetorician in his thinking.

[14] *Le Liber Ordinum en usage dans l'Église wisigothique et mozarabe d'Espagne du 5. au 11. siècle*, ed. Marius Férotin, MEL 5 (Paris: Firmin-Didot, 1904), 149–56. See also Anton Baumstark, "Friede und Krieg in altkirchlicher Liturgie," *Hochland* 13(1915/16): 269f.

[15] Ildefons Herwegen, *Alte Quellen neuer Kraft* (Düsseldorf: L. Schwann, 1920), 86ff.

[16] Even if the well-known tale about the origin of the hymn *Gloria, laus, et honor* is mere legend and not history, the Gallican Theodulf of Orlèans (ca. 750–60 to 821) stands as its author on the hymn, see n. on p. 153; on Theodulf of Orlèans, see Short Biography, no. 178). As its manuscript tradition shows, this hymn gave rise to the growth of a local cult. Beginning in Angers, the way the cult spread is illuminating beyond measure. At the very least, Odo Casel, "Die Präfation der Palmweihe," JLW (1922): 107–10, has demonstrated the Gallic origin of the preface for today's Blessing of Palms, even if in other respects his assessment of this facet of liturgy proves untenable.

Development,* Persistence, Hardening

It may be that—up to this point—the historical study of the liturgy as a field of modern research has known but one practitioner of un- questioned stature: the Englishman Edmund Bishop (1846–1917).[†] To his life's work, reflecting a painstaking attention to detail, he brought the innate moderation of a Giovanni Battista de Rossi (1822–94)[‡] or a Theodor Mommsen (1817–1903).[§] In monographic research, as me- ticulous as one can imagine, he combined the sobriety necessary to exercise the greatest methodological rigor with a genius for discern- ment, enabling him to ascertain both the fundamental truths critical to a historical problem and the central facts governing it.[1] In a brief essay, one of the last to flow from the pen of this indefatigable man,[2] Bishop put great stress on the conservative orientation that—in contrast to the Greek liturgy—the Roman West may share with the Aramaic East.

In fact no notion is more erroneous than this: that a distinctive fea- ture of Greek Christianity is the early onset of sclerosis, the hardening symptomatic of old age. This caricature, picturing Byzantium as an old man, came out of classical philology, but from a period in its de- velopment now long past.[¶] This caricature is passé, both for Byzantine

---

* Although *der Fortschritt* literally means "progress," I have translated it here as "development." In the first place, in American English, the word "prog- ress" has an optimistic and ameliorating connotation. It does not mean "going forward" in a neutral sense of movement, but "going forward to something better." Secondly, Baumstark defines the first law of liturgical evolution as follows: "I shall describe it as the Law of Organic Development ('Organic' and therefore 'Progressive')" (Baumstark, *Comparative Liturgy*, 23). Clearly, his meaning here is closer to "developing" in a more neutral sense than "progress- ing" in a more optimistic sense.

[†] On Edmund Bishop, see Short Biography, no. 38.

[‡] On Giovanni Battista de Rossi, see Short Biography, no. 62.

[§] On Theodor Mommsen, see Short Biography, no. 125.

[¶] Anton Baumstark offers a more extended critique of philology in "Besprechung: Hilgenfeld (ed.) *Ausgewählte Gesänge des Giwargis Warda von Arbel*," OC 4 (1904): 229. See also Frederick S. West, *Anton Baumstark's Com-*

philology in general and for the history of its literature and art in particular. This has been the case for the history of Byzantine literature since the pioneer Karl Krumbacher (1856–1909)* came into the picture and for the history of Byzantine art thanks both to French scholars and to the research work of Josef Strzygowski (1862–1941)† and his school. But this idea is also obsolete in the area of Greek liturgy whose forms quite emphatically did *not* harden at an early stage in its development. Rather, all aspects of Greek Christianity display the rich life produced by an almost compulsive propensity to develop—even into the high Middle Ages. The same dynamic left its stamp on the worlds of Coptic, Syrian, and Armenian Christianity, which came under the influence of Greek church life. Each new effort at liturgical poetry towers above the other. One encounters ever-new lectionaries, at least among the Copts and the West Syrian Jacobites. The Armenian Rite acquired ever-greater variety, first through its connection with the Byzantine Rite and subsequently through contact with the Western liturgy of the Crusaders and the Dominican branch of the Order of the Brothers of St. Gregory the Illuminator (*Fratres Unitores*).‡

---

parative Liturgy in its Intellectual Context (University of Notre Dame: Dissertation, 1988), 151–53, and Fritz West, *The Comparative Liturgy of Anton Baumstark* (Bramcote, Nottingham: Grove Books Limited, 1995), 13–15.

* On Karl Krumbacher, see Short Biography, no. 115.

† On Josef Strzygowski, see Short Biography, no. 169.

‡ The *Fratres Unitores* (ET: Order of the Brothers [or Brothers of Unity or Unifying Brothers or Unifying Friars]) of St. Gregory the Illuminator, an Armenian branch of the Dominicans, resulted from Dominican activity in the Near East. After a time of study and consultation with a Dominican bishop in Persia, some Armenian monks formed the *Fratres Unitores* in 1330. Their monastery and several others united with the Roman Catholic Church and were placed under the Dominicans. Although they adopted the Dominican liturgy, constitution (with exceptions), and habit, these monks were not at first full members of the order. They worked for the union of the Armenian and Roman Churches. In 1356 they were formed into an Armenian branch of the Dominican order (*Fratres Uniti Armeniae*); in 1583 they attained the status of a province. The claims that ca. 1350 the order had fifty priories with seven hundred monks in Armenia, Persia, Georgia, and Crimea is probably exaggerated. The last of them died in Smyrna in 1813. See CE, s.v. "Bartholmew, Apostle to Armenia"; William A. Hinnebusch, *The Dominicans: A Short History* (New York: Alba House, 1975), 56–7. See n. dealing with the Lusignan dynasty, on p. 103.

In contrast to rites exhibiting this sort of development, others are notable for persisting in their liturgical life, the prime example being the liturgy found originally in Aramaic. A pattern of maintaining liturgical customs unchanged from centuries long since past has given that rite a backward and antiquarian character. Significant in this regard are the pericopes used by the Nestorians for scriptural readings. No other lectionary form known comes from an earlier stage of liturgical development—in terms of their structure and stability.[3] On the whole, the Roman liturgy exhibits this conservative tendency even more markedly than the Nestorian, although actually not in regard to its readings. Their determination as a people allows us to understand this all the more. Peasant types have always been conservative. So was the Latin peasantry of the ancient City of the Seven Hills, possibly to a marked degree. When the democratic revolution led by the Gracchus brothers (second century BCE)* started to erode the foundations of political life, this spelled the beginning of the end for Roman greatness, a process that of course dragged on for centuries.[†]

A few facts will suffice to shed light on this general state of affairs. The Roman liturgy is in the same position vis-à-vis the dialogue before the preface, as the Nestorian liturgy is vis-à-vis its order of pericopes. The prayers *Supra quae*[‡] and *Supplices*[§] of the Canon represent a form of the eucharistic prayer that is demonstrably widespread in the East as well as in the West. The Eastern tradition diverged from the form when it introduced into the prayer, at this same location, a petition calling for the Holy Spirit to descend upon the gifts,[¶] to effect their

---

* On the Gracchus Brothers, see Short Biography, no. 77.

† The Western Roman Empire came to an end in 476, with its final defeat by Germanic power.

‡ *Supra quae*, meaning "upon which" in Latin, is the eighth section of the Roman Canon in the Tridentine Roman Rite, which opens, "Upon which look with favor and accept . . ." and recalls God's acceptance of offerings made by Abel, Abraham, and Melchizedek.

§ *Supplices*, meaning "We beseech you" in Latin, is the ninth section of the Roman Canon in the Tridentine Roman Rite, which opens, "We humbly beseech you, almighty God." The prayer requests that the offering be carried up to heaven that those who commune upon earth may receive all heavenly benediction and grace.

¶ At the time of Baumstark's writing, the epiclesis was identified with the East. Though found in all Eastern liturgies, it was not explicit in the Tridentine Rite of the Roman Catholic Church. This became a point of controversy. While

miraculous transformation.[4]* In Jerusalem, as early as the late third century, the baptismal rite included both the renunciation and the adhesion; that is, before descending into the water of rebirth,† it was customary for the baptizand not only to renounce the prince of darkness but also, with equal solemnity, to swear allegiance to Christ.[5] According to evidence found in the *Apostolic Tradition* of Hippolytus (ca. 170–ca. 236),‡ Rome practiced the renunciation of Satan in its baptismal ritual from time immemorial, but never accepted any more than that. Apart from the veneration of the cross that originated in Jerusalem, the Roman celebration of Good Friday displays none of the magnificent and rich ritual with which the East loves to surround the day of our Redeemer's sacrifice on Golgotha.

Especially striking is one phenomenon of far-reaching significance. The oldest liturgical prayer of Christianity simply called upon God, that is, God the Father. Since it had grown out of the euchology of the synagogue, it could do no other. To be sure, even Stephen (d. ca. 35?), on the verge of death, prayed to Christ as the divine "Lord" (Acts 7:59-60),§ and one may assume with certainty that Paul (d. ca. 65?), the apostle to the nations, took a similar stance in his personal prayer life.[6] However, the historical connection with Israel's euchological style retained primary control over the formally structured religious discourse used in communal prayer: it allowed no petitions directly to Christ, but only through Christ to the Father. Then the East—at an early date and to a large extent—began to direct prayers to Christ, not only personal prayers, but liturgical ones as well. It did so under the influence of Hellenism, for the simple reason that Hellenistic converts

---

the East held the epiclesis to be essential to the Eucharist, the West saw its "form" (to use Aristotelian/Thomistic terminology) in the words of institution. An epiclesis was incorporated into the eucharistic prayers of the Roman Missal resulting from the reforms of the Second Vatican Council (1970).

* The word *Wandlung* in the compound neologism *Wunderwandlung* can be translated here as "transformation" or "consecration" or "transubstantiation." For another use of this word in a eucharistic context see p. 169; for use of *die* Verwandlung in a eucharistic context see p. 218.

† In churches constructed after the Peace of Constantine (313), baptismal fonts were often pools built into the floor of a baptistery and entered by descending a few steps.

‡ On the literary tradition referred to as "The Apostolic Tradition," see n. on p. 67; on Hippolytus, see Short Biography, no. 97.

§ On Stephen the Deacon, see Short Biography, no. 166.

to Christianity were not constrained in this regard by the prayer customs of Israel, as were their Jewish counterparts. In this case, significant leadership came from circles of Christians Gnostics, who were outside the church and diverged furthest from Jewish practice.[7] The non-Roman West followed this path as well. There, as late as 397—arguably—an African provincial council held at Carthage expressly and directly forbade the use in the liturgical context of any prayer that was not directed to the Father.[8] Nevertheless, Milan, Visigothic Spain, the indigenous liturgical documents of Merovingian Gaul, and the pre-Roman liturgy of Ireland all follow the Eastern pattern in offering liturgical prayers to Christ. A Gallican prayer for Good Friday, dating from the seventh century at the very latest, seems to anticipate the mystical experience of a St. Catherine of Sienna (1347–80)* or a St. Teresa of Ávila (1515–82)[†] and the "Blood and Wounds Theology" of Nicholaus Graf von Zinzendorf (1700–1760).[‡] Using words from the Song of Songs, it passionately implores the "beloved bridegroom," who is dying, for a kiss from his pale lips.[9] That very same prayer, in two separate instances, went further than we've ever seen liturgical speech go again. It not only addresses the Lord as *auriga supremus* ("highest charioteer") but also applies traits of the ancient sun god to the spiritual "Sun of Righteousness" (Mal 4:2)[§]—a strong indication that its formal style is deeply anchored in Hellenism. However, it is also telling that such a style took hold so firmly in the Spanish-Gallican liturgical area, where Arian Christianity[¶] had decidedly gained the upper hand. One can be certain that the conscious opposition to Arianism, indicated by this style, blazed a wide path into the liturgy for that prayer pattern, which—in directing its prayers to Christ—was still strongly inclined to conform to the consciousness of

---

* Catherine of Siena (1347–80) was particularly dedicated to the Devotion to the Precious Blood. On Catherine of Siena, see Short Biography, no. 42.

† Teresa of Ávila or Teresa of Jesus (1515–82) turned to a life of perfection after praying before a statue depicting the scourging of Christ. On Teresa of Ávila, see Short Biography, no. 170.

‡ Nikolaus Ludwig Graf von Zinzendorf (1700–1760) preached a religion of the heart and developed a theology of Jesus' blood and wounds. On von Zinzendorf, see Short Biography, no. 189.

§ For the Sun Cult, see pp. 81–82.

¶ On Arianism see, n. on p. 101.

the faith found in the earliest Christian community. Here it was the "law of belief" that established "the law of prayer."*

The position Rome took in this regard is all the more worthy of note. From the fifth century on, Rome alone (so far as we can determine) tenaciously adhered to the ancient rule of prayer, which directed prayers solely to the Father through the Son. By this time prose prayers directed to Christ had certainly worked their way into the Roman liturgical books. In every case, however, they are either of Gallican origin or a recent creation of more or less modern character. To be sure, the age-old Roman pattern of prayer enjoys biblical sanction no less than prayers addressed to Christ. While the latter is sanctioned by the prayer that Stephen, the protomartyr (Acts 7:54-60), said lips aquiver, the former is sanctioned by the Lord himself in passages such as John 16:23f.† Surely there is no denying that this latter approach is justified by a central dogma of the faith and is even peculiar to the Roman form of prayer; nor can one deny the magnificent trinitarian integrity of a prayer, which the church—without fail—sends up to the eternal Father, through the only-begotten Son, embraced in the unity of the Holy Spirit. However, one also must not deny that the wording of liturgical prayer as it developed outside Rome was obviously more suited to the theological approach that, since the time of the great Athanasius (ca. 296–373),‡ the struggle against heresy had brought to the fore. This fact should serve as a stern warning against inflating the role of material factors in shaping the Roman manner of praying. Rather, one needs to keep in mind how

* Baumstark is referring to the sentence "Lex orandi statuat lex credendi," credited to Prosper of Acquitaine (ca. 390–ca. 455), who wrote "ut legem credendi lex statuat supplicandi," which translates as "let the rule of prayer lay down the rule of faith." While the sentence asserts that the law of prayer establishes the law of belief, here Baumstark is noting that the opposite pertains. For the original context of this quote, see chap. 8 of *Capitula Coelestini* by Prosper of Aquitaine in PL 51: 209. ET: Prosper of Aquitaine ,"Official Pronouncements of the Apostolic See on Divine Grace and Free Will," in *Defense of Augustine*, trans. P. De Letter, Ancient Christian Writers 32 (Westminister, MD: Newman Press, 1963), 183.

† John 16:23-24 reads, "On that day you will ask nothing of me. Very truly, I tell you, if you ask anything of the Father in my name, he will give it to you. Until now you have not asked for anything in my name. Ask and you will receive, so that your joy may be complete."

‡ Athanasius was a leading opponent of Arianism. On Athanasius, see Short Biography, no. 22.

deeply the formation of liturgical texts is rooted in the spirit of Christian antiquity and in the tremendous power wielded by the classical laws of style—purely in terms of form. The standard stylistic form that Jews used for their prose prayers praising God (in contradistinction to Hellenistic hymnology) was from the outset directed solely to the Father. Adherence to this venerable stylistic form was not the least of the factors influencing the genius of the Roman Rite to resist giving in to the daily demands of the historical development of dogma.

If this example suggests that these liturgical forms somehow hardened far earlier in their development than those of Greek and Oriental Christianity, this should in no way be taken as a strike against Rome's liturgical character. In contrast to the East, which is more easily swayed, Rome demonstrates a prodigious capacity for persisting in its liturgical patterns. This admirable quality, which has safeguarded a venerable legacy from the earliest of days, deserves nothing but thanks. To a remarkable extent, the same thing can be said about another aspect of the Mass rite as well, although on the face of things one is inclined to conclude just the opposite. This aspect manifests itself throughout the West and not only in Rome. It represents the most significant contrast by far with how the East celebrates the Eucharist. Although the East allows the church year to exercise influence over biblical lections and particular sung elements, it categorically denies its sway over the prayer texts of the Eastern Mass. (The only exception to this rule comes from early Christian Egypt: debris from a particular, unique Easter liturgy, preserved in the Coptic language.)[10] Just as fundamentally, the Mass liturgy in the West only uses formularies that are adapted to the course of the church year, that is, formularies that render unique each celebration of the Mass. In this regard, the texts of the Mozarabic Rite vary (and those of the old Gallican Rite varied) even more than Rome and—under Rome's influence—Milan, where at least the Canon essentially eludes this inclination. Yet Milan also goes further than Rome in regard to textual variability: each Mass on principle is assigned its own preface.

One might easily take the textual variability of the West as an indication that it has developed further than the East. From that perspective, the absolute identity of the Eastern texts would be seen as indicative of a monumental hardening. So conceived, this development toward variability would have stalled in Rome halfway, but continued on to its culmination in the Spanish-Gallican liturgical area. The falsehood of such an interpretation quickly becomes apparent, however—at least in regard to the situation pertaining in Rome and northern Italy. We can

see this in documents that predate the papacy of Gregory I (590–604):*
before the seventh century both Rome and Milan had a proper preface
for every Mass, and the text of the canons allowed variations more numerous and significant than today.

Of all the documents extant for the early Roman liturgy, the most valuable one reveals the actual origins of the Western pattern of using variable texts in the eucharistic liturgy. The document is a single incomplete
manuscript, preserved in Verona, Italy, and erroneously identified by its
earliest editors as a sacramentary of Leo the Great (440–61).[11][†] In actuality, it is a private collection of Mass prayers used in the city of Rome. In
this collection one often finds whole series of prayers provided for one
and the same day of the liturgical year, or one and the same occasion.
Frequently, particular prayers can be dated through the allusions they
make to contemporary events. The oldest prayer we are able to date in
this way was first used in March of 483, when it was recited at the grave
of Pope Simplicius (468–83)[‡] following his death.[12] The most numerous
chronological clues, which are also the latest, take us to the time when
Rome was battling the Goths, around the middle of the sixth century.[13]

But clues of the kind—found all through these texts—would have
been excluded a priori had this collection of prayers been originally
designed to provide options for repeated use. References to the ad-
versity of war and the repeated pillaging of the *Campagna Romana*[§] by
enemy troops camped before the city walls, or thanks for an enemy
siege being recently lifted—one would weave allusions such as these
only into the prayers for the Mass said on the one particular day in
that one year when those historical circumstances actually occurred. In
a solemn Mass commemorating a pope's enthronement, the proximity of Easter would only earn mention in a year when the moveable
date of Easter fell near the date of that annual event. In the prayer for
the dead at the burial of a pope, the veneration of St. Lawrence (ca.
225–58)[¶] would play a role only when that burial took place in the
coemeterium adjacent to San Lorenzo fuori le Mura.**

---

* On Gregory I or the Great, see Short Biography, no. 78.
† On Leo I or the Great, see Short Biography, no. 117.
‡ On Simplicius, see Short Biography, no. 163.
§ The *campagna Romana* are the plains surrounding the city of Rome.
¶ On Lawrence, see Short Biography, no. 116.
** This is the cemetery next to the church of St. Lawrence Outside the Walls,
that is, outside the walls of the ancient city of Rome.

From this we can conclude that—up until around the middle of the sixth century—Rome did not yet know a Mass formulary appointed for use on each and every individual occasion and feast day. Frequently popes (or their secretaries) authored the texts for the holy mysteries as occasion required. However, in essence, this is nothing other than the persistence of textual improvisation, the original stage in the formation of liturgical texts, which the East had already grown beyond at least two centuries before, when Serapion of Thmuis (d. 360)* composed his fixed eucharistic prayer without the use of variable texts.[†] The fact that in Rome the prayer texts for the Mass changed, according to the church year or the votive occasion for offering a Mass, was nothing less than an aspect of liturgical history hardening for perpetuity. With conservative tenacity, Rome clung to the freedom that allowed individuals to improvise liturgical texts, or at least to compose each text to suit its specific circumstance, albeit in written form.[‡]

Certainly there were many collections of early formularies similar to this sacramentary, the one allegedly authored by Leo. When the creative juices flagged, one had only to reach into the collection and pull out texts, which were used over and over again on specific days and occasions. The repeated use of texts in a collection of this kind was made possible by bracketing obvious allusions to specific historical events. Musaeus (d. 457/61) in Marseilles,[§] Gregory the Great in Rome, and the editor of the so-called Gelasian Sacramentary[¶] on Gallican soil all had compiled selections of this kind, using the abundant storehouse of liturgical material preserved from the past. The point at which Rome moved beyond this practice, indigenous to the Spanish-Gallican area, was the Canon. Rome developed the main part of this prayer into an essentially invariable, comprehensive eucharistic text; increasingly over time, it even put limits on the textual variations allowed for the preface. In its failure to push on through to the point of creating an inviolable text for the whole eucharistic prayer, Rome once again serves up a surviving remnant. While the Eastern

---

* On Serapion, see Short Biography, no. 157.

[†] For Serapion's prayer book, see p. 91.

[‡] See pp. 94–95 on the early practice of composing eucharistic prayers freely within an accepted framework.

[§] On Musaeus, see Short Biography, no. 126.

[¶] For a discussion of this sacramentary, see p. 120. On Gelasius, see Short Biography, no. 75.

liturgy evolved to that further developmental stage, this Roman remnant maintains one predating it. This makes clear the value of what the Roman type of liturgy rescued. In providing liturgical texts with ample mobility, Rome—in its adherence to the past—has faithfully guarded a priceless treasure.

––––––––––––––

Notes

[1] See the obituaries, full of personal warmth, by Francis Aiden Cardinal Gasquet, "Edmund Bishop: A Personal Appreciation," *Downside Review* 31 (1917): 3–11; Dom André Wilmart, "Edmund Bishop. Homage d'un disciple et d'un âme," *Downside Review* 31 (1917): 12–28; Leo Kunibert Mohlberg, "Erinnerungen an einer Meister liturgiegeschichtlicher Forschung," *Benediktinische Monatschrift* 4 (1922): 44–54; and A. Ferretti, *Scienza Cattolica*, ser., 5, 20 (1921): 436–51 [this citation could not be verified], which comes equipped with a complete list of Bishop's literary works. [For a biography with bibliography of Edmond Bishop, see Nigel Abercrombie, *The Life and Work of Edmond Bishop* (London: Longmans, 1959), 492–508.]

[2] Edmond Bishop, "An Addition by E. B.," *Journal of Theological Studies* 15 (1914): 589–93, an "addition" to a study by Richard Hugh Connolly, *The Work of Menezes on the Malabar Liturgy*, pt. 2 (London: Dauson, 1914).

[3] In this regard, Baumstark, *Perikopenordnungen*, 172–84, offers a summary.

[4] See Anton Baumstark, "'Supra quae' e 'Supplices' del canone Romano," *Roma e l'Oriente* 4 (1912/13): 348–58, 5 (1913): 49–54, 88–96, and 149–58, also published as a single volume as Baumstark, *Le liturgie orientali e le preghiere "Supra quae" e "Supplices" del canone Romano*, Studi liturgici, fasc. 5 (Grottaferrata: n.p., 1913).

[5] Cyril of Jerusalem, Κατηχητικοι λόγοι πέντε [Mystagogical catecheses] I, PG 33, cols. 1065–76 [ET: Edward Yarnold, *The Awe-Inspiring Rituals of Initiation* (Slough: St. Paul's Publications, 1971), 68–95; see also Johnson, *Worship*, II, no. 82-C (selections)]. See Franz Xavier Dölger, *Die Sonne der Gerechtigkeit und der Schwarze. Eine religionsgeschichtliche Studie zum Taufgelobnis*, LF 2 (Münster in Westfalen: Aschendorff, 1918), where admittedly the conditions specific to Rome are not appreciated at all correctly.

[6] See Eduard Alexander von der Goltz, *Das Gebet in der ältesten Christenheit* (Leipzig: J. C. Heinrichs, 1901), 95–101 [available through Google Books].

[7] Illustrations of these prayers are primarily found in the various apocryphal Acts of the Apostles. [While Baumstark does not offer a specific reference here, there are numerous acts of various apostles, as in the Acts of Andrew, Barnabas, John, the Martyrs, Paul, Paul and Thecla, Peter, Peter and Andrew, Peter and Paul, Peter and the Twelve, Philip, Pilate, Thomas, and Xanthippe, Polyxena, and Rebecca, available in various texts and translations. GT: The acts of

John, Peter, Paul, Andrew, and Thomas are available in *Neutestamentliche Apokryphen in deutscher Übersetzung*, 3rd ed., vol. 2, ed. Wilhelm Schneemelcher, rev. ed. Edgar Hennecke (Tübingen: J. C. B. Mohr [P. Siebeck], 1964), 110–372; ET: *New Testament Apocrypha*, vol. 2. trans. Robert MacLachan Wilson (Cambridge: James Clarke & Co.; Louisville, KY: Westminster/John Knox Press, 1991), 75–481. A work dedicated solely to this literature offers texts in Syriac with English translations: *Apocryphal Acts of the Apostles*, 2 vols., ed. William Wright (London and Edinburgh: Williams & Norgate, 1871; repr., Hildesheim: Olms, 1990; repr., Piscataway, NJ: Georgias Press, 2005); selections of passages with liturgical interest from the Acts of John, Paul, and Peter are available in Johnson, *Worship*, I, nos. 18, 19, and 20.]

[8] Third Council of Carthage (397), canon 23, Mansi 3, 384 A, B.

[9] For this text in the Sacramentary of Auxerre, see *Missale Gallicanum*, PL 72, col. 361.

[10] Translated by Henri Hyvernat, "Fragmente der Altkoptischen Liturgie," *Römische Quartalschrift* 2 (1888): 23–25.

[11] For the Leonine Sacramentary, see *Liber Sacramentorum Romae Ecclesiae . . . S. Leoni Papae in vulgatis tributis*, PL 55, cols. 21–156. A critical edition was published by Charles Lett Feltoe, *Sacramentarium Leonianum* (Cambridge: Cambridge University Press, 1896 [repr., Eastbourne, East Sussex: Gardners Books, 2007]).

[12] Constituent to the last Mass for October in the Leonine Sacramentary, PL 55, col. 137. Critical edition by Feltoe, *Sacramentarium Leonianum*, 138.

[13] See Duchesne, *Origines*, 137–39 [ET: Duchesne, *Worship*, 137–40]; Rudolph Buchwald, *Das sogennante Sacramentarium Leonianum, und sein Verhältnis zu den beiden anderen römischen Sakramentarien* (Wien [Vienna]: Kommissions-Verlag, 1908); and Hans Lietzmann, "Zur Datierung des Sacramentarium Leonianum," JLW 2 (1922): 101f.

Chapter 13

Liturgical Language and the Vernacular
Priest and Deacon

In the realm of liturgy, contrasts mark the church. The Greek-speaking area, where the life of the early church has its roots, is characterized by development; its mission field to the East by conservatism; its mission field to the West by a conservatism yet more robust.* This observation is confirmed by how these areas view one of the most delicate issues of liturgical life: the question of liturgical language.

When dealing with an indigenous community speaking a non-Greek vernacular, Christian antiquity never aspired or attempted to retain Greek as its preferred liturgical language. Just as translating the Bible into the local language was simply a top priority for the Greek missionary effort, so was doing the same with the liturgy. Consequently, forms of the Byzantine liturgy and types related to it developed in Armenian, Georgian, and Church Slavonic, whereas the Egyptian liturgy developed a form in Ethiopic (Ge'ez).† No less did the Gothic Arians, when they made their home in the cultural orbit of eastern Europe, possess a liturgy in their Germanic mother tongue, which—in some form—they brought to the west and south.[1]‡ On top of that, in areas where the population had once spoken or understood Greek but were adopting a new

---

* This contrast is elaborated in chapter 12 passim.

† On Ethiopic (Ge'ez), see n. on p. 93.

‡ After migrating from Sweden, the Goths first settled in the basin of the Vistula River and subsequently around the Black Sea as far south as the lower Danube River. Their initial contact with Christianity was on raids to the south. However, Ulphilas (ca. 311–83) is regarded as "the apostle to the Goths" and a source of their Arian faith. Though his family came from Cappadocia, Ulphilas was thoroughly acquainted with their language and culture, for as a child he was raised among them. After being educated in Constantinople and consecrated bishop in 341 by Eusebius, the Arian bishop of Nicomedia (d. 341), he set himself to converting the Goths, which included the crucial work of translating the Bible into their language. Later in the fourth century, when in 376 the Huns invaded and took control of the area around the Black Sea, the Goths divided into two groups. The Ostrogoths (ET: Eastern Goths) accepted Hun hegemony. Others called the Visigoths (ET: Western Goths) moved out of the

tongue, liturgies—responding quickly to the decline of Greek—were translated into the newly ascendant dialects. Instances of this pattern, dating from an earlier period, are (1) the translation of the Egyptian liturgy from Greek into the various Coptic dialects* and (2) those of the liturgy of Jerusalem from Greek into (a) the West Aramaic dialect of the Christian Palestinian population and (b) the East Aramaic language form spoken in Edessa—that is, Syriac†—the linguistic dress clothing the Jacobite and Maronite liturgies.‡ Then in the Middle Ages, the liturgy of the Patriarchate of Antioch was likewise translated into Syriac and Arabic,[2] and even in modern times the Byzantine liturgy was translated into Romanian, in part from the Greek and in part from the Slavonic.[3]§ The

---

region toward the west in two separate migrations. One moved south into the Balkans. Another worked its way militarily across the Danube and into Italy, famously sacking Rome in 410. A Visigothic kingdom established in Gaul and Spain wielded power from the fifth to the seventh centuries.

In this passage Baumstark asserts that, just as the Goths had received the Bible in their own language while in the east, so did they receive such a liturgy, which the Visigoths carried both south (into the Balkans) and west (to Gaul and Spain). In the latter case the liturgy would have evolved into the Mozarabic Rite.

* On Coptic see, n. on p. 93.

† On Aramaic and its Christian form, Syriac, see n. on p. 55.

‡ On the christological controversies and these churches, see n. on p. 48; on the Maronite Church, see n. on p. 47; on the Jacobites, see n. on p. 105.

§ Although texts of the Romanian Orthodox Church began to be translated into the vernacular as early as the sixteenth century, Old Church Slavonic was its official language well into the nineteenth. During the eighteenth century, members of Greek families residing in Phanar, the chief Greek quarter of Constantinople, who had risen to power in the Ottoman Empire, served as princes in the Danubian Principalities (Moldavia and Wallachia) in present-day Romania, with authority over both political and religious matters. During this period (1711–1821), known as the Phanariote epoch of Romanian history, these princes sought to impose the Greek language on their subjects. As a consequence, the use of Old Church Slavonic in the liturgy declined and that of Romanian became more common, particularly in congregations of lower profile. By the end of the eighteenth century, the use of Romanian in the liturgy was widespread, although it was not prescribed for Wallachia until 1862. See *The Blackwell Dictionary of Eastern Christianity*, ed. Ken Parry et al. (Oxford: Blackwell Publishers, 1999), 407–8.

liturgy also adapted itself in places that were thoroughly multilingual. The pilgrim Egeria (fl. fourth century)* reports that, in Jerusalem toward the end of the fourth century, the Greek of the liturgy was orally translated on the spot into Aramaic.[4] An interesting Syrian-Jacobite document, stemming from the close of the fifth century, tells us of a similar instance further to the northeast, where Greek and Syriac were found in the liturgy side by side.[5] Early in the Christian era, monks of different nationalities residing in the Great Lavra of Mar Saba in the Kidron Valley[†] were separated into smaller oratories where they celebrated not only the Liturgy of the Hours but also the Liturgy of the Word as a prelude to the eucharistic celebration. They also came together in the main church of the monastery, but only for the eucharistic service itself, when instead they used Greek for their common liturgical language.[6]

On the other hand, the ecclesiastical language of Eastern Aramaic[‡] was from the outset very different from the Iranian mother tongue spoken by that segment of society won over to Christianity in the Sassanian kingdom.[§] The contrast between it and the latter is perhaps similar to that found in the West—up until the high Middle Ages—between Latin and the vernacular Germanic and Romance languages. As the only liturgical language allowed, it was for the most part retained—with dogged determination—vis-à-vis middle Persian, just as it was later against Arabic. In the first centuries of its missionary efforts, it was only in the church province of Persis[¶] that the Iranian

---

* On Egeria, see Short Biography, no. 65.

† A *lavra* (meaning literally "street" or "alley" in Greek) was a monastic community of the early church in which anchorites dwelling in separate abodes lived under the authority of a single abbot. This *lavra* was founded by Sabas (Arabic: Saba; 439?–532) in the Wadi en-Nar in Palestine, wild country between Jerusalem and the Dead Sea. It became the home of John of Damascus (ca. 650–ca. 750) and significant for the liturgy, as its *typicon* became standard for churches celebrating the Byzantine Rite. On John of Damascus, see Short Biography, no. 109.

‡ The common name for the Eastern Aramaic used by the Christian community is Syriac. On Aramaic, see n. on p. 55.

§ Baumstark is here referring to Middle Persian, often called Pahlavi. In the Sassanian kingdom, Christianity competed with Zoroastrianism and the Manichaean faith. On the Sassanian Empire, see n. on p. 56.

¶ Persis is a church province lying inland from the northeast coast of the Persian Gulf.

vernacular dialect came to be used in the liturgy;[7] as early as the fifth century, we learn not only of liturgies being translated into the nation's new language for worship but even of its use in crafting liturgical poetry.[8] Apart from this one instance, however, it was only at a later date, when the Nestorians advanced farther toward the east, that even their propaganda proved unable to maintain the conservative principle that Aramaic be retained as the liturgical language. The so-called Turfan discovery, made in eastern Turkestan,* provides insight into how the Sogdian language[†] gradually found firm footing in the liturgy, at least for the reading of Scripture.[9] The stone monument from Xi'an-fu, dedicated on February 4, 781, and written in Syriac and Chinese,[‡] tells us that liturgical texts of the Nestorian Rite were translated into Chinese.[10] That occurred sometime after 636. On the other hand, it appears that the Nestorians in India always kept as their

---

* The Turfan discovery of Sanskrit manuscripts was made in the Turfan area of eastern Turkestan (Chinese: Xinjiang) by German expeditions in the first years of the twentieth century, working at places along the northern Silk Road. The publication of these texts began soon after the first expedition returned in 1903. They are described in "Sanskrithandschriften aus den Turfanfunden," part 10 of the *Katalogisierung der Orientalischen Handschriften in Deutschland* (available online at http://staatsbibliothek-berlin.de, search "Sanskrithandschriften aus den Turfanfunden"). An overview of the collection can be found in Klaus Wille, "Survey of the Sanskrit Manuscripts in the Turfan Collection" http://www.bbaw.de/bbaw/Forschung/Forschungsprojekte/turfanforschung/bilder/Wille.pdf.

† Sogdian was a Middle Iranian language spoken in Central Asia in the first millennium of the Christian era, notably in the region of Sogdiana (approximately present-day Uzbekistan and Tajikistan) and in Chinese Turkestan. Extant Sogdian literature includes Christian, Buddhist, and secular texts.

‡ The stone monument from Xi'an-fu (ET: Xi'an Province), now commonly called the Nestorian Stele (or Monument), is a limestone slab a little less than three meters in height and about one meter in width, inscribed with Chinese and Syriac text. Of Chinese workmanship with inscriptions composed by a Nestorian monk, it dates from the Tang dynasty (618–907) and was erected in 781 at the imperial capital city of Chang-an (present-day Xi'an). Its text and lists provide records for 150 years of Christian history in China, mentioning congregations in several northern Chinese cities. The original stele is to be found in the Beilin Museum in Xi'an China.

sole liturgical language the Syriac that had been passed on to them by Nestorian missionaries.*

The Latin West never made concessions like the Aramaic East, which—by accommodating to circumstance—allowed itself to compromise on the principle that their liturgical language be preserved. The West holds its liturgical language to be an inviolable sacred object. It views Latin, honored through time and uniform throughout its rite, to be inseparably bound to the very being of its liturgy. Only once did Rome condescend to allow missionaries to use a vernacular for establishing a liturgy. That was in the ninth century, when the relationship of the Slavic mission to the Western church was at stake. Though Rome did not send Cyril (826–69) and Methodius (815–85) out in the first place, it clothed them with its authority.[11]†

The use of Latin as the liturgical language in the West is more than standing church law. Apart from the fact that the magisterium of the church categorically rejects the argument against the use of Latin (which holds it to be reprehensible and the use of the vernacular to be actually necessary for the liturgy to be fully effective). Apart from all of that, the use of Latin is fundamentally important to the value

---

* According to tradition, the original St. Thomas Christians in India were converts of the apostle Thomas, who arrived in 52 and worked there until martyred in 72. While this cannot be historically verified, there is evidence of contact with Roman traders prior to the Christian era, one "Archbishop John of Persia and Great India" attended the Council of Nicaea (325), and fourth-century fathers—Syrian, Greek, and Latin—make mention of Thomas' work in India. These Christians are concentrated on the Malabar Coast of India and are Nasranis, descendants of the Jewish Diaspora in Kerala. From at least the sixth century they were a part of the East Syrian (Nestorian) Church, functioning under the see of Seleucia-Ctesiphon and calling their liturgy *Qurbana* and using Syriac (*Suryani*) for their liturgical language. However Jewish elements were also mixed into this tradition, as was evident in their day of worship (Saturday), their church architecture, and various beliefs and customs. This unitary tradition splintered under the influence of European powers, beginning with the Portuguese in the fifteenth century. While some entered into communion with Rome, others tied themselves to the West Syrian Church. Today there are some eight separate churches in this tradition. While they all trace their origins back to the missionary work of St. Thomas in India, they have diverged from their shared historic traditions theologically, ecclesiastically, and—to varying degrees—liturgically.

† On Cyril and Methodius, see Short Biography, no. 59, and n. on p. 29.

of the liturgy—and not only as a sign of the unity of church life. It is also crystal clear that the dignity and majesty of the Roman liturgy is greatly enhanced by donning the ancient language of the Roman people for its standard linguistic attire. Nonetheless, one cannot deny that celebrating the liturgy in a dead language, which the bulk of the faithful cannot understand, constitutes the main challenge confronting today's vibrant liturgical movement as it seeks to attain its ultimate goal. That goal can be nothing less than the whole congregation feeling the heartbeat of the liturgy with the same immediacy as they feel their own—just as the assembly did in Christian antiquity. At that time, however, the liturgy was immediately intelligible to the whole assembly, even in its language, and thus the assembly entered into the liturgy with active inner participation, with an involvement as deep as one can imagine. That can never be fully replaced by silently following the liturgy, reading a printed translation of its texts.*

The difficult problem evident here† is found in the East as well, though not with the same urgency—in fact not by far. The problem there: at what point do liturgical and vernacular language finally part company? The lack of urgency around this question in Eastern liturgy is due to the role the East assigns to the deacon. As originally conceived, his office had nothing to do with the liturgy. According to the account of the origins of the diaconate, found in the Acts of the Apostles (Acts 6:1-6), its essence lies in the charitable work of the church. Once again, Rome's conservative temperament is evident, for there *diakonia*‡ remained the church's care for the poor and their district of the city; this only changed when the patterns of church life

---

* For other references to the liturgical movement, see p. 49, pp. 193–94, and pp. 240–42.

† While on a superficial level "the difficult problem evident here" is the relationship of the liturgical language and the vernacular, more fundamentally that relationship and the role of the deacon in the East both raise the issue of comprehensibility and on two levels: on that of history (How does the church attend to the people's understanding of and participation in the liturgy?) and on that of mystagogy (How does the assembly apprehend the mysteries God imparts liturgically?).

‡ Geoffrey William Hugo Lampe, *A Patristic Greek Lexicon* (Oxford: Clarendon Press, 1961), s.v. "διακονία, ἡ." For specific reference to the diaconate, see section B) 5) v) in this entry.

found in the early church had run their course.* In the context of the liturgy, the Roman deacon's only role was to serve at the altar, where he assisted at the eucharistic sacrifice. Already in the legend concerning Lawrence (d. 258), the saint describes this kind of relationship between himself and his pope, Sixtus (257–58),† who went down the path to martyrdom alone, ahead of his deacon.‡ In the context of oriental liturgy, the deacon is infinitely more. There he became the intermediary between the bishop (or priest) and the congregation.

---

* Early on, following the biblical pattern (Acts 6:1-6), there were seven deacons in Rome, of which one, the archdeacon, both served at the altar with the pope and functioned as bursar of the church in Rome. Lawrence (d. 258), mentioned by Baumstark in the following passage, is an example of the latter. Again following the biblical pattern, these deacons were responsible for the charitable work of the church, a role specifically mentioned during the time of Pope Fabian (236–50). To enable this work, the city was divided into seven diaconal districts, where each deacon was responsible for running an administrative center dispensing pensions and alms.

† On Sixtus II, see Short Biography, no. 164.

‡ Sixtus, the bishop of Rome (257–58), went to his martyrdom "alone" only in the sense that Lawrence, the archdeacon who always stood by his side at the altar, did not accompany him. For four deacons died with Sixtus and two later the same day, whereas Lawrence was martyred four days later. Baumstark refers here to an exchange between Lawrence and Sixtus as the pope was being taken away for execution. Wanting to join him in martyrdom, Lawrence said, "Father, where are you going without your son? Wither are you going, holy priest, without your deacon? You were never wont to offer sacrifice without me, your minister. Wherein have I displeased you? Have you found me wanting to my duty? Try me, now, and see whether you have made choice of an unfit minister for dispensing the blood of the Lord" (from the hagiographies for Aug. 10 in Alban Butler, *Lives of the Saints*, vol. 8 (New York and Philadelphia: P. J. Kennedy and Sons, 1895), 344. A poem by Prudentius provides early *acta* of the martyrdom of St. Lawrence. See *Prudentius, with an English translation*, vol. 2, trans. H. J. Thomson (London: William Heinemann; Cambridge: Harvard University Press, 1953), 109–43. A more extended poem, which includes an account of St. Lawrence's protest to Sixtus, comes from medieval England. See *Nigel of Canterbury: The Passion of St. Laurence Epigrams and Marginal Poems*, trans. and ed. Jan M. Ziolkowski (Leiden–New York–Köln [Cologne]: E. J. Brill, 1994), 83–85, lines 187–214. On Lawrence of Rome, see Short Biography, no. 116; on Prudentius, see Short Biography, no. 149; on Sixtus II, see Short Biography, no. 164.

Almost every stand-alone prayer said by the priest in the East is tied to a longer or shorter litany led by the deacon, whose invitations to prayer as well as his introductory formulae and concluding ones are followed by a congregational response.[12] Already before liturgical and vernacular language went their separate ways or when that process never occurred at all, these *diakonika** greatly enhanced the congregation's ability to experience the liturgy with immediacy. Though the *diakonika* were an essential component of the liturgy in their own right, every single member of the congregation was able to understand. Far more than the prayers of the priest they accompanied, their flow of ideas and the way they expressed that oratorically—opened up the liturgy to the people. Sometimes a liturgical language, previously in common use as the vernacular tongue, was completely replaced in everyday speech by a totally different one. In such instances, nothing was more natural than for—at the very least—the responsive prayer exchanged by the deacon and the congregation to be translated into this new vernacular, while the prayer of the priest was able to continue to preserve the older, venerable liturgical language. This is how the Arabic language entered the Greek Byzantine Rite upon Asian soil (that is, the Syriac Rites of the Jacobites and the Maronites) and probably also the Coptic liturgy in Egypt. Once the use of Arabic had actually taken hold alongside one of these languages, it was no longer felt to be a harmful loss of style when that vernacular was also used to proclaim other elements of the liturgy, the first of these being biblical lections, whose sole purpose in the structure of the liturgy is to instruct the assembly. In fact—in the end—there was no obstacle to using the Arabic language for some of the prayers said by the priest, once the desirability of the congregation understanding them had become apparent.

For all their importance in the eucharistic liturgy, the *diakonika* are not only found as a regular feature there; they also recur in every liturgical action of the East—as in the administration of the sacraments, consecration, and burial, but above all even in the church's Liturgy of the Hours. Additionally, last but not least, the greatest merit of this kind of prayer was to open up a bridge to the congregation, providing

---

* The term *diakonika*, used in the Byzantine and Coptic Rites, refers to the liturgical elements recited by the deacon—for example, as he leads the congregation with the petitions of the litanies. See Peter D. Day, *The Liturgical Dictionary of Eastern Christianity* (Collegeville, MN: Liturgical Press, 1993), 68.

them with an avenue for participating in the liturgy through their own contribution. The *diakonika* were also familiar to the Gallic-Spanish liturgical area, although not to the extent described above, and the Mozarabic liturgy was not unique in continuing their use. A diaconal litany, in strictly oriental style, is also heard—even now—in the Ambrosian Mass of Milan, at least on Sundays in Lent.[13] Only the Roman Rite is wholly without this liturgical element—a fact to be counted among its most characteristic features. Understandably, after what we have outlined briefly about the litany, one would be initially hard put to rank this among the most felicitous features of the Roman liturgy. However, in the end, there may be an advantage in not having a deacon participate in the liturgy that probably, even in this case, outweighs its undeniable weakness.*

---

* Baumstark explains his understanding of this weakness in the first paragraph of chap. 14.

Notes

For a general treatment of the conditions found in the Orient, see Anton Baumstark, "Sprache Nation und Kirche im christlichen Orient," *Historisch-politische Blätter für das katholischen Deutschland* 156 (1915): 633–43 and 699–706.

[1] Full particulars can be found in Hans von Schubert, *Geschichte der christlichen Kirche im Frühmittelalter*, vol. 2 (Tübingen: Mohr, 1917–21 [repr., Hildesheim: Olms, 1976]), 23f.

[2] Cyrille Korolevskij [Charon], "Le Rite byzantine et la liturgie chrysostomienne dans les patriarcate melchites (Alexandrie-Antioch-Jerusalem)," Χρυσοστομικα [*Chrysostomika*], 498–635.

[3] See. Ch. Auner, "Les versions romaines de la liturgie de saint Jean Chrysostome," Χρυσοστομικα [*Chrysostomika*], 731–69.

[4] Egeria, chap. 47, no. 3f. Paul Geyer, *Itinera Hierosolymitana saeculi IV–VIII* (Wien [Vienna]: F. Tempsky, 1898), 99; GT: Hermann Richter, *Pilgerreise der Ätheria (oder Silvia) von Aquitanien nach Jerusalem und die heiligen Stätten* (Essen: Baedeker, 1919), 87 [ET: *Egeria's Travels*, trans. John Wilkinson (London: SPCK, 1971), 146f; Johnson, *Worship*, II, no. 83: 2218].

[5] See *Vetusta documenta liturgica*, ed. Ignatius Ephraem Rahmani, Studia Syriaca 3 (Beryti [Beirut]: In Seminario Scharfensi de Monte Libano, 1908), 4–10. Concerning the alternating Greek and Syrian psalmody of two half-choirs in a monastery near Zeugma, see Baumstark, *Literatur*, 141.

⁶ This is according to a fragment of the monastic *typikon*. See Eduard Kurtz, "Review: A. Dmitrijevskij, *Die Klosterregeln des heiligen Sabbas*," BZ 3 (1894): 167–70.

⁷ For a general treatment of the subject, see Eduard Sachau, "Vom Christentum in der Persis," *Sitzungsberichte der Königlichen Preussischen Akademie der Wissenschaften, philologische-historische Klasse* 39 (1916): 958–80. Concerning fragments of a Psalter, arranged for liturgical use and written in Pahlavi, a writing system used for Middle Persian, see Friedrich Carl Andreas, "Bruchstücke einer Pehlewi-Übersetzung der Psalmen aus der Sassanidenzeit," *Sitzungsberichte . . . Preussischen Akademie*, 33 (1910): 869–72, as well as Anton Baumstark, "Die christlich-literarischen Turfan-Funde," OC, n.s., 3 (1913): 328–32, and a corresponding Syrian manuscript of this kind dating from the New Persian period that has been edited by Friedrich W. K. Müller, "Ein syrisch-neupersisches Psalmenbruchstück aus Chinesisch-Turkistan," *Festschrift Eduard Sachau zum siebzigsten Geburtstage gewidmet von Freunden und Schülern*, ed. Gotthold Weil (Berlin: G. Reimer 1915), 215–22.

⁸ These translations were made by one Ma'na born in the city of Shiraz [a city in present-day Iran]. See Baumstark, *Literatur*, 105f.

⁹ See Anton Baumstark, "Die christlich-literarischen Turfan-Funde," OC, n.s., 3 (1913): 329; Baumstark, "Neue soghdisch-nestorianische Bruchstücke," OC, n.s., 4 (1915): 123–28; and Baumstark, *Perikopenordnungen*, 1of.

¹⁰ The best edition and treatment of this text at present is P. Yoshiro Saeki, *The Nestorian Monument in China* (London: SPCK, 1916). See also Baumstark, *Literatur*, 216f.

¹¹ *Epistolae Karolini aevi V*, ed. Erich Caspar, Gerhard Laehr, et al., Monumenta Germaniae Historica: Epistulae 7 (Berlin: Weidmann, 1928; repr. 1978; repr., München [Munich]: Monumenta Germaniae Historica, 1993), 222ff.

¹² Baumstark, *Messe*, 12–16.

¹³ Concerning these Western formularies, see Duchesne, *Origines*, 198–200 [ET: Duchesne, *Worship*, 198–201]; Wilhelm Bousset, *Nachrichten der königlichen Gesellschaft der Wissenschaften zu Göttingen: Philologische-historische Klasse* (Berlin: Weidmannsche Buchhandlung, 1913), 135–62 [citation could not be verified]. Concerning an idiosyncratic development in the rhythmic *preces* of Spain, see the Speyer scholar, Wilhelm Meyer, "Über die rythmischen Preces der mozarabischen Liturgie," *Nachrichten . . . zu Göttingen*, 177–222.

Chapter 14

The Ivy of Poetry

Carrying no stock of diaconal litanies in its liturgical warehouse at all, the Roman liturgy let slip an excellent opportunity for bridge building with the congregation, even over the gulf created by its use of Latin. At the same time, however, the situation allowed the Roman liturgy from its very beginnings to skirt a danger that the East could not avoid. As a responsive prayer exchanged by deacon and congregation, repeated over and over again to the point of true monotony, the diaconal litany threatened to become a framework concealing altogether the priestly liturgy going on behind it.

Liturgical poetry posed a similar danger for the liturgy, but one far more serious yet. While originally intended to serve as a decorative complement to worship and its speech, liturgical poetry exhibits the innate—and universal—tendency to obscure the clear outlines of both, covering them opulently, to an ever-greater degree. Liturgical poetry grows like ivy creeping over some venerable old stonework. Spinning its luxuriant web to work an invasive hold into every crack and joint, the ivy slowly but surely comes to threaten that stonework's very existence. The West felt the danger stemming from this aspect of the liturgy as much as the East. Only the worship of urban Rome showed a kind of intuitive grasp of how serious this danger was. Probably nowhere are the traits characteristic of the Roman liturgy, moderation and clarity, so strikingly apparent at one and the same time, as in Rome's resistance—lasting more than a thousand years—to admit sung pieces of poetry into its liturgy.

The earliest Christian hymns emerged in Greek-speaking areas.[1] Taking as their model the prose translations of the psalms found in the Septuagint, they dispensed with the metrical form. The words of Paul (d. 65?), which contain the earliest liturgical references extant, give us an inkling of the great significance hymns had for early Christian worship. At certain points in the Pauline letters and the Revelation to John, one can catch an echo of these hymns. The Odes of Solomon offers a whole book of such songs, most of which are preserved in Syriac translation, with fragments found in Coptic.[2] Given how quickly

Christianity became Hellenized,* it was only natural that Christian sung poetry would quite soon want—at times—to also make use of metrical forms of poetry found in antiquity. Primarily heretical groups used songs for worship as a way to promote their peculiar doctrines. That aroused fundamental concerns in orthodox circles about the whole idea of hymns. The Council of Laodicea[†] in Asia Minor during the fourth century[3] and in the year 563 the first council of Braga[‡] on the Iberian Peninsula[4] forbade any liturgical use of nonbiblical texts of a poetic nature. Given this state of affairs, only a few odds and ends were able to hold their own; in the context of the liturgy, little has survived from this first spring of song in the young church. The most important two are the Gloria, which in the Western Rite serves universally as a morning hymn,[5§] and a counterpart in the form of an evening song specific to the Byzantine Rite:

> O gracious light,
> pure brightness of the ever living Father in heaven,
> O Jesus Christ, holy and blessed.[6¶]

A martyr Athenogenes (fl. ca. 196)** was erroneously held to be the author of this piece of poetry, in which strains, conveying a profound feeling for nature, throb for the magic of a golden sunset.[7]

Where the eastern dialect of Aramaic[††] was spoken, Bardaisan[‡‡] (154–222) crafted brilliant new heretical "psalms."[8] Then, for the first time, the church overcame its antipathy toward the sung liturgical poetry associated with the heretics and—using the heretics' own weapon against them—changed its tactics to combat them with it. Ranking alongside

---

* See n. on p. 74, and n. on p. 230.

[†] See n. on p. 55.

[‡] See n. on p. 101.

[§] *Gloria in excelsis Deo*, known also as the "Greater Doxology," the "Angelic Hymn," or simply for short the Gloria, became a part of morning prayers in the fourth century, although its origins are earlier. On this hymn, see also p. 69 (chap. 3).

[¶] *Phos hilarion*, sung at Vespers in the Byzantine tradition, is the oldest nonbiblical hymn still in use today. ET: *Book of Common Prayer* (Kingsport, TN: Church Hymnal Corporation and Seabury Press, 1977), 64.

** On Athenogenes, see Short Biography, no. 23.

[††] On Aramaic, see n. on p. 55.

[‡‡] On Bardaisan, see Short Biography, no. 26.

Aswana (fl. before the sixth century)[9]* is one of the oldest catholic hymn writers we hear of in Edessa, the great Ephrem the Syrian (ca. 306–73).[10]†
He was a Christian counterpart to Alcman (fl. mid-sixth to late seventh centuries BCE), the old citizen of Sparta,‡ in that he used choirs of virgins to lead the assembly in singing the melodious liturgical poetry he composed. The genre of these poems acquired the name *madrasha*, meaning "instruction," because—in the battle against heresy—they were frequently used to instruct the faithful. This basic form of Christian Syrian sung poetry is characterized by the length of each individual poem (which is considerable), the repetition in refrain after each individual verse of an invariable shorter one, the inclination to construct the latter out of dissimilar lines of verse, and the propensity to construct the whole composition as an acrostic, usually alphabetical. The *sogitha*, with its penchant for enlivening the liturgy dramatically, is a variation upon the *madrasha*. It makes use of a dialogue carried on between two persons alternating verses, which is joined to a simpler metrical structure and the almost invariable use of an alphabetic acrostic. A similar simplicity in metrical structure as well as a shorter length are peculiar to the *teshbohta*, the "song of praise."§ The *ba'utha* or rogation hymn accompanied rogation processions, held to implore heaven to pour out its mercies upon meadow and field—a response to the climatic conditions that recur in the East on a regular basis, particularly periods of persistent drought. Even a poet so early as Ephrem the Syrian had in fact tried his hand at all of these genres, although the names used for them later were not yet in vogue. In the Syrian liturgy over the coming centuries, the quantity of poetic texts swelled to a virtual avalanche. After the christological schism new genres developed their own separate existence in the various rites using Aramaic.¶ The old textual "property," inherited from a fast-disappearing golden age, was recycled. Perhaps it was broken up to be reused and—now in a new role—mixed into poetic imitations of more recent composition. Even a genre that was originally discursive

---

* On Aswana, see Short Biography, no. 21.

† On Ephrem the Syrian, see Short Biography, no. 66.

‡ On Alcman, see Short Biography, no. 6.

§ "Song of praise" is a translation of Baumstark's German text; the Syriac *teshbohta* is commonly translated into English today as "glorifications."

¶ For the christological division, see n. on p. 48. Baumstark writes of a "separate existence" that reflects this division, which was both doctrinal and linguistic.

rather than melodious, the metrical "speech" of the *memra** had to suffer hymnlike passages being surgically carved out of its texts. Primarily, however, pieces of sung poetry were tied most closely to psalmody.[11] Sometimes an individual psalm verse was sung before each stanza of liturgical poetry; the content of such a verse would be more or less germane to the stanzas following it. Sometimes the individual hymn verses intertwined with those of appointed psalms and biblical canticles. The former occurred in the Nestorian Rite with a style that was unsurpassed.[12] The latter, found among the Jacobites[†] and Maronites,[‡] is the type called *enjana*, or *responsorium*.[13]

All genres of Syrian church poetry use one and the same type of meter, based on syllable count and attention to word stress.[§] A tradition of Greek liturgical poetry employed this new rhythmic meter for crafting verse in place of the quantitative meter used by antiquity. Though dependent on its sister form every step of the way, that is, the older one in Aramaic, this new Greek poetry quickly surpassed it—a reflection of how rich the Hellenistic spirit was.[14][¶] Its earliest creations used single verses, which in their original form at times simply recast words of the great patristic preachers.[15] The name *troparion*, which in the beginning denoted the musical "manner" of these pieces, came to refer to the text itself.[**] The oldest poems of this kind we find in the fifth and sixth centuries, from the region nearby Constantinople, the vicinity of Antioch, and the Palestinian coast. In particular, however, it is the papyrus sheets and shards[††] of Egypt that open up for us a world

---

* Translated, *memra* means "speech" or "voice."

† On the Jacobites, see n. on p. 105.

‡ On the Maronites, see n. on p. 47.

§ I thank Gerard Rouwhorst for pointing out that scholarly opinion now holds that Syriac poetry is based exclusively on the counting of syllables (isosyllabism), without regard for word stress. See Sebastian P. Brock, *An Introduction to Syriac Studies* (Piscataway, NJ: Gorgias Press, 2006), 8–10.

¶ Quantitative meter constructs a line of poetry using a set number of long and short vowels.

** The word *troparion* most likely comes from the diminutive of the Greek word τρόπος, which can mean a way of saying or singing. In the fifth century the term came to refer also to short verses of liturgical poetry placed after those of psalms. In the Orthodox liturgy, *troparia* now come in varying lengths, from one or two verses up to a long poem.

†† In this passage, Baumstark's use of the German word *Tonsherben* is a pun. While literally meaning "shards of clay," a metaphorical reference to fragmen-

pertinent to this tradition—small in compass but rich in documents.[16] Together with some ancient songs preserved by Greek monks in Italy, these Egyptian papyrus texts, the oldest taking us back into the third century, illuminate the developmental path taken by Greek compositions in verse. To be quite specific, this path was influenced by the Syrian *madrasha*.[17] At the end of this development stands the *kontakion*, a fully mature early Byzantine hymn form, whose master is Romanos the Hymnographer (fl. ca. 540),* the greatest poetic exponent of Christian thought prior to Dante Alighieri (1265–1321).† Romanos was born in Aleppo of Jewish parents, coming to Constantinople from Beirut during the reign of Emperor Anastasius I (491–518).‡ A more recent stratum of Greek church poetry, whose texts are composed for insertion into psalmody, corresponds to the Syrian *enjana*. The last forms to appear in this stratum are the so-called canon and *triodion*, which from their beginning were created to be inserted into the biblical *cantica* of the morning office.[18] Jerusalem was the home of canon poetry. In the eighth century, Andrew (660–70), later the archbishop of Crete,§ John of Damascus (ca. 650–ca. 750),¶ and his brother Cosmas (ca. 706–ca. 760)** blazed a new path for the art of composing poetry in the canon form. A second generation of poets, themselves classical masters of this form, took up residence in Constantinople. This generation includes iconophiles like Theophanes, nicknamed "Graptós" (ca. 775–845);†† Theodore of Studios (759–826);‡‡ his brother Joseph, the archbishop of Thessalonica (ca. 762–832);§§ a somewhat younger Joseph "the Hymnographer" (ca. 810–86), with origins in Sicily;¶¶ and others.

The chants found in the Armenian hymnary and the "Antiphonary" of the Copts also consist of the kind represented by the Syrian *enjana*

---

tary evidence, *Ton* can also mean "sound" or "tone" and thus by pun refers simultaneously to "musical" shards.

* On Romanos the Hymnographer, see Short Biography, no. 154.

† On Dante Alighieri, see Short Biography, no. 60.

‡ On Anastasius I, see Short Biography, no. 12.

§ On Andrew of Crete, see Short Biography, no. 13.

¶ On John of Damascus, see Short Biography, no. 109.

** On Cosmas the Melodist, see Short Biography, no. 55.

†† On Theophanes Graptos, see Short Biography, no. 179.

‡‡ On Theodore the Studite, see Short Biography, no. 177.

§§ On Joseph of Thessalonica, see Short Biography, no. 111.

¶¶ On Joseph the Hymnographer, see Short Biography, no. 112.

and the Byzantine Canon (at least for the most part).[19] Finally, the way the poetry for hymns in the East developed in Ethiopic (Ge'ez)* was especially rich and idiosyncratic. Here the image of a St. Yared (525–71),[†] whom Ethiopia venerates as the father of its classical liturgical poetry, fades away into the golden background of legend's half-light.[20‡]

In the Eastern Liturgy of the Hours, this whole varied development created a situation whereby often psalmody was virtually suffocated under the weight of poetic material. Having allowed additions to the psalmody of the hours to increase to unseemly proportions, the proper use of the Psalter, namely, praying all the way through the Psalms over a set period of time, was compromised. In order to shorten the scope of the whole service, this use of the Psalter probably fell away altogether at times. Still more frequently, only just a few individual verses were recited from sung biblical texts. While these texts should have been woven into pieces of liturgical poetry, in actual practice only particular verses were recited, one for each poetic stanza. Of course, today even that is omitted and just the poetic text still recited. What had been intended as a decorative embellishment of the liturgy became a thicket of rank growth, proliferating out of control. At most, only remnants of the liturgy's old structure provide support for that growth—as a kind of flimsy trellis.

Apparently Hilary of Poitiers (ca. 315–67),[§] who became acquainted with the Syrian-Greek hymn form while banished to Phrygia,[¶] was the

---

* On Ethiopic (Ge'ez), see n. on p. 93.

[†] On Yared (or Jared) the Melodist, see Short Biography, no. 192.

[‡] The legend to which Baumstark refers recounts how God, desiring to establish liturgical chant in the Ethiopian Church that had none, sent to Yared three birds from the Garden of Eden, who conversed with him in human speech and carried him off to Heavenly Jerusalem, where he learned the songs sung by the twenty-four priests of heaven. For an English translation of the liturgical hagiography of Yared, see *The Book of Saints of the Ethiopian Church*, vol. 3, trans. E. A. Wallis Budget (Cambridge: Cambridge University Press, 1928), 875–77. For a critical evaluation, see Michael Powne, *Ethiopian Music: An Introduction* (London: Oxford University Press, 1968), 98–101.

[§] On Hilary of Poitiers, see Short Biography, no. 96.

[¶] An area in west central Anatolia. Once an independent kingdom, it became a province under Roman administration. Through the reforms of Emperor Diocletian (284–305), it was divided into two provinces: Phrygia I (or Phrygia Salutaris) and Phrygia II (or Pacatiana), the latter having Laodicea on the Lycus River as its capital and the former Synnada.

first to bring it to the West, when he came out of exile around 359.[21] Be that as it may, his own hymn poetry, along with other examples of the oldest Latin poetry written as hymns—of which valuable odds and ends have been preserved, notably out of Ireland[22]—most unmistakably betrays ties to the East, occasionally even by their content. In the case of longer pieces, this relationship is otherwise evident from their use of refrains and an alphabetic acrostic; in the case of shorter pieces, from being designated for insertion into biblical texts. Following their introduction into Gaul, the only aspect of this poetry to receive a negative reaction in the West (at least its lands to the south) was the change over to the new rhythmic kind of meter. The ties of these lands to the poetic tradition exemplified by the works of Virgil (70–19 BCE)* and Horace (65 BCE–8 CE)† still ran too deep for it to be any other way. Ambrose (ca. 339–97),‡ and even more so the Spaniard Prudentius (348–ca. 410),§ represent a thoroughly classical approach to the Latin Christian hymn. Only a renaissance intent upon reviving the forms of classical antiquity could fully grasp the scope of—and have the understanding required for—a poetry of this kind. This was the significance for Western cultural life of the first renaissance of antiquity,¶ the Carolingian Age.**

---

* On Virgil, see Short Biography, no. 186.

† On Horace, see Short Biography, no. 98.

‡ Ambrose (ca. 339–97), who may be called the father of liturgical hymnody in the West, introduced metrical hymns into the liturgy in Milan. While a number of hymns have been attributed to him, *Aeterne rerum conditor, Deus creator omnium, Iam surgit hora tertia*, and *Intende, qui Regis Israel* are assuredly his. A number of others are attributed to him with less certainty. On Ambrose, see Short Biography, no. 11.

§ On Prudentius, see Short Biography, no. 149.

¶ Baumstark understands the Carolingian Renaissance to be only the first of several renaissances of antiquity that have periodically recurred in Western culture. Another in the twelfth century was marked by exposure to and use of classical writers (notably Aristotle), a third in the period simply named "the Renaissance" revived the classical aesthetic and embraced humanistic ideals, and so on.

** Baumstark refers here to the Syrian-Greek influence upon Gallican liturgy, of which Hilary of Poitiers (ca. 315–67) was one example in regard to hymns. By contrast, the southern Mediterranean cultural area of Western Europe (Italy and Spain) rejected the new rhythmic kind of meter employed by this Eastern genre of poetry, holding instead to the forms of classical Latinity. This state

Were the hymns composed by Hilary—and pieces like them—originally intended for liturgical use?* Were the songs of Prudentius, those about martyrs and for various hours of the day?† To provide definitive answers to these questions probably requires a more detailed knowledge of fourth-century Christian worship in Gaul and Spain than we in fact enjoy. Whatever may have been the case in those lands, hymns did play a role in the liturgical life of Milan, namely those composed by Ambrose, who put them there himself. Others followed the example of the great bishop, as the sixth-century monastic rules of Caesarius (470–542) and Aurelianus (523–51) of Arles attest.[23]‡ At the time that hymn singing became a regular feature of the Office in Gaul, Gallic monasticism was not alone in embracing the practice. The Rule of St. Benedict also provides for singing an "Ambrosian" hymn at each office in the round of daily prayer.[24]§ In the liturgy of the Frankish Kingdom under the Merovingians, the hymn form was used more and more widely, even in churches independent of monastic foundations. This pattern of expansion must have suffered its first setback when that kingdom, under Pepin (751–68)¶ and Charlemagne (king from 768,

---

of affairs changed with the Carolingian Renaissance, which was intent upon reviving the forms of classical antiquity. With this appreciation, the northern part of Western Europe could now join the southern part in also embracing liturgical poetry that drew upon classical antiquity, such as that of Ambrose (ca. 339–97) and Prudentius (348–ca. 410).

* While Hilary of Poitiers (ca. 315–67) is sometimes given the honor of being the first Latin Christian hymn writer, the authorship of many hymns ascribed to him has been disputed. See n. 21 at the end of this chapter.

† *Liber Peristephanon* is a collection of fourteen poems in which Prudentius (348–ca. 410) offers praise for Spanish and Roman martyrs. In *Liber Cathemerinon*, Prudentius provides for daily use twelve lyric poems, which focus upon times during the day and festivals of the church.

‡ This is the monastic rule for the office of Lérins/Arles, first developed by Caesarius of Arles (470–542) and subsequently revised by Aurelianus (523–51), the second person to succeed as bishop of Arles. See Robert Taft, *The Liturgy of the Hours East and West*, 2nd rev. ed. (Collegeville, MN: Liturgical Press, 1993), 100–113.

§ In this instance, Baumstark uses "'Ambrosian' hymn" in the sense found in the Rule of St. Benedict, to refer to the genre of hymns using the quantitative meter of classical antiquity; it does not necessarily refer to hymns composed by Ambrose.

¶ On Pepin III (or the Short), see Short Biography, no. 137.

emperor 800–814),* adapted the Roman Rite. Only resistance to adopting the Roman Rite as it was—witness Alcuin's (735–804) supplement
to the Gregorian Sacramentary!†—gave the hymn form a blanket right
of entry into the liturgy north of the Alps. This right, which the hymn
had enjoyed in the Kingdom of the Franks under the Merovingians,
was thus granted anew and henceforth upheld. At the same time, the
European mainland and Ireland (which worshiped according to ancient monastic tradition‡) differed on the number of standard hymns,
that is, on the minimum size of the inventory of hymns, required to
celebrate the liturgy under normal circumstances. They shared the use
of only a few genuinely Ambrosian hymns and a couple of ancient
Easter songs.[25]

   During the tenth century, the European mainland accepted the selection of hymns used in the Irish Church. The enduring legacy of this

---

* On Charlemagne, see Short Biography, no. 44.

† For Alcuin's work on the *Gregorianum*, see pp. 122–23. On Alcuin, see Short
Biography, no. 7.

‡ The Irish Church, which developed a diocesan structure only late, was
in its early years heavily influenced by monks and monasteries, which both
shaped and directed church life. However, in this passage Baumstark may be
saying something more: that Irish hymnody has ties to Eastern monastic tradition. A liturgical treatise (with incorrect details and a corrupt text), probably
dating from the eighth century, describes this pattern of influence. *Cantuum et
cursuum ecclesiasticorum origo*, a section of *Ratio de cursus qui fuerunt ex auctores*,
accounts for the origins of the songs and orders of various liturgies, including a *Cursus Scottorum* (*Scottorum* in this context meaning "of the Irish"). The
treatise asserts that this *cursus* was widely used by Eastern monastics, brought
to the island Abbey of Lérins in southern Gaul by John Cassian (ca. 360–after
430), and sung there by Germanus of Auxerre (ca. 378–448), who taught it
to Patrick (mid- or late fifth century), the patron saint of Ireland. While the
journey cannot be historically confirmed, there is clear evidence for church
contacts between Ireland and in Gaul, including a visit to Gaul by Patrick. For
a critical edition of the whole document, see "Ratio de cursus qui fuerunt eius
auctores," in *Initia Consuetudinis Benedictinae*, ed. Kassius Hallinger, Corpus
consuetudinum monasticarum 1 (Siegburg: Apud Franciscum Schmitt, 1963),
77–91. For the treatise in Latin and English, see Patrick F. Moran, *Essay on the
Origin, Doctrine and Discipline of the Early Irish Church* (Dublin: J. Duffy, 1864),
243–46. See also *CE*, vol. 3, s.v. "The Celtic Rites," esp. 497d; DACL, s.v. "Cel-
tiques (Liturgies)," and Frederick Edward Warren, *The Liturgy and Ritual of the
Celtic Church*, 2nd ed. Studies in Celtic History 9 (Woodridge, Suffolk: Boydell
Press, 1987), lviii–lxxii, esp. lxix–lxx.

repertoire, insofar as it is still preserved in today's Breviary, consists of the hymns for the Hours, including Compline; the ordinary hymns, that is, those for Matins and Lauds; the longer Sunday and weekday hymns that are sung in winter at Vespers, Matins, and Lauds; the hymns at Lauds and Vespers in the Season of Easter; and a series of texts for the Common of Saints.* Since that time, a mass of hymns has crystallized around this common nucleus. The added hymns spread in various patterns of distribution; their corpus grew more and more in size, to almost incalculable proportions. In the medieval West, the liturgical texts of a poetic nature written for use by a specific locality were more diverse than any other feature of the liturgy; no other aspect even comes close to being so varied. Each monastery and diocese had its own hymnary.†

The tenth century also marked a turning point for liturgical poetry, for it was then that the rhythmic metrical art of the East gained acceptance in the West. That metrical art was primarily bestowed on two new genres in Western liturgical poetry just as they were taking shape, the sequence and the trope—a kind of cradle gift to them at birth. Both genres were most closely tied to choral singing and its use, on occasion, of progressions of notes that seemed like they would never end.

It became customary to use long, drawn-out cadences of this kind to support the final "a" of the Gospel "Alleluia,"‡ the last syllable to die away at the end of the chant sung before the Gospel reading.[26] A monk, fleeing northern France for the Abbey of St. Gall,§ brought along with him a new choral technique, which combined fresh texts with melody in such a way that one syllable was assigned to every single note. The technique had apparently developed in France, since the fugitive monk came from the monastery at Jumiéges,¶ which had

---

* The Common of the Saints contains those parts of the Missal, Office, and Breviary of the Western church used for commemorating saints who do not have propers of the Mass or an office dedicated to them.

† In the West, a hymnary was a liturgical book used in the Middle Ages containing the metrical hymns for the Divine Office, organized by the liturgical year.

‡ The technical term for this vocalized "a" is the *jubilus*.

§ The Abbey of St. Gall, located in Switzerland, was founded ca. 719.

¶ This was the Abbey of Jumiéges, a Benedictine community founded in 634 and located in Normandy on the north bank of the Seine. After being pillaged and burned to the ground by the Normans in the ninth century, it was subsequently rebuilt.

fallen victim to attack by marauding Normans.* Notker the Stammerer (840–912)[†] had to significantly revamp the proposed technique for use in Germany. The genre of songs that thus sprang up was given the name of *prosa* or *sequentia*, the latter applying originally to the note progression itself. Styling poems with meters structured ever more strictly went hand in hand with the introduction of rhyme, which was coming into the poetry of the East at the same time, notably into Syrian church poetry under Arabic-Persian influence. Adam of St. Victor (1179–92)[‡] became not only the unchallenged master of later sequence poetry, but indeed of all liturgical poetry composed for Latin hymns in the Middle Ages.

Yet another phenomenon, the development of the trope, is related, at least in part, to the same manner of composition, namely, texts set to longer series of notes so that—originally—a single syllable was sung throughout the whole progression.[27] Sometimes the trope preceded older liturgical texts as a kind of textual prelude; sometimes it appeared—and this is more often the case by far—as the "filling" for it. The sung elements of (1) the Mass, both (a) the Ordinary and (b) the propers of the Mass, the epistle, and the Gospel, as well as various elements of (2) the Office were expanded in this way.

The successful invasion of the West by liturgical poetry culminated with a final maneuver into daily prayer, charming in its playfulness: the rhymed Office. In this case, even the textual elements that had previously embellished the hours, the antiphons and responses, were reworked into rhymed, rhythmic poetry. Real pearls of this genre have remained in use to the present, especially in the breviaries of orders founded in the later Middle Ages. The Dominican Breviary[§] offers

---

* In a dedicatory preface to his compilation of sequences, the *Liber Sequentiarum*, Notker the Stammerer (Notkerus Balbulus), PL 131, cols. 1003–4, recounts how his work on the musical form that he called *sequentia*, or "sequences," had been inspired by compositions found in a Norman Antiphonary carried to the Abbey of St. Gall by a refugee from the recently devastated Abbey of Jumièges.

[†] On Notker the Stammerer, see Short Biography, no. 131.

[‡] On Adam of St. Victor, see Short Biography, no. 3.

[§] The Dominicans, an order dedicated to preaching and study, were founded in Italy by Dominic (1170–1221) in 1220. They are mendicant, both as individuals and as an order. Because of the priority the order placed upon preaching and study, monks were given considerable leeway to absent themselves from the communal celebration of the Office.

an example in the rhymed Office sung on the feast day of its sainted founder. The dulcet tones in which this extols St. Dominic (1170–1221)* as "the light of the church, the doctor of truth, the rose of patience, the ivory of chastity"† get "stuck in the ear" and are hard to forget.[28]

Although (as just described) the poetry that accumulated on Western soil up until the fourteenth century—nearly overwhelming in quantity—was no less vast than that of the East, this increase had an impact in the West fundamentally different from that upon Eastern liturgy. The abundant vitality of this poetry, urgent and vibrant, can only be compared to the columns and statuary adorning architecture in the Gothic style. Only the ancient and austere liturgy celebrated in the major Roman basilicas‡ refused to open its doors to this abundant vitality, until after the start of the Hohenstaufen Era.§ This way of celebrating the Office survives yet today: in the Roman Rite, all the offices for the final three days of Holy Week and for the Easter Octave, as well as the Vigil for the feast of Epiphany, are marked by their lack of hymns.

When Radulf of Rivo (1350–1403)¶ lamented that the battle for dominance between those basilican rites and the Breviary "of the Roman Curia"** gave victory to the latter, the Western (or Papal) Schism†† was, regrettably, already a reality. To reverse this continuing decline of the church, to find a way out that would save the day, a reform needed to be set in motion—one that would have a decisive impact on the

---

* On Dominic, see Short Biography, no. 64.

† This hymn is sung on August 4, the feast day of St. Dominic.

‡ See pp. 59 and 146.

§ The German Hohenstaufen dynasty ruled the Holy Roman Empire from 1138 to 1208 and from 1212 to 1254.

¶ Following a study trip that took him to France, Italy, and Germany, Radulf (1350–1403) returned in 1398 to Tongres, a city in his native Brabant, to resume his duties as dean. In direct response to the Great Schism, Radulf strived to assert the ecclesiastical discipline he judged the church needed, notably in the area of the liturgy. On Radulf of Rivo, see Short Biography, no. 152.

** See n. on p. 146.

†† The Great Schism of Western Christianity or Papal Schism (also known as the Western Schism) was a division within the Western church lasting from 1378 to 1417. In the end, three men set out competing claims for the papacy. The situation, as much political as religious, was essentially resolved at the Council of Constance (1414–18) and the election of Martin V (1417–31) as pope.

liturgy.* As things happened, this reform did not revert to Rome's previous position; that is, it did not reject liturgical poetry whole cloth. However, the tendrils of poetry, which had climbed over the face of the liturgy and crept into its crevices, were severely pruned back. This trimming was not nearly severe enough to suit Rome's centuries-old attitude toward liturgical poetry. Nonetheless, this curtailment clearly resulted in yet another striking contrast between the Western and Byzantine, that is, Eastern, liturgical styles. As compared to the amount of hymnody medieval hymnaries had supplied, the number of hymns available as propers for particular feasts was greatly reduced. The trope disappeared from the liturgy altogether. As to genuine sequences, apart from Wipo's (ca. 990–after 1048) creation[†] and the Corpus Christi sequence[‡] by Thomas, the citizen of Aquino (1225–74),[§] only that for the feast of Pentecost[¶] was retained. The two other specimens of sequences still featured in the Missal, incidentally

---

* Baumstark is here referring to reforms of the Catholic liturgy instituted by the Council of Trent in the sixteenth century. While usually considered a conciliar expression of the Counter-Reformation, a Catholic response to the Protestant Reformation (or the concerns that gave rise to it), Baumstark here is placing Trent in continuity with an earlier schism of the Western church, the Western or Great or Papal Schism, which commenced in the fourteenth century (see previous n). Be that as it may, it was by action of the Council of Trent that hymnody was curtailed in the liturgy of the Roman Catholic Church. While thousands of sequences, written for various liturgical occasions, come down to us from the Middle Ages, only four survived the reforms of Trent: *Victimae paschali laudes*, *Veni Sancte Spiritus*, *Lauda Sion*, and *Dies Irae*. *Stabat Mater* was reinstated in 1727. Baumstark discusses all five of these sequences in the paragraphs below.

† *Victimae paschali laudes*, a sequence appointed for the Catholic Mass on Easter Sunday, is usually attributed to Wipo (ca. 990–after 1048), but Notker the Stammerer (840–912), King Robert II of France (936–1031), and Adam of St. Victor (d. 1177–92) have all also been proposed as its author. ET: (with Latin text and commentary) Matthew Britt, *The Hymns of the Breviary and Missal* (New York, Cincinnati, Chicago: Benziger Brothers, 1924), no. 59. On Wipo, see Short Biography, no. 191.

‡ The sequence referred to here is *Lauda Sion*; ET: (with Latin text and commentary) Britt, *Hymns*, no. 75.

§ The "Aquinas" in Thomas' name refers to the fact that Thomas was born near Aquino (though actually in Rocasseca) in the Kingdom of Naples. On Thomas Aquinas, see Short Biography, no. 180.

¶ The sequence for Pentecost is *Veni, Creator Spiritus* (Come, Creator Spirit), written by Rabanus Maurus (ca. 780–856) in the ninth century. ET: (with Latin

the most renowned, in fact began as sequences only later, at the close of the Middle Ages. Perhaps *Dies Irae*,[29] most probably composed by the Franciscan Thomas of Celano (ca. 1190–1260) in the first half of the thirteenth century,* was originally a kind of trope on the "Libera," a responsory sung at the bier of the deceased lying in state.[†] This powerful song about the horror of the Last Judgment recalls the hymns composed by Ephrem the Syrian. The *Stabat Mater*,[‡] a Western counterpart to the ancient Syrian-Greek lament heard from Mary at the cross,[§] was passed down in similar fashion as a devotional text for individual use and was still found in prayer books of the fifteenth century. On the basis of uneven evidence, yet another Franciscan is regarded as the poet composing the *Stabat Mater*. This is Jacopone da Todi (1230–1306), who wrote both heartfelt religious songs and biting satires in the Italian vernacular.[30] As a prisoner of Boniface VIII (1294–1303),[¶] he paid

---

text and commentary) Britt, *Hymns*, no. 68. On Rabanus Maurus, see Short Biography, no. 151.

* Thomas of Celano's authorship of sequences, including *Dies Irae*, is in dispute. On Thomas of Celano, see Short Biography, no. 181.

† The name *Dies Irae* (Day of Wrath) is taken from the opening words of the sequence in the Latin Mass for the Dead. The *Libera* song, beginning "Libera me, Domine, de morte aeternus" (Free me, Lord, from eternal death), was a responsory sung at funerals. ET: (with Latin text and commentary) Britt, *Hymns*, no. 87.

‡ *Stabat Mater dolorosa* (The sorrowful mother stood [at the cross]) is a hymn sung during Holy Week that describes in a moving way Mary, the sorrowful mother of Jesus, standing at the foot of the cross of her son. Of unknown authorship, it dates from the twelfth century; the Roman Missal did not prescribe it as a sequence until 1727; ET: (with Latin text and commentary) Britt, *Hymns*, no. 57.

§ Although Baumstark does not specify what hymn he has in mind in the Eastern tradition analogous to the *Stabat Mater*, it is likely the ninth ode in the Matins of Holy Saturday in the Orthodox liturgy (commonly sung today in anticipation on Friday evening), which recurs in subsequent services; for example, on Easter Eve it is sung prior to the midnight resurrection service, as the congregation in the dark church awaits the giving of the holy light at midnight. The ninth ode is comprised of Psalm 119 and intercalated *troparia*. I thank Father Jonathan Proctor for shedding light on this possibility.

¶ On Boniface VIII, see Short Biography, no. 40.

a penalty for enthusiastically joining the Colonna family in their war against the pope.*

---

* In this passage Baumstark is referring to the involvement of Jacopone da Todi (ca. 1230–1306) in an episode of the long conflict between the Guelphs and the Ghibellines, in which Pope Boniface VIII (1294–1303), a Guelph, attempted to limit the power of the Colonna family, who were Ghibellines. Denied by Boniface the opportunity of living the Franciscan Rule in community to strict perfection, Jacopone da Todi joined with the Colonna family, one of the most powerful in Rome, to seek to depose Boniface. In response, the pope excommunicated the Colonna family and successfully went to battle against their forces. For Jacopone da Todi the result was imprisonment.

Notes

For a general survey of the subject, see the following encyclopedia articles: Anton Baumstark, "Hymns (Greek Christian)," ERE, vol. 7, 5–12; A. J. Maclean, "Hymns (Syria Christian)," ERE, vol. 7, 12–15; Guido Maria Dreves "Hymns, Christian, Latin," ERE, vol. 7, 16–25. For an introduction to the ecclesial poetry of the Greek East, one book of texts is still first-rate: *Anthologia Graeca carminum christianorum*, eds., James Mearn, Matthaios K. Paranikas, and Wilhelm von Christ (Leipzig: B. G. Teubner, 1871). Western Latin poetry, together with sample texts, is treated in a way accessible to the reader by Guido Maria Dreves, *Die Kirche der Lateiner in ihren Liedern* (Kempten & München [Munich]: Josef Kösel, 1908).

¹ See Josef Kroll and Programme der Akademie von Braunsberg, *Die christliche Hymnodik bis zu Klemens von Alexandreia* (Königsberg: Hartung, 1921).

² The Syriac texts have been translated by Arthur Ungnad and Willy Staerk, *Die Oden Salomos aus der syrischen Übersetzungen mit Anmerkungen*, KlT 64 (Bonn: Marcus und Weber, 1910). See also Baumstark, *Literatur*, 16f.

³ Council of Laodicea (fourth century), canon 59, Mansi 2, 574 C [ET: Johnson, *Worship*, II, no. 80-C: 2002].

⁴ First Council of Braga (561), canon 12, Mansi 9, 778 CD [ET: Johnson, *Worship*, IV, no. 181: 4747 (under Synod of Braga I, ser. 2)].

⁵ Concerning the various forms of this same text, see Anton Baumstark, "Die Textüberlieferung des 'Hymnus angelicus,'" *Hundert Jahre A. Marcus und E. Weber Verlag, 1818–1918* (Bonn: Marcus und Weber, 1919), 83–87.

⁶ [Mearns,] Paranikas, and [von] Christ, *Anthologia Graeca*, 40.

[7] Although Basil attests to the universal use of this piece around the year 375 in his Περί του Αγίου Πνεύματος [*On the Holy Spirit*], chap. 29, nos. 73–74, PG 32, col. 205, he expressly distinguishes it from the songs of Athenogenes, which admittedly—insofar as content is concerned—appear to be related to it [ET: St. Basil the Great, *On the Holy Spirit*, trans. David Anderson (Crestwood, NY: St. Vladimir's Seminary Press, 1980); *Worship*, II, no. 67-A (selection)].

[8] See Baumstark, *Literatur*, 12–14.

[9] See ibid., 29.

[10] See ibid., 31–52, and on the same topic the admiring introduction written by Otto Bardenhewer for the book: St. Ephrem the Syrian, *Des heiligen Ephräm des Syrers ausgewählte Schriften: aus dem Syrischen und Griechischen Übersetzung*, vol. 1, ed. Adolf Rücker, BKV 37 (Kempten & München [Munich]: Josef Kösel, 1919).

[11] Concerning the relationship between the various forms of oriental church poetry and the recitation of psalms as they developed over time, see Anton Baumstark, "Psalmenvortrag und Kirchendichtung des Orients," *Gottesminne* 7 (1912/13): 260–305, 462–82, 540–58, and 887–902.

[12] For this, see Adolf Rücker, "Die liturgische Poesie der Ostsyrer," *Die Görresgesellschaft im Jahre 1914*, 3rd Vereinsschrift (Köln [Cologne]: J. P. Bachem, 1914), 54–77.

[13] On this subject, see Anton Baumstark, *Festbrevier und Kirchenjahr der syrischen Jakobiten*, SGKA 3, 3–5 (Paderborn: Schöningh, 1910 [repr., New York: Johnson Reprint, 1967]), 72f, and Baumstark, *Literatur*, 244f.

[14] While one publication on this subject attempts a summary, its approach is not at all satisfactory: Karl Krumbacher, *Geschichte der byzantinischen Literatur von Justinian bis zum Ende des oströmischen Reiches*, 2nd ed. (München [Munich]: Beck, 1897), 653–705.

[15] S. Pétridès, "Notes d'hymnographie byzantine," BZ 13 (1904): 421–28.

[16] Comparatively speaking, Theodor Schermann offers the best orientation to this material, for which an easy-to-use compendium would be a great help. Theodor Schermann, *Ägyptische Abendmahlsliturgien des ersten Jahrtausends in ihrer Überlieferung*, SGKA 6, 1 and 2 (Paderborn: F. Schöningh, 1912), 24–30.

[17] From the extensive body of literature dealing with the subject of poetry for the *kontakion* and its master Romanos the Melodist, three may be singled out: Karl Krumbacher, *Die Akrostichis in der griechischen Kirchendichtung*, Sitzungsbericht der Bayrischen Akademie der Wissenschaften 1903 (München [Munich]: Franz in Komm, 1903); Paul Maas, "Die Chronologie der Hymnen des Romanos," BZ 15 (1906): 1–44; and Paul Maas, "Das Kontakion, mit Exkurs über Romanos und Basileios von Seleukeia," BZ 19 (1910): 285. For the most part, in order to examine the great majority of the texts that have been edited, it is still necessary to use the edition by Jean-Baptiste Pitra, *Analecta Sacra Spicilegio Solesmensi parata*, vol. 1 (Paris: A. Jouby et Roger Bibliopolis, 1876 [repr., Farnborough and Westmead: Gregg, 1966]). A good selection of the most venerable pearls of the genre have been critically edited by Paul Maas,

Frühbyzantinische Kirchenpoesie, vol. 1: *Anonyme Hymnen des 5.–6. Jahrhundert*, KlT 52, 53 (Bonn: Marcus und Weber, 1910).

[18] See Wilhelm Weyh, "Die Akrostichis in der byzantinischen Kanonesdichtung," BZ 17 (1908): 1–69. See above, chap. 10, n. 10.

[19] See Ter Mikaelian, *Das armenische Hymnarium. Studien zu seiner Entwicklung* (Leipzig: J. C. Hinrichs, 1905).

[20] See Anton Baumstark, *Die christlichen Literaturen des Orients*, vol. 2 (Leipzig: G. J. Göschen, 1911), 58–60.

[21] The remaining remnants of his poetry can be found in *Hymnographi latini: lateinische Hymnendichter des Mittelalters,* 2nd ser., eds. Clemens Blume and Guido Maria Dreves, AHMA 50 (Leipzig: O. R. Reisland, 1907 [repr., Frankfurt am Main: Minerva, 1961]), 3–8 [ET of three genuine hymns in *The Hymns of Saint Hilary of Poitiers in the Codex Aretinus*, trans. and ed. Walter Neidig Myers (Philadelphia: Ph.D. Thesis, University of Pennsylvania, 1928), 26–75]. At best could one still add the compositions found in *Hymnographi latini,* 148–51, and in *Thesauri hymnologici hymnarium, Die Hymnen des Thesaurus hymnologicus H. A. Daniels und anderer Hymnen-Ausgaben*, vol. 1, ed. Clemens Blume, AHMA 51 (Leipzig: O. R. Reisland, 1908), 9f and 264–71.

[22] See especially in the Antiphonary of Bangor, which developed between 680 and 691, *Antiphonarium Monasterii Benchorensis*, PL 72, cols. 583 [Baumstark cites 585]–606. All this material now can be best found in Blume, *Thesauri*, 257–364.

[23] *Acta Sanctorum quotquote toto orbe coleruntur*, Ianuarii, vol. 1 (Antverpiae [Antwerp]: apud Ioannem Meursium, 1643 [repr., Parisiis (Paris): V. Palmel, 1863]), 735; available online at http://visualiseur.bnf.fr/Visualiseur?Destination= Gallica&O=NUMM-6025 or at http://acta.chadwyck.co.uk/. For the rule of Aurelian, see *Regula ad Monachos*, PL 68, cols. 393–96 [ET: Johnson, *Worship*, IV, no. 171-A (selection)].

[24] *Regula Sancti Benedicti*, chaps. 9, 12, and 17; GT: *Des heiligen Benediktus Mönchsregel*, trans. Pius Bihlmeyer, BKV 20 (Kempten & München [Munich]: Josef Kösel, 1914), 267, 270, and 273 [ET: *The Rule of Saint Benedict*, trans. Leonard J. Doyle, ed. David W. Cotter, OSB (Collegeville, MN: Liturgical Press, 2001); Johnson, *Worship*, IV, no. 155: 4092–93, 4099, and 4106–10].

[25] Clemens Blume, *Der Cursus S. Benedicti und die liturgischen Hymnen des 6.–9. Jahrhunderts in ihrer Beziehung zu den Sonntags und Ferialhymnen unseres Breviers*, Hymnologischen Beiträge 3 (Leipzig: O. R. Reisland, 1908), and accordingly Blume, *Thesauri*, xiii–xxi.

[26] See *Tropi Graduales*, vol. 1: *Tropen zum Ordinarium Missae*, eds. Clemens Blume and Guido Maria Dreves, AHMA 47 (Leipzig: Reisland, 1905), 10–17, a collection that has in part been extensively emended. *Thesauri hymnologici prosarium. Pars prior, Liturgische Prosen erster Epoche aus den Sequenzenschulen des Abendlandes*, eds. Clemens Blume and Henry Marriot Bannister, AHMA 53 (Leipzig: Reisland, 1911), xi–xxviii.

²⁷ Like the diminutive τροπάριον the name "trope" originally did not derive from a textual characteristic, but rather from a musical one (the melisma inserted to lengthen the choral melodies of the *introitus* and the *offertorium*), and it related back only secondarily also to the textual "filler" sung along with this melisma. See *Tropi Graduales*, vol. 2: *Tropen zum Proprium Missarum*, ed. Clemens Blume and Guido Maria Dreves, AHMA 49 (Leipzig: Reisland, 1906), 17, and Blume, *Thesauri*, xvii.

²⁸ This passage in Latin reads in full:

O lumen Ecclesiae
Doctor veritatis,
Rosa patientiae,
Ebur castitatis,
Aquam sapientiae
   propinasti gratis,
Praedicator gratiae,
   nos junge beatis.

For a general discussion of the rhymed Office, see Bäumer, 356–64.

²⁹ For a discussion of *Dies Irae* in this light, see Clemens Blume, "Dies irae, Tropus zum 'Libera,' dann Sequenz," *Cäcilienvereinsorgan* 49 (1913): 55–64. According to Blume and Dreves, *Tropi graduales*, vol. 2, 369–78, "Audi tellus, audi magni maris limbus" is a trope for the *Libera me* that has a relationship to the *madrasha* and *kontakion* poetry of the East, likewise primarily on formal grounds, yet in detail as well.

³⁰ [A typographical error omitted the number for this footnote in the German text.] Disputing his authorship, see especially Clemens Blume, "Der Sänger auf der 'Schmerzenreiche Gottesmutter,'" *Stimmen der Zeit* 89 (1915): 592–98.

Chapter 15

The Demands of Personal Piety

Something else besides liturgical poetry threatened to blur the crisp lines of the liturgy, that is, of the steady flow of liturgical action and the ancient text that accompany it. It was this: the impact upon the liturgy of the liturgical leader's personal devotional needs. Whereas the rampant growth of liturgical poetry primarily endangered daily prayer, at least in the East,* in both the East and the West the priest's personal piety primarily impacted the eucharistic celebration.

The liturgical leader acts and prays for the community and in its name. He has been entrusted with executing or directing the holy celebration of the liturgy, whose social-objective character is essential to its very being. For that reason, the very idea that he might use that celebration to satisfy any kind of personal-subjective need is antithetical to the liturgy's very essence.† Yet a tendency to move in this kind of direction began to set in early on.

In the East, both early and often, a prayer uttered by the celebrant on his own behalf grew out of that said for the whole church and its various hierarchical ministries offered in the course of the general intercessions of the eucharistic prayer.[1] In the West there appear

---

* The statement is unbalanced. As Baumstark just discussed on pp. 210–13, the sequence and trope had a major impact on the celebration of the Mass, both its ordinary and propers, resulting in their being drastically cut back through the reforms of the Council of Trent.

† For a discussion of this understanding of the liturgy and its implications for liturgical method by one of Baumstark's contemporaries, see Romano Guardini, "Über die systematische Methode in der Liturgiewissenschaft," JLW 1 (1921): 97–108, repr. in *Auf dem Wege: Versuche* (Mainz: Matthäus-Grünewald-Verlag, 1923), 95–110. See also pp. 43–44 and pp. 149–50.

217

formularies for a "Mass, which the priest must say for himself."* Spain and Gaul led the way with texts of this kind.[2] Parallels in the Frankish-Roman liturgy were not unknown.[3]

After that the action required to celebrate the Eucharist itself, as both sacrifice and meal, occasioned the formation of a stratum of more recent prayers. Some of these prayers were intended to meet the needs of the celebrant's piety; others related to those needs only more or less directly. Prayers of preparation before the reception of Communion, and of thanksgiving after, fall into the first category. Originally the one celebrating the Eucharist, be he bishop or priest, was only the first of the many gathered to receive the elements of the sacramental meal. This took place after he had said the words of consecration effecting the miracle of transubstantiation[†] and had displayed the Body and Blood of his Christ to the eternal Father as an offering of inestimable value.[‡] His responsibility for dispensing Communion did not leave him time to indulge in personal devotion as well. Eventually, however, actual practice fell short of the early Christian ideal, when the whole community had participated in the holy meal. The more that happened, the more the role of the celebrant changed, becoming something other than what it had been. The more the celebrant's participation in the holy meal became essentially a substitute for what it had originally only set in motion, that is, the communion of the full congregation, the more the Communion of the celebrant acquired a meaning all its own within the structure of the whole celebration. It was only natural that, just before partaking of Communion, when he was

---

* *Missa, quam sacerdos pro se dicere debeat* is the title used for nine Masses found in the *Liber Ordinum*, a Mozarabic text dated 1039, which Dom Marius Férotin (1855–1914) asserts were in use from the fifth century. Of these Masses, four are generic and five designated. Of the latter there are Masses for particular occasions, when a priest is in distress or on a trip, and for particular persons: "for the priest or his substitute" and "for the priest and friends or family" (see n. 2 of this chap.). Masses of this sort are discussed by Jungmann, vol. 1, 221.

† The phrase Baumstark uses here *nachdem das Wort seiner Lippen das Wunder der Wandlung vollzogen [hatte]* translates literally as "after the word of his lips had effected the wonder of transubstantiation." Key to this phrase is *Wandlung*, which can mean "transubstantiation," "transformation," or "consecration." For another use of this word in a eucharistic context, see p. 246; for a use of *die Verwandlung* in a eucharistic context, see p. 169.

‡ With this elaborate phrase, Baumstark refers to the Elevation.

deep in concentration, the celebrant should offer a personal prayer to prepare himself for participating in the holy meal. No Eastern Mass liturgy in its final form is lacking this kind of prayer before Communion; the Byzantine Divine Liturgy, at least, has one after.[4]

In and of itself, the action of placing the eucharistic elements, the bread and the wine, properly upon the altar table was a purely practical necessity, devoid of any meaning beyond that. However, originally, the elements needed for the sacred action were contributed by community members out of their generosity, along with other gifts for the church to be used for the care of the poor. These two kinds of gifts were presented together in the liturgy, the charitable contributions along with the elements.* The memory of the sacrificial character of these gifts, which individuals brought to the community and through it to God, had repercussions for the liturgy. Specifically, it shaped how the handling of these gifts was understood in the context of the liturgy: as an act of offering made by the community, that is to say, in its name. In the East, the Great Entrance, symbolizing the entry of the Lord himself, took the place of the offertory procession performed by the community. With the development of the Great Entrance, which procured the eucharistic elements from the *prothesis* room, the sacrificial action involved in the preparation of the elements moved back earlier in the service to its present place before the word service of the Mass of the Catechumens.[†] Thus there evolved the rite of the *prothesis*, as it is also called in Greek, often an elaborate structure.[5‡] The new

---

* See pp. 194–95 for Baumstark's discussion of the role of Roman deacons in the charitable work of the church.

[†] On the Mass of the Catechumens, see n. on p. 64.

[‡] The idea that the *prothesis* ritual moved from immediately before the anaphora to its present position before the Liturgy of the Word is closely tied to the presumption that there was an offertory procession of the faithful at the beginning of the Liturgy of the Meal, which brought offerings to the table, where they were then prepared for consecration and distribution. If that were the case, then, for the Eastern pattern to evolve, the preparation ritual would have to have been transferred from immediately before the Great Thanksgiving to before the Liturgy of the Word. This is the position taken by Baumstark. However, though well attested in the West, there was no offertory procession of the faithful in the East. There the faithful brought offerings to the church to be handed over to deacons prior to the service. A portion of those offerings, enough to serve the congregation, were then deposited in a "sacristy," either a building outside the church (*skeuophylakion*) or a space within it (*prothesis*

"sacrificial" action of offering in its more recent placement already anticipated the outcome of the consecration in essentially the same way as it had in its previous one. In its more recent location, this happened during the Great Entrance, as the song accompanying it anticipated that outcome when referring to the elements carried in procession as Christ himself.* With this development, however, the notions of "fearful" and "terrible," which were the oriental way of thinking—with its crass realism—came to apply to the actual eucharistic offering of the Body and Blood of Christ, came to refer to the Great Entrance as well.† Consequently, the celebrant came naturally to offer a silent prayer preparing himself for this ritual action just as he did for participating in Communion, while in its original place the priest's private prayer became one of preparing for the celebration of the eucharistic mystery itself.[6] In the framework of the *prothesis*, the ritual that had developed more recently, the priest's private prayer became a global preparation for celebrating the Mass as a whole.

In particular Eastern rites, these same dynamics led the priest to express his private devotions in a variety of ways distinct from the actual "offering prayers." Priest and deacon alternated in commending one another for offering intercession.[7] To a plea from the priest for intercession on his behalf, the congregation responds, petitioning God to mercifully accept his offering.[8] He says a prayer for the forgiveness of sins or one of "absolution," announcing that clergy and people alike are cleansed from the scum that comes from universal human weakness.[9] Finally, the celebrant's preparation became a liturgical act in its own right, found even before that of the *prothesis*.[10] Prayers of varying number and length, taken from the Psalms, play a role here. In the

---

room), where they were prepared for consecration. At the beginning of the Liturgy of the Meal, these preparations were brought from the "sacristy" to the altar in procession. This purely practical procession in time evolved to become what is today the Great Entrance. See Robert F. Taft, *The Great Entrance*, Orientalia Christiana Analecta 200 (Roma [Rome]: Pontificium Institutum Studiorum Orientalium, 1975), 12–34, 178–216.

* In the Divine Liturgy of St. John Chrysostom, the choir here completes the Cherubic Hymn, "That we may welcome the King of All invisibly escorted by angelic hosts. Alleluia! Alleluia! Alleluia!" On this hymn, see p. 77 and n. on pp. 77–78. On the Great Entrance, see pp. 165–66.

† For Baumstark's discussion of the Great Entrance in light of the "impact of Hellenism," see pp. 77–78.

West Syrian and Byzantine Rites, short prayers were said individually as particular articles of liturgical dress were put on.[11] In Ethiopia a comprehensive vesting prayer follows others over the liturgical items to be used in the sacred action.[12] After these prayers, brief ones, with a more concise form, address the priest's devotional needs.[13] In the course of the liturgy, appointed chants are performed or diaconal litanies recited, interrupting the celebrant's liturgical action and the ancient prayer texts that accompany it. These breaks he fills in with silent prayer of more recent composition. In the Byzantine Mass, a "Prayer of the Trisagion" and a "Prayer of the Cherubic Hymn" are notable for both their stirring beauty and their considerable age, which, relatively speaking, is especially great.[14] In the former case, a quiet word of prayer accompanies the hymn "Holy God, holy Mighty, holy Immortal, have mercy on us." In the latter, the prayer is said as the hymn's impressive melody rings out during the procession that carries the eucharistic elements out into the congregation.

It is striking what a close counterpart one finds to all this in the Western Mass *ordo* and the prayers of *accessus ad altare** and *recessus*,[†] which serve as the priest's private preparation and thanksgiving. The *Confiteor*, *Orate Fratres*, and vesting prayers are only some of the most striking parallels. Perhaps one can see here more clearly than anywhere how liturgy develops with a kind of inherent inevitability. In far-flung regions, liturgical development, proceeding independently, leads to the same or similar results. Be that as it may, one can also recognize—with no room for doubt—interaction between East and West. Only the strong influence that Latin worship exercised on the liturgy of the Armenians can account for Psalm 42 being prayed at the beginning of the Armenian Mass and especially for the prologue to

---

* The *accessus* was a ritual preparing the priest for celebration of the Mass, which included a number of psalms, versicles, and prayers. It was found in the *Missale Romanum* from the Middle Ages to 1970. The priest said them either prior to going to the altar or on the way, petitioning God to enable him to offer a sacrifice pleasing to God and rich in blessings, despite the priest's own sinfulness and weakness. See Jungmann, vol. 1, 271–76.

† The *recessus* ritual is a complex of silent prayers that the priest said after the Mass on his way to the sacristy. Found in the *Missale Romanum* from 1570 to 1970, this complex included the *Benedicite*, Psalm 150, versicles, and three orations. See Jungmann, vol. 2, 459–64.

John's gospel being proclaimed at its end.[15]* This influence came into Armenia during the rule of the Lusignans (1342–75), mediated by the Order of the Brothers of St. Gregory Illuminator (Fratres Unitores).† On the other hand, Latin translations of prayers from the Greek liturgies of St. James and St. Basil appear in the more recent strata that fills out the Western Mass *ordo*.[16] A part of the Roman *accessus ad altare* prayer used in the West, which has yet to receive a critical examination, is noteworthy for the further connections it reveals with the eucharistic prayer of the East. Allegedly a composition "of St. Ambrose," sections of this originally integral prayer are today assigned to particular days of the week.‡ It cannot possibly be mere coincidence that here in the

---

* Both Psalm 42 (*Judica me*) and the use of the prologue from the gospel according to John read as the last gospel of the Mass came into the Roman Rite in the late Middle Ages. Both were used initially for priestly devotion, Psalm 42 while vesting or approaching the altar, the Johannine prologue while unvesting, though later it became a pericope of blessing at the end of the Mass. In both the late medieval Roman and Armenian liturgies, the psalm (42 in the Roman, 43 in the Armenian) was used by the priest as he approached the altar at the beginning of the liturgy, and the Johannine prologue followed the dismissal. For their use in the Roman Rite, see Jungmann, vol. 1, 289–90, and Jungmann, vol. 2, 447–51. For the influence of the Western Rite upon Armenian Liturgy, see M. D. Findikyan, "L'influence latine sur la liturgie arménniene," in *Roma-Armenia*, ed. Claude Mutafian (Roma [Rome]: DeLuca, 1999), 340–44, and Gabriele Winkler, "Armenia and the Gradual Decline of Its Traditional Liturgical Practices as a Result of the Expanding Influence of the Holy See from the 11th to the 14th Century," in *Liturgie d'église particulière et liturgie d'église universelle. Conférences Saint-Serge 1975, XXIIᵉ Semaines d'études liturgiques. Paris, 30 June–3 July, 1975*, Bibliotheca "Ephemerides Liturgicae," "Subsidia" 7 (Roma [Rome]: Edizioni Liturgiche, 1976), 329–68. For Western influence on the Armenian rite, see the discussion on the Lusignan dynasty in n. on p. 103.

† See n. on p. 179.

‡ While often ascribed to Ambrose (340–97), as in the title *Orationes Sancti Ambrosii ante Missam singulis hebdomadae diebus distributae*, these prayers are now attributed to Jean de Fécamp (ca. 990–1078), spiritual writer and abbot of the Abbey of the Trinity in Fécamp. Starting in the Middle Ages, they were widely used by priests as private devotions to prepare themselves for celebrating the Mass and were included in the Tridentine *Missale Romanum*. See Jungmann, vol. 1, 275. For the text in Latin with English translation, see http://www.preces-latinae.org/thesaurus/AnteMissam/OrationesSAmb.html.

section for Friday the so-called Epiclesis of the East,* petitioning the Holy Spirit to effect the miracle of transforming the elements, appears in its purest form.[17]

That the text for these prayers is attributed to Ambrose, the Milanese Doctor of the Church (ca. 339–97),[†] is also no accident, any more than are its points of contact with Mozarabic and old Gallican Mass prayers. It was definitely the non-Roman West that produced counterparts—whose bounty just kept on growing in plenty—to the prayers Eastern priests used to express their personal piety. One of the oldest documents relevant to this development, a veritable mine of riches, is the so-called *Missa Illyricus*, which amassed a truly copious amount of material.[18][‡] This extract, a liturgical document without parallel,

---

* See n. on p. 180.

† On Ambrose, see Short Biography, no. 11.

‡ *Missa Illyricus* is the popular name for a collection of prayers from the *Codex Guelferbytanus 1151 Helmstadiensis*, excerpted and published by Matthias Flacius Illyricus (1520–75). The document from which he took this text is an *Orationale* (prayer book), the third of the eight books that Sigebert, the bishop of Minden (d. 1036), had produced ca. 1030 for use in the archbishopric of Minden, a town in northern Germany. While the *Orationale* contains the order for Mass found in the Roman Missal and includes the Canon of the Mass, it is essentially an anthology of prayers for the bishop as presider (and occasionally his assistants) to say in private at various moments and services. Of these prayers, Illyricus excerpted only those from the manuscript's eucharistic section. While initially entitled *Missa Latina*, it soon came to be called *Missa Illyricus* after the compiler, who in 1557 was the first to study prayers from this *Orationale* and publish a commentary on them. Over time, Illyricus' text generated both curiosity and condemnation. As a document it came out in five separate editions during the seventeenth and eighteenth centuries. In his introduction, however, Illyricus takes a Lutheran polemical approach when discussing the *Missa*. This led to the work being placed on the index by Pope Sixtus V (1585–90). In this passage Baumstark assumes knowledge of "Quaedam observationes," the polemical introduction that Illyricus wrote for *Missa Illyricus*. Therein Illyricus dated the *Missa* after the Council of Chalcedon (451), specifically ca. 700, and noted great variety in it. Both of these facts served as grounds for Illyricus to refute the claims made by the Catholic Church in the sixteenth century that the Roman Mass was ancient and immutable. The version of the Roman Mass then current was not ancient, argued Illyricus, because its prayers differed from those found in the *Missa Illyricus*; it was not immutable, he claimed, because its prayers varied from the same. See Fernand Cabrol, "La messe de Flacius Illyricus," RBén 22 (1905): 151–64;

was published in 1577 by Matthias Flacius Francowitz,* the head of the Centuriators of Magdeburg (1520–75).† He regarded it as a principal witness—discovered during the time of the Western (or Papal) Schism—to the relatively recent date of the Roman Mass form.‡ In fact, apart from the fact that the work as a whole is quite disorganized, one has here simply the *ordo* and the Canon of the Mass, albeit overgrown by prayers added from the most diverse sources in a way reminiscent of the suffocating effect liturgical poetry had on the psalm text in the East. New research has suggested its redactor was either Bishop Siegebert of Minden (d. 1036)§ or Alcuin (ca. 735–804),¶ who would have compiled the formulary for his friend, Bishop Arno of Salzburg (ca. 740–821).[19]** If the former were the case, the text would reflect eleventh-century realities; if the latter, those even earlier, at the close of the eighth.

The liturgy of the city of Rome showed the same cool reserve of Roman exceptionalism toward this whole increase of liturgical prose texts that it had toward liturgical poetry. For example, even as late as the second half of the eleventh century, not a single fixed prayer devoted to the "offering" of the presider was to be found in the Ordinary of the Mass. Bernold of Constance (ca. 1054–1100)†† provides express testimony for this in his *Micrologus*, the standard work coming out of the Middle Ages during the earlier phase of literature in the field of

---

and Cabrol, DACL, vol. 5, s.v. "Flacius Illyriens (La messe Latine de)," cols. 1626–35. For a discussion of the history of this text, see Joanne Michelle Pierce, *Sacerdotal Spirituality at Mass: Text and Study of the Prayerbook of Siegebert of Minden (1022–1036)* (University of Notre Dame: unpublished Ph.D. dissertation, 1988), 82–123. For a critical edition of the whole *Orationale* and for a critical commentary, respectively, see Pierce, *Sacerdotal Spirituality at Mass*, 148–276 and 277–446.

* On Matthias Flacius Illyricus, see Short Biography, no. 99.

† The Centuriators of Magdeburg were a group of Lutheran theologians organized by Matthias Flacius Illyricus (1520–75) to write a treatment of church history demonstrating the validity of Lutheranism and disputing the theological claims of Rome. Begun in 1559, its thirteen volumes were completed in 1574.

‡ See n. on p. 210.

§ On Siegebert of Minden, see Short Biography, no. 161.

¶ On Alcuin, see Short Biography, no. 7.

** On Arno of Salzburg, see Short Biography, no. 20.

†† On Bernold of Constance, see Short Biography, no. 37.

liturgical studies.[20] He refers to two formulae familiar to him, which are found in today's Missal and are perhaps of Gallican origin. These are the concluding prayer to the "Holy Trinity"* and the one invoking the Holy Spirit as "Sanctifier, almighty, everlasting, eternal God." With similar wording, this latter invocation recurs in the Mozarabic Rite,[21] where today it is said by the priest when offering the cup.† One first encounters the prayer that accompanies the offering of the host in a collection compiled at the behest of Charles the Bald (840–77).‡[22] To be sure, the use of the formula said as the water is mixed with the wine is indirectly of Roman origin.§ This present use notwithstanding, it occurs as a fixed prayer for Christmas even in the so-called Leonine Sacramentary[23] and, through the Gelasian Sacramentary,[24]¶ spread into the kingdom of the Franks. Whereupon, in this Gallican milieu, it was readied for its present place in the Roman Missal.

---

* There are two prayers to the Holy Trinity in the Tridentine *Missale Romanum*. The priest says this concluding prayer to the Holy Trinity immediately after the dismissal and before the Last Gospel. See Jungmann, vol. 2, 46ff, 437ff. It reads in Latin, "Placeat tibi sancta Trinitas, obsequium servitutis meae; et praesta, ut sacrificium, quod oculis tuae majestatis indignus obtuli, tibi sit acceptabile, mihique et omnibus, pro quibus illud obtuli, sit, te miserante, propitiabile. Per Christum Dominum nostrum. Amen." (May the tribute of my humble ministry be pleasing to thee, Holy Trinity. Grant that the sacrifice which I, unworthy as I am, have offered in the presence of thy majesty may be acceptable to thee. Through thy mercy may it bring forgiveness to me and to all for whom I have offered it: through Christ our Lord. Amen.) For the text in Latin and English, see Bard Thompson, *Liturgies of the Western Church* (Cleveland, New York: World Publishing , 1961), 88–89.

† In the Tridentine Mass, "Veni, Sanctificator omnipotens aeterne Deus et benedic hoc sacrificum tuo sancto nomini praeparatum" occurs in the first set of offertory prayers, just before the water is mixed with the wine. See Thompson, *Liturgies*, 66–67, and Jungmann, vol. 2, 68ff. It is similar to an invocation in the *Missale mixtum*, an eclectic text in the Mozarabic tradition, which was assembled by Alfonso Ortiz (fl. ca. 1500) in Toledo during the fifteenth century. Its invocation reads, "Veni Sancte Spiritus sanctificator: sanctifica hoc sacrificium de manibus meis tibi preparatum." See *Introduction to the Liturgy*, Handbook for Liturgical Studies, vol. 1, ed. Anscar Chupungco (Collegeville, MN: Liturgical Press, 1997), 325–26.

‡ On Charles II (the Bald), see Short Biography, no. 45.

§ See n. on "Veni, Sanctificator omnipotens aeterne Deus . . ." above.

¶ See p. 120, for Baumstark's discussion of the Gelasian Sacramentary and its Gallican use.

The first rite to open up the *ordo* of the Roman Mass to the influx of personal devotional prayer was that used by the papal household in the high Middle Ages. The earliest witness to the new direction this liturgy was taking has to do with the Office. This was Abelard (1079–1142/3)* in the year 1140, in a letter written to St. Bernard of Clairvaux (1090–1153).[25]† As to the eucharistic celebration, some elements found at the beginning of this liturgical text and its end‡ point toward the private chapel of the medieval Lateran palace, located at the head of the *scala sancta*.§ This chapel, preserved as renovated in 1278, has—from time immemorial—been called the *Sancta Sanctorum*, the Holy of Holies.[26]¶ This name came to be associated with the prayers at the foot

---

* On Peter Abelard, see Short Biography, no. 2.

† On Bernard of Clairvaux, see Short Biography, no. 33.

‡ This phrase, which reads in German *des äußersten textlichen Rahmenwerkes* and could be translated as "of the outermost (or furthermost) edges of the text framing this liturgy," is a philological image. One must imagine Baumstark looking at a liturgical text of one page, with the beginning and the ending of the text being literally the "outermost edges of the text framing this liturgy." For what he is referring to includes prayers at the very beginning and the very end of this Mass: the prayer that the pope offers as he is processing into the Sancta Santorum Chapel and "the prayers of thanksgiving said by the priest after the Mass."

§ The *Scala Sancta*, or "Holy Stairs," are a flight of stairs with twenty-eight white marble steps located in Rome near the Lateran. By tradition they were regarded as the staircase once leading to the *praetorium* (i.e., the residence of a procurator or governor of a Roman province) of Pilate in Jerusalem and thus made holy by the feet of Jesus Christ as he tread upon them during his passion. Allegedly brought from Jerusalem to Rome ca. 326 by Helena (246/50–330), the mother of Constantine (306–37), they were known in the Middle Ages as the *Scala Pilati*, the stairs of Pilate. Razing all but the chapel of the old Lateran Palace, which had by now acquired the name *Sancta Sanctorum* (see following n.), Sixtus V (1585–90) reinstalled the *Scala Sancta* at their present location in 1589 as the steps leading up to that chapel. These stairs may be ascended only while praying upon one's knees, a devotion practiced to the present, especially during Lent. See LTK, s.v. "Sancta Scala."

¶ The *Sancta Sanctorum*, or Holy of Holies, is the name given to the old private papal chapel. Dedicated to Lawrence (ca. 225–58), the space got its name from the many relics preserved there. The first mention of an *Oratorium S. Laurenti* is found in the *Liber Pontificalis* under Stephen III (768–72); the name *Sancta Sanctorum* was in common use by the thirteenth century, when the papal private chapel underwent a series of renovations. Work under Innocent

of the altar, notably with their conclusion when the priest begs for the forgiveness of sins "so that, with souls made clean, we may be counted worthy to enter the 'Holy of Holies.'"* With this prayer, which recurs in all of the oldest liturgical documents of the Roman Mass, we probably—in the final analysis—have one going back to the early sixth century at the very least.[27] However, not until this venerable text was understood to allude to the local surroundings of the papal chapel did it become a prayer said during the procession of the pope, who—to offer the Holy Sacrifice—had to take himself from his palace apartments into the papal chapel. The prayer following in today's Mass *ordo* begs for God's clemency with the words, "by the merits of your saints, whose relics are here."† These words, likewise, did not originally have to do with the holy remains of a saint deposited in just any altar, but rather with the vast treasury of relics found in the Sancta Sanctorum Chapel. It will soon be twenty years since the Jesuit Father Hartmann Grisar (1845–1932)‡ undertook an examination of this treasury for the first time, an effort that led to conclusions of the utmost importance for archaeology and art history.§ Finally, the prayers of thanksgiving said by the priest after the Mass point toward this chapel as well: the collect for the feast of St. Lawrence was incorporated into these prayers by virtue of the fact that the chapel is consecrated to the most revered deacon martyr of Rome.¶

III (1198–1216) and Honorius III (1216–27) combined three reliquary altars into a single one and installed the *Salvator* image above it. Then Nicholas III (1277–80) made it as it stands today, its rich decoration being provided by the Cosmati family in 1278. See LTK, s.v. "Sancta Sanctorum."

* This prayer, known by its incipit as *Aufer a nobis*, is the first silent prayer of the Mass. Its full text, in Latin with English translation, can be found in Thompson, *Liturgies,* 58 and 59.

† This prayer, known by its incipit as *Oramus te Domine* may be found in Latin and English in Thompson, *Liturgies*, 58 and 59.

‡ On Hartman Grisar, see Short Biography, no. 85.

§ Hartmann Grisar, *Il Sancta Sanctorum ed il suo tesoro sacra* (Roma [Rome]: Civiltà Cattolica, 1907); GT: *Die römische Kapelle Sancta Sanctorum und ihr Schatz* (Freiburg im Breisgau: Herder, 1908).

¶ On Lawrence, see p. 195 and Short Biography, no. 116.

Notes

[1] The motif is already common to the Greek texts of the Liturgy of St. James and the Liturgy of St. Mark, with Syriac and Coptic texts, respectively, and recurs in the Liturgy of St. Basil. Brightman, 55, lines 4–8; 90, lines 18–25; 130, lines 23–26; and 336, lines 14–22.

[2] One can find such prayers, in a section entitled *Missa, quam Sacerdos pro se dicere debeat*, in the Western Gothic *Le liber ordinum en usage dans l'église wisigothique et mozarabe d'Espagne du cinquième au onzième siècle*, ed. Marius Férotin, MEL 5 (Paris: Firmin-Didot, 1904), cols. 273–82. Prayers of this kind are also found in the Bobbio Missal, in a section entitled *Missa quomodo Sacerdos pro se orare debet*. See *Sacramentarium Gallicanum*, PL 72, cols. 537–38.

[3] The Sacramentary of Fulda offers no less than eleven pertinent formularies. See *Sacramentarium Fuldense saeculi X*, ed. Gregor Richter and Albrecht Schönfelder, Quellen und Abhandlungen zur Geschichte der Abtei und Diozese Fulda 9 (Fulda: Der Fuldaer Actiondruckerei, 1912), 248–57.

[4] Baumstark, *Messe*, 163.

[5] Ibid., 110–12. Concerning the development of the Byzantine *prothesis*, see Placido de Meester, "Les origines et les développements du texte grec de la liturgie de saint Jean Chrysostome," Χρυσοστομικα [*Chrysostomika*], 302–13. For its text, see Brightman, 539–51.

[6] Baumstark, *Messe*, 118f.

[7] It is found thus in the current Greek rite. Brightman, 380, lines 1–24.

[8] It is found thus in the Syriac liturgy of the Jacobites, as well as in the Nestorian liturgy. Brightman, 87, lines 2f. and 274, lines 2–26.

[9] The former is found in the Syriac liturgy of the Jacobites and Nestorians, the latter in the Coptic and Ethiopian liturgy. Brightman 83, lines 6–16 and 274, lines 28–34, and accordingly lines 148f and 205f.

[10] Baumstark, *Messe*, 116–18; de Meester, "Les origines," Χρυσοστομικα [*Chrysostomika*], 302–13.

[11] Brightman, 70 and 354–56.

[12] Ibid., 196f.

[13] Baumstark, *Messe*, 170.

[14] [Brightman,] 313f and 318.

[15] [Ibid.,] 416 and 456.

[16] See above, chap. 6, n. 16, and chap. 9, n. 4.

[17] "Peto clementiam tuam, Domine, ut descendat super panem tibi sacrificandum plenitudo tuae benedictionis et sanctificatio tuae divinitatis. Descendat etiam, Domine, illa Sancti Spiritus tui invisibilis incomprehensibilisque maiestas, sicut quondam in patrum hostias descendebat, qui et oblationes nostras corpus et sanguinem tuum efficiat," etc. Moreover, in medieval liturgical documents in the West, this text is also found almost word for word in numerous instances, as in the *Hanc Igitur* text of the Sacramentary of Fulda

(*Sacramentarium Fuldense*, 169) and in the "Mass" of Flacius Illyricus (for the full reference, see the following footnote), PL 138, col. 1328 [Baumstark cites col. 1528; for a critical edition, see Joanne Michelle Pierce, *Sacerdotal Spirituality at Mass: Text and Study of the Prayerbook of Siegebert of Minden (1022–1036)* (University of Notre Dame: unpublished Ph.D. dissertation, 1988), 228].

[18] To be found as *Missa Latina*, the first section of *In sequentem Missam et Missae fragmentum*, ed. Joannis Bonae, PL 138, cols. 1305–36. [For a critical edition, see Pierce, *Sacerdotal Spirituality at Mass,* 148–259.]

[19] For the former supposition, see Joseph Braun, "Alter und Herkunft der sogenannten Missa Illyrica," *Stimmen aus Maria Laach* 2 (1905): 143–45; for the latter, Fernand M. Cabrol, "La messe de Flacius," RBén 22 (1905): 151–64.

[20] Bernold of Constance, *Micrologus de ecclesiasticis observationibus*, chap. 11 entitled "Quid super oblatione sit dicendum," PL 151, col. 984.

[21] *Missale mixtum*, PL 85, cols. 113 and 536.

[22] Feliciano Ninguarda, *Liber precationum, quas Carolus Calvus Imp . . . colligi mandavit* (Ingolstadii [Ingolstadt]: Ex typographia Davidis Sartorii, 1583), 112.

[23] *Sacramentarium Leonianum*, PL 55, col. 146.

[24] *Sacramentarium Gelasianum*, PL 74, col. 1059. H. A. Wilson, *The Gelasian Sacramentary* (Oxford: Clarendon Press, 1894), 5.

[25] In Letter 10 of Abelard to Bernard of Clairvaux, PL 178, col. 340. [For a discussion of this letter, a summary of its contents, and a critical edition, see Peter Abelard, *Letters IX–XIV*, trans. and ed. Edmé Renno Smits (Groningen: Rijksuniversiteit, 1983), 70–76, 120–376, and 239–47, respectively.]

[26] See Hartmann Grisar, *Die römische Kapelle Sancta Sanctorum und ihr Schatz* (Freiburg im Breisgau: Herder, 1908), 23.

[27] In the Leonine Sacramentary, in a Mass entitled *In natali episcoporum*, it has to do with a formulary used either in the year 538 at the anniversary of the ordination of Pope Vigilius (537–55), or in one of the two years 549 [*sic*] and 558 at that of Pelagius I (556–61): *Sacramentarium Leonianum*, PL 55, col. 119. In the *Gelasianum*, it is found as the *oratio* for Quinquagesima week. See *Sacramentarium Gelasianum*, PL 74, col. 1064, and Wilson, *Gelasian,* 15. In the Gregorian Sacramentary, it is found as "oratio, quando levantur reliquiae." See *Das Sacramentarium Gregorianum nach dem Aachener Urexemplar*, ed. Hans Lietzmann, LQ 3 (Münster in Westfalen: Aschendorff, 1921), 107.

Chapter 16

Reform and Standardization

The final form of the Roman Mass *ordo* is a product of the same kind of conscious reform that set a limit on the amount of poetic material found in the Western liturgy.* The spirit of reform seen at work in both instances found a happy medium between (1) the absolute prohibition that Rome, being conservative by nature, had originally imposed upon both liturgical poetry and the prose prayers expressing personal devotion and (2) the rampant growth of both, against which "the Rite of the Roman Curia"† could no longer serve effectively as a dam.

Far-reaching and intentional liturgical reforms were not unknown in the East, although their frequency there was quite rare. At an early date, around the turn of the eighth century, the learned Jacob of Edessa (640–708),‡ the Jerome (ca. 342–420) of Aramaic-speaking Christianity,§ revised the texts of the Syrian-Jacobite liturgy that had been translated out of the Greek.[1] In this, Jacob acted the reformer, carrying out what was apparently a thoroughgoing revision, with the goal of staying as close to Greek models as possible. The Hellenization of the world of Syrian Christianity, which had just peaked, imperiously demanded the prerogative to wield influence over the liturgy as well.¶ The history

---

* One effect of the liturgical reforms of the Council of Trent (1545–63) was to cut back on the poetic material that had entered the Roman Mass during the late Middle Ages, notably tropes and sequences. For Baumstark's discussion of this, see pp. 210–13.

† See pp. 144–45, p. 210, and pp. 226–27.

‡ Baumstark also makes this same comparison with Jerome on p. 117. On Jacob of Edessa, see Short Biography, no. 103.

§ On Jerome, see Short Biography, no. 106.

¶ The language of church life, including the language used in the liturgy, for West and East Syrian Christianity was Syriac, the Aramaic spoken in Edessa. This has been the case throughout the history of East Syrian Christianity and since the fourth century for West Syrian, which previously worshiped in Greek. (On Syriac and Aramaic, see n. on p. 55). This, however, did not obviate a process of Hellenization, understandable given the widespread use of Greek as a language of prestige in society as a whole as well as in the Christian

of the Russian Church provides another example. Patriarch Nikon of Moscow (1652–66) implemented a thoroughgoing "improvement" of its liturgical books.[2]* In this instance, innovation met decidedly with resistance of the strongest kind; large segments of the church insisted on using the old books and practices. This gave rise to the *Raskolniki*, a schismatic movement, which produced the various "Old Believer" sects of Russia. The case illustrates just how little incursions into the sacred precinct of the liturgy suit the East. Being wholly attuned to mystical experience, Eastern liturgy is not amenable to interventions that are consciously conceived and implemented through the exercise of authority. To Eastern sensibility, liturgical forms, once fully established, appear to be simply inviolable.[†]

---

church. This process of Hellenization included the use of Greek rhetoric for preaching, the translation of Greek texts (of Scripture, theology, hagiography, liturgy, et al.), and the emulation of Greek literary forms. The work of Jacob of Edessa (ca. 640–708) exemplifies the latter two. Baumstark's comment that Hellenization "imperiously demanded" access to the liturgy reflects the fact that Greek was the imperial language of Byzantium. In the seventh century, that imperial power was asserted vis-à-vis the church by Emperor Heraclius (ca. 575–641), who imposed Chalcedonian belief on the various ecclesiastical parties. The West Syrian Church of Jacob of Edessa, Monophysite in belief, rejected this coerced solution to the christological debate. For a description of Hellenism in general, see n. on p. 74.

See Glenn Warren Bowersock, *Hellenism in Late Antiquity*, Thomas Spencer Jerome Lectures 18 (Ann Arbor: University of Michigan Press, 1990), 29–40; Averil Cameron, "The Eastern Provinces in the 7th Century A.D.: Hellenism and the Emergence of Islam" in Ελληνισμός [*Hellenismos*]: *quelque jalons pour une histoire de l'identité grecque: actes du Colloque de Strasbourg, 25–27 octobre 1989*, ed. Susanne Saïd, Travaux du Centre de Recherche sur le Proche-Orient et la Grèce antiques 11 (Leiden, New York: E. J. Brill, 1991), 287–312; Robert Hoyland, "Language and Identity: The Twin Histories of Arabic and Aramaic (and: Why did Aramaic Succeed where Greek Failed?)," *Scripta Classica Israelica. Yearbook of the Israel Society for the Promotion of Classical Studies* 23 (2004): 181–99; Fergus Millar, "The Problem of Hellenistic Syria," in *Hellenism in the East*, ed. Amélie Kuhrt and Susan Sherwin-White (Berkeley and Los Angeles: University of California Press, 1987), 110–33.

* On Nikon of Moscow, see Short Biography, no. 130.

† The Nikonian reforms were instituted vigorously, with support from the civil authorities. Those who refused to accept them came to be called Old Believers or, after their excommunication in 1667, the *Rashkolniki*, that is, the

The mental predispositions the West applies to liturgical reform are essentially different. There the conceptual landscape for the religious dimension of the church is juridical, a perspective basic for Rome. One cannot doubt for a moment that the ecclesiastical authorities use sovereign law as an instrument to oversee the liturgical life of the church, even its most venerable forms. Thought of reform vis-à-vis the Roman liturgy first sprang up at an early date, shortly after the turn of the first millennium. Its proponent at that time was the occupant of the Papal See, Gregory VII (1073–85),* the great champion of the movement coming out of Cluny, which advocated the general reformation of the church. We lack sufficient information about how much this powerful adversary of Henry IV (1071–1106)[†] accomplished in his attempt to bring greater strictness and purity back to the worship of urban Rome. In any event, that being said, these efforts are in complete accord with his larger agenda for church politics and religious reform. For this, his contemporary Bernold of Constance (ca. 1054–1100)[‡] provides express testimony.[3] As for details, one learns that this pope issued not only a ruling on the Ember Days celebrated each quarter but also at least one further reform-minded decree dealing with liturgical matters. Whereas until that time the dates for the observance of Ember Days had been moveable, Gregory regularized them with an arrangement that has remained in force ever since.[4]

The other decree to survive involved statutes for canons regular,[§] which came early in his papacy—arguably from the year 1074.[5] These statutes provided the basis for selecting the psalmody sung at night, a system not abridged until the most recent breviary reform of the ferial and Sunday Office initiated by Pius X (1903–14).[¶] The selection was justified as a revival of earlier usage, required to check the laxity that had crept into liturgical practice. The old Pachomian pattern of twelve psalms coupled with three readings was established as the norm for

---

Schismatics. Despite persecution, sometimes severe, they have survived as a recalcitrant, albeit fragmented, force on the margins of Russian Orthodoxy.

* On Gregory VII, see Short Biography, no. 81.

[†] On Henry IV, see Short Biography, no. 93.

[‡] On Bernold of Constance, see Short Biography, no. 37.

[§] Canons regular are nonmonastic religious living in communities under the Augustinian Rule. A community of canon regulars was attached to a larger church, with responsibility for its liturgical life, including singing the Office.

[¶] On Pius X, see Short Biography, no. 144.

the ferial night choir and for one part—the first of the three—of the Sunday night choir. Three psalms and the same number of readings were to provide the content for the other two Sunday Nocturns, for Matins throughout Easter week, and for one of three Nocturns on all the remaining feast days. Moreover, the decline of the liturgy, which these reforms sought to reverse, was attributed to the German control of the Eternal City.* According to the brief statement by Bernold, the renewal of a strictly Roman form of worship came to be the goal, consciously pursued.[†]

Before adjourning, the Council of Trent (1545–63) gave the pope responsibility for carrying out a new and substantial reform of the liturgical books of the Roman Rite.[6] That reform was launched during the pontificate of Pius IV (1559–65)[‡] and completed under Urban VIII (1623–44).[§] Like all human endeavors, it is best judged in light of its period and the spirit of the times. The church now enlisted into its service the late humanism of the Renaissance, whose culture emphasized the individual and delighted in the senses. The baroque created its rich spaces, inundated by the dazzling light of white stucco and the intensity of resplendent colors. To further its own brilliant rise, the young Society of Jesus fostered both aspects of Renaissance culture. In contrast to the centrifugal forces unleashed by the Protestant Reformation (representing as it did a gigantic defection from the ancient church), a spirit of ecclesiastical centralization—with a discipline as strict as can be imagined—came fully into play in the sixteenth century. This spirit also found in the Jesuits its most trustworthy custodians and self-sacrificing standard-bearers. To do justice to the unique character of the work of liturgical reform in the sixteenth and seventeenth centuries, one must never lose sight of this overall historical situation.[¶]

---

* Henry IV (1056–1105) occupied the city of Rome from 1082–84.

[†] Gregory VII (1073–85) asserted the church as a spiritual power, ascendant over temporal power, notably in his conflict with the German emperor, Henry IV (1056–1105). Baumstark sees this same assertion of Roman prerogative vis-à-vis German control reflected in Gregory's liturgical reform.

[‡] On Pius IV, see Short Biography, no. 142.

[§] On Urban VIII, see Short Biography, no. 184.

[¶] The relationship to the Society of Jesus of the sixteenth-century liturgical reforms in the Roman Catholic Church is multifaceted. First of all, the Society of Jesus established an organizational structure able to promote Roman reforms. Being "the army of the pope," coupling strict discipline with its own

The character of the Tridentine reform, shaped by the times as it was, is apparent above all in how the Breviary was handled.[7] Preliminary work at breviary reform had borne fruit since 1524, undertaken

---

highly centralized organization, it was able to further uniformity in liturgical matters and papal authority at a time when many church structures had been weakened by the Reformation. As Baumstark goes on to speak of the Jesuits and art, it is well to note that Rome sought to centralize aesthetic motifs and themes as well as order, doctrine, and liturgy. See the discussion of Catholic art in Italy, France, Spain, and Flanders after the Council of Trent (1545–63) in Émile Mâle, *L'Art religieux de la fin du XVIe siécle, du XVIIe siécle et du XVIIIe siècle,* 2nd ed. (Paris: Librairie Armand Colin, 1951), 1–108.

A separate question is the relationship of the Society of Jesus to the baroque style of art and architecture. Nineteenth-century scholars held that the baroque constituted a distinctive Jesuit style, evident in the numerous Jesuit churches in that style built after 1575—a position that has been roundly criticized by more recent art historians. For a review of the *status quaestionis,* see Rudolf Wittkower, "Problems of the Theme," in *Baroque Art: The Jesuit Contribution,* eds. Rudolf Wittkower and Irma B. Jaffe (New York: Fordham University Press, 1972), 1–14.

Baumstark's assertion here is subtler, however. He speaks instead of an affinity between certain emphases of late humanism, the Society of Jesus, and baroque architecture, notably the dual emphasis on the individual and the senses. Whereas the Renaissance focused upon the individual within society, Ignatius Loyola (1491–1556) and the Jesuits stressed the salvation of the exercitant, developed in a personal relationship with his spiritual director. Whereas the art of the Renaissance is notable for its sensuality, Ignatius Loyola in *The Spiritual Exercises* regards the senses as a primary means for appropriating spiritual subjects, whose contemplation can lead the individual toward God. Ignatius speaks explicitly of "the applications of the senses" (*Exercises* 121–26) as a tool for contemplating the incarnation and the nativity. However, the appreciation for the senses is apparent throughout this manual for spiritual training. See also, for example, *Exercises* 47, 165–71, 235, and 247–48.

In this passage, Baumstark asserts that baroque architecture accords with Ignatian spirituality in that it addresses the spirituality of the individual through the play of the senses. The appropriation of these two Renaissance emphases for service by the church, Baumstark suggests, was key for the remarkable growth of the Society of Jesus, presumably because of their wide appeal. Founded in 1540, the Society of Jesus numbered 8,500 by the turn of the century. For a discussion of this interplay, albeit in relation to art of churches rather than to their architecture, see Jeffrey Chipps Smith, *Sensuous Worship. Jesuits and the Art of the Early Catholic Reformation in Germany* (Princeton and Oxford: Princeton University Press, 2002), esp. chap. 2, "Sensuous Worship or a Practical Means to a Spiritual End," 31–55.

by the Theatine Order and Pope Paul IV (1555–59), a member of the Carafa family, who came to the papacy from that order.* These efforts invited others to carry on the work of reform. As early as 1535, Diego Fernandez [*sic*] de Quiñones† of Santa Croce (d. 1540),‡ a Spanish cardinal from the Franciscan order, published a breviary reform that repudiated all ties with the past. Its radicalism sounded the alarm against dangers best avoided. In all of this work on the Breviary, two aspects of the Office were the chief foci of reform: the hagiographical readings for the Night Office and the metrical hymns.§

The reform of the hagiographical readings was carried out for the church as a whole under Pius IV and his successor, St. Pius V (1566–72).¶ The new text was created by the Bishop Egidio Foscacari of Modena (1512–64),** who, like Pius V, was a member of the Dominican order. To give it form, he enjoyed the collaboration of the humanist Giulio Poggio (1522–68);†† as to content, he latched onto—in part—what Cardinal Quiñones had done in this department. The main task at hand involved nothing less than using the tools of historical criticism

---

* The early history of the Theatines is inseparable from the biography of Paul IV (1555–59), born Giovanni Pietro Carafa. On Paul IV, see Short Biography, no. 135.

† On Francisco de Quiñones, see Short Biography, no. 150.

‡ Baumstark mentions Santa Croce, and this Breviary was often called the "Breviary of the Holy Cross." The references are to the Basilica Santa Croce in Gerusalemme (Basilica of the Holy Cross in Jerusalem), to which Cardinal Francisco de Quiñones (1475–1540) was named as titular bishop. It was built by Helena (246/50–330) in 325 to house the relics of the passion and dedicated to the True Cross. Quiñones is buried in that church.

§ As to the details of its reform, this breviary for the most part eliminated the difference of rank between the feasts, severely curtailed the readings from the lives of the saints, and set aside antiphons, versicles, the Little Office of Our Lady, as well as many hymns, retaining only the most ancient. At the same time, it aimed to equalize the number of readings and the length of the hours. All 150 psalms were recited within the week and the entire Bible was read within the year. The length of the offices was approximately equal, with only three psalms sung at each and only three readings proclaimed each day at Matins. See Batiffol (Eng. ed.), 181–91, and Robert F. Taft, SJ, *Liturgy of the Hours East and West*, 2nd rev. ed. (Collegeville, MN: Liturgical Press, 1993), 311.

¶ On Pius V, see Short Biography, no. 143.

** On Egidio Foscacari, see Short Biography, no. 72.

†† On Giulio Poggio, see Short Biography, no. 145.

to edit these readings, indeed their very content. This took a stout heart, for their apocryphal legends, having grown rampant, needed thinning.* An additional task was then—as much as possible—to cloth the language of the hagiographies in the ceremonial dress of classical Latinity. To complete this task, the church could not resist enlisting a generation of Latinists who vied with Cicero and Augustan Rome for the palm branch of stylistic mastery.[†] On formal grounds, what this work of reform achieved undoubtedly deserves our unreserved appreciation. As to its content, it often left something to be desired. While the reform showed some critical grasp of this hagiographical material, it is only natural that—from the perspective of today's historical and literary criticism—one could wish they had wrestled with the material even more vigorously.

Early on, soon after it was completed, objections were leveled against one particular "correction" of the Breviary, this one also having to do with form. The revision felt compelled to impose upon the hymns of the Breviary the rules for meter and style used in classical antiquity.[8] Four Jesuits carried out this work under Urban VIII: Famiano Strado (1572–1649),[‡] Tarquino Galluzzi (1574–1649),[§] and Girolamo Petrucci (1585–1669)[¶] of Italian extraction, and Matthias Sarbiewski (1595–1640) of Polish.[**] The pope—himself a poet of no mean gifts—contributed new hymns to their work, composed in the spirit and taste of the times.[9][††] Prior to his efforts, around the turn of the seventeenth

---

* Whereas the Breviary of Quiñones had suppressed some legendary material, the Council of Trent (1545–63) ordered the abolition of yet more. Batiffol (Eng. ed.), 181–91, 193–201, and Taft, *The Liturgy of the Hours*, 311.

[†] Baumstark here pictures the Latinists of the sixteenth century entering a Roman circus to do gladiatorial battle with Cicero (see Short Biography, no. 48) and stylists of his measure. In recognition of his victory, the successful gladiator received a monetary reward as well as a palm branch, which he waved to the crowd on a victory lap around the circus.

[‡] On Famiano Strado, see Short Biography, no. 168.

[§] On Tarquino Galluzzi, see Short Biography, no. 74.

[¶] On Girolamo Petrucci, see Short Biography, no. 140.

[**] On Matthias Casimir Sarbiewski, see Short Biography, no. 155.

[††] Baumstark attributes to Urban VIII (1623–44) hymns for the offices of three female saints in the Breviary: *Martinae celebri* for St. Martina (d. 226 or 228), *Regali solio* for St. Hermenegild (d. 585), and *Domare cordis* and *Opes decusque regium* for St. Elizabeth of Portugal (1271–1336). On Urban VIII, see Short Biography, no. 184; see also n. 9 at the end this chapter.

century, during the papacy of Clement VIII (1592–1605),* Cardinals Silvio Antoniano (1540–1603)[10†] and Bellarmine (1542–1621)[11‡] were similarly engaged in the field of poetry.§ It is beyond dispute that—having had their hitherto unbroken continuity in the liturgy disrupted—the older hymns suffered, losing no little of their power and simplicity at the hands of this classicism, merciless in exercising its pedantic arts. The hymns newly composed in the sixteenth and seventeenth centuries are striking for their "antiquitising," if not to say "paganising," flourishes, even more than for the polish of their verse structure, cool as marble, which for the most part imitates the odes of Horace.¶ In any case, when judging all that history has produced, one must guard against the narrow-mindedness that fundamentally misconstrues the unfamiliar, a criticism that can be justifiably leveled against the "correctors" working under the Barberini Pope.** It was no accident that in 1683 Bernini's (1598–1680)[††] baldachin, with its gigantic spiraled columns of gilded bronze,‡‡ was raised over the papal altar of St. Peter's Basilica at the bidding of this very pope. For an individual whose stylistic bias did not preclude—in any way at all—the enjoyment of baroque church art, for one to whom the soft voice of a soul could sound even through a work such as this baldachin, to that individual even the "antiquitised" hymnody of the golden age of the baroque would still have something to say. Not without emotion is he able to appreciate it for being the form in which the human spirit, having reached

---

* On Clement VIII, see Short Biography, no. 49.

† On Silvio Antoniano, see Short Biography, no. 15.

‡ On Robert Bellarmine, see Short Biography, no. 29.

§ Both Silvio Antoniano (1540–1603) and Robert Bellarmine (1542–1621) served on the commission that Clement VIII (1592–1605) appointed to revise the Breviary. Batiffol (Eng. ed.), 213.

¶ Matthias Sarbiewski, known as "the Polish Horace," memorized all the poetry Horace wrote and composed his own poetry emulating the Roman poet's literary style. On Horace, see Short Biography, no. 98.

** Baumstark is referring here to Urban VIII (1623–44), born Maffeo Barberini. The "correctors" of whom Baumstark speaks are presumably the four Jesuit Latinists mentioned above: Famiano Strado (1572–1649), Tarquino Galluzzi (1574–1649), Girolamo Petrucci (1585–1669), and Matthias Sarbiewski (1597–1640).

†† On Giovanni Lorenzo Bernini, see Short Biography, no. 35.

‡‡ While the angels atop Bernini's baldachin in St. Peter's Basilica are gilded, its four spiral columns are of bronze.

a certain stage in its development, attempted—and it could only attempt!—to ascend to the lyrical praise of the Most High.

There can be no doubt that from then on the approach taken by these revisions to deal with the hagiographical readings and hymns of the Breviary became the prime characteristic of liturgical reform after Trent. Still, however, what came from these efforts in no way exhausted all that Trent had to achieve, indeed not even its central thrust. Despite how keenly attuned that era was to the pulse of life, it refrained from any radical break with tradition. Specifically, it left untouched the way the psalms of the Office were distributed over the particular days of the week and hours as well as the pattern of psalmody that Gregory VII had specifically sanctioned for the nocturnal Office. The goal pursued in the eleventh century* remained crucial even in the sixteenth and seventeenth: to rescue a genuinely Roman form of the Office from the stranglehold of foreign influence.† Most telling in this regard are two pieces of evidence: (1) the indiscriminate trimming of poetic material that had overgrown the text‡ and (2) the similar treatment given to the prose prayers the priest used to express his personal devotion.§

Yet another aspect of Gregory VII's work on the liturgy was picked up again in the sixteenth and seventeenth centuries. Already with Gregory, the attempt to standardize the liturgy used in the West went hand in hand with the internal reform of the Roman Rite. The purified liturgy of Rome was meant to become that of the whole Latin Church. Fundamentally, this liturgical centralization was now a fait accompli. Only a man with the stature of Milan's sainted Cardinal Archbishop Charles Borromeo (1538–84)¶ was able to safeguard the continued existence of his city's traditional liturgy, even one so venerable as the

---

* While the eleventh-century reforms strived to free the Roman liturgy from German influence, a similar dynamic was at play in the ninth, when (as Baumstark suggests on pp. 135–37) the Carolingian liturgical reforms ultimately saved the Roman Rite from "orientalization"—though under German influence.

† Gregory VII (1073–85) reaffirmed old Roman custom in the structure he upheld for the nocturnal psalmody of the Roman Office. See above and Batiffol (Eng. ed.), 126–31.

‡ See pp. 204–10.

§ See pp. 221–27.

¶ On Charles Borromeo, see Short Biography, no. 41.

Ambrosian Rite.* Sixtus V (1585–90)[†] created The Congregation of Sacred Rites as the guardian of liturgical unity.[‡] Through Charlemagne's (king from 768; emperor 800–814)[§] initiative the old liturgy of the city of Rome became the basis for the imperial liturgy, although—in the form given it by the ruler of the Franks—this lasted no longer than his empire.[¶] Following the Council of Trent (1545–63), the liturgy of

---

* Milan was able to keep celebrating the Ambrosian Rite on account of the directive of the Council of Trent (1545–63) that local liturgies with a history of two hundred years or more may continue in use. However, it did not do so without a struggle. With papal permission to have the Roman Mass said in any church he might attend, the Governor of Milan made a move against the rite that Cardinal Charles Borromeo (1538–84) was able to defeat. While the cardinal accommodated Rome with some changes in the rite, he was careful to preserve its essential character. Archdale A. King, *Liturgies of the Primatial Sees* (Milwaukee, WI: Bruce Publishing Co., 1957), 309–11. On the Ambrosian Rite, see pp. 132–33.

† On Sixtus V, see Short Biography, no. 165.

‡ The Sacred Congregation of Rites (*Sacra Rituum Congregatio*) was established on January 22, 1588, by Pope Sixtus V (1585–90) following the Council of Trent (1545–63) to oversee the liturgy of the Roman Catholic Church. Since May 8, 1969, by option of Paul VI (1963–78), responsibility for the liturgy was reconceived and assigned to succeeding bodies, currently the Congregation of Divine Worship and the Discipline of the Sacraments (*Congregatio de Cultu Divina et Disciplina Sacramentorum*). See Jovian Lang, *Dictionary of the Liturgy* (New York: Catholic Book Publishing Co., 1989), s.v. "Acta Apostolicae Sedis," "Congregation for Divine Worship and the Discipline of the Sacraments," and "Liturgical Law"; see also *New Catholic Encyclopedia* (New York: McGraw-Hill, 1967–96), s.v. "Congregation of Divine Worship and the Discipline of the Sacraments." On the *acta* of this congregation, see n. on p. 244.

§ On Charlemagne, see Short Biography, no. 44.

¶ Charlemagne (king from 768; emperor 800–814) adopted the Roman liturgy to match and serve his imperial ambitions. In Baumstark's words, he sought "the renewal of Roman imperial glory through German strength." See p. 134. However, neither his empire nor the liturgy long outlived him. At the end of the reign of Charlemagne's son and successor, Louis I or Pious (813–40), the Frankish Kingdom went into crisis, with a settlement agreed upon at the Treaty of Verdun (843) and final breakup occurring in 889. Nor did the liturgy remain uniform. Josef Andreas Jungmann looks back at this period by reviewing liturgical documents from around the year 1000, grouping them by genus and species. He finds a basic Frankish-Roman type, which includes a number of "species," represented by documents from (1) the episcopal see of Seez in

the Roman Catholic Church became simply the reformed rite "of the Roman Curia," with the claim that, in some sense, it participated in the indestructibility of the church itself and the immutability of its very being. The contest that Rome fought and won against ambitious yet particularistic attempts at reform—above all during the Age of Enlightenment—only served to reinforce this claim.*[12]

Of course the claim that the liturgy participates in the indestructibility and immutability of the church is not irreconcilable with further strengthening certain aspects of liturgical life celebrated according to the Roman Rite. From the beginning, the new Roman administrative authority should have been charged with the responsibility for this kind of consolidation no less than with safeguarding what had been received as a finished product. The position held by the Latin Rite, which as a liturgy of unity seeks on principle to stabilize its worship forms, does not rule out the responsible authority taking up comprehensive reform once again. A renewed effort at breviary reform, initiated by Benedict XIV (1740–58),[†] should have made this apparent;[13] it never came to fruition.[‡] A still more far-reaching liturgical reform was launched by Pius X—and only that.[14] In short order it departed from the principles still upheld by its older post-Tridentine sister; it reverted to the hazardous venture already attempted by Quiñones, a completely new distribution of the liturgical Psalter. Purchased at this

---

Normandy, (2) the archbishopric of Minden on the Weser River in Germany (see n. on p. 223), (3) the monastery of St. Gregory in Alsace, and (4) the monastery of St. Laurence of Liège. See Jungmann, vol. 1, 92–103.

* The Age of Enlightenment inspired a number of reform movements with the potential of loosening ties with Rome: those of Josephinism, a policy of the Holy Roman Emperor King Joseph II (1765–90) of Austria; of the Synod of Pistoia (1786) in Tuscany; and of Ignaz Heinrich von Wessenberg (1774–1860), a reformer in the Diocese of Constance, Germany (where, incidentally, Baumstark was born and spent his early years); as well as of Gallicanism in France. All were vigorously opposed by Rome and ultimately suppressed.

† On Benedict XIV, see Short Biography, no. 32.

‡ The complexity of the Breviary of Pius V (1568) led to revisions being published, notably in France (the Parisian Breviary of 1736). Taking this as an opportunity, Benedict XIV (1740–58) proposed a revision of the Breviary, and congregations met throughout the early 1740s to work on one. However, while Benedict sought a thorough reform of content and calendar, most of his advisers desired merely to modify the existing book. In the end, this work came to naught. See Batiffol (Eng. ed.), 236–83.

price was a relaxation of the demands required to put into practice a principle of supreme value. To pray through the whole Psalter regularly every week: that should have been reaffirmed as the proper footing for constructing the Office.* However, here even the most recent reform takes us down paths leading right back to the early Roman liturgical type, which Gregory VII, as the spiritual student of Cluny, had pursued; even having evolved into a universal liturgy, the liturgy of Rome as such proceeds, in a manner as yet unknown in the East, to reflect upon itself and the long-established features that characterize its essence.†

A return to Christian antiquity as it was minted in Rome, sober and clear, can be singled out as the ultimate and comprehensive goal of a reforming movement of this kind. To speculate about what headway this movement might make toward that goal, in the short or the long

---

* Baumstark here wishes to hold together two requirements: (1) that the whole of the Psalter, all 150 psalms, be recited in the course of the week and (2) that they be recited "through regularly," that is, in the order of their biblical sequence. Traditionally the Roman Office assigned psalmody either to Nocturns (Matins) or Vespers, the former being given Psalms 1–108 and the latter Psalms 109–50, spreading them in these two hours across the week. These were sung in order, save for those few psalms selected for ordinary use (for example, Psalms 148–50 for Matins and Psalm 140 for Vespers). Depending on which psalms fell in which hours, some were longer, others shorter.

While the reform of Pius X (1903–14) did require the recitation of the whole of the Psalter within the week, it also equalized the psalmic material sung on each day and at each office. To do this, it subdivided the longer psalms to create 235 psalmic units of equal length. These 235 units were assigned equally, thirty-three per day, and distributed over the hours. See Batiffol (Eng. ed.), 284–330, esp. 325–30, and Robert F. Taft, *Liturgy of the Hours*, 312–13.

In this system two things were sacrificed. First of all, the sequential order. Longer psalms were divided into segments, and thematic considerations clustered nonsequential psalmic units together. While sequence was one value used for organizing the Psalter, it was no longer the primary one. Secondly, with all hours containing approximately the same amount of psalmody, a certain rigor was lost. Baumstark mourned both of these losses. He honored the sequentiality as venerable tradition; he valued the rigor needed to recite hours of greater length as a kind of spiritual calisthenics, capable of strengthening the virile faith he admired. See pp. 169–73.

† Baumstark mentions the Breviary of Pius X on p. 144, p. 232, and p. 245. See also n. on p. 144.

term, does not fall within the purview of a work such as this, which turns to take a look back at history.*

---

* Baumstark is referring here to the modern liturgical movement as it was emerging during the 1920s. For other passages by Baumstark on this movement, see p. 49, pp. 193–94, and pp. 140–42.

Notes

[1] Baumstark, *Literatur*, 253f.

[2] See Konrad Lübeck, *Die christlichen Kirchen des Orients* (Kempten & München [Munich]: Josef Kösel, 1911), 192.

[3] Bernold of Constance, *Micrologus de ecclesiasticis observationibus*, chap. 14 entitled "De Signis super oblationem," PL 151, col. 986.

[4] For the entire decree pertaining to this from the year 1078, see Samuel Löwenfeld [Baumstark cites Löwenstein], "Ein Aktenstück aus der Ostersynode von 1078," *Neues Archiv für altere deutsche Geschichtskunde* 14 (1889): 620–22. The pertinent regulation can also be found in Decretum Gratiani III, Distinctio V, Caput 16 [for an electronic version of the full Latin text, see http://digital.library.ucla.edu/canonlaw/librarian?ITEMPAGE=CJC1&NEXT].

[5] The complete text can now be found in Germain Morin, *Études, textes, découvertes contributions à la littérature et à l'histoire des douze premiers siècles I* (Maredsous-Paris: A. Picard, 1913), 457–65. The regulation concerning the ordering of the Office is also to be found in Decretum Gratiani III, Distinctio V, Caput 15 [for an electronic version of the full Latin text, see http://digital.library.ucla.edu/canonlaw/librarian?ITEMPAGE=CJC1&NEXT].

[6] See Ludwig von Pastor, *Geschichte der Päpste seit dem Ausgang des Mittelalters* 6 (Freiburg im Breisgau: Herder, 1920), 309–12.

[7] See Bäumer, 410–510. Batiffol (Fr. ed.), 268–339 [Batiffol (Eng. ed.), 177–235].

[8] References for this can be found in Bäumer, 509.

[9] They are the hymns found in the Offices of Saints Martina, Hermenegild, and Elizabeth of Portugal [ET: (with Latin text and commentary) Matthew Britt, *The Hymns of the Breviary and Missal* (New York, Cincinnati, Chicago: Benziger Brothers, 1924), 222–26, 248–50, and 276–78, respectively].

[10] Composed by Cardinal Silvio Antoniani is the vesper hymn *Non virgines*. [This attribution could not be verified. Britt attributes to Antoniani *Fortem virile pectore*, sung at Lauds and Vespers for the Common of Holy Women. ET: (with Latin text and commentary) Britt, *Hymns*, 342–43.]

¹¹ Composed by Cardinal Robert Bellarmine are *Pater superni luminis*, the vesper hymn in the Office of St. Maria Magdalena, and *Custodes hominum*, the hymn for Lauds on the feast of the Guardian Angels [ET: (with Latin text and commentary) Britt, *Hymns*, 278–79 and 295–97, respectively].

¹² See Bäumer, 529–42, and Batiffol (Fr. ed.), 353–68 [Baumstark cites 353–56], who essentially limits his discussion to the course this development took in France [ET: Batiffol (Eng. ed.), 236–46].

¹³ See Bäumer, 562–84 and Batiffol (Fr. ed.), 369–429 [ET: Batiffol (Eng. ed.), 246–83].

¹⁴ This reform, which primarily implemented a reorganization of the Psalter, is assessed from the standpoint of liturgical history in Anton Baumstark, "La Riforma del Salterio Romano alla luce della storia Liturgia comparata," *Roma e l'Oriente* 3 (1911/12): 217–28 and 289–302, which was published as a separate volume: Baumstark, *La riforma del Salterio Romano alla luce della storia della Liturgia comparata*, Studi liturgici, fasc. 2 (Grottaferrata: Tip. "Nilo," 1912).

Chapter 17

The Limits of What We Can Know

Not only the future is closed off from view. In the end, only a portion of the facts—some more significant, some less—ever emerge out of the dim and distant past in focus sharp enough to still be seen clearly. Just like the natural sciences, historical research dares not forget the piecemeal nature of all human knowledge. It too has limits where one distinctly hears the word that humbles our pretensions: *ignoramus et ignorabimus*—we do not know and will never ascertain it.

In this regard, liturgical history may find its position particularly disadvantaged. A comparison of the way things are formed under the authority of the Sacred Congregation of Rites with how they were formed before that congregation existed, or falling outside its domain, lets one easily see why. Certainly a comparative approach to research may fairly often reach the point where general laws of liturgical development can be observed—laws which one may assume to be in play even when external sources are silent. However, such laws govern the course of the liturgy's internal development and there are a great many questions that they are unable answer. Primarily these are the specific questions concerning the when, where, how, and why of the emergence, transformation, and passing of particular phenomena found in practice and text. In this regard, for the Roman Rite and for it alone, we learn of these matters through *acta.** This is because, for as long as there has been a central administration responsible for the ritual development of the Roman Rite, each step involves an official procedure that requires every pronouncement to be duly recorded.

---

* The record of the actions taken by the Sacred Congregation of Rites (*Sacra Rituum Congregatio*) and the bodies that have succeeded it provides a picture of Roman liturgical development since it was created in 1588. Since 1904, the *acta* of all the congregations of the Curia, including the decrees and decisions on the liturgy, have been published periodically, usually monthly, in the *Acta Apostolicae Sedis*, the official journal of the Holy See. Unless otherwise indicated or necessitated, liturgical legislation goes into effect three months after its promulgation. On the Sacred Congregation of Rites and its successor bodies, see n. on p. 239.

However, per se, genuine liturgical development does not involve this kind of a process, one in which decisions—entailing documentary verification—are made by an authority of the church. Both of these features clearly contradict the essence of the liturgy insofar as it manifests itself as a kind of organic growth. Until the sixteenth century, it was universally such that each step in the liturgy's development proceeded in profound silence, as it does still today in the Christian Orient. In the nature of the case, persons living at the time a step in liturgical development occurs are at that point totally unaware of its significance, which only becomes apparent in light of some subsequent development. For this reason, only rarely are such steps recorded by historical tradition.

The forms liturgical life assumed at a specific time and place—no less than the particular steps their development entailed—quite often lie beyond our ken, probably forever. There are even distinct limits to what one can infer about the situation of an earlier time from a subsequent one. Suppose, for instance, that every single bit of information were lost about the arrangement of the days and hours found in the Roman Breviary that was official up to the time of the reform by Pius X (1903–14).* And just imagine what would be involved in reconstructing that arrangement inferentially from the way psalms are distributed today! This example lets us immediately recognize how severely circumscribed our knowledge is. However, in many cases, sources reveal nothing explicit beyond those circumscribed boundaries since—at the time that a liturgical form developed—much was taken for granted. Take, for instance, the experience of a Protestant scholar, who was in time to make contributions of the greatest value to historical research into the liturgy. To him the field owes a debt of gratitude. He began his time in the churches of Rome by making a concerted effort at immersing himself in the organism of Catholic worship.† In the process of doing so, he found himself one day standing utterly clueless before

---

* See n. on p. 144. On Pius X, see Short Biography, no. 144.

† This scholar is likely the German Protestant Hans Lietzmann. Baumstark first met him in Rome during the years 1899–1904, when living at the Campo Santo Teutonico, a German study house located next to the Vatican. A lifelong friend, Lietzmann was instrumental in making it possible for Baumstark to teach on the university level. See Frederick S. West, *Anton Baumstark's Comparative Liturgy in its Intellectual Context* (University of Notre Dame: unpublished dissertation, 1988), 153–68. On Hans Lietzmann, see Short Biography, no. 118.

the fact that—contrary to the text of his newly purchased pocket Missal—the choir in St. Peter's Basilica, at the first Hosanna before the consecration,* interrupted with the singing of the *Sanctus.* One could easily chuckle at the fix he found himself in. When investigating a living rite from the East, the Western Catholic often experiences a similar helplessness when encountering aspects of its practice. In this case as well, practical, firsthand experience of a liturgical structure (which is alien to the Western scholar) is key to understanding much of what is puzzling about a tersely worded rubric, which has been left unchanged—being as it was intended for the oriental Christian whose practical knowledge of the liturgy could be taken for granted. Likewise, direct experience would solve the riddle of the compact wording of an abbreviated text, similarly self-evident to one regular at worship. However, we can have no immediate experience of centuries long past; we cannot bridge their span. What was so familiar to the centuries themselves that the liturgy could be executed without adding a word remains unknown to us, irretrievable from the past—virtually in principle. This is despite the fact that our greatest need, almost as fundamentally, is to experience it firsthand.

Of course, such undeniable difficulties do nothing to diminish the value of a historical encounter with the liturgy. Least impaired is the ability of this encounter to enhance the power of the liturgical experience itself. Science has been criticized for being puffed up. To the contrary, genuine humility is the only ethical stance to assume before the recognition that—on any given subject—one can only know what falls within comparatively narrow parameters, which—sooner or later—will crimp the relentless pursuit of scientific knowledge.

Adopting this attitude, the one participating in the church's liturgical life is readily able to be content with insight into the grand developmental relationships of its history, those that have produced the forms of that life he now experiences. And, at a minimum, those developmental relationships—at least in broad strokes—will not escape his attention. The links of their chain lead him back into the impressive "year of the Lord's favor," whose inauguration those gathered

---

* The German word Baumstark uses here is *die Wandlung,* meaning "transformation," "consecration," or "transubstantiation." See n. on p. 169, and p. 218 for other instances of Baumstark's use of this term, singly or in compound words, in reference to the Eucharist.

in the synagogue of Nazareth once heard proclaimed (Luke 4:19). At the height of the summer of that year, amidst the ripening grain fields of the Palestinian hills, the Redeemer—with his own lips—taught the Our Father to the circle of his first faithful followers (Matt 6:9-13; Luke 11:2-4). Indeed, the development of the liturgy is anchored even beyond the time of the Lord's earthly life, in the forms of worship and prayer life practiced by his people Israel, as well as in the vast Hellenistic milieu, the cultural environment surrounding that small ethnic group, whether they lived in their Jewish homeland or in the Diaspora. This path of development moves from an abundant regional diversity, as rich as one can imagine, toward a unity spanning the globe. The most diverse forces determined the course of this development. Deep contrasts rooted in national character find expression; contrasts of language left their decided stamp on the wording of liturgical texts. The influence of important centers of human activity, belonging to cultural orbits of the distant past, is still felt, up into the present. The vigorous activity of individuals, which in the final analysis creates all things of truly human worth, is also at work, albeit often in discreet obscurity. The quiet world of monasticism and the political expediency of nations pining for power exert a significant influence. Dangers posed by the rampant growth of more recent elements, which threatened the future existence of venerable ones from an earlier time, were exorcized by the fortunate intervention of authoritative reform. What is achieved at each point in the development of the liturgy is such that it justifies—even from our present perspective—the final judgment rendered on the day of creation: "and indeed, it was very good" (Gen 1:31).

When a sense of history enriches the liturgical prayer of today's worshiper, that individual's spiritual perspective takes all of this in. Out of the depths of distant centuries, it comes to meet him as a blaze of color. In the sacred hall of the house of God, as tentative flashes off a mosaic with a golden background, it frees itself from the darkness of dawn's first light. Without the ordering rule of eternal prudence, the believing spirit would not have the power to grasp temporal formation, transformation, and passing—even in general terms. In regard to the historical development of forms, this soul will sense doubly the possibility of revering that rule, where the finite pays the tribute of his adoration to the eternal and he himself experiences the eternal condescending in grace. For the soul thus deeply stirred, the word of the apostle heard so often in the Sunday reading of Prime becomes a commanding imperative for personal confession: "To the Kings of the ages, immortal, invisible, the only God, be honor and glory forever and ever. Amen" (1 Tim 1:17).*

---

* In the Breviary of Pius X (1903–14), this Bible verse was read as the little chapter: "Regi sæculórum immortáli et invisibili, soli Deo honor et glória in saécula saeculórum. Amen." See *The Hours of the Divine Office in English and Latin*, vol. 1 (Collegeville, MN: Liturgical Press, 1963), 90.

Short Biographies

1. Ab(b)a I (d. 552, catholicos from 540), teacher and church leader, converted to Christianity from Zoroastrianism (Mazdaism), studied at Nisibis, learned Greek at Edessa, traveled widely in the eastern Mediterranean, and returned to teach in Nisibis before moving to Seleucia-Ctesiphon to assume his duties as catholicos. Though his tenure was strained by tensions between Persia and Rome, he was able to consolidate the Nestorian Church, notably at a synod he called in 544. He was instrumental in introducing the anaphora of Theodore of Mopsuestia and that of Nestorius to the Nestorian liturgy, which had previously used the anaphora of Addai and Mari. Disputes with Zoroastrians led to his persecution, imprisonment, and exile in Azerbaijan, though before his death he was able to return to Seleucia-Ctesiphon to resume his responsibilities.

2. Peter Abelard, né Pierre de Pallet (1079–1142/3), a philosopher, theologian, and teacher of immense popularity, studied in Paris, where he became an outspoken proponent of nominalism. His ill-fated romance with Héloise (1101–64) resulted in both of them entering monastic life, for which neither was much suited. Bernard of Clairvaux (1090–1153) sought to condemn Abelard as a heretic.

3. Adam of St. Victor (d. 1146), sequence writer, probably born in Breton, was educated in Paris, served at the Cathedral of Notre Dame in Paris, and entered the Abbey of St. Victor. He wrote a large number of sequences, which are notable for combining liturgical austerity with doctrinal precision. See http://www.oxfordmusiconline.com/subscriber/, s.v. "Adam of St. Victor."

4. Agobard (ca. 769–840) became archbishop of Lyons in 816. Though his support of a revolt against Louis I (814–40) led to his deposition in 835, he was reinstated four years later. Original and versatile in his scholarly endeavors, he opposed the excessive veneration of images, trial by ordeal, and belief in witchcraft and magic.

5. Albertus Magnus (1200–1280), medieval theologian, philosopher, and scientist, was born in Germany and studied in Italy, where he

became a Dominican in 1222. Upon returning to Germany, he taught theology, underpinning it with Aristotelian philosophy. For a time he taught at the University of Paris, where Thomas Aquinas was his student. The Roman Church canonized him in 1622 and declared him a Doctor of the Church in 1931.

6. Alcman (fl. mid- to late seventh century BCE), lyric poet, was native to either Laconia or Lydia and active in Sparta. By the late fifth century BCE his poems were regarded as classics. The two "Maiden Songs" (*Partheneia*) are the most important of his works to survive.

7. Alcuin (735–804) is regarded as the inspiration for the Carolingian renaissance. Educated at the cathedral school of York in his native England, he became adviser to Charlemagne (king from 768, emperor 800–814) on religious and educational matters. He wrote widely, established libraries and a school, taught by means of a dialectical method, and required for study Boethius (ca. 480–524 or 525), Augustine (354–430), and the grammarians. Among his students were some of the leading intellectuals of the day, including Amalarius of Metz (ca. 780–ca. 850) and Rabanus Maurus (ca. 780–856). In 796 he became abbot of Marmoutier Abbey near Tours, though he continued to provide Charlemagne with counsel.

8. Alexander II (d. 1073, pope from 1061) succeeded in becoming pope, despite opposition to his election by the German imperial court, which put its whole weight behind an antipope. In 1066 he gave his blessing to the Norman conquest of England (1066) and William the Conqueror's bid for the English crown. Liturgically, he instituted in the Latin Church the suppression of the Alleluia during Lent.

9. Alexander the Great (356–23 BCE, king from 336), the son of Phillip II of Macedon (382–36 BCE), received a classical education, with Aristotle (384–22 BCE) as his teacher. After militarily consolidating Macedonian rule over the Greek city-states, he set out on a ten-year campaign, which took him through the regions of Asia Minor, Syria, Mesopotamia, and Persia, and to places as far-flung as Egypt, Bactria, and India. By conscious design, he promoted Greek civilization in conquered territories, thereby starting the process of Hellenization, whose effects lasted more than a millennium.

10. Amalarius of Metz (ca. 780–ca. 850), a student and admirer of Alcuin (735–804), became prominent in the Carolingian Renaissance. A liturgical scholar, Amalarius' principle treatise, *De ecclesiasticis officiis*,

wielded great influence in the Middle Ages and is valuable today as a source for the history of the liturgy.

11. Ambrose (ca. 339–97) was born in Trier, practiced law, and served in government. In 374 he was made bishop of Milan. Known for his preaching and orthodoxy, he involved himself in the liturgy, monasticism, and the defense of the faith. He influenced more than one Roman emperor as he defended a place for the church within the empire. The conversion of Augustine (354–430), who held him in high esteem, is due in part to him. In the area of the liturgy, he is credited with introducing hymns, some of which he composed, and his work *De Sacramentis* is a valuable source for the history of the liturgy. The Roman Church holds Ambrose to be one of the four traditional Doctors of the Church, along with Jerome (ca. 342–420), Augustine, and Gregory (590–604).

12. Anastasius I (ca. 430–518, emperor from 491), who was greatly admired for his character, won favor for his wise administration of the Byzantine Empire. His reign was marked by wars in the Isaurian Mountains, with the Sassanian Empire, and against invasions by Slavs and Bulgarians. Though theologically Miaphysite, he pursued a path of reconciliation in affairs of the church. Childless, he was succeeded by Justin I (527–65).

13. Known both as a preacher and an ecclesiastical poet, Andrew of Crete (660–740), who was born in Damascus, became a monk at the Great Lavra of St. Sabas near Jerusalem, served as deacon and director of a home for orphans and the aged in Constantinople, and was elevated to become bishop of the Metropolitan See of Gortyne, Crete. An iconodule and sometime monothelite, Andrew inaugurated a canon of nine separate odes, which slowly supplanted the *kontakion*.

14. Ansgar or Anskar or Oscar (801–65), "The Apostle to the North," was born near Amiens and educated at Corbie Abbey in Picardy, where he took monastic vows. He devoted his life to spreading Christianity in northern Europe, under royal patronage and papal recognition. After evangelizing in Jutland (most of present-day Denmark), he helped found Corvey Abbey in Westphalia, conducted mission work in Sweden upon invitation of the king, and served as archbishop of two dioceses: the See of Hamburg and, after that city had been decimated by warfare, the newly constituted See of Hamburg and Bremen. Tradition holds that, at each point along the way, God directed him through visions.

15. Silvio Antoniano (1540–1603) was born in Rome and educated at the University of Ferrara, where he became professor of classical literature. He later taught in Rome at the Sapienza University as well. In 1566 he resigned to study for the priesthood and was ordained in 1568. With an enthusiasm for humanism, he focused on educational problems and wrote his major work on Christian education. In 1593 Clement VIII (1592–1605) appointed him Secretary of Papal Briefs, making him a cardinal in 1599. Antoniano helped produce the Roman Catechism and worked on Clement's revision of the Breviary.

16. Aphrahat (early fourth century), known as "the Persian Sage," ascetic, ecclesiastic, and writer, survived the persecution of Shapur II (309–79) and is the first of the Syriac church fathers. We know him primarily through the twenty-two essays called *Demonstrations*, which survey the Christian faith and are arranged on an acrostic plan. A twenty-third, written in 345, is in the nature of an appendix. His writings, which show an interest in asceticism and orthodoxy, shed light on both early Persian Christianity and the text of the New Testament. See Brock, no. 11, 19–21.

17. Lucius Apuleius (ca. 124–after 170) was a Platonic philosopher, rhetorician, and author. He is remembered for *The Golden Ass*, which he called *Metamorphosis*. Recounting the adventures of a young man changed by magic into an ass, it is valuable to scholars of religion for its description of the ancient religious mysteries. Whether the author was initiated into the Mystery of Isis or not, he was well acquainted with the worship of the Egyptian goddess.

18. Ardashir II (fl. late fourth century, king 379–83) succeeded his brother Shapur II (309–79) as king of the Sassanian Empire in Persia. While governor of the province of Adiabene during his brother's reign, he had been involved in the persecution of Christians. After his brother's death, nobles in his brother's entourage placed him upon the Sassanian throne, though he was advanced in age. His attempts at putting his own stamp upon state policy came to naught and he was shortly deposed.

19. Aelius Publius Aristides (117–81) was an Athenian philosopher and Christian apologist. Drawing upon the Stoics for his conception of the deity, he enumerated the errors of pagan, Hellenistic, and Jewish religion, while defending the quality of the moral life found among the

"new nation" of Christians, as well as their idea of God: Creator of the world through his Son and the Holy Spirit.

20. Arno of Salzburg (ca. 740–821), monk, diplomat, and bishop, was born in Bavaria and entered the monastery of St. Amand at Elnon in France, where he served as abbot from 782 to 808. In that capacity he became a close friend of Alcuin (735–804), who brought his talents to the attention of Charlemagne (king from 768, emperor 800–814). Upon the emperor's urging, Arno became bishop of Salzburg, where he was able to serve Charlemagne, notably as an emissary to the papal court. After Charlemagne's death, he withdrew from politics and once again turned his attentions to matters of the church, including the founding of a library and a school.

21. Aswana lived prior to the sixth century, at one time as a monk in Edessa. A tradition counts him as a teacher of Ephrem the Syrian (ca. 306–73). In addition to various liturgical pieces, he composed songs to the dead in dialogue form using an alphabetical acrostic. See Baumstark, *Literatur*, 29.

22. Athanasius (ca. 296–373), bishop of Alexandria, was a native of that city, where he received a classical education. He was a staunch defender of the Nicene faith and an opponent of Arianism. His use of intimidation and violence led to his deposition in 335 and exile to Trier. With the support of the Western church and empire, he intermittently returned to his see and regained his episcopal office. In addition to apologetical works, he authored *De incarnatione*. A friend to Serapion (d. after 360) of Thmuis, he also gave support to monasticism, befriending both Anthony of the Desert (ca. 251–356) and Pachomius (ca. 290–346).

23. Athenogenes (n.d.), theologian and bishop of Sebaste, Armenia, allegedly died as one of ten martyrs, probably during the persecution of Diocletian (303–11). As he was being led to the stake to be burned, so legend tells us, he sang a hymn to the Holy Spirit that his disciples preserved as a legacy and tradition identifies as *Phos hilarion*. See *A Dictionary of Christian Biography, Literature, Sects and Doctrines*, eds. Sir William Smith et al., vol. 1 (London: John Murray, 1900), 207; LTK, s.v. "Athenogenes"; and Alban Butler, *Lives of the Saints*, eds. Donald Attwater and Herbert Thurston, vol. 3 (New York: Kenedy, 1956), July 16.

24. Augustine of Canterbury (d. 604/5) was prior of St. Andrew's monastery in Rome when in 596 Gregory the Great (590–604) called

upon him to reestablish the church in England. Although welcomed by the king, he had limited organizational skills and failed to reach an agreement with the ancient Celtic Church.

25. Of Berber stock, Augustine of Hippo (354–430), who was born at Thagaste in present-day Algeria, had a pagan father and a Christian mother. He was educated in North Africa and became a Manichaean before converting to Christianity while living in Milan, where he was working as a teacher of rhetoric. After ordination to the priesthood, he became bishop of Hippo in North Africa. A prolific writer, he was active in his opposition to heresies, notably those of the Pelagians, Donatists, Arians, and Manichaeans. The Roman Church holds Augustine to be one of the four traditional Doctors of the Church, along with Jerome (ca. 342–420), Ambrose (ca. 339–97), and Gregory (590–604).

26. Bardaisan (Latin: Bardesanes; ca. 154–222), a philosopher, astrologist, and poet, was born of Parthian parents in Edessa on the banks of the Daisan River, from which derives his name, which means "Son of Daisan." He was learned in Babylonian astrology and, after converting to Christianity, sought to create a speculative synthesis of the two. Attached to the court in Edessa, Bardaisan had to flee to Armenia toward the end of his life. His writing, including 150 hymns, exists only in fragments. His followers formed into a group, the Bardaisanites, which had a tenuous existence for centuries. See Brock, no. 4, 15.

27. Bar Hebraeus, Bar 'Ebroyo, Gregory the Hebrew, or Gregorios Bar 'Ebrâjâ (1126–1286), the common name for Abu-l-Farag, a Jacobite Syrian bishop of Jewish parentage, studied at Antioch and Tripolis, became a monk, was consecrated a bishop in 1246, and was elected mafrian (or metropolitan) of Mosul in 1264. Multilingual, he wrote on philosophy, theology, physics, astronomy, and mathematics; he also had renown as a physician. His *Chronicle* is invaluable as a source for history of the Syrian churches, east and west. See Brock, no. 95, 75–80.

28. Basil the Great (ca. 330–79) received the best in Christian and pagan education in Caesarea, Constantinople, and Athens. He forsook the world to live as a monk, living in rural Cappadocia, until his bishop called him out of monastic retirement to defend orthodoxy against Arianism. In 370 he became bishop of Caesarea, also in Cappadocia, where he earned a reputation for his erudition, organization, eloquence, and holiness.

29. Robert Bellarmine (1542–1621), born in Tuscany, joined the Jesuits in 1560 and was ordained priest in 1570. While professor of theology at Louvain in modern-day Belgium, he encountered thinkers from outside the Roman Church. In 1576 he moved to Rome to teach as professor of controversial theology at the newly established Collegium Romanum. Known as a learned and eloquent adversary of Protestants, he sought to best his opponents through reasoned argument rather than dogmatic claims. Made a cardinal in 1599, he served as archbishop of Capua from 1602 to 1605. At the end of life, Bellarmine turned his scholarly attention to spirituality. His views on the papacy caused his canonization to be delayed until 1930.

30. Benedict (ca. 480–ca. 550), "the Patriarch of Western Monasticism," was born in Nursia and educated in Rome. The licentiousness he witnessed during the years of his youth led him to retire ca. 500 to a cave at Subiaco, where he lived as a hermit. There a community grew up around him. Moving to Monte Cassino with a group of followers ca. 529, he drew up plans for the reform of monasticism and wrote his rule.

31. Though a layman when elevated to the throne of St. Peter by force, Benedict VIII (d. 1024, pope from 1012) became a strong leader of the church in Italy and its proponent abroad. He crowned the German king Henry II (1002–24) as emperor. With strong ties in France and England, he fought for the integrity of Italy and peace within it. Supporting the reformation of the monastery in Cluny, he worked to improve clerical integrity.

32. Benedict XIV (1675–1758, pope from 1740) was born in Bologna and educated in Rome. After years serving in various capacities at the Vatican, he rose to become cardinal in 1728 and archbishop of Bologna in 1731. A man of learning and balance, Benedict had gifts as an administrator, earned the respect of both Catholic and Protestant European courts, exhibited intellectual moderation, and worked to elevate the moral stature of the papacy. Among other writings, he composed a classic treatise on canonization and compiled an influential volume on diocesan synods. He established academies at Rome to further historical studies.

33. Bernard of Clairvaux (1090–1153), of French noble birth and abbot of Clairvaux Abbey, was instrumental in building the Cistercian order. Active in the wider church, he played a significant role in councils,

church politics, and promoting the Second Crusade. Believing in the immediacy of faith and devoted to the Virgin Mary as intercessor, he opposed the rationalism of Peter Abelard (1079–1142/3).

34. Bernard of Porto (d. 1176) was a canon regular of the canonry of San Frediano at Lucca in present-day Italy who came to Rome to serve as prior of the community of canon regulars assigned to the Basilica of St. John Lateran. There he wrote a customary, entitled *Ordo officiorum ecclesiae Lateranensis*, describing its worship "customs." In 1145 he became cardinal priest of San Clemente and in 1152 the archpriest of the patriarchal Vatican basilica. In 1158 he was elected bishop of the See of Porto and Santa Rufina in the suburbs of Rome. On numerous occasions, Bernard represented Rome diplomatically, including traveling on a mission of peace to Pavia for an audience with Frederick I Barbarossa (1152–90). For a biography (with bibliography), see http://www.fiu.edu/~mirandas/bios1145.htm#Bernardo; and also Bernhardi Cardinalis et Lateranensis ecclesiae Prioris, and *Ordo officiorum ecclesiae Lateranensis*, ed. Ludwig Fischer, Historische Quellen und Forschungen 2, 3 (München [Munich]-Freising: Datterer, 1916), xl–xlviii.

35. Giovanni Lorenzo Bernini (1598–1680), an industrious man of wide-ranging talents, worked as a sculptor, painter, architect, and poet. From France and England as well as from Italy, he received commissions to portray royalty, painted on canvas or sculpted in stone. He is best remembered, however, for being an architect active in Rome, where he worked under five popes. There he became superintendent of public works and architect of St. Peter's Basilica, for which he designed, among other things, the baldachin over its altar and St. Peter's Square with its colonnade. His style leans heavily toward the baroque.

36. Berno (ca. 978–ca. 1048), an orator, hymn writer, musician, and liturgist, who became a monk at Prüm near Trier, was named abbot of the Abbey of Reichenau in 1008. Under his leadership, the abbey became a center for learning. He wrote widely, established a scriptorium, revised Gregorian chant, and initiated extensive building projects. He also provided strong support for his royal patrons, Henry II (1014–24) and Henry III (1028–56).

37. Bernold of Constance (ca. 1054–1100), historian and theologian, was born in Swabia, studied in Constance, was ordained in 1084, and became a Benedictine monk ca. 1086. Closely associated with the reforms of Gregory VII (1073–85), he opposed Emperor Henry IV

(1056–1106) in the Investiture Controversy and wrote in defense of Rome. While his hope in authoring the *Micrologus*, an important medieval liturgical treatise, was to restore Roman liturgical practice, he was compelled to incorporate into it material from non-Roman sources.

38. Edmund Bishop (1846–1917) was an English convert to Roman Catholicism and an autodidact, who for a time served as secretary to the English historian Thomas Carlyle. Supporting himself as a civil servant, he otherwise pursued historical studies, with a special focus on the liturgy. As a liturgical scholar, Bishop is unusual for having a full-length biography devoted to him: Nigel Abercrombie, *The Life and Work of Edmund Bishop* (London: Longmans and Co., 1959).

39. Boniface IV (ca. 550–615, pope from 608) was a deacon of the Roman Church prior to his elevation to the throne of St Peter. As pope, he was able to make the Parthenon into a Christian church, the first instance of a building built for pagan worship being so converted. He attended to affairs of the English church. As Roman citizens regarded him as the man among them who was closest to God, they blamed Boniface for the hunger, illness, and flooding that the city suffered during his pontificate. He died in monastic seclusion.

40. Boniface VIII (1234–1303, pope from 1294) studied in Italy before becoming canon at Paris, Rome, and elsewhere. In 1276 he commenced his career in the Curia, engaging in diplomacy and intrigue. A great defender of the absolute power of the papacy, Boniface entered into a long and drawn-out struggle with Philip IV (or the Fair) of France (1285–1314), which eventually resulted in the pope's death. He was more successful in his campaign against the Colonna family. After defeat by the papal armies, many members of that family had to flee to France for refuge.

41. Charles Borromeo (1538–84), born to nobility on the shores of Lake Maggiore, became one of the leaders of the Counter-Reformation. Though he studied law and civil engineering in Pavia, he was set on the path to the priesthood at a young age. At twenty-two he became cardinal and archbishop of Milan, exercising influence on the third session of the Council of Trent (1545–63). Within his see he initiated reform, raising standards for both clergy and laity, strengthening the diocesan administration, establishing seminaries, and improving the instruction of children. He was renowned for his pastoral care. Though his reforms were strongly opposed in some quarters, his influence was widespread. He was canonized in 1610.

42. After a period of solitude and penance, Catherine of Siena (1333/47–80), a Dominican tertiary, felt called to care for the poor, the sick, and sinners. Soon she was acting as an intermediary in matters of conflict, both in her native Siena and in higher circles. Due to her sanctity, wisdom, and personality, people were drawn to her. Central to all her writings is Christ crucified, especially his blood, which she took to be a sign of his love and a cause for ours. Although she succeeded in convincing Gregory XI (1370–78) to move back to Rome from Avignon in 1377, his death and the Great Western Schism followed shortly thereafter, a factor contributing to her early death.

43. Born of plebian parents, Marcus Porcius Cato the Elder (234 BCE–149 BCE), statesman, soldier, and agriculturalist, at first followed family tradition in becoming a soldier and an active landowner. A man of strict discipline, conservative temperament, great talent, personable manner, and eloquent speech, he went to Rome, where he became a senator and was elected consul. The first author of importance to write Latin prose, he composed manuals and histories in addition to publishing his orations.

44. Charlemagne or Charles the Great (ca. 742–814, king from 768, emperor from 800) extended the lands he inherited from his father, Pepin the Short (751–68), in all directions of the compass. In 800 he was the first to be crowned emperor of the Holy Roman Empire. Throughout his territory, he developed a strong and consistent system of imperial government; his support of ecclesiastical reform and scholarship were essential to the flourishing known as the Carolingian Renaissance.

45. Charles II or the Bald (823–77, king from 840, emperor from 875), the youngest son of Louis the Pious (814–40), was first ruler of the West Frankish Kingdom and then—as Charles II—Emperor of the Holy Roman Empire. Though in conflict with his brothers and unpopular among his nobles, Charles was educated, cultured, and a friend of the church, a source of his political support. Charles commissioned beautifully illuminated editions of at least seven books to be produced out of his palace school, including the prayer book referred to by Baumstark on p. 225. See Rosamond McKitterick, "The Palace School of Charles the Bald," in *Charles the Bald: Court and Kingdom*, eds. Margaret T. Gibson and Janet L. Nelson, 2nd rev. ed. (Aldershot: Variorum, 1990), 333.

46. Chrodegang (d. 766), bishop of Metz from 742, was one of the chief ecclesiastical reformers of his day. Perhaps related to Pepin the Short (751–68), he served Charles Martel (716–41) as his private secretary, chancellor, and chief minister, even after his elevation to the episcopacy.

47. John Chrysostom (ca. 347–407, patriarch from 398) received a pagan education in the law at Antioch before studying theology at Tarsus. After spending time as a monk, he was ordained to serve in Antioch, where he gained renown for his preaching, because of both his eloquence (Chrysostom means "golden-tongued") and his insight into Scripture. Upon becoming patriarch of Constantinople, his reforming zeal earned him disfavor. Despite popular support, he was condemned, deposed, exiled, and, through enforced hardship, killed.

48. Marcus Tullius Cicero (106–43 BCE) was a Roman statesman, lawyer, scholar, and writer. Remembered as the greatest Roman orator, he wrote books on rhetoric, philosophy, and politics, and published his orations as well. In the years that civil war threatened the republic of Rome, he strived without avail to defend republican principles.

49. Clement VIII (1536–1605, pope from 1592), the son of a prominent Italian lawyer, was a man of admirable character. He involved himself deeply in politics, in and out of the church. Encouraging the revision of service books, he saw published new editions of the Vulgate Bible, *Missale*, *Breviarium*, *Caeremoniale episcoporum*, and *Pontificale*.

50. Little is known about Clement of Alexandria (ca. 150–ca. 215), save that he was a theologian. After studying the Christian faith and pagan philosophy, perhaps in Athens, he settled in Alexandria where he taught. In his writings he sought to follow a via media between Gnosticism and Christian simplicity, holding Christianity to be the fulfillment both of the promises of the Old Testament and of the pursuit of pagan philosophy.

51. Biographical information on Clement of Rome (fl. ca. 96) is meager. Tradition has it that Peter (d. 67?) appointed Clement bishop of Rome. While a body of literature has been ascribed to him, the First Epistle to the Corinthians is assuredly genuine and provides information on the Roman Church in the first century CE, including references to the liturgy. During the subapostolic era, this letter was regarded as inspired and read widely in churches.

52. Clovis I (466–511, king from 481), founder of the Merovingian dynasty, was the first king to bring all of the Frankish tribes together under one ruler. Of utmost significance for the history of the church is his baptism (496) as a Catholic Christian, the faith of the majority of his subjects. This aligned him with Rome and against the Goths, adherents of Arian Christianity who ruled over much of Gaul. Most likely Clovis was converted under the influence of his wife, Clotilde or Clothilda (475–545).

53. Constantine the Great (272–337, emperor from 312) became a competitor for imperial power in 306, defeating one rival at the battle of Milvian Bridge in 312 and another in 324. In the earlier battle and ever after, he rode under the *labarum*, a standard on which the Chi-Rho symbol for Christ replaced pagan emblems. Although baptized only shortly before his death, initiatives in the state and for the church served to strengthen the faith. Under his rule as emperor, Christianity was both tolerated and received imperial favor. He involved himself directly in the affairs of the church, including the Donatist schism and the Arian dispute, the last of which led him to call the Council of Nicea (325). Upon gaining uncontested power in 324, he established his imperial capital at Byzantium, which he rebuilt, renaming it Constantinople.

54. Cornelius (d. 253, pope from 251) was elected pope after the persecution instituted by Emperor Decius (249–51), which left the See of Rome vacant for more than a year. Though two synods supported Cornelius, he faced opposition in the Novatianists, who wished to take a hard line against the *lapsi* of the persecution. Due to persecution, he himself was forced to flee Rome for Centumcellae (present-day Civitavecchia) where he died, probably not as a martyr. When his body was later taken to Rome, he was not buried in the chapel of the popes, but in the cemetery of Callistus, perhaps in an area reserved for the *gens Cornelia*. See J. N. D. Kelly, *The Oxford Dictionary of Popes* (Oxford and New York: Oxford University Press, 1998), s.v. "Cornelius, St."

55. Cosmas the Melodist or of Maiuma or the Hagiopolite (ca. 706–ca. 760), a writer of Greek liturgical hymns, was born in Jerusalem, where, after being orphaned, he was adopted by the father of John of Damascus (ca. 650–ca. 750). He studied with John under an Italian monk also named Cosmas, entered the Great Lavra of St. Sabas near Jerusalem, and was made bishop of Maiuma near Gaza. He composed fourteen canons for the feasts of Easter, Christmas, and the Exaltation of the

Cross, all of which are now found in the Byzantine liturgy, while some of them have been translated into Syriac.

56. Cosmas and Damian (d. ca. 287) were twin brothers martyred at Cyrrhus, a city in the Euphratensis Province of Syria, from where their cult spread widely. They were known for their miraculous cures and became the patron saints of physicians. As they desired no payment for their ministrations save the faith of those healed, they received the moniker of "moneyless" or "silverless."

57. Cyprian (d. 258), bishop of Carthage, was a pagan rhetorician who was consecrated bishop shortly after converting to Christianity. After the persecution instituted by Emperor Decian (249–51), he engaged in controversy over the lapsed and the schismatics, insisting on discipline for the former and rebaptism for the latter. His writings, some of theological significance, many apologetic and pastoral, were widely read. On Sept. 14, 258, he was martyred in Carthage during the persecution of Emperor Valerian (253–60).

58. Cyril (376–444, patriarch from 412), patriarch of Alexandria, received a classical education in Alexandria, where he rose to assume the patriarchate held by his uncle Theophilus (385–415). He was known for refined theology and bare-knuckle politics, both civic and ecclesiastical, even to the point of violence. Though he prevailed in his opposition to Nestorius over the nature of Christ, his victory was bittersweet, as it resulted in the permanent division of the church of the East into the oriental and orthodox spheres.

59. Cyril (826–69) and Methodius (815–85), "The Apostles to the Slavs," were brothers born to a senatorial family of Thessalonica who became priests and moved to Constantinople. Upon the request of the emperor, they took up the work of evangelization, initially journeying in Caucasia and Crimea among the Khazars, a people of Turkic stock, who were wavering between Judaism, Islam, and Christianity. On a journey to Moravia, again under royal patronage, Cyril and Methodius translated some of the Bible and the Byzantine liturgy into Slavonic, inventing for the purpose the Glagolithic alphabet, from which the Cyrillic alphabet (named after Cyril) was later derived. After the death of Cyril, Methodius continued to evangelize the Slavs under the aegis of Rome, yet using the Eastern liturgy.

60. Dante Alighieri (1265–1321), a Florentine politician and writer, is esteemed for being the father of the Italian language. He was embroiled

in the Guelph-Ghibbeline conflict, on the side of the Guelphs, whom he joined in battle. Because of this political allegiance, he spent the last twenty years of his life exiled from Florence, during which time his interests in philosophy and literature deepened and he concentrated on his writing. His most renowned works, *De Monarchia* and *The Divine Comedy*, are fruits of this activity.

61. The only evidence we have for Bishop Decentius (fl. fourth century), the earliest known bishop of Gubbio in Umbria, Italy, is a letter dated March 19, 416, a reply to questions he had put to Innocent I (402–17) concerning the liturgy and church order.

62. Though employed as an archivist at the Vatican Library, Giovanni Battista de Rossi (1822–94) undertook to explore the archaeology of Rome. Ahead of his times, he recognized the value both literary sources and geology had for archaeological work. Specializing in the catacombs, he rediscovered the lost Catacomb of Callistus along the *Via Appia Antica*.

63. Dionysius the Pseudo-Areopagite (fl. ca. 500), mystical theologian, is the name given to the author of a body of theological writings attributed to the Dionysius converted by Paul (d. 65?) in Athens (Acts 17:34). These writings were quoted in Christian literature for the first time ca. 513, when Severus of Antioch (ca. 465–538) appealed to them to defend the theological position of the Monophysites. During the Middle Ages the thought of Dionysius the Pseudo-Areopagite was also influential on Christian thinking in the West.

64. Dominic (1170–1221), born in Spain, educated in arts and theology, became a canon regular, following the rule of St. Augustine. Encountering the Cathars, whom Rome regarded as heretical, he resolved to win them back for the Catholic faith through preaching. There grew up around him a group of followers, later established as an order dedicated to the charisms for which he was renowned: an austere life style and preaching with intellectual rigor in a popular style.

65. Egeria, also Etheria (fl. fourth century), traditionally thought to be a nun or an abbess, perhaps from Spain but more probably from Gaul, wrote a pilgrimage account notable for its keen observations. This journal, describing a trip to the Holy Land between 381 and 384, is a key source for the liturgy of Jerusalem in the late fourth century.

66. Ephrem the Syrian (ca. 306–73), Syrian biblical exegete and ecclesiastical writer, was born in Nisibis where he was ordained a deacon,

though near the end of his life he settled in Edessa. He was known for his learning, his authorship of *madrasha* (teaching songs or hymns), and refutations of heretics (Arius, Marcion, Mani, and Bardaisan). His writing is profoundly scriptural and mostly in verse. See Brock, no. 12, 22–28.

67. Epictetus (ca. 55–ca. 135 CE) was a Greek Stoic philosopher, probably born a slave at Hieropolis in Phrygia. He resided in Rome until he was exiled to Nicopolis in Greece, where he lived most of his life, remaining there until his death. Epictetus taught that philosophy is more than an intellectual endeavor; it is in fact a way of living. His *Discourses* were put down in writing by a disciple, Arrian (ca. 86–160).

68. Eugene IV (1383–1447, pope from 1431), a native of Venice who entered an Augustinian monastery there, was called into the service of the Roman Church while still young. His papacy was marked by turmoil, in the church as well as in the political arena, sometimes resulting in armed conflict. His political struggles led to a ten-year exile from Rome, which he regained by force of arms; within the church, his opposition to the conciliar movement, notably at the Council of Basel (1431–45), resulted in the decline of that movement and a strengthening of the papacy. His numerous proclamations on slavery have been seen as providing papal blessing for the trade.

69. Very little is known about Eustasius, Eustachius, or Eustathius (fl. fifth century), save that he succeeded Venerius (431–52) as bishop of Marsilia (now Marseilles). See *A Dictionary of Christian Biography, Literature, Sects and Doctrines,* eds. Sir William Smith et al., vol. 1 (London: John Murray, 1900), 381.

70. Julius Firmicus Maternus (d. after 360) was a rhetorician, likely of Sicilian origin, and an adult convert to Christianity. He wrote *Matheis,* the book to which Baumstark refers on p. 84, while still a pagan, the most complete work on astrology to come down from antiquity. As a Christian apologist, he wrote *De errore profanarum religionum,* in which he condemns paganism and calls upon the emperor to suppress it by force.

71. Venantius Honorius Clementianus Fortunatus (ca. 530–ca. 610), Latin poet and ecclesiastic, was born near Venice and educated in Ravenna. After a pilgrimage to the tomb of Martin of Tours, he settled in Poitiers (now in France), where he won the favor of the court and in time became bishop. Fortunatus put pen to paper in an attempt to

maintain classical Latin culture before the swelling influence of the German tribes. Eleven works of poetry in various genres survive, including a number of Latin hymns, *Vexilla Regis* and *Pange lingua gloriosi* being the best known.

72. Beginning as a teacher of theology, Egidio Foscacari (1512–64) became bishop of Modena in 1550. A short imprisonment on charges of heresy did not prevent him from participating in the Council of Trent (1545–63), where he played an important role. He collaborated in both the composition of the Roman Catechism and the revision of the Breviary. See LTK, s.v. "Egidio Foscacari."

73. Gabriel of Qatar, Arabic: Jibril bar Lipeh Qatraye (fl. sixth to seventh centuries) was a Nestorian scribe and writer from Bet Qatraye. He studied at the School of Nisibis, where he may have met the future Ishoyabh III (649–59), who was also a student there. In addition to writing a liturgical commentary, Gabriel produced a copy of the gospels. See Sebastian P. Brock, "Gabriel of Qatar's Commentary on the Liturgy," *Hugoye: Journal of Syriac Studies* 6:2 (2003), also available online at http://syrcom.cua.edu/Hugoye/Vol6No2/HV6N2Brock .html#S4; and Adam H. Hecker, *Fear of God and the Beginning of Wisdom* (Philadelphia: University of Pennsylvania Press, 2006), 1–6.

74. Tarquino Galluzzi (1574–1649), orator, poet, and translator, was born in the Sabina region just east of Rome and joined the Society of Jesus in 1590. He lived mostly in Rome, where he taught rhetoric and ethics before becoming rector of the Greek College. Having mastered the style of classical poetry, he was invited to work on the hymns of the Breviary by Urban VIII (1623–44). Admired for his eloquence and learning, he was invited to deliver funeral orations for such notables as cardinals Arnaud d'Ossat (1537–1604) and Robert Bellarmine (1542–1621). His writings include *Carminum libri tres* (Three books of poems), a commentary on Virgil, and a translation with commentary of Aristotle's *Nicomachean Ethics*. See *Jesuit Latin Poets of the 17th and 18th Centuries: An Anthology of Neo-Latin Poets*, eds. James J. Mertz and John P. Murphy (Wauconda, Illinois: Bolchazy-Carducci Publishers, 1989), 185.

75. Gelasius I (d. 496, pope from 492), born either in Rome or Africa, was the most prolific writer among the early popes. He continued a struggle with the Eastern Roman Empire, in which he asserted the primacy of Rome over the entire church, Eastern and Western. In the

city of Rome he sought to strengthen religious life by forbidding the celebration of Lupercalia, an ancient pagan festival, and working to suppress the Manicheans, who had a large population there.

76. Gerontius (395–480/85), monk and priest, archimandrite of cenobites in Palestine, native of Jerusalem, joined the monastery for men started by Melania the Younger (ca. 385–438/39) on the Mount of Olives and served as chaplain to her community of women. He died in the desert, where he had been forced to flee because of doctrinal struggles. His *Life of Melania the Younger* is significant for the history of the liturgy.

77. Tiberius Sempronius Gracchus (168/63–33 BCE) and Gaius Sempronius Gracchus (154–21 BCE) were brothers, elected to serve as tribunes in Rome. Both championed the cause of the common people against the interests of the Roman Senate and aristocracy, won popular followings, and came to violent deaths.

78. Gregory I or the Great (540–604, pope from 590), the son of a senator, who at one point became prefect of Rome, gave all his wealth to the poor and became a Benedictine monk. After serving first as a deacon in Rome and then as representative of the pope in Constantinople, he returned to become abbot of his community and subsequently pope. He is known for furthering the temporal power of the papacy and enhancing the stature of Rome, the evangelization of England, work on behalf of the poor, support of monasticism, and an interest in the liturgy and its music. The Roman Church holds Gregory to be one of the four traditional Doctors of the Church, along with Jerome (ca. 342–420), Augustine (354–430), and Ambrose (ca. 339–97).

79. Gregory II (ca. 669–731, pope from 715) came from a noble Roman family and served Popes Sergius I (687–701) and Constantine I (708–15). During his own pontificate, cracks first appeared in the relationship between Rome and the Byzantine government, while ties were strengthened to the German world. Gregory condemned the policy of iconoclasm pursued by the Eastern Roman Empire, but maintained peaceful relations with the Lombards ruling in Italy. As for the liturgy, he prepared new Masses for Lent.

80. Although Gregory IV (d. 844, pope from 827) forthrightly acknowledged the rule of Louis I (814–40), relations with the Holy Roman Emperor (as well as the Frankish bishops) deteriorated because of his involvement in internecine struggles between Louis and his sons. In

Rome, Gregory rebuilt the Basilica of San Marco. In the mission field, he appointed Ansgar (801–65), the "Apostle to the North," to serve as the archbishop of the See of Hamburg and Bremen.

81. Gregory VII (ca. 1015–85, pope from 1073) was born in Tuscany and educated in Rome, where he became a monk and served more than one pope. In his reforms, inspired largely by Cluny, he sought to raise the moral tenor of the Roman Church and its clergy, notably through his condemnation of simony. His position met with widespread opposition, sparking the Investiture controversy and including a showdown with the German emperor, Henry IV (1050–1106).

82. Of noble birth, Gregory IX (ca. 1148–1241, pope from 1227) was educated in Paris and Bologna. A nephew of Innocent III (1198–1216), he became a cardinal upon his uncle's accession and cardinal-bishop of Ostia in 1206, serving as papal delegate on various missions. A personal friend of Francis of Assisi (1181/82–1226), he was appointed Protector of the Franciscan Order in 1220 and helped develop the Third Order. As pope he canonized Francis (1181/82–1226) in 1228, and later Antony of Padua (1195–1231) and Dominic (1170–1221). A proponent of the Crusades and an opponent of Frederick II (1220–50), he worked without success for a union with the Eastern church.

83. Gregory XI (1329–78, pope from 1370), who was born in France and studied in Perugio, was a skilled canonist and theologian. The last French pope, he was elected at Avignon, where he remained for the time being. His papacy focused with limited success upon quelling the rebellion in the Papal States. Returning to Rome in response to entreaties from Catherine of Siena (1347–80), Gregory spent the last year of his papacy and life disappointed, in an inhospitable Rome. The Great Western Schism followed upon his death.

84. Due to Arian opposition Gregory (of) Nazianzus, Gregory Nazianzen, or Gregory the Theologian (330–89/90, patriarch from 379 to 381) served only briefly as patriarch of Constantinople. Trained in rhetoric and philosophy, he was highly skilled in rhetorical style. Imbued with the Hellenistic tradition, he set the course for Byzantine theologians and ecclesiastics, with his trinitarian theology being especially influential. The Liturgy of Gregory (Nazianzus) is one of the three Coptic liturgies of Egypt.

85. Hartmann Grisar (1845–1932) studied in both Münster and Innsbruck before being ordained a priest and entering the Society of Jesus.

In 1871 he became professor of church history at Innsbruck, but after 1895 spent much of his time in Rome researching the treasury of the papal chapel. In addition to archaeology (especially that of Rome) and the early history of the popes, he wrote extensively on Martin Luther, bringing a critical Catholic perspective to bear upon the Protestant reformer.

86. Hadrian I (d. 795, pope from 772) was born of Roman nobility. While this pope offered strong support to Charlemagne (king from 768, emperor 800–814), the increase in the emperor's power inevitably constrained some actions of the Roman Church. The relationship of the two men was for the most part friendly, though they concurred on some ecclesiastical matters and differed on others. Hadrian had skills in administration, as reflected by the building projects he initiated for the city of Rome.

87. Hadrian II (792–872, pope from 867), of noble Roman birth, was already elderly when elected pope. He became embroiled in both Frankish imperial politics and Byzantine ecclesiastical affairs. Like his predecessor Nicholas I (858–67), Hadrian sought to strengthen the position and power of the papacy in the West.

88. Hadrian of Canterbury (d. 709), of African origin, became abbot of a monastery on the island of Nisida near Naples. When Pope Vitalian (657–72) designated him bishop of the See of Canterbury, then vacant in Britain, he declined, recommending Theodore of Tarsus (ca. 602–90) in his stead. While following Hadrian's advice, the pope also sent him to England along with Theodore to tend to the doctrinal and cultural aspects of the mission.

89. Al-Harith ibn Jabalah (d. 569, king 529) was the king of the Ghassanids, an Arab people who lived on the eastern edge of the Byzantine Empire. He was honored by Emperor Justinian I (483–565) for supporting the Byzantine Empire in its struggle against the Sassanian Empire. As a Miaphysite Christian, Harith strove to find a via media between Nestorianism and Eutychianism. In the complicated christological controversies of the day, Chalcedonians held Miaphysites to be adherents of Monophysitism, a charge the former refuted. However, in rejecting the teachings of the Council of Chalcedon (451), Harith offered implicit support to others who opposed the council, notably the Monophysites, and in so doing encouraged the growth of the Syrian Orthodox Church.

90. Haymo of Faversham (d. 1244), Franciscan friar, theologian, and ecclesiastic, was born in England and educated in Paris. While teaching at Oxford, he served both his order and Pope Gregory IX (1227–41) in various diplomatic capacities. He was elected general of the Franciscan Order in 1240. At the request of Innocent IV (1243–54), he revised the ordinals for the Roman Breviary, Missal, and grace before and after meals.

91. Helisachar or Elisachar or Elisigarus (d. after 837) was a cleric, scholar, and government official. In addition to being the chancellor of Louis I (814–40) from 814 to 819, he also served as archchaplain, with responsibility for the palace clergy. Intelligent and observant, he found Frankish chant in disarray and, upon becoming abbot of Saint-Riquier near Abbeville in 819, worked to reform it.

92. Henry II (973–1024, king from 1002), the last of the Ottonians, was gentle and devout, encouraged the Cluniac movement, and sent out missionaries from his court to the new bishopric of Bamberg. He also elevated royal control over the churches and abbeys to a principle of government, endowed by God.

93. Henry IV (1050–1106, king from 1056–1105) rose to become Holy Roman Emperor (1084–1105), the third in the Salian dynasty. A towering figure in the eleventh century, he struggled mightily with the papacy during the Investiture Controversy, when Pope Gregory VII (1073–85), by asserting Rome's right to name clergy to church positions, challenged a prerogative previously exercised by the crown. During his turbulent reign, Henry succeeded in consolidating imperial power at home and expanding the empire's boundaries. He was forced to abdicate, however, in the year before his death.

94. Herman the Lame or Cripple or Hermannus Contractus (1013–54), Christian poet and chronicler, was educated in the monastery at Reichenau, where he later took vows. In addition to his poems, he wrote on mathematics, astronomy, and chronography. *Salve regina* (Hail, Holy Queen) has been attributed to him. While this hymn, one of the oldest Marian antiphons, found its way into the Mass, its original and common setting was monastic prayer. In addition to Herman, however, *Salve Regina* has been ascribed to Adhémar, the bishop of LePuy (d. 1098); Peter, the bishop of Compostela (d. 1003); and Bernard of Clairvaux (1090–1153).

95. Ildefons Herwegen (1874–1946), who entered the Benedictine novitiate in 1895, was ordained in 1901 and elected abbot of the Abbey

of Maria Laach in 1913. Under his leadership, the abbey, which had embraced a liturgical apostolate already before World War I, became renowned for it in the years after the war. Herwegen was a strong proponent of liturgical science and a leader in the liturgical movement. Politically conservative, he initially welcomed the rise of the NSDAP (National Socialist Democratic Workers or Nazi Party), but soon realized its ideology was incompatible with the teachings the Roman Catholic Church.

96. Hilary of Poitiers (ca. 315–67), theologian and ecclesiastic, was converted from neoplatonism, became bishop of Poitiers, and engaged in the Arian controversy. His staunch defense of orthodoxy led Emperor Constantius II (337–61) to exile him to Phrygia, where he stayed for four years before returning home.

97. A Christian ecclesiastic named Hippolytus lived in Rome around the turn of the third century. He has been identified as a Roman ecclesiastical writer and antipope, vigorous in his opposition to heresy. While a corpus of writing has been attributed to "Hippolytus" from the fourth century, including the *Apostolic Tradition*, there were a number of persons remembered by the early church who bore that name, more than one writer may have produced the literary corpus, and neither the provenance of the writings nor Hippolytus's community are known for certain.

98. Quintus Horatius Flaccus (65 BCE–8 CE), known in English as Horace, a Roman lyric poet and satirist, was the son of a freed slave and well educated, first in Rome and then in Athens. Following the assassination of Julius Caesar (44 BCE), he joined forces with Brutus, who was defeated. With amnesty and his return to Italy, a job at the treasury allowed him to practice his poetic arts; his writings rank as classics of the golden age of Latin literature. From the Renaissance until the decline of romanticism, the style of his poetry was closely studied and often emulated.

99. Matthias Flacius Illyricus, the Latinized name of Matthias Vlachich or Matthias Francovich (1520–75), Lutheran theologian, was born in Istria (Illyricus), a peninsula on the northeasterly shore of the Adriatic. After studying for the priesthood, he became a Lutheran, university professor, and zealous defender of what he understood to be true Lutheran doctrine, even against the likes of Phillip Melancthon (1497–1560). Though he lived for a time in Wittenberg, his argumentative nature caused him to move frequently.

100. Innocent I (d. 417, pope from 402) involved himself in ecclesiastical matters in Africa, the Holy Land, and the Eastern Empire, defending the claims of the authority of Rome and the papacy. His letter to Bishop Decentius of Gubbio (fl. fourth century) is notable for the light that it sheds on the Canon of the Mass, the episcopal prerogative to confirm, and the rites of unction and penance.

101. Ishoyabh, Isho'yahb, Yeshuyab, or Ishu'yabb III (ca. 580–659; catholicos from 649), monk, scholar, and ecclesiastic, was born in the province of Adiabene to a well-to-do Persian family, studied in Nisibis and became a monk at the convent of Beth 'Abe. He served as bishop of Nineveh from 628, metropolitan of Arbel from 637, and catholicos until his death. In collaboration with another monk, he edited the *Hudra*. See LTK, s.v. "Ischo'jabh III; Brock, no. 54, no. 54.

102. Jacob Baradaeus or Bûrde'ânâ (ca. 500–578), from whom the Syrian Orthodox Church received its moniker "Jacobite," was born in Tella and received his education at the monastery of Phesilta, near Nisibis. With hospitality from Empress Theodora I (ca. 527–48), who supported the Monophysite party, he lived in Constantinople for fifteen years. Secretly ordained bishop of Edessa in 541/42, he spent the remainder of his life on the road, furtively setting up a separate Monophysite hierarchy, ordaining priests, and encouraging the East Syrian church. His nickname "Bûrde'ânâ," meaning in Syriac "the man who has a horse cloth," may have stemmed from his use of a horse blanket for disguise, which was common dress in his time for the poor, or it could be a good-humored reference to his constant travel by horseback. See Diarmaid McCullough, *Christianity: The First Three Thousand Years* (New York: Viking, 2009), 237.

103. Jacob of Edessa (ca. 633–708), bishop and author, a native of Antioch, studied at the monastery of Qennesrin and in Alexandria before being appointed bishop of Edessa. A man of superior knowledge and literary skill, he wrote in the areas of theology, philosophy, exegesis, history, and grammar. See Brock, no. 61, 57–59.

104. Jacopone da Todi (ca. 1230–1306) was a Franciscan poet who allegedly authored the *Stabat Mater*. After studying law and living a worldly life, the death of his wife precipitated a turn to religion and his becoming a Franciscan lay brother. In addition to poetry in both Latin and the Umbrian dialect, he wrote satires attacking Pope Boniface VIII (1294–1303). Although excommunicated and imprisoned for

his opposition to Boniface, he was freed by his successor, Pope Benedict XI (1303–4), and died in a Franciscan monastery.

105. Along with the apostle Peter (d. 67?), James the Just or Adelphotheos ("Brother of the Lord"; d. 62) was a leader of the apostolic community in Jerusalem. After Peter's departure, James seems to have exercised primary authority, presiding over the Council of Jerusalem (Acts 15) and being chosen bishop. Jewish Christians held him in great esteem. Tradition attributes to him the Liturgy of St. James.

106. Jerome (ca. 342–420), a biblical scholar and apologist, was born in Illyria and began his studies in Rome, where he converted to Christianity. Until the middle of his life, he traveled widely, from Gaul to Egypt, studying and writing. He then settled in Palestine where, living as a hermit in Bethlehem, he dedicated himself to biblical commentaries and translation, producing the Latin version of the Bible that came to be known as the Vulgate. The Roman Church holds Jerome to be one of the four traditional Doctors of the Church, along with Ambrose (ca. 339–97), Augustine (354–430), and Gregory (590–604).

107. Though raised in poverty, Cardinal Francisco Jiménez de Cisneros (1436–1517), a Franciscan, early caught the attention of princes in both the church and the state, rising to become a cardinal. Through his role as confessor to Queen Isabella I (1474–1504), he exercised considerable influence at the Spanish court, twice serving as regent for the king. As Grand Inquisitor, he was instrumental in the forcible conversion of the Spanish Muslim population. He advanced scholarship in founding the university at Alcalá de Henares and sponsoring the publication of the first polyglot version of the entire Bible. He worked to ensure a future for the Mozarabic liturgy.

108. John III (d. 574, pope from 561) was the son of the *vir illustris*, Anastasius. Little is known about this pope, who reigned during the Lombard invasion of the Italian peninsula, when he drew upon the Byzantine Empire for help.

109. John of Damascus or Damascene (ca. 650–ca. 750), teacher, preacher, and author, was born of a prominent Arab Christian family. He studied with Cosmas of Maiuma (ca. 706–ca. 760) under an Italian monk also named Cosmas, became a monk at the Great Lavra of St. Sabas near Jerusalem, was ordained priest after 705, and like his father served under the caliphs. Productive in writing as a theologian, John also composed at least eight of the canons that celebrate the

principal feasts of the Lord, as well as a number of hymns in the so-called *Octoechos*.

110. Nothing is known of John, bishop of Syracuse (fl. sixth to seventh centuries), save that Gregory I or the Great (590–604) wrote to him a number of letters between 595 and 603 and conferred the pallium upon him.

111. Joseph of Thessalonica (ca. 762–832), preacher, poet, and bishop, was born in Constantinople, the brother of Theodore the Studite (759–826), and—like him—received an excellent religious and secular education. He entered a monastery in Bithynia where their uncle was abbot and became archbishop of Thessalonica, but, because of his opposition to the iconoclasts, suffered exile and persecution. Most probably, the many hymns of the *Octoechos* attributed to Joseph the Hymnographer (ca. 810–86) are his work. See LTK, s.v. "Joseph von Thessaloniki."

112. Joseph the Hymnographer (ca. 810–86), Greek hymn writer, was born in Sicily, but, when Arabs invaded his homeland, fled to Thessalonica to live as a monk. He later moved to Constantinople. On a trip to Rome, he was captured by Arab pirates and enslaved on Crete, but escaped to return to Constantinople, where he established a monastery. He reputedly composed one thousand canons, two hundred of which, using an acrostic of his name, are found in the *Menaion*.

113. Justin Martyr (ca. 100–ca. 165), an early Christian apologist, was born in Samaria of pagan parents, but converted to the Christian faith ca. 130, eventually becoming a teacher of Christianity, first in Ephesus and later in Rome. Around 165, Justin, along with some of his disciples, was denounced for his faith; upon refusing to offer sacrifice, they were scourged and beheaded. Justin's writings contain important liturgical references, as in *First Apology* 67, which contains the earliest extant description of an order for Christian worship.

114. Justinian I (483–565, emperor from 527) was the most energetic of the early Byzantine emperors. For the church, he brought about the construction of a number of basilicas, including Hagia Sophia in Constantinople, and, though a defender of orthodoxy, attempted—probably on the urging of his wife, Empress Theodora (ca. 500–548)—to reconcile with the Monophysites. Politically, he published the Code of Justinian, which sought to reestablish the political and religious unity

of the Roman Empire and became influential in the development of Western canon law.

115. Karl Krumbacher (1856–1909), professor and scholar, was a pioneer in the modern study of Byzantine culture. Educated in the classics, he concentrated on medieval Greek literature. His *Geschichte der byzantischen Literatur* (1891) went through a number of editions. In 1892 he founded the journal *Byzantinische Zeitschrift* and in 1897 was appointed to the newly established chair in medieval and modern Greek studies at the University of Munich.

116. Legend tells that Lawrence (d. 258) was born in Tarraconensis in present-day Spain and educated in Rome under Archdeacon Sixtus. Upon becoming bishop of Rome in 257, Sixtus II (257–58) ordained Lawrence deacon, giving him responsibility for the administration of the church's charitable work among the Roman poor. He was martyred in 258, when Sixtus and the seven deacons of Rome became victims of the persecution under Valerian (253–60). However, Lawrence did not go to his death with Sixtus and six other deacons, but rather went four days later, grilled on a gridiron. For bibliography see n. on p. 195.

117. Leo I or the Great (ca. 400/410–61, pope from 440) came from Italian aristocratic stock. With support from the Roman Emperor Valentinian III (425–55), he was able to considerably enhance the authority of the papacy. When Attila (434–53) led his army into Italy and threatened Rome, Leo went out to meet him and was able to help save the city from siege. Although unable to similarly avert the sack of Rome by the Vandals (455), he sought to mitigate the harshness of their occupation. Leo is admired for his prose.

118. Hans Lietzmann (1875–1942), born in Düsseldorf, was a German theologian and church historian. A student of the philologist Hermann Usener (1834–1905), who wrote on the festival of Christmas, Lietzmann in time succeeded Adolf von Harnack (1851–1930) at the University of Berlin. He worked in the areas of church history, New Testament studies, archaeology, classical philology, and papyrology. In the field of liturgical studies, he edited *Das Sacramentarium Gregorianum nach dem Aachener Urexemplar* (1921) and authored the influential *Messe und Herrnmahl* (1926), ET: *Mass and the Lord's Supper* (1944). He died in Switzerland in 1942.

119. Louis I, the Pious, or le Débonnaire (778–840, emperor from 814), was the third son of, and successor to, Charlemagne (king from 768, emperor 800–814). Although weak and indecisive as a ruler, he was a patron of learning, with a decidedly religious temperament. During his reign, much of the scholarly work of the Carolingian Renaissance came to fruition.

120. Lucian of Samosata (ca. 120–after 180), Greek rhetorician, pamphleteer, novelist, and satirist, was born in Samosata, a part of the Roman province of Syria. Trained in rhetoric, he was itinerant in Ionia, Greece, Italy, and Gaul, delivering entertaining talks and clever lectures. The fame he earned makes it difficult to determine the extent of his literary corpus, as authors made use of his name to lend prestige to their work. Of his writings the best known are *A True Story*, *Dialogues of the Gods*, and *Dialogues of the Dead*.

121. Marcus Aurelius Antoninus Augustus (121–80 CE, emperor from 161) was both a Roman emperor and an important Stoic philosopher. His reign as emperor saw wars in Asia, Gaul, and north of the Danube. The last of the "Five Good Emperors" in the Nervan-Antonine line, whose reigns ran from 96 to 180 CE, his *Meditations*, composed in Greek, are valued for their reflections upon the task of governing as service and duty.

122. Melania the Younger (ca. 385–438/39), granddaughter of Melania the Elder (ca. 342–410), married her husband, Valerius Pinian (d. 431/32), in Rome. Upon the death of their two children in infancy, the two converted to Christianity and dedicated themselves to lives of celibacy. Melania gave the inheritance she received from her parents to the poor. By way of Sicily, the couple traveled to Africa, where they got to know Augustine of Hippo (354–430) and founded monasteries in his native Tagaste. After a stop in Alexandria, they made their way to Palestine, where they joined Jerome (ca. 342–420) at Bethlehem, entering monasteries there. Melania established a convent for women on the Mount of Olives and, after her husband's death, also founded both a monastery for men and a church.

123. Michael I Cerularius (ca. 1000–1059, patriarch of Constantinople from 1043) was highly critical of Rome, both for incorporating the *filioque* clause into the Nicene Creed and for using unleavened bread in the Eucharist. Attempts at reconciliation having failed, members of a Roman delegation laid a notice excommunicating Michael on the altar

of Hagia Sophia; Michael responded with reciprocal excommunications and anathemas. These events occurred in 1054, conventionally regarded as the date for the schism of the church between East and West.

124. Mimnermus (fl. ca. 630 BCE), an early Greek elegiac poet from Colophon in Ionia, Asia Minor, lived in difficult times, when the Ionian cities in Anatolia were struggling to stay independent from the kings of Lydia, who were gaining in power. Writing his poems to be sung with a flute, he was the first to make use of elegiac verse for composing love poetry.

125. Theodor Mommsen (1817–1903) was a German historian, jurist, and statesman whose particular focus was the history of Rome. He produced more than one thousand publications and was instrumental in organizing of a number of series, including the significant *Monumenta Germaniae Historica*. In 1902 he was awarded the Nobel Prize for Literature.

126. Musaeus (d. 457–61) was known for his piety, grace, and insight into Scripture. His scriptural selections were used both in worship and for education; the work he composed on the sacraments combined liturgical material with a treatise on the liturgy. Valued as a preacher, his sermons were read for edification.

127. Nestorius (b. after 351, d. after 451, patriarch from 428), a native of Syria, entered a monastery in Antioch, probably studying with Theodore of Mopsuestia (350–428). There he adopted the principles of the Antiochene school of theology. Known for his outstanding preaching, Nestorius was invited by Theodosius II (408–50) to fill the See of Constantinople. Although Nestorius regarded himself as a defender of orthodoxy, his teachings were definitively condemned at the Council of Ephesus (431). In 436 he was banished to Upper Egypt, where he lived until the end of his life.

128. Nicholas II (d. 1061, pope from 1059), who was elected in opposition to the antipope Benedict X (1058–59), claimed the papacy by force of arms in an alliance with the Normans. This alliance gave him independence vis-à-vis the Western and Eastern Empires. He led the Roman Church to electoral reforms, notably that popes be elected by the College of Cardinals assembled in Rome, thereby reducing the influence of the Roman aristocracy on the papacy.

129. Nicholas III (1216–80, pope from 1277), born to a noble Roman family, was a natural politician, who served under eight popes. He was able to secure the political position of the papacy in Italy. On Aug. 14, 1279, he issued the papal bull *Exiit qui seminat*, an attempt to clarify the rule of poverty for the Franciscan Order. He was, however, known for his extreme nepotism, which earned him the mockery of Dante, who, when writing *The Inferno*, assigned him a place in the Eighth Circle of Hell, reserved for those guilty of simony.

130. Nikon of Moscow (1605–81, patriarch from 1652 to 1658), priest and abbot of the Russian Orthodox Church, rose to power through his close connection with Czar Alexis I (1645–76). Upon election as patriarch of Moscow, he initiated "purifying" reforms that sought to bring the Russian liturgy in line with Greek practice, though in fact the Greek practices he introduced were of more recent origin than the Russian "corruptions." These reforms, which he implemented through the raw use of state power, and the opposition they aroused ultimately led to Nikon's downfall as patriarch and defrocking as a priest. He withdrew to a monastery to live out his last days as a monk.

131. In his youth, Notker the Stammerer or Notkerus Balbulus (ca. 840–912) entered the Benedictine monastery at St. Gall, which he served as librarian, guestmaster, and master of the monastic school. He introduced sequences to the liturgy and compiled them in *Liber hymnorum*, one of his various literary works.

132. Origen (ca. 185–ca. 254), a prolific biblical critic, exegete, theologian, and spiritual writer, was born in Alexandria. Raised in a Christian home, he also studied pagan philosophy. After teaching for years in Alexandria, he was expelled and, in 231, found refuge in Caesarea, where he established a school. Essentially a biblical scholar, he is best known for employing neoplatonism in his allegorical interpretation of the Scriptures. In 250, during the persecution under Emperor Decius (d. 251), he was imprisoned and tortured. He died shortly thereafter.

133. Born of pagan parents, Pachomius (ca. 290–346), after a stint in the army, converted to Christianity and was baptized. Around 320 he established a monastic community at Tabennisi near the Nile River in the Thebaid, a region in southern Egypt, and his reputation soon drew large numbers of monks. Upon his death, Pachomius was abbot general over nine communities of men and two of women. His rule, extant

only in Jerome's (ca. 342–420) Latin translation, influenced monasticism in both the East and West.

134. Paul I (d. 767, pope from 757) served as a Roman deacon until becoming pope. On the throne of Peter, he worked out an alliance with Pepin the Short (751–68) whereby Rome served as sponsor of the Frankish throne and the Franks as protectors of Rome, first against the Lombards and later against the Byzantine Empire. In the face of Byzantine inroads, he defended church doctrine on the veneration of icons and on the Trinity.

135. The future Paul IV (1476–1559, pope from 1555) was born into a distinguished Neapolitan family and became bishop of Chieti (Theate) in 1504. Disturbed by the abuse in the Roman Church from a young age, he resigned his see in 1524 to join Thomas Cajetan (1480–1547) in founding the Theatine Order, whose name derives from his former see. With an apostolate of reforming the church, this order included in its rule a novel feature: the intention to produce a revised version of the Roman Breviary for their use. Upon returning to the hierarchy and eventually becoming pope, Paul both remained influential in the order and continued to work for its aims, including the reform of the Roman Breviary for use throughout the church. See Batiffol, *Breviary*, 191–94.

136. Paul the Deacon (ca. 720–ca. 800), born into a noble family of Lombardy, received an exceptional education. After Charlemagne (king from 768, emperor 800–814) conquered Paul's home region in 774, Paul was banished to Monte Cassino, where he joined the Benedictine Order. Yet, on a visit of Paul to Charlemagne's court, the emperor was impressed by his learning and set him to work upon a number of literary tasks, including the *Homilarium* mentioned on pp. 122–23.

137. Pepin III, the Short, or the Younger (ca. 714–68, king from 751), was the first king of the Carolingian dynasty. Upon the death of Pepin's father, Charles Martel (ca. 716–741), the power to rule the Frankish kingdom was divided between Pepin and his brother Carloman (706/16–54). Since, however, military prowess was a requirement for leadership, they placed the Merovingian Childeric III (743–51) on the throne as king. Over time, however, Childeric proved weak, whereas Pepin acquired both military experience and the effective rule of the kingdom. At this juncture, Pepin persuaded Pope Zacharias (741–52) to deem him king de jure as well as de facto. On the strength

of a papal bull recording this and with a show of force, an assembly of Franks elected Pepin king. Later in Paris, Pepin was anointed by Pope Stephen II (752–57), who bestowed upon him the further title of *patricius Romanorum* (patrician of the Romans).

138. Peter Fullo or the Fuller (d. 488, patriarch from 470) received his nickname from his original trade as a fuller of cloth. After possibly beginning in the church as a monk, he used influence and guile to become patriarch of Antioch. Opposed to Chalcedon, he imposed his Monophysite beliefs upon his patriarchate, in part through adding to the Trisagion the phrase "who was crucified for us." During his tenure, which was marked by interruptions in his reign and turmoil in his patriarchate, he fell in and out of imperial favor. Though at the end of his life he stood condemned by Rome and opposed by the emperor, he died a patriarch.

139. Little is known about Bishop Peter of Lerida (Latin: Ilerda), who lived in Spain in the fifth and sixth centuries.

140. Girolamo (Latin: Hieronymus) Petrucci (1585–1669), a Jesuit, wrote *De Christi Domini cruciatibus ad Urbanum VIII* (1627), and, under Urban VIII (1623–44), worked on revising the hymns of the Breviary, See *Jesuit Latin Poets of the 17th and 18th Centuries: An Anthology of Neo-Latin Poets*, eds. James J. Mertz and John P. Murphy (Wauconda, IL: Bolchazy-Carducci Publishers, 1989), 2.

141. Photius (ca. 810–95, patriarch from 858), of noble extraction and great erudition, first served in the imperial entourage. When still a layman, he was appointed patriarch of Constantinople and consequently became embroiled in imperial politics and disputes with Rome, notably over doctrinal issues and missionary territory. He was the first theologian of note to challenge as an innovation Rome's addition of the *filioque* clause to the Nicene Creed.

142. Born in Milan, Pius IV (1499–1565, pope from 1559) was educated in medicine and law before coming to Rome, where he served in the Curia and rose to the throne of Peter. In addition to producing the Roman Catechism, he is best remembered for bringing the Council of Trent (1545–63) to a close and starting the process of implementing its decrees. He reestablished amicable relations with the Holy Roman Empire, but was unpopular for his nepotism and heavy taxation of the Papal States.

143. Pius V (1504–72, pope from 1566) became a Dominican at a young age and after ordination, in addition to holding offices in his own order, taught philosophy and theology. Rising to the episcopate and cardinalate, he served on several inquisitorial missions. With his election as pope, he brought ascetical discipline to bear on the papal household and reform to the Roman Church. He continued implementation of the decisions of the Council of Trent (1545–63), notably the reform of the Breviary (1568) and Missal (1570). He also initiated the publication of a new edition of Thomas Aquinas's (1225–75) works. In the political sphere, his excommunication of Elizabeth I, Queen of England (1558–1603), brought disfavor upon Roman Catholics in that country, but allied with the Spaniards and Venetians, he was able to defeat the Turkish fleet at Lepanto in 1571. He was canonized 1712.

144. Born in Upper Venetia, Pius X (1825–1914, pope from 1903) rose in the Roman Church to become bishop of Mantua and (as cardinal) patriarch of Venice. When pope, he struggled with the relations of church and state (primarily in France), laid the foundation for the Catholic Action movement, condemned modernism, encouraged the study of Thomism, and initiated work on canon law. He gave early encouragement to the liturgical movement through a number of initiatives in the area of the liturgy: a reform of the Breviary, as well as decrees on music and the frequent reception of Communion. Pius X was canonized in 1954.

145. Giulio Poggio or Julius Poggiani (1522–68), a writer born in Suna, Italy, on Lago Maggiore, showed an early aptitude for classical languages. Moving to Rome, he became a tutor of future clerics and secretary to various prelates. Subsequently becoming a trusted associate of Charles Borromeo (1538–84), the cardinal of Milan, he served the Council of Trent (1545–63) as secretary and Latinist. Notably he contributed to the text of the Roman Catechism and the reform of the Breviary. See *Biographie Universelle* (Paris: Ch. Delagrave et Cie, n.d.), s.v. "Poggiani, (Jules)."

146. Polycarp (ca. 69–155), bishop of Smyrna, was a staunch defender of orthodoxy and a Quartodeciman. On a trip to Rome, he was arrested at a pagan festival and, refusing to recant his Christian faith, burned to death.

147. Ferdinand Probst (1816–99), priest, teacher, and liturgical scholar, was ordained in 1840, appointed professor of Pastoral Theology at

Breslau in 1864, and became Dean of Breslau Cathedral in 1896. While a man of immense erudition and capacity for work, his profound respect for church tradition led him at times to fail to fully appreciate the historicity of the Roman liturgy.

148. Nothing is known of Bishop Profuturus of Braga (fl. sixth century), metropolitan of Gallicia, apart from the fact that he wrote a letter to Pope Vigilius (537–55) inquiring about various liturgical matters, to which the pope responded with a decretal that was read at the Council of Braga (561).

149. Prudentius Aurelius Clemens (348–ca. 410), Latin poet and hymn writer, was born in Spain, practiced law, and enjoyed success as a civil administrator. In retirement he turned to expressing his Christian faith in the written word. Most Western breviaries included excerpts from his hymns, which employ classical meters and typically run to one hundred lines or more.

150. Francisco de Quiñones (1475–1540) was born of a noble Spanish family, entered the Franciscan order in 1498, and became cardinal in 1528. He held several offices in the Franciscan order and was active in papal diplomacy. By order of Pope Clement VII (1523–34), Quiñones dedicated himself to producing a new Breviary, which was published in 1535. While originally intended only for private use, it became widely popular, with more than one hundred editions appearing between 1536 and 1566. Quiñones served as titular bishop of the Basilica of the Holy Cross in Jerusalem, where his remains were laid to rest.

151. Rabanus Maurus (ca. 780–856), theologian, poet, and educator, was instructed at Fulda and Tours under the direction of Alcuin (735–804). As Abbot of Fulda and archbishop of Mainz, he advanced the evangelization of Germany. Reputedly the most learned man of his age and famed as a teacher, he made Fulda a center for learning during his lifetime. Rabanus composed hymns for the feasts of St. Michael the Archangel and of All Saints, as well as the well-known *Veni Creator Spiritus*.

152. Radulf or Radulph of Rivo (1350–1403), historian and liturgist, was born in Brabant and studied in France, Germany, and Italy before eventually becoming dean of Rivo (or Tongres) in present-day Belgium. He wrote works on grammar, history, and the liturgy in addition to working for liturgical reform, by which he meant a return to the practices of ancient Rome.

153. Remigius of Rouen (d. ca. 771, serving as archbishop from 755–762), the son of Charles Martel (716–41), was educated at the Frankish court. On a political mission to Rome in 760, he became acquainted with Roman chant and liturgy. Returning from that visit, he brought back to Gaul monks from Rome who could instruct his diocese in that chant tradition and introduce it into the Gallican Church.

154. As his moniker suggests, Romanos the Hymnographer or Melodist (fl. ca. 540) was gifted in music. Born of Jewish parents in Syria, he worked later as a Christian in Constantinople, where he composed Greek religious poetry, poetical songs, and metrical sermons for chanting. His most renowned composition is the first *kontakion*, the one for the feast of the Birth of Our Lord.

155. The Jesuit poet Matthias Casimir Sarbiewski or Sorbiewski or Sarbevius (1595–1640) became known as "the Polish Horace," whose complete poetic corpus he committed to memory. Going to Rome for study and ordination, he there received favor from the Barberini family. One of their number, Pope Urban VIII (1623–44), who called him "my Maecenea" (70–8 BCE) and crowned him *poetus laureatus*, engaged him to work on the Breviary. Upon return to Poland, Sarbiewski taught and preached, becoming chaplain and preacher to King Wladyslaw IV (1632–48). Gifted in music and the fine arts as well as in letters, he was remarkably productive as a poet using classical styles, of course that of Horace (65–27 BCE), but also that of Pindar (522–443 BCE). See *Jesuit Latin Poets of the 17th and 18th Centuries: An Anthology of Neo-Latin Poets*, eds. James J. Mertz and John P. Murphy (Wauconda, IL: Bolchazy-Carducci Publishers, 1989), 1–3.

156. Lucius Annaeus Seneca or Seneca the Younger (ca. 4 BCE–65 CE) was a Roman philosopher, statesman, orator, and tragedian. Around the middle of the first century, he was the leading intellectual light in Rome. Between 54 and 62 CE, the early years of Nero's rule (54–68), he and his circle were the de facto rulers of the Roman world.

157. From ca. 339, Serapion (d. after 360) was bishop of Thmuis, a town in the Nile delta. A close friend of Athanasius (ca. 296–373) and a companion to Anthony of the Desert (ca. 251–356), he wrote doctrinal and literary works as well as a compilation of prayers that bears his name.

158. Sergius I (d. 701, pope from 687) was born in Antioch and educated at Palermo. He took an active interest in developing church life

in Britain and resisted an attempt to grant Constantinople the same ecclesiastical standing as Rome. Among his liturgical innovations are the introduction of the *Agnus Dei* into the Mass and the addition of a procession, accompanied by a litany, to each of the four chief Marian feasts.

159. Severus of Antioch (ca. 465–538, patriarch from 512–518) studied in Alexandria and Berytus (Beirut), was baptized in 488, and in time became a monk. An important theologian among moderate Monophysites, he was elevated to the patriarchate of Antioch. After being excommunicated by a synod of Constantinople in 536, he took refuge in Egypt under the protection of the Monophysite patriarch of Alexandria, Timothy IV (517–35).

160. Shapur or Sapor II or the Great (309–79), ninth king of the Sassanian Empire of Persia, may have been the only king in history to be crowned in utero, the crown being laid upon his pregnant mother's belly. As a result he came out of the womb coronated, his reign commencing on the day of his birth. After assuming the responsibilities of the throne, he launched an invasion across the Tigris River in an attempt to recapture Armenia and Mesopotamia, both of which had been lost to the Romans by his predecessors. Although the state religion of the Sassanian Empire was Zoroastrianism (Mazdaism), Christianity was widespread. With Constantine's (312–37) toleration of Christianity after 313 and the subsequent Christianization of the Roman Empire, Shapur came to regard Christians as a fifth column in his kingdom. To combat this "subversive" influence within the realm, he introduced a policy of persecuting and forcibly converting Christians.

161. Siegebert of Minden (d. 1036), who is unknown prior to his elevation as bishop of Minden, was a loyal servant of the Salian court and a much-beloved pastor. There exist manuscripts bearing his name of no less than eight liturgical books, including the *Orationale* from which Matthias Flacius Illyricus (1520–75) excerpted the *Missa Illyrica*. See *Biographisch-Bibliographisches Kirchenlexikon* (Herzberg: Verlag Traugott Bautz, 1995), s.v. "Sigebert von Minden."

162. Simeon bar Sabbae (ET: Simeon son of a dyer; d. 344 or 341), bishop of Seleucia-Ctesiphon in Mesopotamia and martyr, was an opponent of his predecessor Aggai (285–326/27). Though elected bishop upon Aggai's deposition, Simon did not take office until the latter's

death, at a time when the East Syrian Church was suffering internal difficulties and persecution under Shapur II (309–79). Suspecting Simeon of Byzantine (read: "Roman") leanings, Shapur first imprisoned him and then later put him to death along with five others, including his sister. This was the first group of Christians martyred by the Sassanian dynasty.

163. Simplicius (d. 483, pope from 468), a native of Tivoli, Italy, is known for working to maintain Rome's standing in the church, notably through his defense of the Council of Chalcedon (451) against the heresy of Eutyches (ca. 380–ca. 456). He reigned as pope when German tribes marauded Italy, which resulted in the deposition of the last Western Roman emperor, Romulus Augustulus (475–76).

164. Sixtus II (d. 258, pope from 257) may have been of Greek birth. During his short tenure as pope, he reestablished ties with the North African and Eastern churches. He died a martyr during the persecution under Emperor Valerian (253–60), beheaded along with numerous bishops, priests, and deacons. Writings of his may have survived.

165. Sixtus V (1521–90, pope from 1585), the son of a gardener, entered the Franciscan order at the age of twelve and was ordained at twenty-six. Renowned as a preacher and dialectician, he was a friend of Ignatius Loyola (ca. 1491–1556) and Philip Neri (1515–96). Sixtus edited the works of Ambrose (ca. 339–97). His active role in the Inquisition earned him advancement in his order and the Roman Church as well as enemies. As pope he initiated serious reform within both the administration of the church and the Papal States. Interested in physical Rome, he completed numerous building and city planning projects, including additions to and renovations of the Lateran Palace, a new building to house the Vatican Library, bringing the cupola of St. Peter's Basilica to completion, and the construction of a water supply system for the city capable of feeding twenty-seven fountains. The edition of the Vulgate Bible he inaugurated remained the typical edition until the late twentieth century.

166. Stephen the Deacon (d. ca. 35?), one of the seven deacons of the apostolic Christian community of Jerusalem, was the first Christian to die for his faith, which earned him the title of "protomartyr." See Acts 6:1–8:2.

167. Stephen of Liège (ca. 850–920) was a hagiographer and composer of church music. After serving as the abbot of Lobbes Abbey in

present-day Belgium and as a canon of the cathedral in Metz, he was elected bishop of Liége in 901, where he remained until his death.

168. Famiano Strado (1572–1649), historian and moralist, member of the Society of Jesus, taught rhetoric and Latin at the Collegium Romanum. Under Urban VIII (1623–44), he worked on the hymns of the Breviary. His best-known book is a history of the Dutch War of Independence, written at the request and with the help of Alessandro Farnese, the Duke of Parma (1545–92). Published in 1632 as *De Bello Belgico decades duae*, by 1700 it had been translated into Dutch, French, Italian, English, and Spanish. See *Biographie Universelle*, (Paris: Ch. Delagrave et Cie, n.d), s v. "Strada (Famian)," http://www.jrank.org/literature/pages/18015/Famiano-Strada.html#ixzz0lEkmi9G6, and http://nl.wikipedia.org/wiki/Famiano_Strada.

169. Josef Strzygowski (1862–1941), an art historian born in Austrian Silesia (now Poland) and a member of the Vienna school of art history, taught in Austria first at the University of Graz and subsequently at the University of Vienna. To conduct his research, he traveled widely in the Mediterranean basin and the Near East. He and his school developed a revisionist approach to art history, which argued that influences flowed from East to West rather than from West to East. Specifically, he argued that Rome was the recipient rather than the source of artistic influence. He developed his theories using a comparative approach, which exercised an early influence on Anton Baumstark (1872–1948), who as a young man met Strzygowski in Rome. Over the years Strzygowski's theories became increasing polemical, ahistorical, and anti-Semitic, factors in his support of the NSDAP (National Socialist Democratic Workers or Nazi Party).

170. Teresa of Ávila or Teresa of Jesus (1515–82) was a Spanish Carmelite nun and mystic. Writing during the Counter-Reformation, she was a theologian of contemplative life and prayer who turned to a life of perfection after praying before a statue depicting the scourging of Christ. Within her order she worked for reform. She was canonized in 1622 and in 1970 named a Doctor of the Church.

171. Quintus Septimus Florens Tertullian (ca. 160–ca. 225), an African church father, was raised in Carthage, where he benefited from an education in literature and rhetoric. In 197 he converted to Christianity, later joining the Montanist sect. He authored numerous apologetic, theological, polemical, and ascetical works in Latin and Greek. The li-

turgically significant *De baptismo* raises the problem of infant baptism, a practice he criticized.

172. Theodora I (ca. 500–548, empress from 527), wife of the Emperor Justinian I (527–65), may have been the most powerful woman to reign in antiquity. A commoner, she was an actress and a courtesan before an encounter with Monophysite Christianity on travels to the East caused her to reform her ways. Her marriage to Justinian in 1523 required repeal and enactment of laws, whereby Theodora was raised to the rank of patrician. She brought a lively personality, a keen intelligence, life experience, and energy to her responsibilities as empress and coregent. Though involved in all aspects of governing, she had a special interest in the church, in both the complex theological issues of the day, in which she became deeply engaged, and its charitable work.

173. In 830 Theodora the Armenian (ca. 815–67), the daughter of an aristocratic family of Armenia, married the Byzantine emperor Theophilus (829–42), also of Armenian origin. Although he was an iconoclast, she was a devoted iconophile. After her husband's death, she served as regent for her son Michael III (842–67), ruling with strength. However, court intrigue resulted in the assassination of her son and her banishment to a monastery.

174. Theodore Balsamon (ca. 1140–after 1195, patriarch from 1191) was a Greek canonist. Although elected patriarch of Antioch, actions by the Latin Crusaders prevented him from exercising his duties. He remained in Constantinople, where he wrote extensively in the area of canon law.

175. Theodore of Mopsuestia (350–428) studied theology and biblical exegesis in Antioch, along with his friend John Chrysostom (347–407). In 392 he became bishop of Mopsuestia, a city in Cilicia, located in southeastern Anatolia. Theodore was known for his scholarship and orthodoxy, although his doctrine of the incarnation was condemned by the Councils of Ephesus (431) and Constantinople (553).

176. Theodore of Tarsus (ca. 602–90) was a monk from Greece. When Pope Vitilian (657–72) consecrated him archbishop of Canterbury in 668, he was a member of a monastic community that spoke Greek, though located in Rome. Anxious that Theodore's Greek background not compromise the orthodoxy of this Roman mission, the pope sent Benedict Biscop (ca. 628–90) and Hadrian (d. 709) along with him to

England, where Theodore did much to strengthen the organization of the church.

177. Theodore the Studite (759–826), monastic reformer and theologian, was born in Constantinople. Along with his brother, Joseph of Thessalonica (ca. 762–832), he received an excellent religious and secular education. Theodore entered the monastery in Bithynia where his uncle was abbot and was ordained there. After succeeding his uncle, he moved the community to Constantinople to revive the dormant monastery of Studios. Theodore contributed to the development of hymn meter and was a productive hymn writer, composing canons on the adoration of the cross and one to be sung upon the burial of a monk. He was active as an adversary of the iconoclasts. See Alice Gardner, *Theodore of Studium, His Life and Times* (New York: Burt Franklin Reprints, 1924), 236–44, 247–52.

178. Theodulf of Orléans (ca. 750–821), ecclesiastic, poet, and theologian, was a native of Spain, of Gothic descent, and a protégé of Charlemagne (king from 768, emperor 800–814). While serving as bishop of Orléans and abbot of Fleury nearby, he was also active at court, even being present in Rome at Charlemagne's coronation (800). Theodolf himself represents the intellectual life and inclinations of the Carolingian Renaissance. Writing in a variety of genres (poetry, epigrams, hymns, chronicles, and treatises), his episcopal statutes were particularly influential and his revision of the Vulgate a scholarly tour de force. Theodulf's hymn "All Glory, Laud, and Honor" became the processional for Palm Sunday in the Western church.

179. Theophanes Graptos (ca. 775–845), Byzantine poet and patriarch, was born in Palestine and professed as a monk at the Great Lavra of St. Sabas near Jerusalem. Moving to Constantinople, he opposed the iconoclasts, suffering torture and exile; he and his brother Theodorus (ca 775–842) both bear the moniker *Graptos*, "written upon," because they each had twelve lines of verse "written" into their skin. After the iconoclastic controversy (842), Theophanes became the metropolitan of Nicaea. As to liturgical hymns, his authorship of nineteen *idiomela* and 160 canons is assured; he is credited with a great number of anonymous canons and liturgical books as well.

180. Thomas Aquinas (1225–75), philosopher and theologian in the scholastic tradition, was born in Roccasecca (in present-day Italy) and educated at Monte Cassino, Naples, Paris, and Cologne. Resolved to

pursue an intellectual apostolate, he joined the Dominicans, teaching in Paris and at various places in Italy. His *Summa Theologica*, in which he strived to put the philosophy of Aristotle in the service of the church, is a preeminent work in the history of Christian thought and became definitive for Catholic theology. Known as *doctor angelicus*, he was not only granted the honored status of Doctor of the Church, but also ranked with the four great Latin doctors—Jerome (ca. 342–420), Ambrose (ca. 339–97), Augustine (354–430), and Gregory (590–604).

181. Thomas of Celano (ca. 1190–1260), poet and hagiographer, was one of the first disciples of Francis of Assisi (ca. 1181–1226) and, before settling in Italy, helped to spread the Franciscan Order into Germany. He seems to have known Francis personally. His authorship of two lives of Francis and a record of his miracles is assured; the attribution to him of a life of Clare (1194–1253) and of sequences, including *Dies Irae*, is disputed.

182. Thomas of Edessa (d. before 544), Nestorian author, studied at Nisibis under Mar Ab(b)a I (540 to 552), traveling to Constantinople to immerse himself in Greek learning. His writings are contained in *Thirteen Expositions of the Feasts of the Economy*, a work containing compositions of various authors. Although he was commissioned to write on the eight principal feasts of the liturgical year, before his death he was only able to produce explanations of two, Christmas and Epiphany (nos. 1 and 3 in the collection). A fellow pupil and successor of Thomas, Cyrus of Edessa (fl. sixth century), completed his commission.

183. Urban II (ca. 1035–99, pope from 1088), who supported the reforms of Pope Gregory VII (1073–85), was nominated by Gregory as a possible successor and, once pope, continued his policies. Urban is renowned for initiating the First Crusade (1095–99) and establishing the Roman Curia, modeled after a royal court, as a body to assist the pope in administering the Roman Church. While opposed by the antipope Clement III (1080–1100), Urban was supported by synods both in his reforms of the church and in the continuing contest with Emperor Henry IV (1050–1106).

184. Urban VIII (1568–1644, pope from 1623), a member of the Barberini family, received a doctor of law degree from the University of Pisa. Rising in the Roman Church through family influence, Urban in turn enhanced his family's position through nepotism and favors. He

condemned heliocentrism, having Galileo Galilei (1564–1642) tried for heresy. Serving as pope for twenty-one years of the Thirty Years' War (1618–48), Urban was the last pope to extend the papal territories. Himself a poet, he was a generous patron of the arts. However, his endeavors, both political and artistic, left the papacy deeply in debt.

185. Venerius (431–52), reputedly a disciple of John Cassian (ca. 360–435) at the Abbey of St. Victor, became bishop for the See of Marsilia (present-day Marseilles). He got caught up in a bitter rivalry between the sees of Arles and Marseilles, even being accused of welcoming the assassination of his fellow bishop. At his request, Musaeus composed both a lectionary and a work on the sacraments. See *A Dictionary of Christian Biography, Literature, Sects and Doctrines,* eds. Sir William Smith et al., vol. 4 (London: John Murray, 1887), 1105–6.

186. Publius Vergilius Maro, known commonly in English as Virgil or Vergil (70–19 BCE), the son of a farmer or a landowner, became one of Rome's greatest poets. He moved in imperial circles, living at a time when the republic was crumbling and the empire rising. Public life is one theme of his poetry, with three complete works being extant. His last poem, the national epic *Aeneid,* which tradition holds was commissioned by Augustus (27 BCE to 14 CE), came to exercise enormous influence upon European literature.

187. Vigilius (d. 555, pope from 537) was born into a noble Roman family. His nomination to the papacy by his predecessor was judged uncanonical and was nullified. However, he had gained favor in the East as an emissary to the court of Justinian I (483–565, emperor from 527) and Constantinople helped him acquire the throne of Peter. As pope, he was caught up in a controversy over Chalcedon, being pressured by the court in the East to compromise and by the church in the West to hold fast.

188. Vitalian (d. 672, pope from 657) did much to improve relations between the church in the East and the West, as indicated by Vitalian's name being placed on the diptych of the Byzantine Church and the Byzantine emperor being received in Rome. At the same time, Vitalian sought to assert Roman authority in both Ravenna and the East. He strengthened the church in England, reinforcing the practice of Roman customs there by sending out Theodore of Tarsus (ca. 602–90) to head the English Church, accompanied by Hadrian (d. 709) and Benedict Biscop (ca. 628–90).

189. Nikolaus Ludwig Graf von Zinzendorf (1700–1760) was a Protestant evangelist and the founder of the Brüdergemeine (the "Moravian Brethren"), which was formed from groups fleeing religious persecution in Moravia and Bohemia. Welcoming these refugees onto his manor estates in what is now southeastern Germany, he established them in a settlement given the name of Herrnhut (House of the Lord), organized on evangelical principles. This model community provided the pattern for settlements established by Moravians around the world. Deeply influenced by German Pietism and preaching a "religion of the heart," von Zinzendorf's primary interest was evangelism. Through Friedrich Schleiermacher (1768–1834), who had a Herrnhut education and defined religion as "a feeling of absolute dependence," he influenced nineteenth-century theology, notably in Germany.

190. Wala (ca. 755–836), statesman and Benedictine monk, was a member of a Carolingian family and educated at the palace school. After serving Charlemagne (king from 768, emperor 800–814) and Louis I (814–40), he entered the abbey of Corbie, where he became abbot in 826. Wala was subsequently elected abbot of the abbey in Bobbio, Italy.

191. Wipo (ca. 990–after 1048), priest, poet, and royal biographer, served the Salian court as both cleric and chronicler. Chaplain to Emperors Conrad II (1029–39) and Henry III (1028–56), his chronicles are of value as a historical source, notably for the reign of Conrad II. Though prolific as a poet, most of his verse has been lost. He composed the sequence *Victimae paschali laudes* to be sung on the day of Easter.

192. Yared (or Jared) the Melodist (525–71) is honored in Ethiopia for introducing hymnody to that church during the reign of King Gabra Maskal (550–57). He is regarded as the father of Ethiopian church music and credited with inventing a system of musical notation for recording hymnody, creating three modes for use on various occasions, and composing the whole body of Ethiopian liturgical music. He spent his later years in monastic seclusion. For citations, see n. on p. 204.

193. Zacharias or Zachary (679–d. ca. 752, pope from 741), a Greek born in Calabria, then a part of the Byzantine Empire, was the last of the Byzantine popes. Through tact and diplomacy, he was able to establish political alliances that saved the exarchate of Ravenna from Lombard attack. Zacharias involved himself similarly in Frankish politics. He confirmed the deposition of the last Merovingian,

Childeric III (743–51) and had Boniface, the "Apostle of the Germans" (ca. 672–754), solemnly anoint Pepin the Short (751–68), the first ruler of the Carolingians (along with his consort). In Rome, Zacharias engaged in construction projects, building a church upon the site of a temple to Minerva and renovating the Lateran Palace.

Index of Subjects

Christianity, kinds of
  Aramaic, 116, 117, 230
  Armenian, 102, 116, 179
  Catholic, 119
  Coptic, 179
  Eastern, xvi, 166
  Egyptian, 48, 184
  Egyptian Monophysite 141
  Greek, 117, 119, 178, 179, 184
  Nestorian, 145
  Orient/Oriental, 184, 245, 246
  Palestinian Rite, 119
  Protestant, 11, 21
  Slavic, 129
  Syrian, 179, 201, 230
  Western, 210
  see also Celebrations; Liturgy; Rites
Christological Parties
  Arianism, 101, 182, 183
  Chalcedonian, 47–49, 118
  Jacobite. See Jacobites
  Julianist, 105
  Manichaen, 191
  Miaphysite hierarchy, 118
  Monophysite, 48, 125, 231
    Egyptian, 141
    Syrian, 118
    and Syrian Orthodox
      Church, 117
  Monothelite, 47
  Priscillianism, 58
Churches
  Anglo-Saxon Church, 110
  Armenian (National Church,
    Apostolic Church, Catholic
    Church), 22, 46, 47, 65
  Assyrian Church. See Syrian
    Orthodox
  Coptic, 23, 103, 116, 196
  East Syrian. See Syrian Orthodox
  Frankish, 120–22
  Greek, 20, 69, 75
  Maronite, 23, 47–49, 56, 152,
    190, 196, 202

Nestorian. See Syrian Orthodox
Oriental (Monophysite), 101, 109
Orthodox (Eastern), 48, 51, 101,
  131, 143
Orthodox (Egypt). See Egypt
Roman Catholic, 3, 14, 25, 28,
  40, 179, 211, 233, 239, 240
  calendar, 41
  liturgical movement, 27, 39, 40,
    49, 193–94, 240–42
  Saints, 116
  St. Peter's Basilica, 237, 246
  Vatican, 4, 107
Romanian Orthodox, 174, 190
Russian, 231, 232
Syrian Orthodox, 22, 47–49, 56,
  90, 100, 115, 116, 117, 118, 145,
  150, 157, 180, 192, 193, 202
Uniate, 46, 47
West Syrian (Jacobite), 23 49, 105,
  116,117, 179, 191 (see also
  Jacobite/s)
Colonna family, 213
Constantinople. See Patriarchal Sees
Copts. See Egypt
Councils and Synods
  Councils
    Alexandria, 101
    Braga, First, 101, 111, 113, 200,
      213
    Braga, Second, 101
    Carthage, Third, 188
    Chalcedon, 48, 129, 223
    Constance, 210
    Constantinople, 101, 108
    Ecumenical, Seventh, 128
    Ephesus, 49, 116
    Frankfurt, 138
    Gerunda, 110
    Laodicea in Asia Minor, 55, 60,
      200, 213
    Nicea, 101
    Orange, Second, 166

God, 25, 31, 32, 43, 53, 63, 70, 79, 80,
    85, 99, 101, 149, 165, 166, 169, 181–
    83, 204, 218, 219, 221, 234, 247, 248
    Mother of, 173
Goths, 189
    Ostrogoths, 170, 189
    Visigoths, 170, 189, 190
Graeco-Roman religious thought, 82
Greece, 54, 56, 99, 108
Greek/s, 136
    burial ceremony, 79
    Byzantine, 124
    Christianity, 119, 178, 179
    Church. *See* Church, Greek
    East, 91, 137
    monastery, 138
    poetry, 173
    See also Liturgy, kinds of;
        Church, Greek; Christianity,
        Greek
Guelphs, 213

Hellenism (Hellenistic).
    See Liturgical Development
Hellenistic Religion. *See* Religions
Hohenstaufen Era, 210
Holy Spirit, 223, 225
Hungary, 129
Huns, 189

Iberian Peninsula, 109
India, 15, 22, 26, 116, 192, 193
International Committee on
    English in the Liturgy, 69
Iran, 82, 198
Iraq, 162
Ireland, 15, 26, 120, 182, 205, 207
Islam. *See* Religions, Islam
Israel, 53, 66, 181, 182
Italy, 91, 104, 120, 135, 146, 170, 184,
    185, 205

Jacobite/s, 48, 56, 65, 105, 117, 145,
    147, 148, 151, 152, 190, 191, 196,
    202

Jerusalem. *See* Patriarchal Sees
Jesus Christ, 3, 25, 44, 62, 65, 66,
    77–82, 87, 93, 94, 99, 101, 105, 130,
    151, 165, 166, 171, 174, 181–83, 212,
    218, 220, 226
Jewish Liturgy, 14
    Eighteen Benedictions, 68
    Shema, 63, 68, 70
Jews. *See* Religions, Judaism
Judaism. *See* Religions, Judaism

Kingdoms. *See* Empires and
    Kingdoms

Language, 5, 6, 10, 20, 162
    linguistics, xxiii, 163, 201
    literature, 164
    liturgical, 194, 196
    Monophysites and, 103
    vernacular, 194, 196
Languages
    Arabic, 56, 75, 111, 140, 189–91, 196
    Aramaic, 55, 56, 103, 104, 106,
        162, 163, 173, 180, 190–93,
        200–202, 230
    Armenian, 159
    Bohairic, 93, 111, 156
    Chinese, 192
    Coptic, 93, 103, 105, 111, 116,
        156, 184, 190, 199
    Egyptian, 93
    English, xxiii, 36, 53, 159, 160,
        176, 188, 201, 207, 222, 227
    Ethiopic (Ge'ez), 93, 106, 141,
        151, 189, 204
    French, xxiii
    German, 35, 36, 45, 78, 176, 189,
        191, 202
    Greek, 35, 49, 55, 75, 77, 103–6,
        111, 115, 143, 151, 156, 159,
        162–64, 189, 190, 191, 193,
        197, 199, 202, 203, 216, 222,
        230, 231
    Hebrew, 56

Dionysius, Cult of, 77
Gnosticism, 182
Hermes Trimegistos, 83
Hermetics, 83
Isis, cult of, 77
Mithraism, 81, 85
Mystery, 74, 78
Stoicism, 84
Zeus Sosipolis, 76
Islam, 47, 103, 118
Judaism, 14, 18, 43, 53, 54, 56,
62–64, 68–71, 74, 75, 77, 79, 89,
90, 92–94, 105, 181, 182, 184,
193, 247
Roman
Arval Brethren (or Brothers), 168
Sun worship, 81, 82
Zoroastrianism, 191
Ring Katholischer Deutscher
Burschenschaften, 24, 25
Rituals, Liturgical
baptism, 57, 77, 86, 87, 181
Blessing of Palms, 177
Communion, 76, 78, 218, 219, 220
Eucharist, 53–58, 60, 66, 76, 77, 81,
87, 91, 93, 95, 99, 105, 107, 120,
131, 141, 151, 165, 181, 184, 186,
191, 195, 196, 218, 219, 226, 246
exorcisms, 76
Great Entrance, 219, 220
Holy Sacrifice, 227
initiation, 76
Rituals, Non-Christian
festival of Ambarvalia, 167
festival of Robigalia, 167
imperial, 19
Jewish, 20
Pindar beatitude, 86
Romanian/s, 174, 190
Orthodox Church, see under
Church

Roman Empire. See Empires and
Kingdoms
Roman Religion. See Religion, Roman
Russia, 28
Russian Church, see under Church

Sacramentary. See under Liturgical
books. For specific sacramentaries see
Liturgical Documents
Sacred Congregation of Rites. See
under Rites
Satan, 181
Scandinavia, 20, 129
Seleucia-Ctesiphon, 90, 116, 151, 193
Semitics, 164
Shema. See Liturgy, Jewish
Slavic/Slavs, 20, 129, 174
Smyrna, 109
Spain, 58, 98, 101, 130, 152, 164, 186,
190, 198, 205, 206, 218
Sweden, 128, 189
Synagogue. See Judaism
Synods. See Councils and Synods
Syria, 50, 55, 56, 117, 118, 130, 136,
142, 163, 203

Tajikistan, 192
Treaty of Verdun, 19, 128, 239
Turkestan, 192
Turks, Seljuk, 102, 103

Uzbekistan, 192

Versailles Treaty, 8, 173
Vikings, 172

Wend people, 129
World War I, 7, 8, 24, 173
World War II, 174

Zoroastrianism. See Religions

Index of Historical Figures

Citations found in Baumstark's text have been placed in **bold** type.

Bernold of Constance, **224**, **229n20**, **232**, **233**, **242n3**, 256
Boniface IV (Pope), **65**, 257
Boniface VIII (Pope), **212**, 213n., 257
Borromeo, Charles, 134n., **238**, 239n., 257

Caesarius of Arles, **206**, 206n.
Callistus I (Pope), 41n.
Carafa family, **235**
Cassian, John, 143n., **147n12**, 207n.
Castiglione, Branda da, 133n.
Catherine of Siena, **182**, **258**
Cato, Marcus Porcius, the Elder, **168**, **176n11**, 258
Chararich (King), 101n.
Charlemagne (Charles the Great) (King) (Emperor), 19n, 23, 24, 25, **122**, **133–35**, **137**, **161n23**, **172**, **206**, **207**, **239**, 258
Charles II (the Bald), 128n., **225**, 258
Charles Augustus (Emperor). *See* Charlemagne
Chrodegang of Metz, **121**, 259
Chrysostom, John, **71nn5** and **14**, **72n17**, **100**, **116**, **141**, 150n., 259
Cicero, Marcus Tullius, **84**, **87n25**, **236**, 259
Cleanthes, 85n.
Clement IV (Pope), 145n.
Clement VIII (Pope), **237**, 259
Clement of Alexandria, **74**, 259
Clement of Rome, 64n., **66**, **72n18**, **163**, 259
Clovis I (King), **119**, 260
Conrad II (Emperor) (King), 124n., **153**
Constantine the Great Emperor), **57**, 81n., **104**, 105n., 130n., 226n., 260
Cornelius (Pope), **163**, 260
Cosmas and Damian, **146**, 261
Cosmas the Melodist, **203**, 260
Cosmati family, 227n.
Cyprian, **95**, **97n16**, 261

Cyril and Methodius, **128**, **129**, **193**, 261
Cyril of Alexandria, **141**, 150n., 261
Cyril of Jerusalem, **187n5**

Dagobert I, 119n.
Damian. *See* Cosmas and Damian
Dante Alighieri, **203**, 261
David (King), 102n.
Decentius, **91**, 262
Dietrich of Berne, **170**
Diocletian (Emperor), 81n., 204n.
Dionysius the Pseudo-Areopagite, **156**, **160n16**, 262
Dominic, **210**, 262
Duke of Milan, 133n.
Durandus, **138n8**

Egeria (Etheria), **23**, **57**, **58**, **106**, **108**, **113n23**, **147n11**, **191**, **197n4**, 262
Elisachar/Elisigarus. *See* Helisachar
Elizabeth of Portugal, 236n., **242n9**
Ephrem the Syrian, 23, 49n., **94**, **152**, **201**, **212**, **214n10**, 262
Epicteutus, **84**, 263
Eugene IV (Pope), **132**, 133n., 263
Eusebius, 189n.
Eustasius (or Eustachius or Eustathius), **155**, 263
Eutyches, 48n.

Fabian (Pope), 195n.
Fécamp, Jean de, 222n.
Firmicus Maternus, Julius, **84**, **88n26**, 263
Fortunatus, Venantius Honorius Clementianus, 101n., **153**, 170n., 263
Foscacari, Egidio, **235**, 264
Francis of Assisi, 59n.
Francovich, Matthias. *See* Illyricus Matthias Flacius
Frumentius, 116n.
Fullo (or the Fuller). *See* Peter Fullo

Gabriel of Kashkar, 145n.

Gabriel of Qatar (Jibril bar Lipeh Qatraye), **157**, **160n20**, 264

Galluzzi, Tarquino, **236**, 237n., 264

Gelasius I (Pope), **120**, **121**, **152**, **186**, 264

Gennadius of Massilia, **159n13**, **176n13**

Germanus of Auxerre, 207n.

Gerontius, **56**, 265

Gracchus, Gaius Sempronius, **180**, 265

Gracchus, Tiberius Sempronius, **180**, 265

Gregory I (or the Great) (Pope), 23, 28n., **110**, **136**, 137n., **151**, **158**, **159**, **160n21**, **166**, 167n., **169**, **176n13**, **185**, **186**, 265

Gregory II (Pope), **57**, **159**, 265

Gregory IV (Pope), **123**, 265

Gregory VII (Pope), 23, **132–34**, 154n., **232**, **238**, 238n., **241**, 266

Gregory IX (Pope), **59**, 266

Gregory XI (Pope), **59**, 266

Gregory (of) Nazianzus (the Theologian), **111n2**, **151**, **176n6**, 266

Gregory the Hebrew, **117**, 254

Hadrian (Emperor), 105n.

Hadrian I (Pope), **122**, **123**, **133**, **161n23**, 267

Hadrian II (Pope), **158**, 267

Hadrian of Canterbury, **110**, 267

Harding, St. Stephen, **61n13**

Harith ibn Jabalah, Al- (King), **117**, 267

Haymo of Faversham, **59**, 268

Helena, 104n., 226n., 235n.

Helisachar (or Elisachar/Elisigarus), **122**, **123**, **127n19**, 268

Henry II (King), **125**, 268

Henry III (Emperor) (King), **153**

Henry IV (King, Emperor), **232**, 268

Henry V (King), 124n.

Heraclius, (Emperor), 75n., 231n.

Herman the Lame (or Cripple or Hermannus Contractus), **153**, **154**, 268

Hermenegild, 236n., **242n9**

Herodotus, 83n.

Hilary of Poitiers, **204**, 206n., 269

Hippolytus (of Rome), **66**, **95**, **163**, **181**, 269

Hitler, Adolf, 8

Honorius III (Pope), 227n.

Horace, **205**, 237n., 269

Hugh Candidus, 132n.

Humbert of Romans, 145n.

Illyricus, Matthias Flacius (Matthias Vlachich or Matthias Francovich), 223n., **224**, **229n19**, 269

Innocent I (Pope), **91**, 270

Innocent III (Pope), 226n.

Ishoyabh (or Isho'yahb or Yeshuyab or Ishu'yabb III), 23, **157**, **158**, 270

Isidore of Seville, **159n5**

Izates, 162n.

Jacob Baradaeus (or Bûrde'ânâ), 105n., **117**, 118n., 270

Jacob of Edessa, **117**, 156n., **230**, 231n., 270

Jacopone da Todi, **212**, 212n., 213n., 270

James the Apostle, **105**, 150n., 271

Jerome, **117**, 143n., **159n13**, **230**, 271

Jiménez de Cisneros, Francisco, **102**, 271

John III (Pope), **107**, 271

John bar Aphtonia, 156n., 157n.

John of Damascus, **159n9**, 191n., **203**, 203n., 271

John of Persia, 193n.

John of Syracuse, bishop, 137n., **158**, **160n21**, **176n13**, 272

John the Baptist, **78**, 78n., 118n., 136n.; *see also* Bible passages

John the Evangelist, 108n., **187n7**

Venerius, **155**, 288
Victor I (Pope), 92n.
Vigilius (Pope), **109**, 110n., **229n27**, 288
Virgil, **176n9**, **205**, 288
Vitalian (Pope), **110**, 288
Vlachich, Matthias, *see* Illyricus,
  Matthias Flacius

Wala, **123**, 289
Wessenberg, Ignaz Heinrich von,
  240n.

Wipo, **153**, **170**, **211**, 211n., 289

Xanthippe, **187n7**

Yared (or Jared) the Methodist, **204**,
  204n., 289

Zacharias (or Zachary, Pope), **121**, 289
Zeno of Citium, 84n., 85n.
Zinzendorf, Nikolaus Ludwig Graf
  von, **182**, 182n., 289

Index of Authors, Compilers, Editors, and Translators

Citations found in Baumstark's text have been placed in **bold** type.

Moultrie, Gerard, 78n.
Müller, Friedrich W. K., **198n7**
Muratori, Ludovico Antonio, **50n2**
Murphy, G. Ronald, 174n.
Mutafian, Claude, 222n.
Myers, Walter Neidig, **215n21**

Neale, John Mason, xv
Nestle, Eberhard, **112n18**
Netzer, H., **126n13**
Neusner, Jacob, **96n13**
Niederwimmer, Kurt, **60n1**, 69n.,
    73nn24 and **26**, 79n., **87n15**, **95n2**
Ninguarda, Feliciano, **229n22**
Norden, Eduard, **19n53**, **87n23**
North, W. L. N., 123n.

Ortiz, Alfonso, 102n., 225

Panfoeder, Chrysostomus, 3
Paranikas, Matthaios K., **213n(head)**
Parry, Ken, 190n.
Pastor, Ludwig von, **242n6**
Paverd, Frans van de, **72n17**, 100n.
Petit, L., **148n16**
Pétridès, S., **214n5**
Phenix, Robert R., Jr., **61n6**
Phillips, L. Edward, 67n., **72n19**,
    175n1
Pierce, Joanne Michelle, 224n., **229n18**
Pitra, Jean-Baptiste, **147n8**, **214n17**
Powne, Michael, 204n.
Probst, Ferdinand, xvi, **89**, **95n1**, 279

Raabe, Richard, **60n6**
Rackham, H., **87n25**
Rahmani, Ignatius Ephraem, **197n5**
Ramsey, Boniface, **147n12**
Rasmussen, Niels, 155n.
Ratti, Abrogio, **51n3**
Ratzinger, Joseph Cardinal, 5n13
Rauschen, Gerhard, **95n3**
Rays, Joseph, 79n.
Reid, Alcuin, 4, 5n13
Reithmayr, Franz Xavier, x

Reitzenstein, Richard August, **86n7**,
    87n22
Renaudot, Eusèbe, xiii, **50n2**, **111n2**,
    146n1, **147n5**
Richter, Gregor, **147n4**, **228n3**
Richter, Hermann, **61n10**, **113n23**,
    147n11, **197n4**
Riedlinger, Albert, **10n29**
Roll, Susan K., 81n.
Rossi, Giovanni Battista de, **178**, 262
Rousseau, Olivier, 33n113
Rouwhorst, Gerard, 19n53, 202n.
Rücker, Adolf, **111n13**, 145n., **214n10**

Sachau, Eduard, **198n7**
Sachsen, Max Prinz von, **51nn5** and **6**
Saeki, P. Yoshiro, **198n10**
Saïd, Susanne, 231n.
Sallis, Arnold von, **87n17**
Saussure, Ferdinand de, 10n29
Schaff, Philip, xii
Scheindlin, Raymond, **70n(head)**
Schermann, Theodor, x, **50n1**, **72n19**,
    86n5, **87n24**, **96n6**, **175n1**, **214n16**
Schmidt, Carl, **87n22**, **96n11**
Schneemelcher, Wilhelm, **187n7**
Schneider, Irmela, **31n106**
Schönfelder, Albrecht, **147n4**, **228n3**
Schroeder, Otto, **86n13**
Schubart, Hans von, **197n1**
Schubart, Wilhelm, **87n22**
Schüer, Emil, **70n(head)**
Schwartz, Eduard, 72n20
Schwerin, Claudius Freiherr von,
    171n.
Scott, Robert, 164n.
Sechehaye, Albert, 10n29
Sherley-Price, Leo, **114n31**
Sherwin-White, Susan, 231n.
Silvas, Anna M., **147n13**
Skutsch, Felix, **88n26**
Smith, Jeffrey Chipps, 234n.
Smith, Munroe, 171n.
Smits, Edmé Renno, **229n25**